Sophia Taylor

A new commentary on Genesis

Sophia Taylor

A new commentary on Genesis

ISBN/EAN: 9783744650595

Printed in Europe, USA, Canada, Australia, Japan

Cover: Foto ©Lupo / pixelio.de

More available books at **www.hansebooks.com**

A

NEW COMMENTARY

ON

GENESIS.

BY

FRANZ DELITZSCH, D.D.,

LEIPZIG.

Translated by

SOPHIA TAYLOR.

VOL. II.

EDINBURGH:
T. & T. CLARK, 38 GEORGE STREET.
1894.

[*This Translation is Copyright, by arrangement with the Author.*]

VI.

THE TOLEDOTH OF TERAH, XI. 27–XXV. 11—
continued.

PROMISE OF AN HEIR AND THE PROMISE OF THE LAND CONFIRMED BY A COVENANT, CH. XV.

Two solemn revelations open in ch. xv. the second section of the life of Abraham. The narrative falls into two halves. It is impossible to regard all from beginning to end as occurring in vision. For (1) if one revelation takes place at night, or at least with a transposition to night, the other is made in the day, and indeed at eventide, the sun being at ver. 12 about to set, and at ver. 17 actually set. And (2) the account of Abraham's believing reception of the promise of a posterity numerous as the stars of heaven ver. 6 separates what preceded from what follows, which though it appears from the ויאמר אליו, 7a, to have immediately succeeded, has yet its own special introduction. Dillmann here carries analysis even farther beyond the bounds of the discernible than Wellhausen does. The safest criterion from Gen. i. to Ex. vi., and one which must only be relinquished for cogent reasons, is the Divine names. The use of these is in both halves of ch. xv. the same. In both יהוה is the prevailing one, and with it occurs once in each אדני יהוה, to be read according to the punctuation אֲדֹנָי אֱלֹהִים, a combination of Divine names which, thus written, is unusual. This אדני יהוה, here twice used, gives to this historical picture in its two departments, as to the prophetic image, Isa. l. 4–9, where it is four times used, its own peculiar stamp; and as this אדני יהוה is only found elsewhere in the Pentateuch at Deut. iii. 24, ix. 26, it may be concluded that it is Jahvistic. Dillmann has in his 5th edition deliberately omitted his former view, that יהוה had been added by *R* to the original אדני of *B* (xx. 4, but there in the address). Equally weak is also Wellhausen's assertion (*Composition des Hexateuchs*, i. 413), that "אני and Ur Kasdim are not Jahvistic." Ur Kasdim is not Jahvistic, if it is here denied to *J*, which is but an arbitrary assertion and not a proof (see on xi. 31); and אני in the formula אני יהוה is so stereotyped (see on vi. 17) as to be common to every Pentateuchal source; it is Deuteronomic, xxix. 5, and also Jahvistic, Gen. xxviii. 13. The reference, too, xxiv. 7, to the covenant promise, xv. 18, and the list of the ten nations, xv. 19 sq., point to *J* as the narrator. The latter is indeed unique in this completeness, though still most akin to the list of seven, Deut. vii. 1; comp. Josh. iii. 10, which also closes with היבוסי. Nevertheless, ch. xv. is not throughout by *J*, ver. 2 being undoubtedly derived from another source, probably from *E*. Also in consideration of הָאֱמֹרִי as a synecdochical designation of the ancient population of Canaan, which is one of the tokens of the older Elohist, it may obviously be assumed that the narrative of the covenant sacrifice with its explanation was originally found in *E*, and derived in its present form from *JE*. Dillmann's opinion, that *R* inserted the glance at the future, vv. 12–16, "from his own resources," must be rejected, if only because the Divine directions stand in symbolic relation to the disclosures which follow them. It cannot be inferred either from רְכוּשׁ (see the Introd. to ch. xiv.) or from בשיבה טובה, which occurs only once more in the Pentateuch, xxv. 8, that *Q* had any share in fashioning the material of the narrative.

A Divine revelation is made to Abraham, which is connected with the conflict he has just victoriously waged, ver. 1: *After these events the word of Jahveh came to Abram in a vision, thus: Fear not, Abram: I am thy shield, thy reward is very great.* The parenthetical formula אַחַר הַדְּבָרִים הָאֵלֶּה (here and xxii. 1, 20, xxxix. 7, xl. 1, xlviii. 1) states that what is to be related followed what preceded after the lapse of some undefined time. The revelation בַּמַּחֲזֶה, which is confined to no time of the day, is a step higher than בַּחֲלוֹם. Abram is to have no fear in the midst of his strange and hostile surrounding, for Jahveh is his shield (the consolatory figure is repeated, Deut. xxxiii. 29). Luther translates farther: and (I am) thy very great reward. But God does not give Himself to him as a reward (comp. Wisd. v. 15, ἐν κυρίῳ ὁ μισθὸς αὐτῶν), but promises him one, and that very great,—only so can Abram's answer be understood, ver. 2: *And Abram said, O Jahveh, Lord of all, what wilt Thou give me, since I depart childless, and the inheritor of my house is Damascus (is) Eliezer.* A contrasted adverbial sentence begins, as at xviii. 13, with וְאָנֹכִי. "Depart" is certainly meant, as at xxv. 32, 2 Chron. xxi. 20, Ps. xxxix. 14, and frequently, of death. עֲרִירִי in itself means "alone," "lonely," here childless, like Lev. xx. 20 sq. With Abram all the fulness of the Divine blessing falls into the background in presence of his childlessness at that time; a man who is not his own flesh and blood having every prospect of being his heir. The unusual מֶשֶׁק is used to symphonize with דַּמֶּשֶׂק. The evident intention protects דמשק (הוא) from the suspicion of being a gloss (Hitzig, Tuch, Olshausen). The LXX. has the unmeaning υἱὸς Μασέκ; Syr. Targ. Jer. II. prefer leaving out the not understood משק; others, apparently deriving it, according to the formation כָּרָר, from שָׁקַק, "to run about busily," translate: son of my household business (Onk. Targ. Jer. I. Samar. Theod.) = my steward, for which we should rather have expected בַּעַל מֶשֶׁק, or: *filius procuratoris domus meae* (Jer. comp. Luth.), but מֶשֶׁק in this concrete sense is, though possible, improbable. The verb מָשַׁק, ܡܫܩ (related to מָשַׁךְ), which, as stem of מֶשֶׁק, is nearest, means, to draw to oneself, to seize, to take possession of, as is evident from מִמְשַׁק, Zeph. ii. 9; and בֶּן־מֶשֶׁק is the correct expression for one who has the reversion or right of taking possession. Thus the inheritor of my house is דַּמֶּשֶׂק אֱלִיעֶזֶר. Lagarde views דמשק as a prefixed apposition in the sense of the Arabic دمشق اليدين (according to Kâmûs, one is nimble with his hands), but this would yield a eulogy of Eliezer, not an allusion to his position. Dillmann, in accordance with Ew. § 286c, places the two words in genitival relation: the son of possession of my house is Damascus of Eliezer; but the subject aimed at is surely not the town, but the person whose rightful home it is. If however the narrator intended to say: Eliezer who is of Damascus (Ges. *Lehrgeb.* p. 648), אליעזר דמשק would be required in the reverse order (like 2 Sam. xxiii. 24; comp. on Prov. xxx. 1). There is thus nothing left but to take אליעזר as the more closely defining permutative of דמשק: the inheritor of my house is Damascus is Eliezer. It is just because the latter is aimed at that it is not said בת־משק, as might have been expected if דמשק had been the main subject.[1] The sense is clear: Damascus will inherit me, *i.e.* in the person of Eliezer, viz. (comp. 1 Chron. ii. 34 sq.) the Damascene. The Moslem tradition calls Abram's servant exactly دمشق, *Dimašk*, regards him according to the Arabic view as an Abyssinian, and says that he built Damascus and called it after his own name (*DMZ.* xvi. 701 sq.). Profane history is acquainted with a sojourn of Abram at Damascus on his journey from Chaldea to Canaan. Justinus the epitomizer of Trogus names Abram as one of the ancient kings of Damascus (xxxvi. 2); and Nicolaus Damascenus (in Josephus, *Ant.* i. 7, comp. *Fragm.*, ed. *Orelli*, p. 114) says in B. iv. of his *Universal History* that "Abram, a foreigner who had come thither with an army from the so-called land of Chaldea above Babylon, ruled in Damascus. Not long afterwards he went forth and transplanted himself hence (Damascus) with his people to the land

---

[1] The view that הוא דמשק is a marginal gloss to משק, which has got into the text (see Driver in the *Expositor*, vii. 6), makes the words the result of an incomprehensible silliness.

now called Judæa, then Cauaan, where his descendants became very numerous." "The name of Abram," adds Josephus, "is still held in great honour in Damascus, and a village owing its origin to him is shown and called Abram's dwelling ('Αβράμου οἴκησις)." Perhaps Berzat-el-Chalîl, "the marriage tent of Abraham," is meant, a village which lies one league north of Damascus, where the ravine of the Wadi *Macrabâ* opens into the *Gûṭa*, and where the memorial day of the patriarch's wedding, a popular festival of the Damascenes, is annually kept in spring (Wetzstein in *DMZ.* xxii. 105), so vivid is still the remembrance of Abram in and around Damascus. He is the most renowned of all the great men of antiquity in the mouths of the Bedouin tribes of the neighbourhood, who, if asked concerning their religion, call themselves *Dîn Ibrâ hîm.* Ver. 2 is followed by the same saying of Abraham in a more comprehensible form, ver. 3: *And Abraham said: Behold, to me hast Thou given no seed: and, lo, the son of my house is my heir.* No hereditary claim existed, but Abram had, as is seen from vv. 2 and 3, destined the inheritance to his tried and faithful servant, in case he should die childless. The promise of God however raises him above this grievous force of circumstances, ver. 4: *And, behold, the word of Jahveh to him, saying: This man shall not be thine heir, but he that shall go forth out of thine own body, he shall be thine heir.* Instead of וַיְהִי, we have here וְהִנֵּה, which presents an object to the mind, and instead of מֵחֲלָצֶיךָ, xxxv. 11, מֵעִים only used of the wife in the more recent custom of the language (xxv. 23), but here, as in 2 Sam. vii. 12, xvi. 11, of the husband: מִמֵּעֶיךָ. The ecstatic condition of Abram is to be conceived of as continuing, ver. 5: *And He led him into the open air, and said: Look towards heaven, and count the stars, if thou canst count them. And He said to him: So shall thy seed be,* numerous as the stars of heaven (xxii. 17, xxvi. 4; Ex. xxxii. 13; comp. the fulfilment, Deut. x. 22). Demeanour of Abram with regard to this promise, so paradoxical in itself, ver. 6 : *And Abram believed in Jahveh ; and He reckoned it to him for righteousness.* The conclusion of the first portion of the narrative, as ver. 18 sqq. is of the second. The *perf.* states in ver. 6 the basis, as the *Imperf. consec.* does the fact of the imputation (comp. on i. 2). The verb אָמֵן, of whose various use we may take a survey even within the Pentateuch, means to be firm, certain, whence אֱמוּנָה, Ex. xvii. 12, in its first physical meaning firmness and אֱמֶנֶת = אָמְנָה (adverbially אָמֵן, אָמְנָה and אָמְנָם), truth as firmness and certainty, transitively: to secure, to support, whence אָמְנָה, pillar, as that which supports, and אֹמֵן, a nurse, as he who supports, holds in leading strings, has care of. The *Niph.* means in a temporal sense to be wearisome, Deut. xxviii. 59; in a local sense, to be firm, unchangeable, see Isa. vii. 9, 1 Sam. ii. 35, and frequently; then to be certified, to be verified, to be proved true, xlii. 20, by man or God: to show oneself trustworthy, *partic.* genuine, faithful, Num. xii. 7; Deut. vii. 9. As נֶאֱמָן signifies faithful, πιστός, the *Hiph.* הֶאֱמִין signifies to trust, πιστεύειν, the cherishing and manifesting a frame or disposition, which is certain of its object and relies upon it; with לְ of the person or thing, Ex. iv. 8 sq., whose testimony is believingly accepted (comp. Lane under آمن); with בְּ of the person or thing, Deut. xxviii. 66, which is believingly rested on as a firm foundation, a certain warrant. Both constructions are met with to designate the attitude towards God. האמין לה׳, Deut. ix. 23, but more frequently האמין בה׳, xv. 6; Ex. xiv. 31; comp. iv. 31, xix. 9; Num. xiv. 11, xx. 12; Deut. i. 32. The LXX. translates here, καὶ ἐπίστευσεν Ἀβραμ τῷ Θεῷ; one of the New Testament phrases, πιστεύειν εἰς or ἐπὶ τὸν Θεόν, ἐπί or ἐν τῷ Θεῷ, would have been more in conformity with the text. For האמין בה׳ denotes the faith, not as *assensus*, but according to the *fiducia* or *acquiescentia* in which it is perfected. We are not merely told that Abram believed the testimony of Him who promised, but that he relied upon

His person, and believingly rested in or upon Him. Jahveh reckoned it, this faith, to him (which is the proper meaning of חשׁב, حسب, here with לְ of the person, like Ps. xxxii. 2) as righteousness (צְדָקָה, comp. לִצְדָקָה, Ps. cvi. 31, according to which the LXX. has καὶ ἐλογίσθη αὐτῷ εἰς δικαιοσύνην, like Rom. iv. 3; Gal. iii. 6; Jas. ii. 23). No external legal work whatever, but faith justified Abram before God, while as yet uncircumcised—a prechristian Scripture testimony that not in the way of law, but in the way of the promise which brings him salvation, does man attain to a righteousness valid before God, and that this righteousness, far from being self-effected, is as to its foundation a righteousness imputed in faith, which grasps the salvation offered in Christ. The promise too, here made to Abram, has truly Christ for its object (*sub innumerabili illa posteritate latebat Christus*, as Hunnius remarks); the faith in which he receives it, is faith in the promised seed, and Jahveh, in whom Abram believingly rests, is God the Redeemer. But that this faith is meant to be regarded as the motive power of a new life, is shown by the passage, Ps. cvi. 31, which bears the same relation to Gen. xv. 6 that St. James does to St. Paul. From the righteousness of faith proceeds a righteousness of life, which, for the sake of the source whence it comes, is, like faith itself, reckoned by God as צְדָקָה.

According to the law, "To him that hath shall be given," the faith of Abram is rewarded with a renewed promise of the possession of the land, ver. 7 : *And He said to him: I am Jahveh that led thee out of Ur-Casdim, to give thee this land to take possession of it.* This self-testimony of Jahveh is the preliminary stage to that of Ex. xx. 2—the one conditions and demands the other. It sounds Jahvistico-Deuteronomic. It is then no relapse to unbelief, no fit of weak faith, when Abram says, ver. 8: *O Lord of all, Jahveh, whereby shall I know that I shall possess it?* On בַּמָּה, with euphonic Dagesh, see Ewald, § 243*b*; and on יָדַע, with בְּ of the means, comp. xlii. 33; Ps. xli. 12; Job xii. 9. It is a question, like Gideon's, Judg. vi. 36 sq., and Hezekiah's, 2 Kings xx. 8, not of doubt, but of supplication. God does not leave this justifiable desire of faith ungranted, ver. 9: *And He said to him: Take to thee a heifer of three years old, and a she-goat of three years old, and a ram of three years old, and a turtle dove and a young pigeon.* The *part. Puhal* מְשֻׁלָּשׁ means here, having reached three, *i.e.* three years. So most ancient translators (LXX. Sam., Targ. jer., Syr. Jer.); comp. also 1 Sam. i. 24, ἐν μόσχῳ τριετίζοντι, where LXX. Syr. read בפר משלש. In spite of the various modes of expression, Isa. xv. 5, Judg. vi. 25, Ex. xii. 5 and elsewhere, no other meaning is possible, neither: having reached the third part of full maturity (which מְשֻׁלָּשׁ, *Baba mezia* 68a, as a Denominative from שָׁלִישׁ, a third of full maturity, means), nor: tripled (*i.e.* three calves, like Onkelos), nor: divided into thirds, for Abram divided them not into thirds, but halves, ver. 10: *And he took to him all these, and divided them in the midst, and laid the piece of each over against the other, and the birds he divided not.* On אִישׁ בִּתְרוֹ, each, its piece=the piece of each, see on ix. 5. צִפּוֹר is as collective as at Ps. viii. 9, cxlviii. 10; Ezek. xxxix. 4. They are the five clean sacrificial animals according to the future sacrificial ritual, which Abram is to take; his leaving the turtle and the dove undivided is also in conformity with it (Lev. i. 17). From his laying the בְּתָרִים opposite each other, it may be inferred that he also laid the turtle dove opposite the pigeon, so that four portions lay on each side. This arrangement was to subserve a Divine purpose, the attainment of which was however endangered, ver. 11: *And the birds of prey came down upon the carcases, but Abram drove them away.* He knows not what purpose that which has been thus brought is to serve, but he seeks to preserve it uninjured for a purpose which he hopes to learn. And now preparation is made for the revelation about to be connected with the sacrifice thus lying ready, ver. 12: *The sun was just about to go down, and a deep sleep befell Abram, and, lo, terror, great darkness settled upon him.* On the construction וַיְהִי לָבוֹא, see Ges. § 132, note 1: תַּרְדֵּמָה is deep sleep, ii. 21, here a violent plunging of the natural life of perception and thought into unconsciousness and inactivity, a cessation and, as it were, a casting into slumber of the ordinary activity of the mind and senses, for the purpose of unsealing the inner eye. The LXX. here, as also ii. 21, has ἔκστασις. The succession of accents in אֵימָה חֲשֵׁכָה גְדֹלָה is the same as at vi. 9. The awful and great darkness is supernatural, for it falls only on Abram, and indeed before sunset. After everything earthly has been rendered invisible to him, God lights up the future, vv. 13-16: *And He said to Abram: Thou art to know, that thy seed shall be a stranger in a land not belonging to them, and they shall serve them, and they shall oppress them four hundred years. And again the nation, whom they shall serve, shall be judged by me, and afterwards they shall depart with great possessions. And thou shalt go to thy fathers in peace, and be buried at a good age. And in the fourth generation they shall return hither, for the iniquity of the Amorites is not yet full.* The strange land, viz. Egypt, is first expressly named to Jacob. The subject of וַעֲבָדוּם is the descendants of Abram: they are to serve the inhabitants of the strange land (עבד, with an acc., like xxix. 15; Ex. xxi. 6; Deut. xx. 11). The LXX. has wrongly καὶ δουλώσουσιν αὐτούς, they shall enslave them (thy descendants), which would be וְעָבְדוּ בָם. The Divine retribution begins with וְגַם. The expression תָּבוֹא אֶל־אֲבֹתֶיךָ is like Ps. xlix. 19, and differs from xxv. 8. This is the first time in Holy Scripture that we meet with the word שָׁלוֹם, which (coming from √שׁל) means release, deliverance from care and want, and therefore peace, in the sense of both contentment and satisfaction. וְדוֹר רְבִיעִי is an acc. of time (comp. xvi. 4b). The LXX. correctly has: τετάρτῃ δὲ γενεᾷ. The synecdochic designation of the inhabitants of the Promised Land as הָאֱמֹרִי is a different one from that at xii. 6, xiii. 7. Thus the sojourn in Egypt is to last 400 years, so that דּוֹר (as in Nestor, γενεά, ii. 1. 250) is a *seculum* of 100 years—a round number, instead of which we find, Ex. xii. 40 (*Q*), the more accurate statement, 430 years, with which the genealogy, Ex. vi. 16 sqq., apparently agrees. For the 137 years of Levi, the 133 of Kehath, the 137 of Amram, and the 80 of Moses at the exodus, undoubtedly the representatives of the four generations, give above 400 years, but only if they are added together without regard to synchronism. Hence the LXX. already reckons, Ex. xii. 40, in the 430 the sojourn in Canaan. This is the view handed down in the synagogue (*e.g. Pesikta de Rab Cahana*, ed. Buber, 47*b; Mechilta* Parasha, בא, c. 14), and thence among the Syrians, from which also St. Paul proceeds, Gal. iii. 17. For if we reckon the 25 years from Abraham's entrance into Canaan, and the first promises given him to the birth of Isaac, the 60 years from Isaac's birth to that of Jacob, the 130 thence to Jacob's going into Egypt, together 215 years, with the 215 years of the Egyptian sojourn, they come to 430 years. The genealogy, Ex. vi. 16 sqq., with the numbers of the years of life of Levi, Kehath, and Amram, which together amount to 407 years, prove at least that a generation might at that period be reckoned at 120 (in round numbers 100) years; and we must at any rate estimate a generation according to the numbers in Ex. xii. 40, and not lessen the numbers to suit it. This is however a problem, the discussion of which belongs to Ex. vi. 16 sqq. or Ex. xii. 40, and not to our passage. The revelation here made to Abraham is both in its special and general meaning a new disclosure: he learns that the race, of which he is destined to become the ancestor, is to go through suffering to glory—henceforth a law in the history of redemption (comp. Luke xxiv. 26 ; Acts xiv. 22). What preceded this revelation now appears in the symbolical light thrown upon it thereby. The three years of age of the heifer, the goat and the ram impress upon what is in question the stamp of holiness, for three is the number of God in His nature (comp. the number seven, Judg. vi. 25). The carcases of the animals lying opposite each other in fours allude to the four seasons; the birds of prey rushing down like harpies upon the pieces (comp. Virgil, Æn. iii. 244 sqq.) to the nations hostile to the Lord's people (comp. Deut. xxviii. 49); and the awful darkness presents an anticipation and prefiguration of the fact that the light of glory will arise only from the dark background of previous suffering. But before God manifests Himself in perceptible majesty, it gets yet darker within and without, ver. 17: *And it came to pass, the sun went down and deep darkness took place, and behold a smoking furnace and a flaming torch which passed between these pieces.* The name of the sun, generally masculine, is here as elsewhere, only, Nah. iii. 17, Isa. xlv. 6, Mal. iii. 20, feminine. What follows ויהי, is fashioned according to the scheme of contemporaneousness, like xxvii. 30, comp. vii. 6; the two perfects coincide, the state of the case is essentially the same at 12*a* (Driver, § 165). With sunset the darkness of night set in (הָיָה for הָיְתָה, according to Ges. § 147, note 2), then between the parts of the sacrifice there passed an appearance as of a smoking furnace (עָשֵׁן, adj. = עָשֵׁן), *i.e.* (the point of comparison being only the cylindrical form[1]) of a pillar of smoke and a flaming torch rising up from it. It is Jahveh, whose glory is in its manifestation a shining light from a dark background, who has ordained for all His creatures darkness as the substratum of light, and who also permits His people to attain to light in no other way than through darkness. Thus manifesting Himself, He confirms

[1] See on *tannûr*, Assyr. *tinûru*, Friedr. Delitzsch, *Proleg.* 146; D. H. Müller in the *Wiener Zeitschrift für die Kunde des Morgenlandes*, i. 23 sq.; and for confirmation of the fundamental meaning there accepted, "hollow, concave vessel," Wetzstein in the *Transactions* of the Anthropological Society, 1882, p. 467. A detailed history of the word is given by Rud. Dvorak in the *Zeitschrift für Keilschrift-forschung*, 1882, but with the inadmissible result, that it is a word derived from the Persian.

what He had promised, vv. 18–21: *On that day Jahveh made a covenant with Abram, saying : To thy seed I give this land, from the river of Egypt to the great river, the river Euphrates—the Kenite and Kenizzite and Kadmonite, and the Hittite and Perizzite and the Rephaim, and the Emorite and Canaanite and Girgashite and Jebusite.* The perfect נָתַתִּי applies, as at i. 29, ix. 2 sq., to what is determined; elsewhere as at xx. 16, to what is performed at the time of speaking. It is nowhere else promised that the land of Israel is to reach to Egypt, hence the נְהַר מִצְרַיִם here, and the ποταμὸς Αἰγύπτου, Judith i. 9, is the נַחַל מִצְרַיִם (*naḥal Muṣur* in Asurbanipal's account of the war) often named as the southern boundary of Palestine, the *Wâdi el-'Arîs*, which, now as a shallow brook, now as a rushing torrent, runs through the entire northern portion of the Sinaitic peninsula, and falls into the Mediterranean near the village *el-'Arîs*, the ancient 'Ρινοκόλουρα, the "nose-docked town" (from κόλουρος, dock-tailed, then docked in general = κολοβός) of the Ethiopian conqueror 'Ακτισάνης, Diodor. i. 60. The appellation of this boundary stream as שִׁיחוֹר מִצְרַיִם, 1 Chron. xiii. 5, comp. 1 Kings viii. 65, Josh. xiii. 3, may arise from its having been erroneously regarded as the most westerly portion of the net of channels of the Nile, though it might also, as Ebers admits, have been so called as the first Egyptian water met with in coming from Palestine. On the names of the Euphrates, see on ii. 14. The nations cited are exactly ten. The Kenites dwelling in the farthest south-east, whose name corresponds with *al-Kain*, a branch of the Arabian tribe *Kodā'a* (*DMZ.* xl. 181), the likewise southern Kenizzites (comp. on xxxvi. 15) and the Kadmonites, *i.e.* as it seems the Arabs dwelling farthest to the north-east, are first mentioned. Beginning thus from the border of the land, the enumeration proceeds in a zigzag from south to north to express absolute perfection, whose symbol is the number ten. Instead of the ten, six nations are named, Ex. iii. 8, 17, xxiii. 23, Deut. xx. 17 ; and seven, Deut. vii. 1,

Josh. iii. 10. In both instances the קַדְמֹנִי, קְנִזִּי, קֵינִי and רְפָאִים here enumerated are omitted. The number seven is completed by the here unmentioned חִוִּי. Where only six are named, the גִּרְגָּשִׁי reckoned among the seven are wanting.

The transaction here designated by כרת ברית consists in the engagement, ver. 18, comp. 7, and its pledge. This transaction has always been regarded (see *e.g.* the Targums) as the entering into a covenant by means of a covenant sacrifice; and not incorrectly, although neither a covenant proper is entered into nor a sacrifice proper offered. There is no proper entering into a covenant; for God grants and confirms a promise to Abram, on which account it is He only who passes between the portions of the sacrifice. Hence it is not a covenant in the sense of a *pactio*, but of a *sponsio*. כרת ברית is also elsewhere used, both of the promises of God to man, Ex. xxxiv. 10 (also כרת alone, 2 Chron. vii. 18 ; comp. Hag. ii. 5), and of the promises of man to God, Ezra x. 3. Nor is a proper sacrifice offered, for this laying of the pieces (בְּתָרִים or גְּזָרִים) is not the same as the laying of the portions of the sacrifice upon the altar. Nor is it said that the fire of Jahveh consumed them (comp. Judg. vi. 21; 1 Kings xviii. 38) ; hence the expression of Josephus, *Ant.* i. 10. 3, θυσίαν προσφέρει τῷ Θεῷ, is unsuitable. On the other hand, it is still a sacrificial transaction, to which, indeed, although the central mark of a sacrifice—the *oblatio*—does not apply, its fundamental mark —the *sacratio*—does, for it is for the purpose of worship that Abram slays the animals and lays the pieces. Hence the animals slain and divided into pieces on the occasion of entering into covenants are also called in Latin and Greek ἱερεῖα and *hostiæ*, and the oath combined with this rite is designated in Demosthenes as ὀμνύναι καθ' ἱερῶν or καθ' ἱερῶν τελείων, in Pausanias as ὅρκον διδόναι ἐπὶ τομίων (comp. Hesych. *s.v.* τόμια), although the pieces of the animals were neither burnt in honour of God nor partially eaten, but buried or thrown into water, and the eating of them, as affected by the curse, interdicted. Accordingly we find in this case the performance of what the word בְּרִית (from בְּרָא=בָּרָה, to cut) originally means, and what the phrases בָּרַת בְּרִית (Aram. וְגֵזַר קְיָם), ὅρκια τέμνειν, fœdus ferire, i.e. ferienda hostia, facere fœdus (comp. Pers. *peimân burîden*, to cut an alliance, Turkish *kabini kymak*, to cut in pieces = to conclude a marriage settlement) properly state. God accommodates Himself, says Ephrem (*Opp.* vol. i. p. 162), in this transaction to the custom of the Chaldeans, for it was their solemn usage to pass torch in hand between the divided carcases of the animals, laid opposite each other in an appointed order, and so to inaugurate the covenants they entered into. They thus imprecated upon themselves a like death with these animals (comp. διχοτομεῖν, Luke xii. 46) in case they transgressed the covenant. Comp. Liv. ix. 5: *ut eum ita Jupiter feriat quemadmodum a fetialibus porcus feriatur*; xxi. 45: (*Dii*) *ita mactarent, quemadmodum ipse mactasset agnum*, and also the ancient oath, *per Jovem lapidem*, in which the swearer held a stone in his hand, and (according to Paulus Diaconus) said: *Si sciens fallo, tum me Dispiter salva urbe arceque bonis ejiciat uti ego hunc lapidem*. Here, where it is Jahveh who binds Himself by a covenant, self-imprecation seems out of the question. But it is just this which is essential in this custom, and that this was the case in Israel also is shown by Jer. xxxiv. 18, where Jahveh gives this reference to the עָבַר בַּבְּרִית. The passing of Jahveh between the pieces is an act of deepest condescension, to the same effect as His elsewhere swearing by Himself, xxii. 16, or by His life, Deut. xxxii. 40, or still more anthropomorphically by His soul, Amos vi. 8; Jer. li. 14. It is thus that the occurrence is also viewed by St. Luke, Acts vii. 17, in his reproduction of the speech of Stephen. Jahveh condescends so deeply that He may testify to Abram as palpably, impressively, and memorably as possible, τὸ ἀμετάθετον τῆς βουλῆς αὐτοῦ (Heb. vi. 17). But the deeper His condescension, the more majestic is His appearance. God's manner of manifesting Himself in His intercourse with the patriarchs is on other occasions more gentle and familiar. Here it is purposely more sublimely terrible than elsewhere.

THE EVENTS PRECEDING THE BIRTH OF ISHMAEL, CH. XVI.

The second portion of the second section, ch. xvi., which relates the birth of Ishmael, shows us once more how everything went on in the family of Abram contrary to human thoughts and ways. Sarai remains barren after the covenant as before. She rashly gives up the hope of being called to take part in the realization of the promise, and associates her Egyptian maid with Abram, by whom the latter becomes the mother of Ishmael. The narrator is *J;* but ver. 3 shows itself to be from *Q*, and the birth of Ishmael, ver. 15 sq., also is related in words from *Q*, because this source had in this case the advantage of greater accuracy.

A verse stating the circumstances precedes and is then followed by the facts aimed at in the historical manner, vv. 1–4: *And Sarai, Abram's wife, bare him no child: and she had an Egyptian maid, whose name was Hagar. And Sarai said to Abram: Behold, now, Jahveh has restrained me, that I should not bare. Go in, I pray thee, to my maid, perhaps I may obtain children from her. And Sarai, Abram's wife, took the Egyptian Hagar, her maid, after the lapse of ten years since Abram's dwelling in the land of Canaan, and gave her to Abram her husband to wife. And he went in unto Hagar, and she conceived, and when she perceived that she had conceived, her mistress became little in her eyes.* 1*a* is not a repetition of xi. 30: the barrenness of Sarai continued in Canaan also. Probably Hagar was one of the female slaves bestowed upon Abram by Pharaoh, ch. xii. 16. The historic nature of the name is supported by the national name of the הַגְרִים (הַגְרִיאִים). Being Sarai's handmaid, she was, as is still the custom, entirely at her mistress's disposal. Sarai resigns her to Abram to use her as אִשָּׁה (i.e. אִשָּׁה פִּילֶגֶשׁ), that she may herself be built up, i.e. obtain children by her (xxx. 3; comp. 1 Pet. ii. 5). The idea is a different one from when, with reference to the cottage or arbour set up for the nuptials of a newly-married pair (*DMZ.* xxxii. 153), it is said of the man in relation to the woman in Arabic بَنَى عليها, or in Bedouin diction عَرَّسَ عليها. The family is represented as a house, procreation as building, and becoming a mother as being built up. He who begets is called in Assyrian *bâni*, "my father," *abû bânija*; she who begets *bânîtu*, and that which is begotten *binûtu* or *nabnîtu*. The original form of בֵּן is *banj* (بِن), according to Arabic grammarians = بَنْو), as that of עֵץ is *'aṣj* (عَصْو=عَصًا). בוא אל to a woman is the same as دخل بها, he went in unto her, viz. into the marriage chamber. Abram consents to Sarai's request, מְבַקֵּשׁ זֶרַע אֱלֹהִים (Mal. ii. 15). The intention was good, but also nothing farther. Ten years had then elapsed since Abram settled in Canaan (לְשֶׁבֶת without the tone on the first syllable, because it subordinates genitivally the following subject). When Hagar found that she had conceived she felt herself raised above her former position, and behaved herself as if she had taken Sarai's place, her mistress, to whom she was indebted for her new position, being henceforth little accounted of by her. וַתֵּקַל, impf. Kal, with *a* of the intransitive, עע has an accented ultima, comp., on the contrary, וַיֵּרַע; the accentuation vacillates, Ges. § 67, note 3. Sarai now complains of the arrogant conduct of the concubine, and so requites it that she flees, vv. 5, 6: *And Sarai said to Abram: My suffering wrong is thy fault. I gave my maid into thy bosom, and now that she sees she has conceived, I am little in her eyes—Jahveh judge between me and thee. And Abram said to Sarai: Behold, thy maid is in thy power, do to her as seems good to thee. And Sarai dealt hardly with her, and she fled from her.* With חֲמָסִי עָלֶיךָ Sarai makes her husband responsible for the injury she suffers (comp. Jer. li. 35), and appeals to the judgment of God. וּבֵינֶיךָ has a super-punctuated second Yod, because בֵּין, with the suffix of the second person, elsewhere has always the singular form. Abram saw his closest relation disturbed, and left it to Sarai to deal according to her own judgment with her slave, who was indeed entirely at her disposal. *Hic se Abram ostendit*, says Augustine, *non amatorem servum, sed genitorem liberum.* Sarai abundantly requited Hagar's arrogance by unkind treatment; and Hagar, who found the situation unendurable, took flight. Her name, הָגָר, corresponds (we know not whether accidentally or intentionally) with this fact. For *haǵara* (whence the name *Hiǵra* and the erotic وصل, هجر union and separation) means to break off intercourse with any one, to separate oneself, to depart, in opposition to which ברח has the meaning of to flee from the perverse, the crooked (comp. בְּרִיחַ, cross-piece of timber) direction entered upon.

What a number of mishaps ensued from this course of action, which endeavoured arbitrarily to bring about the fulfilment of the Divine promise instead of patiently waiting for it! God's faithfulness to His covenant however turned all into blessing, ver. 7: *And the angel of Jahveh found her by the fountain of water in the wilderness, by the fountain on the way to 'Sûr.* Hagar was purposing to flee to Egypt by the way of Beersheba. She made use of the road at all times the most frequented: the way to שׁוּר, a place no longer ascertainable (xx. 1) in מִדְבַּר שׁוּר (Ex. xv. 22), *i.e.* (according to Saadia) in the desert region of *el 'Gifâr* (الجفار), from five to seven days' journey long, between the south-west of Philistia and the north-east of Egypt, reaching as far south as beyond Kulzum (Suez), and including the *Tîh beni Isrâil* (the wilderness of Pharan). The angel of Jahveh there appears to her. This is the first time we meet with this kind of revelation of God by means of an angel. How are we to understand it?

Is the angel of God God Himself, making Himself visible as an angel, or only an angel of whom God makes use as the organ of His self-manifestation? The angel is called explicitly יהוה (xviii. 33; Judg. vi. 14; Zech. i. 13, iii. 2, and frequently), אלהים and אל (xxxii. 25 sqq.; Hos. xii. 5, comp. 4), and designates Himself as the God of salvation (xxxi. 13; Ex. iii. 2, 6 sqq.). On the other hand, the very name מלאך (from לאך, لَاكَ الّكَ, Aeth. *la'áka*, to cause to go, to bid go, hence: sending, properly, as the Arabs rightly interpret their الّكَ, the accessory, and presumably the root-form of الّكَ, *n. verb. abstr.*, then one sent) already leads to the personal distinction of the sender (xxiv. 7; Ex. xxxiii. 2; Num. xx. 16) and the sent. We have here then a problem with important pros and cons. The ancient synagogue regards the angel of God as a created angel, calls him מטטרן, *metator*, as he who marches before and is the pioneer of Israel, and explains his speaking as though he were Jahveh Himself by Ex. xxiii. 21, according to which "his name is as the name of his Lord" (*Sanhedrin* 38*b*). The ancient Church, on the contrary, sees in this angel the appearance of the Son of God, the Logos, in the form of an angel. Παντὶ δῆλον—says Basil, *adv. Eunom*. ii. 18—ὅτι ἔνθα καὶ ἄγγελος καὶ Θεὸς ὁ αὐτὸς προσηγορεύεται ὁ μονογενής ἐστι δηλούμενος. This prevailing ancient ecclesiastical view found welcome support in Isa. ix. 5, LXX. (μεγάλης βουλῆς ἄγγελος), and Isa. lxiii. 9, LXX. (οὐ πρέσβυς οὐδὲ ἄγγελος, ἀλλ' αὐτός). On the other hand, the view that the angel of God is everywhere a created angel, is found in the ancient Church only in the Clementines (*Hom*. xx. 7, in the closing portion made known by means of Dressel). It is also found in Augustine, Jerome, Gregory the Great, most decidedly in Theodore and Theodoret, and more recently in Grotius, Clericus, and Calixtus. This view has now for a long time been discredited, because Jewish expositors since the Middle Ages (see Levi b. Gerson on Gen. xvi. 7) have maintained the creaturehood of the angel of Jahveh in an antichristian, and Socinians in an antitrinitarian interest. More recently however Steudel has been the first to attempt its complete establishment, and v. Hofmann, Baumgarten and Köhler (*Comm. on Zechariah*, 1861) are on the same side. The history (xviii.–xix. 28) will show that the LORD is conceived of as being in each of the three angels there appearing; that not one is, in preference to the others, Jahveh Himself in visible manifestation, but that all three are so, though in different manners, according to the will of God, who is using them as His organs, hence that all three are finite spirits made visible (Philo, *Opp.* ii. 17: ἱεραὶ καὶ θεῖαι φύσεις, ὑποδιάκονοι καὶ ὕπαρχοι τοῦ πρώτου Θεοῦ, so too Josephus and the Talmud, *Mezia* 86b). Where then the מלאך ה׳ appears, it will not be Jahveh Himself, but the angel (הַפַּלְאָךְ, xlviii. 16), or an angel (מלאך) without an art., Ex. xxiii. 20, xxxiii. 2; Num. xx. 16; Hos. xii. 5) in whom Jahveh is and of whom He makes use as His organ. That the angel of Jahveh can, without being Jahveh Himself, call himself and let himself be called Jahveh, takes place, according to *Berachoth* ver. 5, מפני ששלוחו של אדם כמותו, *i.e.* because the delegated is equal to the delegator. With this may be compared that in the *Iliad*, 18. 170 sqq. Iris, the messenger of Juno, speaks as though she were herself Juno, and Talthybios, 4. 204, as though he were the person who sends him; and further, that in Herodot. i. 212, the messenger of Tomyris speaks to Cyrus as though he were Tomyris himself; Psamenit, Herod. iii. 14, to the messenger of Cambyses, as though he were Cambyses; Cyrus, in Xenoph. *Cyrop.* 3. 3. § 56, to the ambassador of Cyaxares, as though the latter were in his presence. We have too, in Zech. ii. 12 sqq., a remarkable example of the words of Jahveh and His angel being intermixed, and at Rev. xxii. 6 sqq. a New Testament parallel entirely corresponding to the manner of the מלאך ה׳. Here the very same angel, who elsewhere distinguishes himself in the most decided manner from God and His Christ (xxii. 9), says: ἰδοὺ ἔρχομαι ταχύ. The angel of Jahveh, speaking from himself, prays to Jahveh, Zech. i. 12: How long wilt Thou not have mercy on Jerusalem and the cities of Judah? And at Zech. iii. 2 he says to Satan: Jahveh rebuke thee! which, according to Jude 9, is only said by one who οὐ τολμᾷ κρίσιν ἐπενεγκεῖν βλασφημίας (see Köhler on *Zech*. p. 60). When then he says to Moses, Ex. iii. 6: I am the God of thy fathers, the God of Abraham, Isaac and Jacob, it is the invisible God who is speaking from him who is His organ. This is how the New Testament regards it. For Stephen, Acts vii. 30, calls the angel who appeared to Moses in the burning bush ἄγγελος κυρίου, or, according to A. B. C. S., merely ἄγγελος, and he cannot have thought of the angel, of whom he says, ver. 38, that he spake with Moses on Mount Sinai, as a Divine Being, since he says, ver. 53: ἐλάβετε νόμον εἰς διαταγὰς ἀγγέλων, with which also St. Paul agrees, Gal. iii. 19 and Heb. ii. 2. The law is, as distinguished from the direct revelation of God in Christ Jesus, διαταγεὶς δι' ἀγγέλων, is δι' ἀγγέλων λαληθεὶς λόγος—these New Testament statements are absolutely opposed to the identification of the angel of Jahveh and the Logos. Equally unfavourable to this view is it, that the author of the Epistle to the Hebrews, xiii. 2, where he alludes to Gen. xviii. 19, would certainly have expressed himself differently if he had regarded one of the three angels as directly God (a fact to which Augustine appeals, *de civ*. xvi. 29). Also, that in the two first chaps. of St. Matthew's Gospel, the parallelism of which with the Pentateuchal primitive histories is unmistakeable, the Old Testament angel of Jahveh is transformed into ἄγγελος κυρίου (an angel of the Lord). Hence the New Testament Scriptures are on our side if we say, that Jahveh manifests Himself in the מלאך, in a manner which prefigures and prepares the way for the incarnation, by means of a finite spirit, which becomes visible. The angel of Jahveh is Jahveh's פָּנִים, and yet he is not.[1] He is פָּנָיו, Deut. iv. 37, but מַלְאַךְ פָּנָיו, Isa. lxiii. 9. He is not that direct Presence of God which mortals cannot look upon, and therefore Manoah's fear proved groundless, when he feared he should die because he had seen God, Judg. xiii. 21 sqq. The angel of Jahveh is an angel in whom Jahveh lets His face be seen (xxxii. 31); but this is brought to pass by means of a created being, for no man can see it directly without dying, Ex. xxxiii. 20. He is, as שְׁמִי בְּקִרְבּוֹ in the unique passage, Ex. xxiii. 20–22, declares, the medium and mediator of God's self-manifestation, but not God manifest Himself. The angelophanies of God were a prefiguration of His Christophany. Hence the mediator of the new covenant is called, Mal. iii. 1, מַלְאַךְ הַבְּרִית (comp. Isa. xlii. 6, xlix. 8, and also Heb. iii. 1). He is called thus, not as the incarnate angel of Jahveh, but as the man in whom Jahveh fulfils the covenant, for the realization of which He was preparing the way by appearing in His angel. It is significant that in our passage the angel of Jahveh appears first, not to Abram, but to Hagar, and indeed after the concluding of the covenant, ch. xv. If he were the God of the revelation Himself, his appearance would have been no new event, since Jahveh had not only spoken, but also appeared (xii. 7) to Abram before, ch. xv. If, on the contrary, the appearance by the means of the angel is a new and peculiar manner of revelation, this explains the fact of its not taking place till after the conclusion of that covenant, the purpose of which it was appointed to serve, by being a means of that gradual realization of its promise which was now commencing.

Hagar is resting by a fountain when he finds her; וַיִּמְצָאָהּ, like 1 Chron. xx. 2, for קָ—. A fountain is called עַיִן, as though

---

[1] The section, Ex. xxxii. 30–xxxiv. 10, can no more than Ex. xiv. 19 be turned to account in ascertaining what is the idea of the מלאך ה׳, without critical analysis.

it were a weeping eye of earth, in Spanish Arabicized as *ojo de agua*. Shakespeare, in the *Winter Night's Tale*, compares a beautiful landscape to a female face, and the surface of the water to its eyes. Here at the fountain the angel sends Hagar back to her mistress, vv. 8, 9: *And he said: Hagar, Sarai's maid, whence camest thou and whither goest thou? She said: I flee before Sarai, my mistress. And the angel of Jahveh said to her: Return to thy mistress, and bow thyself under her hands.* Upon this condition he promises her, again taking the initiative, an innumerable posterity, ver. 10: *And the angel of Jahveh said to her: I will increase, yea increase thy seed, and it shall not be able to be numbered for multitude.* Then taking the initiative for the third time, he promises her the son through whom the promise made to Abram, xv. 5, shall find a reflected fulfilment in her case, on the ground of her belonging to the patriarch's family, vv. 11, 12: *And the angel of Jahveh said to her: Behold, thou art pregnant, and shalt bear a son, and shalt call his name Jišmaʿêl; for Jahveh hath heard thy affliction. And he shall be a wild ass of a man; his hand shall be against every one, and the hand of every one against him. And he shall dwell eastward of all his brethren.* Together with the participial adj. הָרָה, as at xxxviii. 24 and frequently, comp. 2 Sam. xi. 5, stands יֹלַדְתְּ, the unaltered root-form of יֹלֶדֶת, as at Judg. xiii. 5, 7; comp. on the contrary, xvii. 19; Isa. vii. 4. Elsewhere also in J, from iv. 1 onwards, the mother appears as the giver of the name, as the father does in Q, from v. 3 onwards. In the reason for the name יִשְׁמָעֵאל we have יהוה instead of the more obvious אלהים, xxi. 17. The genitival combination פֶּרֶא אָדָם, a wild ass of human species, is like כְּסִיל אָדָם, a fool of human species, *i.e.* one conspicuous in it as such, Prov. xv. 20. This image of the פֶּרֶא, Arab. *ferâ*, the beautiful and swift animal which when grown cannot be caught, described Job xxxix. 5–8, brings vividly before us the unbounded love of freedom of the hardy and frugal

Bedouin, who despises the life of cities, and roves about, spear in hand, in the desert on his camel (*delul*), or subsequently on his horse. The words יָדוֹ בַכֹּל=לְפֹל וגו׳ describe an incessant war of attack and defence, as an Arabic poet says: I have fraternized with war; if I do not stir up the war myself, I am the shield of him who stirs it up.[1] The words עַל־פְּנֵי וגו׳ (like xxiii. 19, xxv. 18) state the eastern dwelling-place of the Ishmaelites among those of the Abrahamites: the peninsula between the Tigris, the isthmus of Suez and the Red Sea, which became the cradle of wandering hordes for the tropical latitudes of North Africa and South Asia, an active human fountain whose streams have flowed for millenniums far and wide, eastward and westward, conquering the nations from the Ebro to the Oxus, and remaining themselves invincible. Hagar rightly recognises in the angel who had thus placed before her eyes the future of her son, the Presence of Jahveh, ver. 13: *And she called the name of Jahveh who spake to her: Oh, Thou God of sight; for she said: Have I here also looked after him that seeth me?* She calls him אֵל רֳאִי, God of seeing, *i.e.* the All-seeing, whose all-seeing eye the helpless and forsaken does not escape, even in the remotest corner of the wilderness; for — as she says — have I here (הֲלֹם, elsewhere *huc*, Ex. iii. 5, here *hic*), even here in the wilderness, far from the patriarch's home, looked after him who is seeing me (who has seen me?). רֳאִי is generally, but wrongly, taken for a pausal form of רָאִי, which must have been רֹאִי, with the tone on the penultima, like צֳרִי, from צְרִי, Ezek. xxvii. 17, found at Job vii. 8 (see Baer) as a various reading, but as a masoretically authenticated one, only at 1 Sam. xvi. 12. And רָאִיתִי is usually understood, as already by Onkelos, in the sense of *videns = vivus* (like ὁρέων or δεδορκώς = ζῶν) *mansi*, which would have required אֶרְאֶה or אֲנִי רֹאֶה, or better, as Wellh. (*Proleg.* 2nd edit. p. 339,

---

[1] Schwarzlose, *Die Waffen der alten Araber* (1886), p. 34.

note 2) reads, according to Judg. vi. 22, xiii. 22, Ex. xxxiii. 20: רָאִיתִי וָאֶחִי. But this וָאֶחִי makes אחרי ראי inexplicable, which cannot mean "after my seeing" (so already *Gesch.* 344), for which אחרי רְאוֹתִי is the expression required. Hence אחרי ראי must be taken together, אחרי in a local sense, like Isa. xxxvii. 22, and the "looking after" in the sense of Ex. xxxiii. 23. Jahveh appeared to her in His angel. While he was speaking to her he saw her, but it was not granted her to look him in the face; however, as he was disappearing, she could look after him, whose gracious Providence had not overlooked her in her misery. The fountain also received a name from the occurrence, ver. 14: *Therefore the well was called Beër lachai roï; it lies between Kadeš and Bered.* It was in remembrance of Hagar's experience a sacred place, xxiv. 62, xxv. 11. The ל in the name is the Lamed of dedication, like Isa. viii. 1. If רָאִיתִי, 13*b*, could mean *vivus mansi*, the explanation, "He who sees me is (remains) alive," might commend itself; but then God or the angel would be the speaker, which is inconceivable. Hence it is, on the contrary: the well of the Living One, my beholder, *i.e.* who sees me (like Job viii. 8, instead of רֹאִי), Isa. xxix. 15, or רֹאִי, Isa. xlvii. 10). Onkelos, with real correctness, has: Well of the angel of the Living One (מַלְאַךְ קָיְמָא), who made himself visible to me. For קָדֵשׁ and בֶּרֶד the Syriac has: between רקם and נדר, בית, Onkelos: between רקם and חגרא (which in him, ver. 7 = שׁוּר), Targ. Jerus.: between רקם and הלוצה (Elusa); the Targums elsewhere render Kadesh-Barnea by (רְקַם גֵּיאָה (גֵּאָה). The problematic situation of Kadesh was spoken of at xiv. 7. John Rowlands, whose observations H. Clay Trumbull found on the spot to be perfectly trustworthy, discovered Hagar's well, or at least that which is now esteemed such, at *Muweilih* (مويلح, the name of the black camel, which is esteemed the best), a place still provided with water, south of Beersheba. It is a chief station on the caravan road from

Beersheba along the *'Gebel es-Sûr* which runs from north to south, and is combined by Rowlands with שׁוּר. The Bedouins not only connect the well of Muweilih, but also a rocky dwelling in the neighbourhood, with Hagar, perhaps because ھاجر and حجر (rock) seem to them as much combined as in the Text. Rec. of Gal. iv. 25. It is certainly this very well of which Jerome says: *hodieque Agar puteus demonstratur.* Here the fugitive Hagar seems to have had that manifestation of God by which she was directed to return to Abram's house. She also showed herself obedient, and became the mother of Ishmael, vv. 15, 16 : *And Hagar bore Abram a son : and Abram called the name of his son, whom Hagar bare, Jišmaʿel. And Abram was eighty-six years old when Hagar bare Jišmaʿel to Abram.* That what the angel had predicted came to pass is told by *J* also, but the Redactor preferred to reproduce it as found in *Q*. The birth of Ishmael took place in Abram's eighty-sixth year, for he was seventy-five years old at his entry into Canaan, and ten years (ver. 4) together with the time of Hagar's pregnancy had elapsed. Abram has now a son, but is he the seed which the promises of God have in view? This question Abram cannot himself answer. He must often have asked it of God, till at last he received the answer related ch. xvii.

THE SIGN OF THE COVENANT, THE CHANGE OF NAME, AND THE PROMISE OF THE BIRTH OF ISAAC, CH. XVII.

The third section of Abram's life begins with ch. xvii., a portion characteristic of *Q*. Elohim seals His covenant with Abram, giving him the name of promise, Abraham, and instituting circumcision as the sign of the covenant (1–14). Sarai also receives the name of promise, Sarah, and is now distinctly designated as the mother of Isaac, who, while to Ishmael also are awarded abundant blessings, is to receive the one all-surpassing blessing, that God will make with him and with his seed an everlasting covenant (15–22). Elohim, who has since the Fall been enthroned far from men, and since the Flood far from the earth, having reascended, Abraham in his ninety-ninth year, and in Ishmael's thirteenth, circumcises himself, his son and his whole household (23–27). Thus this first portion of the third section, which corresponds with and continues the first portion of the second section, falls into three strictly distinct divisions. This strophic artistically rounded off design, with its terminating exclamations, its frequent repetitions like strokes upon the same nail, the Divine names אלהים and שׁדי אל, the whole system of favourite expressions grouped about these names and always found with them (הוֹלִיד, בֶּד־נֶכָר, אֶרֶץ בְּנַעַן, אֲחֻזָּה) not מְאֹד מְאֹד, לְדֹרֹתָם, כָּל־זָכָר, בְּרַת בְּרִית not נָתַן בְּרִית, הקים בְּרִית, יָלַד, לִבְרִית and לַאֲחֻזַּת עוֹלָם, וְנִכְרְתָה הַנֶּפֶשׁ הַהוּא מֵעַמֶּיהָ, מִקְנַת־כֶּסֶף, מִגָּרִים, פָּרָה וְרָבָה, בְּעֶצֶם הַיּוֹם הַזֶּה, עוֹלָם), in short all and everything bears the mark of Q, who here gives completely in its historical place an important portion of the Thorah, which is afterwards taken for granted in the Codex, Lev. xii. 3, without farther explanation. Elsewhere too he refers to this fundamental confirmation of the covenant, Ex. vi. 3 sq., and when xvii. 16 sq. is compared with xviii. 10–15, shows himself to be an independent and separate narrator. בְּרִית is repeated thirteen times, whence an ancient eulogy of circumcision (*Nedarim* 31*b*, comp. *Berachoth* 48*b*) says: גדולה מילה שנכרתו עליה שלש עשרה בריתות.

There has been much contention as to whether a custom existing elsewhere was transferred by Divine sanction to the race of the promise, or whether the origin of all circumcision is to be traced back to its Divine sanction for Abram. The circumcision of boys of thirteen, already existing among the Arabic Ishmaelites before Mohammed (Joseph. *Ant.* i. 12. 2), refers itself to the patriarch as a component part of the *Dîn Ibrâhim* (the religion of Abraham). There is however, besides these two possibilities, still a third. When Herodotus testifies to the customariness of circumcision among the Colchians, Egyptians and Æthiopians, among the Syrians at the rivers Thermôdon and Parthenios, among the Phœnicians and Macronians, and remarks that the Palestinian Syrians and the Phœnicians confess to having learnt it from the Egyptians, as the Syrians at the Thermôdon and Parthenios do to having it from the Colchians (ii. 104): its dissemination by way of imitation among this circle of nations (to which belong also, according to Diodorus, iii. 32, the Troglodytes, and apparently, according to Jer. ix. 25, Edom, Ammon and Moab) is indeed still conceivable; and we may assume, with Ewald, that the still existing custom among the Ethiopian Christians, the negroes of the Congo, etc., is the remnant of an ancient African view of the matter which started from the valley of the Nile. But we also meet with circumcision in America among many Indian tribes, *e.g.* the Salivas, the Guamos, the Otamocos on the Orinoco, who circumcise infants of both sexes on the eighth day after birth, as also among the inhabitants of Yucatan and the Mexicans (see Martius, *Indianer Südamerika's*, p. 582 sq.). It has likewise been found in the South Sea Islands, *e.g.* in the Fiji Islands, in a manner similar to the Jewish, and among the most southerly negro tribes, *e.g.* the Damaras (Owaherero) in tropical South Africa, whose chiefs, we are told by Francis Galton, slew half a dozen oxen on a circumcision day, as on a day of festivity. Here we cannot imagine any connection with either the Abrahamic or the ancient Egyptian circumcision, unless we were, with the crack-brained author of the *Palaeorama* (1868), to transfer the primitive history of mankind from Asia to America, and let it be played out originally in the latter, and only imitatively in the former. The case is the same with heathen circumcision as with heathen sacrifice. As sacrifice arose from the feeling of the need of an atonement, so did circumcision from the feeling of the impurity of human nature. This too is the point of sight under which it is placed in Israel. The uncircumcised is esteemed as טָמֵא, the foreskin עָרְלָה as טֻמְאָה κατ' ἐξ., on which account hereditary spiritual uncleanness is figuratively called (Lev. xxvi. 41; Deut. x. 16, xxx. 6 and frequently) עָרְלָה of the heart, while circumcision is regarded as the taking away of טֻמְאָה (whence it is in Arabic simply called *ṭuhûr* or *ṭathîr*, purification), and as the first of all covenant duties for every member of the holy nation, Ex. xix. 6; comp. Num. xvi. 3. The uncircumcised appeared not merely as one standing outside the holy covenant, but also as one naturally unclean (comp. Ex. xii. 48 with Lev. vii. 20). The natural and ethical prerequisites of circumcision are however implied in each other. The reason for circumcision appearing as a requirement of bodily purity, is to be found in the fact that human natural life culminates in the intercourse of the sexes, and therefore its carnalization culminates in the flesh κατ' ἐξ. (בָּשָׂר, Lev. xv. 2; Ezek. xvi. 26), that there is the chief seat of both moral and natural impurity, and that there sin prevails most unrestrictedly and is transmitted in ever new combinations from parents to children. Hence also the injunction that the child is to be circumcised on the eighth day after birth (ver. 12; Lev. xii. 3), for both the male child and she who bare him are in a state of uncleanness for seven days, and the child is not to be subjected to circumcision till after separation for the embryonal aliment. To the physico-ethic prerequisites of circumcision is also added the historical, viz. that a nation of redemption is to be begotten, that it may become the redemption of the nations. There is therefore no place of human nature which could be more in need of a sign of the Divine approval than the place of generation. Circumcision is intended to show that God approves of generation, notwithstanding the sinful corruption which has taken possession of it, and purposes to use it in that work of redemption to which history is tending. The circumcised man is to know himself to be a member of a tribal and national society, with which God has entered into an eternal covenant, upon the ground of promises which have for their contents the redemption of mankind, and whose generations form a genealogical chain issuing in the redemption of the world. Circumcision is to remind him of the covenant into which he has entered with God, and of the high calling in which he has a share, is to be to him a perpetual reminder, warning not to obstruct in rude immoral lust his power of generation, and also, in its natural use, not to forget its impurity and need of sanctification. So far circumcision certainly is also, as Philo says, a sign of the ἡδονῶν ἐκτομὴ αἳ καταγοητεύουσι διάνοιαν. It told the man that he had Jahveh for his bridegroom, to whom he was betrothed by the blood of circumcision, Ex. iv. 25; hence not only the Jews, but the Ishmaelites and the Moslems in general, call the day of circumcision the circumcision marriage, and celebrate it with the solemnity of a wedding. Still circumcision is no sacrament in the New Testament sense, and differs from baptism in this respect also, that it is no initiatory rite properly so called. It is not circumcision which makes the Israelite an Israelite, *i.e.* a member of the Israelite Church. He is this by birth. For in the Old Testament the nation and the Church are one and the same. Every בֶּן יִשְׂרָאֵל belongs as such to the קְהַל יִשְׂרָאֵל, for God has placed Israel in covenant relation to Himself, and in virtue of this position the nation is at the same time a religious community. This covenant relation involves however covenant obligations, which again have as their correlative covenant promises. The first of all these covenant obligations is the מִילָה. The reception of circumcision is for the born Israelite the fulfilment of his first covenant obligation. The born Israelite does not thereby become a member of the קְהַל ה', but proves himself to be such. The case is however different with the Gentile. He can in no other manner enter the community of the covenant than by submitting to the first covenant obligation, the מִילָה, by which he at the same time takes upon himself all the duties of a born Israelite, and receives all his privileges and benefits. Circumcision, which is to the born Israelite only the seal of the relation in which the seed of Abraham is placed toward Jahveh, is to the non-Israelite the rite of admission, which qualifies him henceforth to keep the Passover with Israel (Ex. xii. 43—49), and so incorporates him into Israel that there is no difference between the circumcised גֵּר and the אֶזְרָח (Ex. xii. 48). So far then as it compensates in the case of the non-Israelite for birth among the covenant people, and in that of the Israelite is a seal of that birth, Circumcision and Baptism may certainly be compared as means of grace, incorporating into the Church. They are also similar, in that both are a recasting of an already existing rite of purification, for the sacrament of Baptism is in conformity with the טבילת גרים (the baptism of proselytes), and at all events with that of John the Baptist. In other respects however they essentially differ. Circumcision impresses an outward characteristic, Baptism an inward one. Circumcision places a man in relation, by way of promise, to the coming redemption; Baptism, by way of impartation, to the redemption that is come. Circumcision is for the seed of Abraham, and only secondarily for those who enter it; Baptism is for the whole human race without national prerogative, and also without distinction of sex. Circumcision is a sign in the flesh; Baptism is a spiritual transaction, which is but transitorily represented in the earthly element of water, $\pi\epsilon\rho\iota\tau o\mu\grave{\eta}$ $\grave{a}\chi\epsilon\iota\rho o\pi o\acute{\iota}\eta\tau o\varsigma$, Col. ii. 11. For the Old Testament Church is the visible organism of a nation; the New Testament Church is, on the contrary, the body of Christ, *i.e.* the invisible organism which the Lord, who is the Spirit, has produced for Himself. It is the vocation of the New Testament Church to carry on the development of that spiritual life which is its true nature, and to procure for it an ever more and more commanding, sanctifying influence upon the natural, both within and without her body; it is, on the other hand, the vocation of the Old Testament Church more and more to internalize and spiritualize the sanctified natural life which is its true nature. The tendency of the New Testament Church is from within outwards, from the centre to the circumference, from the world to come to this world, to raise the latter to the former. The tendency of the Old Testament Church, on the contrary, is from without inwards, from the circumference to the centre, from this world to that which is to come.

The name 'ה just appears, ver. 1, for the purpose of connecting ch. xvii. with ch. xvi. (comp., on the other hand, xxxv. 11): *Abram was ninety and nine years old when Jahveh appeared to Abram, and said to him: I am El 'Saddai: walk before me, and be spotless.* It was then twenty-four years after his migration, thirteen after the birth of Ishmael, and at least fourteen after the entering into covenant of ch. xv., when Jahveh appeared to him to seal the covenant by the institution of a sign. The divine name שַׁדַּי is, according to ancient interpretation, the same as שֶׁ דַּי, He who is self-sufficing— the All-Sufficient ἱκανός (= αὐτάρκης), which can in no respect be accepted. Neither is it an original plural: *potentes mei* (Nöldeke), the form being opposed to this interpretation, and no trace appearing of the position of the word in the address; but it is from שָׁדַד (according to the form חַי), which, from the root-meaning of making fast or tight, *i.e.* knotting, barring, barricading, contained in the Arabic شد, advances to that of powerful intervention, and not from a synonymous שָׂדָה, which the usage of the Hebrew language does not exhibit, nor from a synonymous שׁוּר, whence שַׂר, the powerful, the Lord, plur. שָׂרִים. Friedr. Delitzsch thinks differently,[1] and would refer this Divine name to the Assyrian *šadû*, to be high. But even supposing that the proper name שְׂדֵיאוּר is to be explained according to the Assyrian *šadê ûru*, the rise of the morning (= עֲלוֹת הַשַּׁחַר), which is very tempting, and granting also that

---

[1] See his *Prolegomena*, p. 95 sq. It is worthy of notice that the LXX. translates שַׁדַּי אֵל, xvii. 1, by merely ὁ θεός σου, xxviii. 3, ὁ θεός μου, Ex. vi. 3, θεὸς ὢν αὐτῶν, and Ps. lxviii. 15, τὸν ἐπουράνιον.

the form שַׁדַּי, not שַׁדַי, can be referred to a verb לָה, we find the meaning, "the All-Powerful," far more sensible than the meaning, "the All-elevated," for which the Hebrew has a whole series of other words, as עֶלְיוֹן (מָרוֹם) רָם, מַעֲלָה, נִשְׂגָּב. The most ancient feeling for language derived שַׁדַּי from שדד, as may be inferred from Joel i. 15, and the former meaning is in any case more helpful to the understanding of Ex. vi. 2 sq. than the latter. The Divine names, יהוה, אל שדי, אלהים, are the signs-manual of three degrees of Divine revelation and Divine knowledge. אלהים is the God who so made nature that it exists, and so preserves it that it consists. אל שדי is the God who so constrains nature that it does His will, and so subdues it that it bows to and subserves grace. יהוה is the God who carries out the purposes of grace in the midst of nature, and at last puts a new creation of grace in the place of nature. אלהים is the God who created the soil of nature. אל שדי (explained by Ibn Ezra and Kimchi: מנצח המערכת העליונה, by Nachmani: שודד את־המזלות, He who breaks through the *influxus siderum*, and therefore the course of nature) is the God who omnipotently ploughs it and scatters therein the seed of promise. יהוה is the God who brings this seed of promise to its flower and fruit. Hence the covenant with Noah and the Noachidæ was made in the name אלהים; for this covenant is by its very nature a renewal and guarantee of the order of creation, which had been broken through by the Flood; the covenant with the patriarchs in the name אל שדי, for it is by its nature the subdual of corrupted and perishable nature and the foundation of the marvellous work of grace; and the covenant with Israel in the name יהוה, for it is in its nature the completion of this work of grace and its carrying on to the climax of its perfection, to which אֲנִי יהוה, when occurring in the history of the patriarchs (xv. 7, xxviii. 13), prophetically points. The times of the patriarchs are the period of El-Shaddai. Their characteristic is the violence done to the natural to make it subserve the purposes of salvation. The

GENESIS XVII. 2–5.

ethic prerequisites of this new state are, with respect to Abram, a walk with constant regard to God and a disposition entirely devoted to Him (תָּמִים, see on vi. 9). Thereupon God offers, ver. 2: *So will I make my covenant between me and thee, and will increase thee beyond measure*, properly with weight, weight *i.e.* in the most important and intense manner. The phrase נתן ברית (here as at ix. 12; Num. xxv. 12) designates the covenant as a gracious free offer of God. The impression made upon Abram by the appearance and word of God, ver. 3a: *And Abram fell upon his face.* Continuation of what God will perform in accordance with His covenant and change of Abram's name, 3b–5: *And Elohim talked with him, saying: As for me, behold, my covenant with thee, and thou art to become the father of a multitude of nations. And no longer shall thy name be called Abram; but thy name shall be Abraham, for the father of a multitude of nations have I appointed thee.* אֲנִי here, like אָנֹכִי at xxiv. 27, stands first, in an absolute sense, correlatively with וְאַתָּה, ver. 9. Because the covenant implies something that is to be, וְהָיִיתָ may be used in continuation, in the sense of "thou art to become." The ו before וְהָיָה after a preceding לֹא has, as at xlii. 10, the meaning of כִּי־אִם. The accusative of the object is found with passives as at 5a, also at iv. 18, and frequently, it is an ordinary construction. לְאָב instead of לְאָבִי is said with reference to the name אַבְרָהָם, in which אָב, as also elsewhere *e.g.* אֲבִשָׁלוֹם (with אֲבִישָׁלוֹם), is the form of combination. המון (from המה, to roar, to rush), which symphonizes with the last syllable of אַבְרָהָם, is purposely chosen instead of קָהָל, xxxv. 11, xlviii. 4, xxviii. 3. And while, where this promise is made to Jacob xxviii. 3 (לִקְהַל עַמִּים), xxxv. 11 (קְהַל גּוֹיִם), and to Joseph xlviii. 4 (לִקְהַל עַמִּים), עמים (גוים) is meant of the national tribes to which the sons of Jacob should grow, we must here, where as nowhere else הֲמוֹן גּוֹיִם is used, understand not Israel alone, but all the nations of whom Abraham became the ancestor: the Arab tribes descended from him through Hagar and Keturah and the Edomites. The quotation too (Rom. iv. 17) presupposes that the promise extends beyond Israel—the apostle placing it in the light of xii. 3, and understanding it spiritually. The name אַבְרָם means exalted father, or, the father is exalted, which certainly is to be understood as a word of acknowledgment with respect to God, like אֱלִיאָב, God is a father, אֲבִיעֶזֶר, the father is a support, and the like (see Nestle, *Eigennamen*, pp. 182-188). By the change to אברהם, the acknowledgment of God on the part of him who is named becomes God's acknowledgment of him. For אַבְרָהָם means—and this is certainly the best explanation — father of a רָהָם (=הָמוֹן), of a rushing, *i.e.* a noisy, multitude (Arab. رهام ; comp. Isa. xvii. 12, 13) ; nor is it perhaps accidental that a ה, the fundamental letter of יהוה, is interwoven in it. After the name of the patriarch is made the prophetic cipher of his high destiny, the promise is further unfolded and repeated in grander terms than ever before, vv. 6-8 : *And I will make thee exceedingly fruitful beyond measure, and appoint thee to be nations, and kings shall come forth from thee. And I will establish my covenant between me and thee and thy seed after thee, according to their generations, for an everlasting covenant, to be a God to thee and to thy seed after thee. And I will give unto thee, and to thy seed after thee, the land of thy pilgrimage, the whole land of Canaan, for an everlasting possession, and I will be their own God.* This fact to which the promise returns is the climax of the covenant: God promises Himself, with all that He is and purposes and can effect, to the descendants of Abraham. Henceforth the narrative no longer speaks of the patriarch as *Abram,* but as *Abraham.*

The Divine address having now reached the goal so admirably prepared for, begins again, vv. 9-11 : *Elohim said also to Abraham: And as for thee, thou shalt observe my covenant, thou and thy descendants after thee, according to their generations. This is my covenant, which ye shall observe, between me and you and thy seed after thee: Every male among you shall be circumcised. Ye shall circumcise the flesh of your foreskin, and it shall be the sign of a covenant between me and you.* The obverse to אֲנִי, 4a, follows in this וְאַתָּה, thou, on thy part. As הקים ברית means at one time the making, at another the confirmation, of a covenant, so does ברית mean at one time a covenant promise, at another, as here, a covenant obligation or condition. To circumcise (comp. on the notion, Job xxiv. 24) is called מָלַל (√ מל, perhaps related to מר, from the drawing backwards and forwards of the cutting instrument), *Niph.* נִמַּל, whence נְמַלְתֶּם=נְמַלְתָּם (with an accus. of the object, as is also the case with the passive at vv. 5, 14, 24), not from a verb נָמַל, which does not exist in this sense, and probably also the *impf.* יִמַּל (Ps. xxxvii. 2; Job xiv. 2, xviii. 16); or מאל (post-biblical מָהַל), *Niph.* נָמוֹל (according to the post-biblical formation, נִדֹּן, נִצּוֹל, נִוֹּף, Luzz. *Gramm.* § 521), whence the imperatively used *inf. abs.* הִמּוֹל, 10b. The mode of performance is now more particularly defined, the law of circumcision specialized, vv. 12–14: *And eight days old shall every male be circumcised according to your generations: the home-born and the bought with money of all strangers, who do not belong to thy seed. Circumcised, yea, circumcised shall be thy home-born and he that is bought with thy money, and my covenant shall be in your flesh for an everlasting covenant. And an uncircumcised one, a male, who is not circumcised in the flesh of his foreskin—this soul shall be extirpated from his fellow-countrymen, my covenant has he broken.* Circumcision is to be performed on a child when he is eight days old, in which injunction seven days are reckoned, according to Lev. xii., for purification from the uncleanness which adheres to the child as well as to the mother directly after birth. It is also to be performed on every slave of the patriarchal family, whether *vernae* or *mancipia*, so that the family may be esteemed a unity which is neither accidental nor one merely serving the earthly. Especially must this be the case with the nation developing in this family, into which all who are susceptible of salvation in the heathen world are to be incorporated by circumcision as subsequently by baptism. Extirpation (וְנִכְרְתָה) from the national society is to be the lot of the uncircumcised. The same threat is found with the command to observe the Sabbath, there including the capital punishment to be inflicted by the congregation, Ex. xxxi. 14, comp. also xxxv. 2, Num. xv. 32–36 ; its proper meaning however is the being snatched away by direct Divine judgment, according to tradition the premature and childless death of one who is uncircumcised and of full age. In this threat of the so-called *Carath*, מֵעַמֶּיהָ (for which Ex. xxxi. 14 has מִקֶּרֶב עַמֶּיהָ) is interchanged with the synonymous מִיִּשְׂרָאֵל, Ex. xii. 15, Num. xix. 13, or מֵעֲדַת יִשְׂרָאֵל, Ex. xii. 19, Num. xvi. 9. The plural עַמֶּיהָ does not assume that the singular עַם may signify a single fellow-countryman (as the post-biblical גוֹי means also a single heathen); עַם means the people as a whole, and עַמִּים the parts of the whole nation (tribes, families and individuals, בְּנֵי הָעָם, Lev. xix. 18, comp. 16). The reason אֶת־בְּרִיתִי הֵפַר implies that it is not *defectus*, but *contemtus*, which incurs the penalty of the Carath ; on the pausal הֵפַר like הֵתַל, Isa. xviii. 5, see Ges. § 67, note 6.

The Divine address begins again. Sarai's name, which she brought with her from her heathen ancestral home, is also to be transformed, in accordance with the new times rich in promise, which were to begin with Abraham, vv. 15, 16: *And Elohim said to Abraham: Sarai thy wife— thou shalt not call her name Sarai, for Sarah shall her name be. And I will bless her and also give thee a son of her, and will bless her and she shall become nations. Kings of nations shall arise from her.* The fundamental letter of the name יהוה is entwined in the name of the ancestress also of that promised seed, which is the germ and star of the promised future. The warlike (שָׂרַי, LXX. Σάρα, from שׂרה, to struggle, to fight, with "the old feminine suffix,

which still occurs in the Syriac as *ai*, and is written ܣ
in the Arabic, *é* in the Ethiopic," *DMZ*. xl. 183) becomes
a princess (שָׂרָה, fem. of שַׂר, prince, LXX. Σάρρα, with
double ρ as a compensation for the length of the *a*;
Assyr. *šarratu*, fem. of *šarru*, according to Friedr. Delitzsch,[1]
from *šarâru*, to rise brilliantly, to beam forth). She is to
become גּוֹיִם, the twelve tribes of Israel, and the multitude
of the heathen spiritually incorporated therein being traced
back to her. The promise now included Sarah also in its
miraculous circle. Impression made upon Abraham by the
glorious yet paradoxical announcement, ver. 17: *And
Abraham fell upon his face and laughed, and he said in
his heart: Shall a child be born to one a hundred years old,
or shall Sarah — shall one that is ninety years old bear?*
The succession of interrogative particles הֲ...וְאִם...הֲ is more
emphatic than at Num. xi. 12, 22, and the Dagesh in
הַלְּבֶן is like xviii. 21, xxxvii. 32. His desire concerning
the son whom he already has, ver. 18: *And Abraham said
to God: Would that Ishmael might live in Thy sight!* That
he might only remain an object of God's loving care! (Prov.
iv. 3). This shall suffice him; he ventures to ask and to
hope for nothing higher. God's answer to the petition which
thus evades His promise, vv. 19—21: *And God said: Nay,
but Sarah thy wife shall surely bear thee a son, and thou
shalt call his name Isaac, and I establish my covenant with
him for an everlasting covenant, with his seed after him.
And as for Ishmael, I have heard thee: Behold, I have blessed
him and made him fruitful and increased him exceedingly;
twelve princes shall he beget; and I have appointed him for
a great nation. But my covenant I establish with Isaac,
whom Sarah shall bear unto thee about this time in the next
year.* The particle אֲבָל (apparently from √ בל, whence also
בֵּל, בַּעַל, to be powerful = *potenter, vero*) introduces a counter-
assurance, and then an assurance in general (comp. *Erubin*

---

[1] See the satisfactory proof in his *Prolegomena*, p. 92.

20b, אמרו להן אבל, they answered: certainly). The לְ of לְיִשְׁמָעֵאל is that of reference, as at xix. 21, xlii. 9; comp. Isa. xxxii. 1b. On the twelve נְשִׂיאִים of Ishmael, see xxv. 12-16. Ishmael also is abundantly blessed, but the covenant surpassing all that is earthly is made with Isaac, who will be born about this time, בַּשָּׁנָה הָאַחֶרֶת, in the year next following, properly that coming behind the present; comp. ὄπισθεν, afterwards = future (see this referred to, xxi. 2). The name *Jishak* (laugher) is to be the continuous expression of the impression made upon Abraham by the promise. Its matter was so immensely great that he fell in adoration on the earth, so immensely paradoxical that he could but involuntarily laugh. Contrast is the essence of the ridiculous. What אל שדי does, takes nature captive to the obedience of grace, and reason to the obedience of faith.

Cessation of the Divine address, ver. 22: *And when He had ended His speaking with him, Elohim went up leaving Abraham.* Jerome also marks the period thus: *ut desiit loqui cum eo,* etc. 22a being logically an accessory sentence, the subject אֱלֹהִים is reserved for the principal sentence. ויעל can signify that God went away from Abraham, withdrew from him (comp. Ex. xxxiii. 1); but the parallel passage, xxxv. 13, shows that ascension to heaven is intended,—the heavenly one then had descended, for since the Fall God is far from man, and since the Flood the place of His throne has been super-terrestrial. Abraham now executes the order of Him who has disappeared, vv. 23-27: *And Abraham took Ishmael his son and all his servants born in his house and bought, every male among the people of Abraham's house, and circumcised the flesh of their foreskin on the same day, as Elohim had said unto him. And Abraham was ninety - nine years old when the flesh of his foreskin was circumcised. And Ishmael his son was seventeen years old when the flesh of his foreskin was circumcised. On one and the same day was Abraham circumcised and Ishmael his son.*

And all the people of his house, the home-born and those bought of a stranger, were circumcised with him. The בְּ of בְּאַנְשֵׁי, 23a, is partitive, like vii. 21, xxiii. 18, and like the מִן of מִבֶּל, 12b; while, on the other hand, מֵאֵת, 27a, according to Lev. xxvii. 24, comp. Gen. xxiii. 20 (=מִיַּד, xxxiii. 19), belongs to מִקְנַת. עֶצֶם in biblical Hebrew serves to denote naturally lifeless, as נֶפֶשׁ does a naturally living being, hence *eo ipso die, eodem die.* On account of the great importance of circumcision, the obligation of which is presupposed in subsequent legislation, its performance is related as circumstantially and accurately as possible.

THE HEAVENLY MESSENGERS AT MAMRE AND SODOM, CHS. XVIII.–XIX.

1. *Renewed promise of a son by Sarah,* xviii. 1-15.

The Elohistic introduction, ch. xvii., which, by relating the inauguration of a new period for Sarah and Abraham, at the same time prepares for the birth of the son of promise, is followed by the second portion of the third section of Abraham's life, chs. xviii.–xix. In this the angelic visits in the grove of Mamre and in Sodom, together with the promises in the former case and the infliction of judgment in the latter which accompanied them, are, with the exception of xix. 29, narrated throughout by that master of the epic art, J. He is at once recognisable by the flowing, vivid and graphic mode of statement which both enters into details and stedfastly pursues its conscious object, by the Divine name יהוה, together with אדני, by the promise that the nations shall be blessed in the seed of the patriarchs, xviii. 18, comp. xii. 3, and by certain favourite expressions, such as הִנֵּה־נָא xviii. 27, 31, xix. 2, 7, 19, 20 comp. xii. 11; כִּי עַל־כֵּן xviii. 5, xix. 8 comp. xxxiii. 10, xxxviii. 26; Num. x. 31, xiv. 43; לְפָּה זֶּה xviii. 13 comp. xxv.

22, 32, xxxiii. 15. The style touches closely upon the Deuteronomic, *e.g.* in the frequent energetic imperfect form in אָן, xviii. 28–32, and in the אַל contracted from אֱלֶה, xix. 8, 25 comp. xxvi. 3, 4, Deut. iv. 42, vii. 22, xix. 11 (elsewhere only once in the Law of Holiness, Lev. xviii. 27 and 1 Chron. xx. 8). The first part of this historical picture, extending from xviii. 1 to xix. 28 (29), and continuing in the appendix, xix. 30 sqq., viz. xviii. 1–16, is (within the extant composition of extracts from sources), as it were, the continuous historical development of xvii. 21. For the promise, which forms the central point of xviii. 1–16, is not very differently expressed, vv. 10 and 14. Hence it was not long after the institution of circumcision that the heavenly visitants made their appearance. Theophanies increase in frequency in proportion as that great event in the history of redemption, the birth of Isaac, draws near.

What follows is in accordance with its nature introduced as an appearance of Jahveh, ver. 1: *And Jahveh appeared to him by the terebinths of Mamre, as he was sitting at the door of the tent in the heat of the day.* The grove of Mamre has continued to be the abode of Abraham since xiii. 18, xiv. 13. פֶּתַח הָאֹהֶל is, like 10*b*, the accus. of the place. He was sitting outside in the shadow of the tent, when suddenly a surprising sight appeared, ver. 2: *And he lifted up his eyes and looked, and, lo, three men standing at a short distance from him. He saw and ran to meet them, and bowed himself to the earth.* The impression of the uncaused is enhanced by the expression וְהִנֵּה. To remain standing was, according to custom, an unassuming appeal to hospitality. עָלָיו over against him is equivalent to at some, but not at a great distance from him. The invitation and its acceptance, vv. 3–5: *And he said: O Lord, if now I have found grace in Thine eyes, pass not away from Thy servant. Let a little water be fetched and wash your feet and rest under the tree. And I will bring a piece of bread, and strengthen ye* *your heart, after that ye may go farther, for therefore are ye come to your servant!—They said: So do as thou hast said.* With the expression of the condition is blended in אִם־נָא, the wish that it may be so; so too at xxiv. 42, xxxiii. 10, xlvii. 29, l. 4; Ex. xxxiii. 13, xxxiv. 9; compare the simple אָם, Num. xxxii. 5, xi. 15. The washing of the feet was, especially when sandals were worn, the first kind office rendered to travellers on their reception (*e.g.* in the N. T. 1 Tim. v. 19, νίπτειν τοὺς πόδας), and before they were entertained. הִשָּׁעֵן means here to rest thoroughly by leaning and propping oneself. To recline at table was not an ancient Semitic custom. פַת־לֶחֶם sounds modest; courtesy makes little of its own doings. Food and drink were, according to the ancient view, the strengthening of the heart, Judg. xix. 5, 1 Kings xiii. 7, comp. Acts xiv. 17. אַחַר is here an adv. as at x. 18, xxiv. 55, Num. xxxi. 2 and frequently. Therefore—thinks Abraham—it has so fallen out, that I might have the opportunity of showing kindness to you; כִּי עַל־כֵּן, as at xix. 8, xxxiii. 10, xxxviii. 26, Num. x. 31, xiv. 43, comp. אֲשֶׁר עַל־כֵּן, Job xxxiv. 27, not everywhere the same as כִּי עַל־כֵּן or עַל־כֵּן־אֲשֶׁר: therefore that = because, but so conceived as it reads: for this purpose. The three men then accept the kindly persuasive invitation. דִּבַּרְתָּ, as at xix. 21, has not a pausal Kametz. Abraham's hospitable preparations, vv. 6–8: *And Abraham hastened into the tent to Sarah and said: Fetch quickly three Seâh of fine meal, knead, and make cakes. And Abraham ran to the herd and took a calf tender and good and gave to the servant, and he hasted to dress it. And he took butter and milk and the calf which he had dressed, and placed it before them, while he stood by them under the tree, and they ate.* The tone in הָאֹהֱלָה (according to Baer's text) is upon the ultima, but in xxiv. 67 upon the penultima.[1] עֻגוֹת (from עוּג, to curve, to round) is a usual dish

---

[1] But see Frensdorff's edit. of the *Darche ha-Nikkud* of Moses Punctator (1877), pp. 21 and xxxiii.

of hospitality, which the Bedouin women prepare rapidly and even while riding upon the camel; the addition of three סְאָה (Aram. סָאתָא, Assyr. *sûtu*), hence ⅜ = 1 ephah, was superabundant for three men, comp. Ex. xvi. 16. Butter and milk served, according to Bedouin custom, for the basting of the meat; the traditional explanation of Ex. xxiii. 19 and elsewhere rejects this. It was also a requirement of good manners that Abraham should not sit with his honoured guests, but remain standing and awaiting their commands. The narrative—says Lane (*Sitten und Gebräuche*, ii. 116)—contains a perfect description of the manner in which a Bedouin Sheikh of the present day entertains a traveller arriving at his tent. And General Daumas (*Die Pferde der Sahara*, p. 195) says: "A stranger appears before the Duâr, he remains at some distance and says, *Deif rabbî*, i.e. a guest sent by the Lord. The effect is magical, all spring up, hasten towards him, and bring him into the tent . . . the master of the tent keeps him company all day long . . . there is never the impertinent question: Whence comest thou, or whither goest thou?"

Now follows, ver. 9 sqq., the conversation at table. The guests beginning it, ver. 9: *And they said to him: Where is Sarah thy wife?* *And he said: There in the tent.* The fact that אֵלָיו has איו super-punctuated may point to a various reading לוֹ, and is favourable to the view that a model copy is the basis of the Masoretic text. The promise and its impression upon Sarah, vv. 10-12: *And he said: Return, yea return will I to thee about the time when it revives, and, lo, Sarah thy wife has a son; but Sarah heard it in the door of the tent, and this was behind him. And Abraham and Sarah were old, well stricken in age; the rules, after the manner of women, had ceased with Sarah. And Sarah laughed within herself, saying: After I am worn with age should I have pleasure now, when my lord is old?* The definition of time, כָּעֵת חַיָּה, means at the reviving time, or rather, since חַיָּה is without an article, at the time when it revives, Ges. § 109. 2*b*; comp. the synonymous expression περιπλομένου ἐνιαυτοῦ, 1 Sam. i. 20. וְהוּא, 10*b*, refers to the door, according to others (LXX.) to Sarah, which is contrary to the traditional text. The door was behind him who gave the promise, hence she heard without being seen by him. כַּנָּשִׁים is the monthly purification (comp. xxxi. 35, LXX. translates classically τὰ γυναικεῖα), which is the condition of the power of conception. These so-called rules had long been discontinued in the case of Sarah, hence what had been promised made her laugh. On the Perf. הָיְתָה־לִּי (should it yet be to me), see on xxi. 7. Her calling her husband אֲדֹנִי is quoted in her praise, 1 Pet. iii. 6. Her laughter however was that of contemptuous doubt, the laughter of Abraham that of delighted astonishment. He needed to have his faith encouraged, she to be brought back to the humility of faith, vv. 13, 14: *And Jahveh said to Abraham: Why then did Sarah laugh, thinking: Should I also really bear, when I am old? Is anything unattainable for Jahveh? At the set time I return to thee, at the time when it revives, and Sarah has a son.* With אַף אָמְנָם, "in very truth" (reality), comp. אַף אָמְנָם, "yea certainly," Job xxxiv. 12, xix. 4. יִפָּלֵא is a synonym to יִבָּצֵר, xi. 6. Instead of מֵיְהוָֹה,[1] like xxiv. 50, 1 Sam. i. 20, Hahn and Theile have here erroneously מֵיְהוָה. Sarah's vain evasion, ver. 15: *And Sarah denied, saying: I laughed not: for she was afraid. But he said: Nay, thou didst indeed laugh.* Matter of great and eternal importance is here related in plain and childlike words. Brought back to the humility of faith. Sarah received indeed the strength

---

[1] The writing מֵיְהוָֹה (= מֵאֲדֹנָי with audible א) follows the Masoretic rule, משה מפיק (מוציא) וכלב מכניס, *i.e.* Moses led (Israel) forth, and Caleb led (him) in, *i.e.* grammatically: the letters מ, ש, ה make the א of אֲדֹנָי audible; ב, ל, כ, on the contrary, make it quiescent, *e.g.* בַּיהוָה (with Metheg of the counter-tone) and also וַיהוָה=וַאֲדֹנָי. The *vox memorialis*, which includes also the ו, is נֶעְלָם בּוֹ כֹּל, all in Him is mysterious, *i.e.* grammatically: the prefixes כ, ל, ב, ו have after them a latent (quiescent) א.

of the naturally impossible, ἐπεὶ πιστὸν ἡγήσατο τὸν ἐπαγειλ-
λάμενον (Heb. xi. 11). The fulfilment itself was the repeated
appearance of Jahveh after the space of a year, for the God of
the promise was Himself present to effect its fulfilment.

Dillmann is of opinion, with Knobel, that the three were
Jahveh and two angels, and besides, regards the אֲדֹנָי, 3*a*, as
erroneous, because premature. But it is just this אֲדֹנָי which
leads to the true meaning of the narrator. It is not the case
that one of the three angels is the appearance of Jahveh, but
that there are three heavenly messengers, in whom Jahveh
manifests Himself, three by reason of the threefold nature of
their vocation, which is not to promise only, but also to punish
and to deliver. Because however the message of grace to
Abraham is a higher one than the messages of judgment and
of mercy to Lot, the two are subordinate to the one, and
Jahveh is specially present to Abraham in the one, whom he
recognises as above the other two and addresses as אֲדֹנָי, Lord
of all (קרי according to the Masora, in distinction from
אֲדֹנָי, my lords), because He has made upon him the impression of a being in whom God is, and whom he is to receive
as God Himself. A Greek legend tells of a similar event to
that related in chs. xviii. and xix.: Jupiter, Mercury and
Neptune visit an old man of the name of Hyrieus, in the
Bœotian town of Tanagra, he prepares a meal for them, and
at his request obtains, though hitherto childless, a son, Orion,
Ovid, *Fast.* v. 494 sqq.; *Palœph.* ch. v. And then—as a
pendant to ch. xix.—Jupiter and Mercury are travelling in the
form of men; no one will receive them but Philemon and
Baucis, an old and childless couple, wherefore the gods deliver
them, taking them away with them to a mountain, and trans-
forming the inhospitable neighbourhood of the hospitable cottage into a pool, and the cottage into a temple, Ovid, *Metam.*
viii. 611–724. Here the three and then the two angels
become respectively three and then two Gods; but Abraham
recognises in the three and especially in the one, and Lot in

the two, the presence of the one God. They treat them nevertheless as human travellers, for the Godhead in them is concealed, and only manifest to the eye of the spirit. Josephus, *Ant.* i. 11. 2, explains their eating as mere appearance: οἳ δὲ δόξαν αὐτῷ παρέσχον ἐσθιόντων. So too Philo (*Opp.* ii. 18): τερδστιον καὶ τὸ μὴ πεινῶντας πεινώντων καὶ μὴ ἐσθίοντας ἐσθιόντων παρέχειν φαντασίαν, and also the Targum, Talmud *Mezia* 86b, Midrash, Tob. xii. 19, Ephr. Procop. and most of the Fathers. It must however be differently explained, whether we hold that the human form in which they appeared was only a symbolization of their invisible being, or that it was, as Tertullian, *adv. Marc.* iii. 9, asserts: *non putativa caro, sed veræ et solidæ substantiæ humanæ*. In the first case they ate, "as we say of fire that it consumes everything" (Justin, *dial c. Tr.* c. 34); in the other they ate, as the risen Christ did, of whom Augustine says: *Quod manducavit, potestatis fuit, non egestatis. Aliter absorbet terra aquam sitiens, aliter solis radius candens: illa indigentiâ, iste potentiâ*. The intercourse of Jahveh with the patriarch was just at this time more humanely intimate than ever, because the birth of Isaac, the great type of the human appearance of God in Christ, was the subject of the message. At the beginning of the period of the νόμος, which brought to consciousness the infinite distance between the Holy God and the sinful creature, Moses heard from the burning bush the call: "Draw not nigh hither: put off thy shoes from thy feet!" Ex. iii. 5. The patriarchal period is more evangelical, as the time before the law it is a pattern of the time after the law.

2. *Abraham's transaction with God concerning Sodom and Gomorrah*, xviii. 16 sqq.

This second part of the Jahvistic portion, chs. xviii.–xix., forms a transition to what follows, as the first part was a connection with what preceded. It prepares for the history of the destruction of Sodom and Gomorrah. Departure of the three, ver. 16: *And the men rose up from thence, and looked toward Sodom, and Abraham went with them, to accompany them.* According to an interesting tradition (Jer. *Ep. cviii. ad Eustochium*), he accompanied them as far as the site of the subsequent Caphar-berucha, whence the *solitudinem ac terras Sodomœ* may be perceived; עַל־פְּנֵי, like xix. 28, Num. xxi. 20, xxiii. 28. Resolution of Jahveh, vv. 17–19: *And Jahveh said: Shall I hide from Abraham what I am about to do, since Abraham shall surely become a great and mighty nation, and all the nations of the earth shall be blessed in him? For I knew him, that he will command his children and his household after him, that they keep the way of Jahveh, to do justice and judgment; that Jahveh may bring upon Abraham what He has spoken of him.* He knew him, *i.e.* He chose him in preventing love (ידע, like Amos iii. 2, and New Testament γινώσκειν). The purpose of that loving communion with Himself to which He has admitted him follows in מַעַן=מַעֲנֶה, לְמַעַן אֲשֶׁר (مَعْنًى). He is to inculcate upon the present, and indirectly upon the future members of his family, the religion of Jahveh (דֶּרֶךְ ה׳, like Ps. xix. 10, יִרְאַת ה׳), that they may practise צְדָקָה וּמִשְׁפָּט (so here and Ps. xxxiii. 5; Prov. xxi. 3; comp. Deut. xxxiii. 21, instead of the more customary משפט וצדקה), so that Jahveh may realize to him what He has promised in respect of his great vocation in the redemptive history. The LXX., as also the Syr., adds to ἀπὸ ʼΑβραάμ, τοῦ παιδός μου (עבדי), for which Philo has τοῦ φίλου μου (comp. Jas. ii. 23). There is scarcely a passage where this עַבְדִּי (xxvi. 24) or אֹהֲבִי (Isa. xli. 8, 2 Chron. xx. 7) would be more in place than just here. Abraham is the friend of God,—an appellation which has become among Moslems a surname to his name, خليل الله, the insinuate, *i.e.* the intimate of God, or merely الخَليل, whence also Hebron is called *Beit-el-chalîl* or *El-chalîl*, and from a friend we keep nothing secret. Hence Jahveh dis-

closes to him the judgment which He purposes to inflict, vv.
20, 21: *Then Jahveh said: The cry of Sodom and Gomorrah
is become really great, and their sin really very heavy. I will
however go down and see if they have altogether done according to
the cry concerning it, which has come to me; or if not, I will investigate.* The circumstantializing perfect ויהוה אמר is followed
by the principal fact, viz. the communication, with ויאמר יהוה.
The cry of Sodom is the cry for punishment which comes up
thence demanding it. The assuring כִּי (the case is such that
then = *revera*) stands elsewhere also in the middle of the
sentence, xli. 32; Ps. cxviii. 10 – 12, cxxviii. 2. רַבָּה is
Milel, and therefore 3rd pr.; comp. on the other hand, Hos.
ix. 7. He will go down to see the state of the case (quite
like xi. 5), viz. into the valley of the Jordan district, will in
the long-suffering of His wrath see whether their behaviour
entirely corresponds with the cry for vengeance which has
proceeded from it. The *Athnach*, ver. 21, is rightly placed, the
second member of the disjunctive question being made inde-
pendent by a verb of its own. The *Pasek* between עָשׂוּ | כָּלָה
shows that כָּלָה here is to be understood, not as in the
phrase עָשָׂה כָלָה, "to put an end to," but as at Ex. xi. 1, as an
adverb in the meaning of *omnino*. הַבָּאָה is, according to the
penultimate tone, not a particip. but a *finitum*, hence (הֵל)
has, as at xlvi. 27, Job ii. 11 (comp. Ges. § 109), the value of
a relatively used demonstrative pronoun, just as *al* (*alli*) and
hal (*halli*), with the meaning "that which," are quite common
(*DMZ.* xxii. 124) in the Bedouin speech and in the book
language also, *e.g.* الْيَرْضَى بِه, *is qui acceptus habetur*, may be
said. The departure for Sodom, ver. 22: *And the men turned
thence, and went toward Sodom, and Abraham remained still
standing before Jahveh.* A parallel verse to ver. 16; there
all three are going farther, here two (xix. 1). But it is
Jahveh who betakes Himself to Sodom in the two, while, on
the other hand, He remains behind, Abraham continues stand-

ing before the one in whom Jahveh specially manifests Himself to him, and through whose angelic-human form he rightly discerns the LORD. According to tradition, 22b is a תקן סופרים, *correctio scribarum* (see my *Commentary on Habakkuk*, pp. 206-208, and Perles' *Biographie Salomo's b. Adereth*, 1863, pp. לר—לב), and was originally ויהוה עודנו עמד לפני אברהם, which seemed unworthy of God, עמד לפני being the usual expression for standing to serve. The originality however of the existing reading is defended by xix. 27. The two others departed, while Abraham still retained the third, and in him Jahveh.

To Him he turns with intercession for Sodom, vv. 23-25: *And Abraham drew near, and said: Wilt Thou then utterly cut off the righteous with the wicked? Perhaps there are fifty righteous in the city, wilt Thou really cut off and not forgive the place for the fifty righteous' sake that are therein? Far be it from Thee to do thus, to kill the righteous with the wicked, so that it should happen to the righteous as to the wicked that be far from Thee. Should not the Judge of all the earth do right?* The particle אף, ver. 23 sq., means *etiam*, not as at iii. 1 in the sense of *adeo*, but of *revera* (Saad. يَقِينًا). נשא with לְ, like Num. xix. 19 and frequently, means to grant acceptance and forbearance, *i.e.* forgiveness. In כַּצַּדִּיק כָּרָשָׁע, כ is conceived of as a noun, like the Latin *instar*: in such correlative repetition of the objects to be compared, it may either precede, as here, comp. xliv. 18, Hag. ii. 3, or follow. חָלְלָה לְּךָ means, as is shown by the Targumico-Talmudic חֻלִּין הוּא לָךְ, to the unholy *ad profanum;* חָלִיל in this sense is permitted for use, shown *licitus* by حَلِيل ; חֲלִילָה however is not a feminine with a retraction of the tone, for the penultimate accentuation is not found only before the monosyllabic לְךָ, but elsewhere also, *e.g.* xliv. 7, before לַעֲבָדֶיךָ. The question, 25b, is like that at Rom. iii. 3. Jahveh agrees, ver. 26: *And Jahveh said: If I find in Sodom fifty righteous within the city, I will forgive the whole place for their sake.* Abraham reduces the number by five, vv. 27, 28: *And Abraham answered and said: Behold now, I have taken upon me to speak to the Lord, who am but dust and ashes. Perhaps there may lack five of the fifty righteous: wilt Thou destroy the whole city for lack of five? He said: I will not destroy it if I find there forty-five.* The אֲדֹנָי interchanging here and vv. 31, 32, as at xviii. 3, with יהוה, belong to the קְלֹד וּדְאָין, *i.e.* the 134 true (really written) אדני. The pair of words עָפָר וָאֵפֶר symphonize like הוֹד וְהָדָר, נִין וָנֶכֶד, and the like. On the construction of the verb חסר with the acc. of what is lacking, comp. Ges. § 138. 3. בַּחֲמִשָּׁה, 28a, is equivalent to בַּעֲבוּר חֲמִשָּׁה, for the sake of so few less as five. He again reduces the number by five, ver. 29: *And he continued to speak to Him, and said: Perhaps forty will be found there. He said: I will not do it for the forty's sake.* He grows bolder, and deducts ten, ver. 30: *He said: Let not the Lord be angry that I speak: perhaps thirty may be found there. And He said: I will not do it if I find thirty there.* On חָרָה לְ he grows hot, he falls into the heat (of anger), see iv. 5. On the cohortative וַאֲדַבֵּרָה, see Ges. § 128. 2. From thirty down to twenty, ver. 31: *And he said: Behold now, I have taken upon me to speak to the Lord: perhaps there shall be found twenty there. He said: I will not destroy it for the twenty's sake.* From twenty down to ten, ver. 32: *And he said: Let not the Lord be angry that I speak yet but this once: Perhaps ten will be found there. And He said: I will not destroy it for the ten's sake.* Immediately after this promise Jahveh disappears, ver. 33: *And Jahveh went away, when He had finished speaking to Abraham, and Abraham returned to his place.* It is the syntactic scheme of the coincident, like vii. 6. Jahveh departed (not to Sodom, as Wellhausen, expunging עֵינֵי, xix. 1, thinks), *i.e.* He withdrew from the further importunity of the bold petitioner, and the latter, perceiving the limit thus placed, returned to the grove of Mamre.

This intercession of Abraham, which, with increasing

boldness six times takes advantage of concession, is somewhat· singular. While however it excites laughter in a Voltaire, and while Hausrath and Gesenius find impressed upon it the stamp of the Jewish "trading spirit" (see Geiger's *Jüdische Zeitschr.* x. p. 157), it moved a Lavater to admiration. "As for the whole dialogue, — I exclaim as publicly as I can,—where in all the world is its equal in greatness and simplicity to be found!" It is, to begin with, highly significant that Abraham does not intercede specially for his relatives in Sodom; that he believes in the existence of righteous persons among the heathen therein; that his intercession proceeds from the assumption that man as such is his neighbour; that it applies to the cities of those seven nationalities on which the Mosaic law inflicts unsparing extermination (Deut. vii. 2, xx. 16). The subsequent different measurement of the duty of Israelites towards fellow-countrymen and foreigners did not as yet exist; religion had not yet assumed its temporary intermediate and national form. And what depths of Divine condescension, what heights of human faith do we here meet with! Accompanied, indeed, by a boldness which New Testament piety does not sanction with respect to God. The intimacy borders on irreverence. Even the Son of man finds the ἵλεώς σοι of Peter (Matt. xvi. 22) unbearable, and how could we, in presence of the actual experience that war and calamities carry off, as Job ix. 22 says, both the righteous and the wicked, appeal to God's justice for the contrary? We must lay our hand upon our mouth, hoping for a solution in another world of the enigmas of this. Old Testament piety is still affected by a residuum of polytheism, the gods of which were more human than Divine. The reduction too of the numbers from fifty to ten is more childish than child-like, but Jahveh condescends to this childish ἀναίδεια (Luke xi. 8) of bargaining intercession. All answers to prayer depend upon such condescension. For when God created free beings, He at the same time granted the possibility of allowing His actions to be determined by their conduct, and of permitting their prayer, *i.e.* their invocation of His goodness and mercy, to influence Him. The bold familiarity of the intercessor reduced to ten the number of the righteous, for whose sake Sodom was to be spared. But ten were not found. His intercession did not however fall to the ground. Four were found, Lot, his wife and his two daughters—these did not suffice to be the means of saving Sodom, but they were themselves not destroyed with the wicked, but delivered.

3. *The destruction of Sodom and Gomorrah by fire, and the deliverance of Lot,* xix. 1–29.

In accordance with Deut. xxix. 22, the prophets frequently refer to the matter of this third part of the second portion by holding up, as a warning to the people of God, the fate of Sodom and the other cities (Amos iv. 11; Hos. xi. 8; Isa. i. 9 sq., iii. 9 and elsewhere), just as the "days of Gibeah" (Judg. xix.) are also remembered for a like purpose (Hos. ix. 9). Arrival of the two Divine messengers, ver. 1: *And the two angels came to Sodom at evening, as Lot was sitting in the gate of Sodom. And Lot, perceiving them, rose up to meet them, and bowed himself down with his face towards the earth.* The gate is usually in the nearer East a vaulted entrance, with large recesses on both sides. It was here, beneath or near the gate, that people assembled either for business purposes, or to discuss, in larger or smaller circles, the affairs of the town (xxxiv. 10; Deut. xxi. 19). It was here that Lot was sitting, and when he saw the angels coming he rose up and went to meet them, greeting them no less reverently than Abraham had done, ver. 2: *And he said: Behold now, my lords, turn aside, I pray, into your servant's house, and stay the night and wash your feet and rise up early and go your way. But they said: Nay, we will spend the night in the street*. Only here is הִנֶּה־נָא written instead of הִנֵּה־נָא. And only here do we incidentally find אֲדֹנָי with Pathach, which the Masora distinguishes as חֹל, κοινόν, from אֲדֹנָי as קֹדֶשׁ. Lot's spiritual vision is weaker than Abraham's, he greets the men with only the courteous "my lords;" he does not at first recognise them as angels, nor as the LORD, who was manifesting Himself in them. He invites them in the kindest manner, but they refuse, just as Jesus (Luke xxiv. 28) seemed at first about to refuse the disciples at Emmaus. Their nay (Ven. πώμαλα) is לֹא, written with emphatic Dagesh, as at 1 Sam. viii. 19, 1 Kings xi. 22. At last they yield to his solicitation, ver. 3: *And he urged them much, and they turned in unto him and entered his house, and he prepared a meal and baked sweet cakes, and they ate.* Sweet cakes, מַצּוֹת (from מצץ, to suck in and out), are unleavened cakes, which would be the sooner ready. But before the guests retired, the sin of Sodom is manifested, vv. 4, 5: *They had not yet lain down, when the people of the city, the people of Sodom, surrounded the house, from the boy to the old man, the whole people from the utmost end. And they called to Lot and said to him: Where are the men which came to thee this night? bring them out to us, we will know them.* The construction of טֶרֶם is like ii. 5, and, in a like connection, Josh. ii. 8. Instead of מִקָּצֶה ··וְעַד־קָצֵהוּ, xlvii. 21, from one end to the other, we have here and Jer. li. 31 מִקָּצֶה, from the end, *i.e.* of the city in its whole extent. Without respect to hospitality, they say shamelessly what they desire: חַטָּאתָם הִגִּידוּ לֹא כִחֵדוּ, Isa. iii. 9. The travellers are young and beautiful (Mark xvi. 5), the inhabitants of Sodom desire to "know" them, Judg. xix. 22; their unnatural lust, according to Rom. i. 27 a curse of heathenism, according to Jude 7 a copy of demoniacal error, according to the Mosaic law (Lev. xviii. 22, xx. 13) a תּוֹעֵבָה to be punished with death (named by Ezekiel, xvi. 49 sq., as the worst among the sins of Sodom), wears no mask, no æsthetic nimbus, as in Greece. Lot now tries his utmost to save his guests, vv. 6-8 : *And Lot went out to them to the entrance and shut the door behind him. And he said: Pray, brethren, do not so wickedly. Behold, I have two daughters who as yet have known no man. I will bring them out to you, and do ye to them as seems good to you, only to these men do nothing, for therefore have they come under the shadow of my roof.* The formation הַפֶּתְחָה is like קָדְשָׁה, Judg. iv. 10, the former from פֶּתַח, the latter from קָדֵשׁ הָאֵל for הָאֵלֶּה, here 8*b*, as at 25*a*, xxvi. 3 sq., Lev. xviii. 27, Deut. iv. 42, vii. 22, xix. 11, and elsewhere only at 1 Chron. xx. 8, is no archaism; the Arabic *ulâ*, Ethiop. *ellâ*, Aram. *illên, illêch*, showing that this demonstrative originally terminated with a vowel (perhaps *illai*). כִּי עַל־כֵּן (see xviii. 5) is said of the purpose of their becoming guests, viz. to be protected. Lot acts like the old man in Gibeah of Benjamin, Judg. xix. 23 sq.; he is willing to sacrifice his duty as a father to the duty of hospitality, and commits the sin of desiring to prevent one sin by another. But this also is of no avail, ver. 9: *But they said: Stand back! And they said: This one came to sojourn, and is playing the judge: now will we deal worse with thee than with them! And they pressed upon the man, upon Lot, and came near to break the door.* The exclamation גֶּשׁ־הָלְאָה has the meaning of move away! הָלְאָה (comp. the verb, Micah iv. 7) has the tone upon the *penult.*; it is the locative of הָל, which directs to a distance. They threaten Lot, the one man, who is enjoying among them the rights of hospitality, and yet . . . (*imperf. consec.* of the contrasting context, the paradoxical result, like xxxii. 31; Prov. xxx. 25–27; Job ii. 3). The *inf. intens.* to וַיִּשְׁפֹּט emphasizes this troublesome censorious behaviour as incessant (Ges. § 131. 3*b*). To take, with Hupfeld, the ה of הָאֶחָד interrogatively, like Num. xvi. 22, Neh. vi. 11, comp. Judg. xii. 5, and also הָאָדָם, Deut. xx. 19, is not advisable, the determinative of אֶחָד (this one) being indispensable. The עַתָּה is conclusive: they will consequently deal worse with him than with his *protégés*. The permutative combination בְּאִישׁ בְּלוֹט is like בסדום ··בתוך העיר, xviii. 26. They prepare to break the door, when Lot's guests become his protectors, vv. 10, 11 : *And the men stretched out their hand and took Lot in unto them, into the house, and shut to the door. And the men who were at the entrance of the house, they struck with blindness, from the least unto the greatest, and they wearied themselves to find the entrance.* Instead of the more usual בַּעֲוִרוֹן, Zech. xii. 4, Deut. xxviii. 28, we here have בַּסַּנְוֵרִים, from סַנְוֵר, to make blind, a *Shaphel*—the original causative form—with נֵוֵּר = نَوَّرَ, to blind. Summons to Lot to escape with his family, vv. 12, 13 : *And the men said to Lot: Whom hast thou here? Son-in-law, and thy sons and daughters, and all that belongs to thee in the city, bring them out of the place: for we are about to destroy this place, because the cry concerning them is become great before the face of Jahveh, and Jahveh has sent us to destroy it.* The suffix of צַעֲקָתָם (to be understood like xviii. 20 sq., *Clamat ad cœlum vox sanguinis et Sodomorum*) refers to the inhabitants, and the suffix of לְשַׁחֲתָהּ to the city. חָתָן is purposely an indefinite collective singular. Lot finds no audience with his sons-in-law, ver. 14 : *And Lot went out, and spake to his sons-in-law, who had taken his daughters, and said: Get you up, go out of this place, for Jahveh is about to destroy the city, — but he was as one who mocked in the eyes of his sons-in-law.* The LXX. and Targ. Jer. I. have correctly: τοὺς εἰληφότας τὰς θυγατέρας αὐτοῦ, not : *qui accepturi erant filias ejus* (Jerome), for in ver. 15 the two daughters, still at home, are distinguished from those who were married; and the two saved with Lot have not, ver. 30 sq., to lament the loss of bridegrooms. Those offered to the Sodomites were still his virgin and, as may be also inferred from ver. 8, his unbetrothed daughters. In קוּמוּ צְאוּ the צ has the emphatic Dagesh to ensure its clear pronunciation between two *u* sounds (comp. Ex. xii. 31; Deut. ii. 24). This carelessness, when destruction was close at hand, is referred to Luke xvii. 28. Even Lot does not follow his preservers with the gratitude of a joyful faith, vv. 16, 17: *And as soon as the dawn began, the angels urged Lot to hasten, saying: Arise, take thy wife, and thy two daughters, which are here, that thou be not consumed in the iniquity of the city. But he lingered; then the men seized his hand and the hand of his wife and of his two daughters, by reason of the forbearance of Jahveh ruling over him, and led him out, and let go of him outside the city.* While the biblical כְּ is always merely a preposition, כְּמוֹ serves here like כַּאֲשֶׁר as a conjunction, which its analogous formation from כְּ and מה=מוּ permits, comp. Isa. xxvi. 18; Ps. lviii. 8. The daughters still in the parental house are called הַנִּמְצָאוֹת in distinction from those already married, as is explained *Bereschith rabba* c. 50, and in Ephrem. The angels urge Lot to hasten, but he delays: he is no Abraham, and it is not gladly, but with inward reluctance, that he leaves the beautiful city and his home in it. The angels are obliged to bring him and his family out by force, and this takes place בְּחֶמְלַת ה' עָלָיו. Olshausen would prefer בְּחֶמְלַת, but in the Psalms also בְּחַסְדְּךָ, xxv. 7, and בְּחַסְדְּךָ, xxxi. 17, are interchanged. They do not let go of him (הִנִּיחַ, different in use from הֵנִיחַ) till he is outside the city. Here Jahveh, speaking by the angels, invites him to save himself by hastening straight onward, ver. 17: *And it came to pass when they* (the angels) *had led them* (Lot and his family) *forth, He* (Jahveh) *said: Escape for thy life, look not behind thee, stay not in all the plain; escape to the mountain, that thou be not consumed.* Jahveh is in the two angels, as in the three: they are all three messengers, *i.e.* organs of God present in them (as the apostles were messengers and organs of Christ present in them). Without looking backwards (אַל־תַּבִּיט instead of the more regular אַל־תַּבֵּט), he is to seek to place himself in safety by reaching the (subsequently Moabite) mountains. But here too he shows how weak and defective is his faith and obedience, vv. 18–20: *And Lot said: O Lord, not so. Behold now, Thy servant hath found grace in Thy sight, and Thou hast magnified Thy favour, which Thou hast showed to me to preserve my soul alive; and I cannot escape to the mountain, misfortune might overtake me, and I die. Behold now, this city is near to flee thither, and it is indeed but small: let me escape thither—it is indeed so small—that my soul may live.* The deprecative אַל strengthened by נָא (Ruth i. 13) is followed by two sentences, each commencing with הִנֵּה־נָא, and apparently marking two premisses, the first of which, ver. 19, gives, as a reason for the request, the mercy of God and the impotence of the suppliant, the second, 20*a*, the smallness of the thing requested, and then by אִמָּלְטָה־נָּא the conclusion. Lot now knows that it is Jahveh Himself who has snatched him as a brand from the burning; he no longer says אֲדֹנַי, but אֲדֹנָי; yet even with this nearness of God to him and care of God for him, he does not attain to entire obedience: the mountain is too far for him; he fears lest the approaching catastrophe should catch him (תִּדְבָּקַנִי, with uniting vowel *a*, like xxix. 32; Ges. § 60, note 2); he would rather flee to the small town which is near, and whose insignificance might excite compassion. Jahveh agrees, vv. 21, 22: *And He said to him: See, I favour thee in this also, not to destroy the city of which thou hast spoken. Hasten to escape thither, for I can do nothing till thou art come thither—therefore the name of the city was called Ṣoʿar.* The phrase נשׂא פני means to let the presence, appearance, or person of any one make an impression and find access. The לְ of לַדָּבָר is that of reference. הַפְּנֵי has בְּ, according to the Masora, like בְּנָפוֹ, Ex. xii. 27. מַהֵר is an adverbial infinitive, like Ps. lxix. 18. The city was that regarded by Lot as מִצְעָר, a trifle, a small matter, and hence called צֹעַר (smallness), at the south-eastern entrance of the then valley of Siddim. The crusaders found it still existing under the name of *Segor* (صغر or زغر, LXX. Σηγώρ), pleasantly situated among palm-trees, *girato lacu a parte australi*, hence, after going round the southern end of the Dead Sea on its eastern side, where it lay, not as Irby-Mangles and Robinson suppose, upon the peninsula jutting far into the southern half of the sea from the east, but, as Wetzstein has pointed out, on the south-eastern end, in that part of the Arabah which is now called *Gôr es Ṣâfieh*. The catastrophe, vv. 23-25 : *The sun was risen upon the earth, and Lot was come to Ṣo'ar. Then Jahveh rained down upon Sodom and Gomorrah brimstone and fire from Jahveh from heaven. And He overthrew those cities and all the plain, and all the inhabitants of the cities and that which grew on the ground.* By sunrise Lot had already arrived at Zoar. צֹעֲרָה has in Baer an accented local *ah*, but Heidenheim accentuates this word like הָאֹהֱלָה according to Moses Punctator as *Milel*. The causative הִמְטִיר has for its object rain proper, ii. 5; hail, Ex. ix. 18, manna, Ex. xvi. 4, here גָּפְרִית וָאֵשׁ (for which we have אֵשׁ וְגָפְרִית, Ps. xi. 6 ; Ezek. xxxviii. 22). הָפַךְ, in the sense of *evertere*, refers not only to cities but to men (as at Prov. xii. 7 ; Isa. i. 7) and plants. Brimstone and fire came through the intervention of God present in His angels from (מֵאֵת, like Micah v. 6) Him who is enthroned in heaven. The statement distinguishes still more decidedly than Hos. i. 7, Zech. x. 12, 2 Tim. i. 18, the supermundane and the historically manifested God. But we should be more correct to say that the mundane presence of God in the angels was a prefiguration of the ἐφανερώθη ἐν σαρκί, than to agree with Justin, Eusebius, and the Council of Sirmium, which decreed, after these authorities: *Pluit Dei filius a Deo patre*. Not only Sodom and Gomorrah, but Admah and Zeboiim, the two other cities of the Pentapolis (xiv. 2), as we are told, Deut. xxix. 23 (the fundamental passage for Hos. xi. 8), or, as it is here said, the whole plain, Zoar alone excepted, perished by fire and brimstone—a catastrophe to which Strabo, Tacitus, and Solinus Polyhistor also testify, and which, in the subsequent literature down to the Apocalypse, is often both alluded to and directly mentioned (*e.g.* Ps. xi. 6). Fate of Lot's wife, ver. 26: *And his wife looked back from behind him, and became a pillar of salt.* She was following him and, whether from affection, compassion, or curiosity, looking about behind her, and became, in consequence of this disregard of the Divine command, a prey to the catastrophe. She was covered with a saline incrustation and changed, as it were, into a statue of salt. In the time of the author of the Book of Wisdom this στήλη ἁλός, Wisd. x. 7 (comp. Clement, *ad Cor.* c. xi.), was still pointed out. Josephus (*Ant.* i. 11. 4) declares that he had seen it: ἱστόρηκα αὐτήν, ἔτι γὰρ καὶ νῦν διαμένει. A poem among the works of Tertullian (ed. Oehler, ii. 773) relates of it, that when it is mutilated it completes itself again, which Irenæus (iv. 31. 3, 33. 9) explains typically. These are legends which have their very obvious rise in the partly cylindrical, partly pyramidal cones of salt still found, in consequence of the winter rains, on the salt-mine track, *Haǵar Usdum*, which extends not far from the eastern shore of the Dead Sea, two leagues and a half towards its southern extremity (see Tuch, *Quæstio de Flav. Josephi loco B. J.*, iv. 8. 2, 1860). What is related in ver. 26 however is regarded as history in the New Testament also (Luke xvii. 32, comp. ix. 62). The disappearance of Eurydice when Orpheus, contrary to the command of Proserpine, looks round at her when brought from Hades before arriving at their native land, as related in the Greek legend, is somewhat similar. What Abraham had to behold next morning, vv. 27, 28: *And Abraham got up early in the morning to the place where he had stood in the presence of Jahveh, and looked toward the face of Sodom and Gomorrah and toward the whole face of the country of the plain, and beheld, and, lo, the vapour of the land went up as the vapour of the furnace.* Instead of עִיר,

smoke (Ex. xix. 18), we have here the less usual קִיטוֹר (Arab. قُتَار), steam or vapour (Ps. cxix. 83); comp. Wisd. x. 7, καπνιζομένη χέρσος, and Brocardus: *mare mortuum est semper fumans et tenebrosum sicut os inferni, ut oculis meis vidi, ob tetrum vaporem inde fumantem.* So far the account of J, to which is now joined the sketch of Q, ver. 29: *And it came to pass, when Elohim destroyed the cities of the plain, then Elohim remembered Abraham and led Lot out of the overthrow, when He overthrew the cities in which Lot had dwelt.* Thus Lot was delivered for the sake of Abraham, and indeed for the sake of his intercession. "In which" is the same as in one of which, like Judg. xii. 7. Instead of הֲפֵכָה, occurring here only, מַהְפֵּכָה is the Deuteronomico-prophetic word.

The Dead Sea, as it appears at present, has no kind of odour; its water is clear as crystal, and has in fair weather the blue colour of heaven like other seas. Flights of birds are frequently seen passing over its waters. It nevertheless gives an impression of awe. Neither fish nor other living creatures are hidden in its bosom, those who enter it with the current from the Jordan dying immediately, and its lonely shores are entirely devoid of vegetation. The atmosphere over its waters is purest at night, but never quite pure. If it is agitated by a storm, the spray that is driven about covers everything with an incrustation of salt. Liquid bitumen is not found, but the Moses and Asphalt stone so frequent on the coast lead to the conclusion, that a great bed of asphalt forms the bottom of the sea. After the earthquake of 1837, which destroyed Tiberias, a mass of asphalt the size of a house appeared upon the surface, it was driven on to firm ground on the western side not far from Usdum, and furnished the Arabs with 150 ctr. of asphalt.[1] The length of this unique waste of waters amounts to 40, and its average breadth to 8 miles; at its

---

[1] See Zincken, *Fossile Kohlen und Kohlenwasserstoffe*, 1884, pp. 327–331 (*Bituminöse Schichten und Emanationen Palästina's*).

southern extremity its whole breadth is fordable. According to Symond's measurement it lies 1231 feet, while the Sea of Tiberias is only 308 feet below the surface of the Mediterranean. As Moore found the bottom to be in some places 1700 feet deep, it reaches to almost 3000 feet beneath the surface of the Mediterranean. The Lake of Achen in Tyrol, and especially Lake Baikal in Asiatic Russia, are far deeper, but their situation is incomparably less deep, that of the Dead Sea being one of the deepest depressions on the surface of the globe. The view advocated by great authorities (Ritter, v. Schubert, Daubeny, J. B. Roth), that the Jordan, the Dead Sea and the Gulf of Akaba originally formed one connected waterway, has been proved untenable by more recent investigations (Russegger, Robinson, Thornton, Fraas). The land between the Arabian Gulf and the Dead Sea rises to a height of 2100 feet above the level of the sea, and it can be geologically proved that the Wadi Arabah has undergone no elevation since the existence of the present basins. Lartet, who accompanied the Duke de Luynes, arrived at the result that the Dead Sea had at all times been a basin for the deposits which fell on its declivities, and that its surface was at the end of the Tertiary period 100 metres higher than at present; but that volcanic catastrophes subsequently took place at the east and north-east in the form of effusions of basalt, and that hot mineral springs, bituminous eruptions and earthquakes were, in historic times, the last forces which shaped the basin of the Dead Sea. Fallmerayer too (1853) is of opinion that the southern part of the Dead Sea, between the great peninsula jutting in on its eastern side and the hill of lava, ashes and salt, *'Gebel Usdum*, was originally the dry land of the plain of Siddim, and was covered with water in consequence of a catastrophe. He thinks that the Dead Sea has advanced, and has volcanically overwhelmed tracts of land, which formerly lay beyond its reach, and in the enjoyment of sunlight. That where to-day are the bare peninsula and the Dardanelle current, there was once the termination and southern boundary of the Dead Sea. And that the formerly flourishing and abundantly watered Vale of Siddim, the Lectonia (ii. 14, 283 sq.) of Canaan, of which only the great Delta in Southern ·Gôr remains besides its extremely irregular borders on the east and west, extended from this natural enclosure to the wall of hills across the Wadi Arabah. With this agrees also the result arrived at by Capt. Lynch, who undertook in 1848 an expedition to the Dead Sea in two boats, one of iron, the other of copper, which were brought thither over land. It was ascertained that the bed of the sea forms two sunken plains, one from 1000 to 1200, the other on an average only 13 feet below the surface. This shallower southern part, as may now be considered almost settled, would thus have to be regarded as the submerged Vale of Siddim. Fritz Noetling however judges otherwise in the three articles on the Dead Sea which he has published in the *Berliner Tageblatt*, Aug. 1886. He denies that there is any kind of connection between a catastrophe in the time of Abraham and this body of water which has always existed in the deepest part of the Ghôr, regards the Wadi Zerka as the only conceivable place of the site of Sodom and Gomorrah, and is convinced that the volcanic action in the region of the Dead Sea was still operative when the district had already almost exactly its present relief; for "the most recent streams of lava have flowed down from the plateau into the valleys, which were already hollowed out to their present depth." It is however evident from the circumstance that the stream of lava that has descended from the Attarus mountain chain appears to be sawn through the midst by the never resting water of the Wadi in such wise that its two portions adhere to both sides of the slopes of the valley in the form of terraces, that this last outburst of volcanic force in Palestine took place in the Alluvial period thousands of years previously. The narrator certainly does not tell us in ch. xix. that the cities were submerged in the sea which arose in consequence of the fiery judgment, only xiv. 3 seems to proceed from this view.

4. *The incestuous generation of Moab and Ben-Ammi*, xix. 30–38.

The second portion of the third section of Abraham's life closes with xix. 30–38. What is here related is closely linked with xix. 1–28, and there is no valid ground against our admitting that it is still *J* who here continues the narrative. The distinction of age by בְּכִירָה and צְעִירָה occurs also with him at xxix. 26, and חַיּוֹת רָע at vii. 3. It is he also who relates how the hero of the Flood committed himself ix. 20 sqq., after having stood such a test of his faith; and if the histories of Abraham, Gideon, David and other models of faith terminate with a fall from their ideal height, this is the less amazing in the case of Lot.

He moved from Zoar, and dwelt in a cave in the mountain, vv. 30–32: *And Lot went up out of Ṣo'ar, and dwelt in the mountain, and his two daughters with him. And the first-born said to the younger: Our father is old, and there is no man in the land to come in unto us according to the manner of all the world. Up, we will give our father wine to drink, and we will lie with him and will propagate the race from our father.* When invited to escape to the (Moabite) mountain, Lot had requested permission to flee to Zoar; but it was just there that he now felt himself insecure and departed thence to the mountain, whither he had formerly desired not to go. There was this former nomad compelled by poverty and fear to become a dweller in a cave (בַּמְּעָרָה with the article of the species, unless it has the meaning of the definite cave known as the birthplace of the two nations). The two daughters of Lot, called by Mas'ûdi, Zewî and 'Arva, are those who were still unmarried at the catastrophe. In the absence of all prospect of marriage, the younger is persuaded by the elder to the desperate resolve of lying with their father after they have made him drunk; דֶּרֶךְ כָּל־הָאָרֶץ is here the usual human manner of sexual intercourse, as the husband in the Jewish marriage articles promises: ואנא אעל לותך כאורח כל־ארעא. Not as if they supposed that the Divine judgment had extirpated all men (so *e.g.* Irenæus, iv. 31. 2); but that they felt themselves so branded as the remnants of an accursed city, that they feared that their family must die out with themselves who were without husbands and their aged father. It was not lust, but the wish to keep their race from perishing, that impelled them. The means was however worthy of Sodom, and Lot became the blind instrument of an infamy punishable by the subsequent law with death by fire. He is, as F. G. v. Moser designates him, a memorable example of an impure man, or, to speak more correctly (comp. 2 Pet. ii. 7), of a very frail righteous man. The proposal carried out, vv. 33–36: *And they gave their father wine to drink that same night, and the first-born came and lay with her father, and he knew neither her lying down nor her rising up. And it came to pass the day after, that the first-born said to the younger: Behold, I lay last night with my father, we will give him wine to drink this night also, and come thou, lie with him, and we will propagate the race by our father. And they gave their father wine to drink that night also, and the younger arose and lay with him, and he knew neither of her lying down nor of her rising up. And the two daughters of Lot were with child by their father.* On two successive nights Lot became the blind instrument of a desire which obtained its satisfaction in a sinful manner. בַּלַּיְלָה הוּא, ver. 33, for בלילה ההוא, ver. 35, is in itself the more possible (xxxviii. 21; Ps. xii. 8), and here, as at xxx. 16, xxxii. 23, 1 Sam. xix. 10, the preferable expression by reason of the hiatus. מִפָּחֳרָת, thus pointed, may be contracted from מִפְאָחֳרָת, like the Aramæan יוֹמָחֳרָא; but מָחָר comes from מחר, to be in front, commonly used in the Assyrian and meaning the approaching day, which forms, as it were, the front of the present line of time. On אֶמֶשׁ, the previous evening, the evening (the night, the day before), from מָשָׁה, to graze, to touch (said of the sun sinking on the horizon), here, ver. 34, used as an accus. of time: to pass the night, *i.e.* the past night, see Fleischer on Job xxx. 3. With the writing, וַתִּישְׁקִיןָ, comp. Ges. § 47, note 3. יָדַע has בְּ of the object, like I's. xxxi. 8; Job xii. 9, xxxv. 15. The formation שִׁכְבָה is like מִכְרָם, Amos ii. 6, with מִכְרָהּ, Ex. xxi. 8; Ewald, § 225*d*. The wine and evil lust combine to plunge Lot, not indeed into absolutely passive unconsciousness, but into animal insensibility, in which he surrendered himself without moral consideration to mere blind instinct. The point over the second ו of ובקומה is said, according to the opinion of the Midrash, to indicate שבשכבה לא ידע ובקומה ידע (*Nazir* 23*a*), which Jerome also relates, but it certainly has only critical and not actual significance. Birth of the children, vv. 37, 38: *And the firstborn bare a son, and called his name Moab, he is the father of Moab to this day. And the younger she too bare a son, and called his name Ben-'Ammi, he is the father of the Bené-Ammon to this day.* In consequence of their crafty incest they became the ancestresses of two nations, of the Moabites, who took possession of the dwellings of the Emim, and of the Ammonites, who took possession of the dwellings of the Zamzummim, Deut. ii. 9–21. The LXX. adds to the naming of Moab: λέγουσα Ἐκ τοῦ πατρός μου. That Moab means begotten by my father is clear, and according to מֵאָבִינוּ, vv. 32, 34, and מֵאָבִיהֶן, ver. 36, it seems to be equivalent to מֵאָב. But it is also possible that it may be equivalent to מֵי אָב, *aqua patris* (מוֹ=מַי, from מָוָה, *diffluere, fluidum esse,* like גֵו, from גָּוָה), for *semen patris* (comp. Num. xxiv. 7, Prov. v. 16, also Isa. xlviii. 1, according to the extant text, though there מִמְּעֵי may be intended for מִמֵּי), to which בְּמוֹ, *Keri* בְּמֵי, Isa. xxv. 10, seems to allude. The name בֶּן־עַמִּי means, according to the narrative, the son of parents of the same stock; עַמּוֹן, the belonging to a nation (*abs.* then *concr.*), is related to עַם as אֲנָשׁוֹן is to אֱנָם.

The people is called בְּנֵי עַמּוֹן, for which עַמּוֹן is first used at a later period of the language (Ps. lxxxiii. 8, comp. 1 Sam. xi. 11, Heb. with LXX.).

Lot is not again mentioned, nor even his death. His history terminates the collateral line of Haran, and at the same time relates the origin of two nations interwoven in the history of Israel. De Wette, Tuch, Ewald, Knobel, Böhmer, and Dillmann see in this narrative the invention of Israelite national hatred. But how should this be the root of the legend, when their descent from Lot is reckoned an honour to the Moabites and Ammonites, Deut. ii. 9, 19, and Israel is directed to leave unmolested the land awarded to them as בְּנֵי לוֹט, and consequently congeners? It was not till they had behaved in an unbrotherly manner to Israel, that they were excluded from the congregation of the Lord,—on no other grounds but just this unbrotherly conduct, Deut. xxiii. 4 sq. And if lewdness (Num. xxv.) and want of natural feeling (*e.g.* 2 Kings iii. 26 sq.) subsequently appear to be fundamental in the character and cultus of both nations, we are at least equally justified in assuming that these their hereditary sins are derived from their origin, as that the legend fashioned their origin accordingly.

SARAH'S PRESERVATION AT THE COURT OF ABIMELECH, CH. XX.

The long Jahvistic section in four parts is now followed by an Elohistic one, relating how the honour of Sarah, which had been endangered by her being taken into the harem of Abimelech, was preserved. This narrative is a pendant to the Elohistic narrative, xii. 10 sqq., where it is the harem of Pharaoh into which Sarah is carried off. Whether the two histories are two forms of the same legend or not, the narrators are at all events different. If *Q* is however regarded as the narrator of ch. xx., it is but a shallow inference to esteem him as such from the use of the Divine name אֱלֹהִים. Ilgen (*Urkunden des Jerusalemer Tempelarchivs*, 1798) already distinguished two Elohists, and the same perception dawned quite independently upon Hupfeld (*Quellen*, 1853), especially with regard to ch. xx. Apart from אלהים (ח), which is besides exchanged, ver. 4, for אֲדֹנָי, there is nothing which absolutely leads to Q, the tone of the language being more closely related to that of J (*e.g.* הארץ לפניך, xx. 15, xiii. 9 ; וַיַּשְׁכֵּם בַּבֹּקֶר, xx. 8, xix. 27 ; עַל־דְּבַר, xx. 11, xii. 17 ; עשה חסד עם, xx. 13, xix. 19 ; רק, xx. 11, xix. 8), but also characteristically differing from it (*e.g.* אָמְנָה, xx. 12, comp. אָמְנָם, xviii. 13 ; אלהים with a plural of the predicate, xx. 13, like xxxv. 7, the אֲמָהוֹת peculiar to him, xx. 7, with the usual שִׁפְחֹת, xx. 14). It is also here only that Abraham is called נָבִיא, xx. 7 (comp. Ps. cv. 15), and the mediatorial position implied in this notion appears here in an instructive and ancient light; the direction of Abimelech to the intercession of the patriarch recalls Job xlii. 8. It was in *E* that *R* found this narrative, which he here inserts retrospectively and not in its original place, as *e.g.* the Synoptists bring in the purification of the Temple, which took place in the first Jerusalem Passover, in the third.

Abraham's departure to the south, ver. 1: *And Abraham departed thence to the land of the south, and dwelt between Kadeš and 'Sûr.* He leaves Mamre and its curse-stricken neighbourhood and journeys אַרְצָה הַנֶּגֶב ; so here instead of הַנֶּגְבָּה, xii. 9, xiii. 1, with *He locale* to the connecting form, like xxiv. 67, xxviii. 2, xliii. 17, xlvi. 1 ; Ew. § 216*b*. The southern part of Canaan, the subsequent territory of the tribes of Judah, Benjamin and Simeon, is divided by the features of the country into four distinctly separate parts. The mountainous (הָהָר) or high land, on whose western slope lies a hilly district which gradually sinks into a plain (שְׁפֵלָה), forms the centre; while towards the east the wilderness (מִדְבָּר) inclines towards the Jordan valley and the Dead Sea, to the south the South-land (נֶגֶב, Josh. xv. 21) forms in several plainly marked terraces a spur of the mountains towards the Petræan peninsula. It was here that Abraham sojourned in the district between

Kadesh and Shur (where was, according to xvi. 7, 14, the well of Hagar), wandering occasionally from these his headquarters to Gerar south of Gaza (see on xxvi. 17). Here in the south-west of Canaan already dwelt the Philistines; for though the narrator both here and xxi. 22-34 calls Abimelech only king of Gerar, and not, as the narrator in ch. xxvi., king of the Philistines, yet this is not to be regarded as his abstinence from a non-historical anticipation (Bertheau, Kn.); it was an actual tradition that the Philistines had settled on this coast long before Israel became a nation (Hitzig, *Philist.* p. 146). Unlike as the Philistines of the patriarchal age are to those of the times of the Judges, Ewald refers to the unmistakeable similarity of the proper names, especially אֲבִימֶלֶךְ, according to P. Haupt, not = *Abimalki* but *Abimilki*, father of the council, and masculine proper names in *ath*, as אֲחֻזַּת and פִּילַת. Abraham fares in this pre-Mosaic Philistine kingdom as according to ch. xii. he had done in Egypt, ver. 2: *And Abraham said of Sarah his wife: She is my sister, and Abimelech king of Gerar sent and took Sarah.* He did not say it to her, but to others of her, אֶל like לְ, 13b, Obad. ver. 1, comp. Ps. ii. 7, xli. 6. In the position which is given to the history by *R*, we should have to admit that Abimelech was not concerned for sensual enjoyment, but that he desired to ally himself as brother-in-law to Abraham the wealthy nomad prince. But this time also Elohim interposes in her behalf, vv. 3-5: *And Elohim came to Abimelech in a dream of the night, and said unto him: Behold, thou must die because of the woman whom thou hast taken, since she is the wife of a husband.* And *Abimelech had not come near her, and he said: Lord God, wilt Thou destroy also a righteous nation? Did he not say unto me: She is my sister? and did not she herself also say: He is my brother? In the integrity of my heart and the cleanness of my hands have I done this..* We may hesitate as to whether הַלַּיְלָה here and xxxi. 24, 1 Kings iii. 5, is meant for an acc. of time or a dependent gen.; the accentuation assumes the latter, and indeed correctly (Targ. בְּחֶלְמָא דְלֵילְיָא). A dream, as the experience of one who is asleep, is the lowest grade of revelation, hence Elohim comes to Abimelech and Laban in a dream of the night; but Jacob also, xxviii. 12, xxxi. 11, and Joseph, xxxvii. 5, receive Divine disclosures בחלום (different from the vision of the night, xlvi. 2). It is *E* who delights in relating these Divine revelations by night. A married woman is called בְּעֻלַת בַּעַל, as at Deut. xxii. 22, in post-biblical terminology אֵשֶׁת אִישׁ. Death is placed before the king as certainly at hand by *en te moriturum*. He was then (according to vv. 7, 17) sick like Hezekiah, Isa. xxxviii. 1, and even on that account he had not come near her (Isa. viii. 3). אֲדֹנָי here, as at xix. 18, is one of *E*'s points of contact with *J*. The original text was perhaps הֲגַם צַדִּיק, at all events גוֹי, if it here meant an individual heathen (Targ. Jer. בר עממין), would have to be regarded, as by Geiger, *Urschr.* 365, as a later insertion; גוֹי however is like עַם (comp. on xvii. 14), an elastic notion, Abimelech is generalizing, which as king he had a right to do. The question is similar to xviii. 23, but there it is אַף, *adeo*, here גַּם, ὅμως, Ew. § 354*a*: a nation which is nevertheless righteous. In וְהִיא־גַם־הִוא, הִיא and the double-gendered הוּא stand incorrectly together. בְּתָם־לְבָבִי, in the innocence of my heart, is the usual expression, not בתם לִבִּי. "Cleanness of hands," as in the phrase "to wash the hands in נקיון," Ps. xxvi. 6, lxxiii. 13. Abimelech's exculpation admitted, vv. 6, 7: *And God said to him in a dream: I also know that thou hast done this in the integrity of thine heart, and I also withheld thee from guilt towards me; therefore have I not suffered thee to touch her. And now give back the man's wife, for he is a prophet and will pray for thee, and thou shalt live; but if thou do not give her back, know that thou shalt die, thou, and all thine.* On the form מֵחֲטוֹ, see Ges. § 75, note 21*c*; and with the construction with לְ, comp. *e.g.* Ps. li. 6. נתן with an accus. and לְ means either authorization, or as here and xxxi. 7, making possible, permitting. God commands the king under a fresh threat at once to restore Abraham's wife, for he is a נָבִיא. Such is the term applied to one who makes known, proclaims, speaks, viz. of God and Divine mysteries, xviii. 17–19, and not the authorized, the inspired, the God-counselled, or any other kind of passive meaning, but like חָסִיד, נָדִיב, פָּלִיל, the intensive of the *part. act.*, as shown in Fleischer's excursus to the former edition of this commentary. The Assyrian, which presents for *nabû* the general meaning to call, to name, to reckon, does not alter it. From the fact that Abraham as נביא is an acceptable petitioner, an interceding mediator, we see that according to the scriptural view the official characteristic of the prophet presupposes the general one of piety and personal association with God (Wisd. vii. 27; 2 Pet. i. 21 comp. iii. 2).[1] The imper. וִחְיֵה is not equivalent to וְתִחְיֶה, it declares, like Prov. iv. 4 and elsewhere, as well the means as the end intended. The God-fearing heathen monarch accepted the reproof of God, but not without taking Abraham to task, vv. 8–10: *And Abimelech rose up early in the morning and called all his servants and told them all these things audibly; and the men were much afraid. And Abimelech called Abraham and said to him: What hast thou done unto us? and wherein have I been guilty against thee, that thou hast brought on me and on my kingdom a great guilt? Deeds which ought not to be done, hast thou done to me. And Abimelech said to Abraham: What sawest thou, that thou hast done this thing?* To speak בְּאָזְנֵי of another means not confidential, but (comp. *e.g.* xxiii. 10) audible and unreserved communication. With 9*b* (what ought not to be done) comp. xxxiv. 7, and with מָה רָאִיתָ, Ps. xxxvii. 37. God's prophet thus put to shame seeks to excuse himself, vv. 11–13: *And Abraham said: Because I thought, Surely there is no fear of God in this place, and they will kill me for my wife's sake. And she is besides really my sister, the daughter of*

---

[1] Kuenen (*Einl.* § 13, note 20) thinks that the designation of Abraham as נביא points to the century in which the prophets undertook the spiritual guidance of the people and were honoured as the confidants of the Deity, an inference on the ground of self-made history and devoid of internal necessity.

my father, but not the daughter of my mother, and she became my wife. And it came to pass, when Elohim led me forth from my father's house, that I said to her: This is thy favour which thou mayst show me; wherever we come, say of me: He is my brother. כִּי, 11a, gives the reason for the understood sentence: I did it, comp. xxvii. 20, xxxi. 31, Ex. i. 19, like the understood "thou shalt" at Ex. iii. 12. כִּי is restrictive, then, because what is simply thus and not otherwise is certainly the case, affirmative (as also at Num. xx. 19; Ps. xxxii. 6). By the statement of Abraham that Sarah is his half-sister (ὁμοπάτριος), what preceded at xi. 29, xii. 13, is incontestably completed. What he says too as to the time of his agreement with Sarah is easily reconcilable with xii. 11. Nor is it strange that he should speak of his wanderings according to outward appearance, reserving to himself their motive and purpose. Hence too הִתְעוּ אֹתִי אֱלֹהִים may be an accommodation to heathen modes of thought and speech, but Israelite piety does not elsewhere shun to speak of the one God in the plural, *e.g.* xxxv. 7; 2 Sam. vii. 23; Josh. xxiv. 19; Ps. lviii. 12; 1 Sam. xvii. 26. אֶל־כָּל־הַמָּקוֹם stands for בְּכָל־הַמָּקוֹם, attracted by what follows (comp. with respect to the art., Ex. xx. 24). Abimelech's obedience and generosity, vv. 14, 15: *And Abimelech took sheep and oxen and men-servants and maid-servants and gave them to Abraham, and restored to him Sarah his wife. And Abimelech said: Behold, my land is open to thee; dwell where it seems good to thee.* He also compensates Sarah, ver. 16: *And to Sarah he said: Behold, I give a thousand shekels of silver to thy brother: behold, let this be to thee a covering of the eyes for all those with thee, and in the presence of all, then art thou righted.* The thousand silver shekels (Ges. § 120, note 2) are not the money's worth of the presents given for appeasing Abraham, ver. 14, but a special present, the purpose of which referred personally to Sarah, delivered to Abraham himself. It is clear what is meant by כְּסוּת עֵינַיִם: a covering of the eyes, which renders one blind to what has happened (comp. Job ix. 24), and makes it as though it had not happened (comp. xxxii. 21). The only question is whether it was Sarah or those around her whose eyes the present was to cover. Dillm. explains it with Hofmann (*Schriftbeweis*, 2nd edit. i. 233): let it be to thee a covering of the eyes for all who constitute thy surrounding, that they may no more see dishonour in thee. Then לָךְ, as *dat. commodi*, would precede the dative of destination. לְכֹל, which is improbable, and כְּסוּת עֵינַיִם has indeed the meaning of a propitiatory present, and as such befits Sarah, on which account לְכֹל cannot be equivalent to לַכֹּל; hence לָךְ is, on the contrary, the dative of destination, and לְכֹל the dative of relation: with relation to all or for all who are with thee. We translate further: and in the presence of all—then (ו *apod.*, like xxii. 4, then he lifted up) art thou proved (Passive to הוֹכִיחַ, Job xiii. 15, xix. 5), *i.e.* to be one to whom a propitiation is due. According to the most obvious view, וְנֹכָחַת is equivalent to וְנוֹכַחְתְּ; the *Dagesh lene* is however lacking, as indeed it would be also at xxx. 15, if וְלָקַחַת were there equivalent to וְלָקַחְתְּ. The punctuators however always place *Dagesh lene* in such formations, *e.g.* שְׁמָעֵךְ for שְׁמָעֵךְ, 1 Kings i. 11 and frequently, and distinguish the second pers. וְקָרָאתְ, xvi. 11, from the third pers. וְקָרָאת, by the added Sheva (according to which Olsh. § 35*b*, must be corrected). They therefore took וְנֹכָחַת as a participle, but scarcely like Gesenius (*Thes.* p. 700, 592): and she was convicted (of her fault), since not shame, but the preservation of her honour is awarded to Sarah; but ונוכחת stands elliptically for וְנוֹכַחַת אַתְּ (comp. xxiv. 30; Hab. ii. 10; Ps. vii. 10, xxii. 29, lv. 20; Isa. xxix. 8, xl. 19), unless we prefer with Dillmann to point it וְנוֹכָחַתְּ (comp. König, *Lehrgeb.* i. 423). By a truly royal extra present, Abimelech makes amends for the wrong done to Sarah, inasmuch as he thereby manifests a respectful acknowledgment of the marital relation against which he had unconsciously almost offended. Abraham accepts the money, because it was meant in all seriousness as an atonement. His prayer is heard, ver. 17: *And Abraham prayed to God, and Elohim healed Abimelech and his wife and his maid-servants, and they bare children.* We have here אֲמָהוֹת instead of שְׁפָחוֹת, the notion of service adhering more to שִׁפְחָה than to אָמָה, 1 Sam. xxv. 41—the ה in this plural formation, for which the Arab. is *amavât*, is a compensation for an original י. The Arabic diminutive *umajja* (little maid) gave a name to the dynasty of the Umajjades. We here first learn that Abimelech and the women of his house were visited with sickness, according to which וַיֵּלְדוּ seems to include Abimelech, and hence to be meant, as at Hos. ix. 16, of the power of procreation as well as of birth. Ver. 18 too may be understood of a hindrance to both conception and bringing forth. Ver. 18: *For Jahveh had fast closed every womb of the house of Abimelech for the sake of Sarah, the wife of Abraham.* The additional clause rightly originates from the fact, that the sickness and recovery of the women took place in the short period of time between the carrying off and the release of Sarah. Those who were pregnant had to lament the absence of travail pains, or their lack of result; the הרחם עצר (בעד) comprises both, when as here it means incapacity of giving birth, Isa. lxvi. 9, and not as at xvi. 2, comp. xxix. 31, xxx. 22, incapacity of conception. It is here construed with בְּעַד, as in a like sense with סגר, 1 Sam. i. 6. עַל־דְּבַר is found in both *E*, ver. 11, and *J*, xii. 17, xliii. 18. Ver. 18 might in itself well be a free exegetical addition; but the diction gives it, like xxii. 15-18, the appearance of conformity to the source.

BIRTH OF ISAAC AND EXPULSION OF ISHMAEL, CH. XXI. 1–21.

This fourth portion of the third section of Abraham's life is divided into two parts, the first of which, xxi. 1–5, relates the birth of Isaac, the second, xxi. 9–21, the expulsion of

Ishmael from the parental house. Apart from the parenthesis, ver. 1, the first part, xxi. 1–5, is essentially from *Q*: it falls back upon ch. xvii., and forms one whole with it. The second part, xxi. 6–21, is, on the other hand, from *E*, in ver. 6, the counterpart to xviii. 12, and from *J*, in vv. 9–21, the counterpart to ch. xvi. The diction of this older Elohist nearly approaches the Jahvistico-Deuteronomic. Thus the likewise Jahvistic formula וַיַּשְׁכֵּם בַּבֹּקֶר is here repeated, ver. 14, as at xx. 8; and עַל־אֹדוֹת, vv. 11, 25, is not less Jahvistic, xxvi. 32. The noun אָמָה, vv. 10, 12, 13, is moreover so very Deuteronomic, that שִׁפְחָה occurs with it only once, xxviii. 68, in Deuteronomy.

The occurrence in Gerar, according to the order here preserved, took place in the year which had been fixed, xviii. 10, 14, to elapse until the birth of Isaac. Ver. 1 points back to this promise given in Mamre: *And Jahveh visited Sarah as He had said, and Jahveh did unto Sarah as He had spoken.* The structure of the verse is like ii. 5*a*, and its contents are, as it were, the obverse of xx. 18. We have to give up the perception of the origin of these two verses; enough that they form a transition from an extract from *E* to one from *Q*, for in ver. 2 follows the text of *Q*: *And Sarah conceived, and bare Abraham a son in his old age, at the appointed time which Elohim had said.* Following ch. xvii. 19, 21, the reference back to xvii. 21 strikes one immediately. According to xxv. 7, Abraham attained the age of 175, hence at Isaac's birth he had still a long life before him, and yet he was in זְקֻנִים (only found besides here, xxxvii. 3, xliv. 20), and was, looking backwards, well stricken in years. He gives to his new-born son the name prescribed, xvii. 14, ver. 3: *And Abraham called the name of his son who was born to him, whom Sarah bare him, Isaac.* It is impossible that הַנּוֹלַד, thus written with Pathach, should be a participle, it is 3 pers., the article standing for אֲשֶׁר, as at xviii. 21, xlvi. 27. The circumcision of Isaac as prescribed,

xvii. 12, ver. 4: *And Abraham circumcised his son Isaac when he was eight days old, as Elohim commanded him.* Abraham's age at the time, ver. 5: *And Abraham was one hundred years old when his son Isaac was born.* This refers back to xvii. 17. The construction of the Passive with אֶת (here and ver. 8, comp. on iv. 18) is, in the Pentateuch, no indication of a source. The extract from *E* now begins with an historical statement of the motive for the name of Isaac, ver. 6: *And Sarah said: Elohim has prepared laughter for me; every one who hears it will laugh at me.* The Pentateuch always has צחק, and never שׂחק, for to laugh. As at xvii. 17 (comp. Ps. cxxvi. 2), it is the laughter of joyful surprise that is intended, but here not unmingled with some feeling of shame. In יִצְחָק־לִי, as in הִתְמַלִּךְ, Jer. xxii. 15, the union of the syllables is loosened, Ges. § 10, note 2. Sarah is in a state of solemn maternal rapture, hence her words have a poetic elevation and arrangement. As ver. 6 is a distich, ver. 7 is a tristich: *She said also: Who would have said to Abraham: Sarah shall give children suck! For I have borne him a son in his old age.* Tuch translates: Who will announce to Abraham: Sarah is giving children suck! and takes the words as a call to take the joyful news to the father. But then instead of מִלֵּל we should expect יַגִּיד, and instead of הֵינִיקָה rather מֵינֶקֶת, and instead of בָּנִים the more definite בֵּן. In Num. xxiii. 10, Lam. iii. 37, also מִי, with a perfect following, means: who has done, *i.e.* ever ventured or been able to do. So here: Who has ever said to Abraham, for which we should say: Who would have said (and yet it is so); comp. on this use of the perfect in questions, xviii. 12, Num. xxiii. 10, Judg. ix. 9 sq., 2 Kings xx. 9 (where חָלַךְ means *iveritne*), Ps. xi. 3, Job xii. 9, Zech. iv. 10 (*quis contemserit*). Only with this meaning is the general plur. בָּנִים (comp. בָּהֵן, xix. 29, as also Isa. xxxvii. 3, 1 Sam. xvii. 43) in place. The expression is brief, well turned and choice (מִלֵּל, a poetic Aramaism, occurs in the Pentateuch only here). Festival at weaning, ver. 8: *And the child grew, and was weaned: and Abraham prepared a great feast on the day of Isaac's weaning.* This took place in his second or third year, a child being, in the East, often nourished by its mother or wet-nurse till its third year (1 Sam. i. 23 sqq.; 2 Macc. vii. 27). To be weaned is called הִגָּמֵל, from גָּמַל, related to גָּמַר, كمل; from the fundamental meaning "to fill, to complete," may be explained all the meanings: to perform = to do actually, to develop fully = to ripen, *Niph.* to be suckled to the end = to be weaned. The announcement, the birth, the weaning of the child—all furnish matter for varied and joyful laughter; יִצְחָק means one who laughs, who has abundant joy. Our Lord (John viii. 56) expresses the deepest cause of this joy. Sarah the wife of the one, by becoming the mother of Isaac, became the mother of Israel, Isa. li. 1 sq., comp. Mal. ii. 15, Ezek. xxxiii. 24, and by becoming the mother of Israel, the ancestress, and thus indirectly the mother of the Messiah, who has flesh and blood from Isaac through Israel, and in whom Abraham became a blessing to all nations. Hence at Verdun the birth and circumcision of Isaac and the birth and circumcision of Christ are correctly placed together on the altar; while above is the announcement of Isaac on the same line as the salutation of the angel. The ancient synagogal Haggadah, that Isaac was born on the night of the Passover, that night of redemption, also fits in to this historical chain. St. Paul, Gal. iv., equally regards what is further related, xxi. 9–21, as typical and allegorical history. Ishmael behaves insolently to his brother, ver. 9: *And Sarah saw the son of Hagar the Egyptian, whom she bore to Abraham, mocking.* The masoretically testified reading is מְצַחֵק, with a small Pathach, *i.e.* Segol in pause, comp. לְצָחֵק, Ex. xxxii. 6; יָרֵחֶף, Deut. xxxii. 11, and the pausal transition of עַד into עָד. The word does not here mean innocent joking, but insolent rudeness (comp. xxxix. 14; Ezek. xxiii. 32, synon. הֵלִיץ לְעַג). The contemptuous attested in word and deed, which Isaac suffered from Ishmael, is regarded by the apostle as a prophecy of the persecution which the believing Church of Christ suffers from the bondmen of the law given in the desert of Sinai, and thus in the Hagarene land. Hofmann closely connects ver. 9 with 8: At the festival of Isaac's weaning, Ishmael, instead of sharing in the joy of the family, was mocking at the son of his father. Sarah's demand, ver. 10: *And she said to Abraham: Cast out this bond-woman and her son; for the son of this bond-woman shall not be heir with my son, with Isaac.* This request vexed Abraham, but God bade him comply with it, vv. 11-13: *The thing appeared very displeasing to Abraham because of his son. But Elohim said to Abraham: Let it not be displeasing to thee because of the boy and because of thy bond-maid; in all that Sarah says to thee, hearken to her words; for through Isaac shall thy seed be named. And also the son of the bond-maid will I make a nation, because he is thy seed.* Sarah's request, in which proud contempt was mingled with just displeasure, was very repugnant to Abraham, not indeed on account of Hagar, who was and continued nothing more to him than his wife's bond-maid, but on account of his son whom she had borne, and whom he loved as his own flesh and blood (עַל־אֹדֹת, on account of the turns, conditions, circumstances; comp. احوال, from حال, to turn, an ancient "on account of" occurring outside the Pentateuch only Josh. xiv. 6, Judg. vi. 7, Jer. iii. 8, comp. the corrupt passage, 2 Sam. xiii. 16). God however requires of him the denial of his natural feeling, basing this denial on the promise כִּי בְיִצְחָק יִקָּרֵא לְךָ זָרַע, and making it easier by the promise that He would also make the son of the bond-maid the ancestor of a nation, even him (a retrospective pron. like xlvii. 21), because he is his seed. Three explanations of this ἐν Ἰσαὰκ κληθήσεταί σοι σπέρμα (Rom. ix. 7; Heb. xi. 18) are possible: after Isaac's name shall thy seed be called (v. Hofm., comp. Ges. § 154. 3*a*), or: in, through, from Isaac shall seed be called into existence for thee (Drechsler), or: in Isaac, through him shall it happen, that a seed of Abraham is spoken of (Bleek), or more accurately: through him shall a seed be bestowed on thee, who shall bear thy name, and propagate the blessings connected with it in a direct line (Kn. Dillm.). Since with the first view we should have expected בְּשֵׁם, Isa. xliii. 7, xlviii. 1, and moreover the nation of the promise is only once, Amos vii. 9, called יִשְׂחָק, and since קָרָא has indeed the meaning "to call into existence," Isa. xli. 4, Rom. iv. 17, but never so without an addition, the third view must be preferred. In Isaac shall the nation, which is and is called the genuine seed of Abraham (Isa. xli. 8), have its point of departure. Abraham understands this in a vision of the night, or a dream, for he acts in the morning according to the Divine direction, ver. 14: *Then Abraham arose early in the morning, and took bread and a skin with water, and gave it to Hagar, laid it upon her neck, and the boy, and sent her away. And she went and wandered in the wilderness of Beĕrŝéba'.* He obeyed the voice of God, much as his attachment to the child and his mother, and his compassion for both, strove against it. Ishmael having been at Isaac's birth, xvii. 25, thirteen years of age, must now have been fourteen, and yet Abraham puts him together with the bread and water upon Hagar's neck. So indeed according to the LXX., καὶ ἐπέθηκεν ἐπὶ τὸν ὦμον αὐτῆς τὸ παιδίον, which Dillm. looks upon as the original wording. But even supposing that *E* was not as aware of the age of Ishmael as *Q* was, why should he have looked upon him as a little child to be carried by his mother? why should וְאֶת־הַיֶּלֶד, governed by וַיִּתֵּן, be a harmonistic correction? The state of the case is in reality similar to וְאֶת־בִּנְיָמִן, xliii. 15. Hagar no more took Ishmael astride upon her neck than his brothers took Benjamin in their hand like the money; שָׂם, like שָׁפַל, xviii. 14, is the perf. of the accessory action (Driver, § 163). וַתֵּתַע is *impf. Kal* from תעה, not יעה. From Hagar's wandering in the wilderness, afterwards called that of Beër-sheba, we may infer that Abraham at that time resided in the Negeb. Nor does it follow from vv. 15, 16 that the narrator regarded Ishmael as a little child : *And the water in the skin was spent, then she cast the child under one of the shrubs, and went and sat over against, about a bow-shot off; for she said : Let me not look upon the death of the child—therefore she sat over against and lifted up her voice and wept.* The appellation יֶלֶד (comp. iv. 23 ; 1 Kings xii. 8 ; Dan. i. 4 ; Eccles. iv. 13) leaves the age undecided. To cast is like Matt. xv. 30 (comp. to cast into prison, Jer. xxxviii. 6), to lay down hastily, here said of the sudden resolve of hopeless resignation. The store of water was spent, and Ishmael in a state of extreme exhaustion was unable to drag on any farther, and she laid him down under a שִׂיחִם. The branchy woody perennial desert plant which furnishes the usual fuel, and in the shade of which a scanty vegetation exists in the hot season, is still called شيح. Under such a shrub she laid him, that he might at least die in the shade, and sat down over against הַרְחֵק בִּמְטַחֲוֵי קֶשֶׁת, at the distance of shootings of the bow (Gen. like Jer. iv. 29), *i.e.* according to the usual *comparatio decurtata* : as far as bow-shots are accustomed to carry, from מָטָה, original form מָטוּ, *Pilel* מָטֲוָה, like שַׁחֲוָה, Ges. § 75, note 18. Maternal love was not able to look upon the death of the child (רָאָה בְּ, said of compassionate beholding, as at xliv. 34, xxix. 32 ; Num. xi. 15), but at the same time could not lose sight of him. A voice of comfort then resounded from heaven, vv. 17, 18 : *Then Elohim heard the voice of the boy, and the angel of Elohim called to Hagar from heaven, and said to her : What aileth thee, Hagar? fear not, for Elohim has heard the voice of the boy where he is. Arise, lift up the boy and hold him with firm hand ; for I will make him a great nation.* God heard (as the name יִשְׁמָעֵאל signifies); He who had entered into covenant with Abraham, even the Angel of the covenant, proclaimed from heaven words of comfort and encouragement to the mother. בַּאֲשֶׁר הוּא שָׁם, where (= בִּמְקוֹם אֲשֶׁר, 2 Sam. xv. 21) he now is (in so helpless a state). With הַחֲזִיקִי בוֹ is here placed אֶת־יָדֵךְ, which elsewhere has to be supplied, *ex quo manifestum est*, as Jerome remarks, *eum qui tenetur non oneri matri fuisse, sed comitem*. The immediate help, ver. 19: *Then Elohim opened her eyes, and she saw a spring of water, and went and filled the skin with water and gave the boy drink*. Elsewhere (as at xxvi. 15) בְּאֵר means a well dug by human hands, here a spring that might be seen, Assyr. *bêru* (differing from בְּאֹר=בּוֹר, cistern, *i.e.* a receptacle for rain water, Assyr. *bûru*), as at xiv. 10, with חֵמָר, the bitumen spring.[1] A spring from which water was flowing appeared before her eyes, which had become enlightened, and with it she refreshed the exhausted boy. How it afterwards fared with Ishmael, vv. 20, 21: *And Elohim was with the boy, and he grew up, and dwelt in the wilderness and became an archer. And he dwelt in the wilderness of Pharan, and his mother took him a wife out of the land of Egypt*. Entrance into adolescence is meant by וַיִּגְדַּל. The sentence concerning the vocation may be translated: growing up, he became an archer; רֹבֶה, from רָבָה, to increase = to grow, comp. on Prov. xxviii. 28; Arab. رَبَا, to grow up (whence رَبّ, according to the spirit of the Arabic: educator, guardian, master). In the Mishnic too רֹבֶה means the youth (plur. רֹבִים), according to which R. Chananel and other ancient expositors (see Abulwalid's *Lexicon*) and the Targ. translate רַבְיָא קַשָּׁתָא, *juvenis sagittarius*. But it is better to take רֹבֶה as the more general word, which is more particularly explained by קַשָּׁת, a caster (shooter), viz. an archer, a permutative combination as at xiii. 8; 1 Kings i. 2, v. 29; Ges. § 113. The LXX. too took רבה in the sense of רבב, to shoot (like xlix. 23; Ps. xviii. 15; Job xvi. 13), translating the two words together τοξότης, and hence read רֹבֵה קֶשֶׁת in the same sense as רֹמֵה קֶשֶׁת, according to which Onkelos also translates (as Gr. Ven.

---

[1] See my article on the song of the well, Num. xxi. 17 sqq., in Luthardt's *Zeitschr.* 1882, pp. 449-451.

does, βάλλων τόξῳ), and for which Hitzig on Jer. iv. 29, Hupf. on Ps. lxxviii. 9, Kn. Olsh. Dillm. decide. מִדְבַּר פָּארָן is the name of the entire desert plateau, bounded on the west by *Gebel Helâl* and *Gelek*, on the east by the Edom country, on the north by the southern mountains of Judæa, on the south by *el-Tih* proper, which here as a whole extending far and wide is opposed to the מִדְבַּר בְּאֵר שֶׁבַע. Hagar, herself an Egyptian, representing herein the father (xxxiv. 4, xxxviii. 6), took for her son a wife from Egypt.

TREATY BETWEEN ABRAHAM AND ABIMELECH, CH. XXI. 22–34.

The fifth part of the third section of the life of Abraham (xxi. 22–34) relates the solemn conclusion of a treaty between Abimelech and Abraham. The narrator is *E*, the same who related Sarah's preservation in Gerar, and the expulsion of Ishmael and his mother; the scene is everywhere the south country, with the neighbouring Gerâr and the great wilderness opening somewhat farther southwards. The diction of the narrator here too has points of contact with *J*, it contains specially classical expressions. The conclusion of the covenant (denoted by כרת ברית, only used by *J* and *E*, never by *Q*) is represented with the same archæological preciseness as the history of the redemption by the Goel in ch. iv. of the book of Ruth. Only at the end does *R* complete and frame the narrative of *E* by an extract from *J*. The desire and proposal of Abimelech, vv. 22, 23: *And it came to pass at that time, that Abimelech spake, and Phicol, the captain of his host, to Abraham thus: Elohim is with thee in all that thou doest. Now then swear unto me by Elohim, on the spot, that thou wilt not be faithless to me, nor to my offspring and posterity, that the same kindness that I have shown thee, thou wilt show to me and to the country in which thou sojournest as a guest.* A friendly relation, introduced by Abimelech, already exists; the question is concerning its establishment for all future time. Phicol accompanies Abimelech, to be present as a witness. The LXX. adds, from the Jahvistic counterpart (xxvi. 26), the name of אֲחֻזַּת. The appellations of the king and his official are Canaanite, as are also the Philistine names of the cuneiform inscriptions. הֵנָּה, locative of the demonstrative הֵ, urges an immediate compliance. וָנִ֫י נֵ֫כֶר are a pair of words alliterating like an acrostic, found elsewhere only Job xviii. 19; Isa. xiv. 22. Abraham consents, ver. 24: *Then Abraham said: I swear.* אָנֹכִי added to אִשָּׁבֵעַ (with the original *i* instead of *ĕ*, like אֵפֶס, Judg. xvi. 26, together with אֶשְׁפֹּט, Ezek. xx. 38) is as emphatic an expression as 2 Kings vi. 2; Prov. xxiv. 32. He swears, yet not without a "but," ver. 25: *And Abraham reproved Abimelech on account of the well of water, which the servants of Abimelech had taken away.* The article points to some definite well, for an indefinite one would have been called בְּאֵר מַיִם (xxi. 19). The king declares that he has had no part in this unjust appropriation of Abraham's property, ver. 26: *Then Abimelech said: I know not who has done this, and neither hast thou told it to me, nor have I heard it except to-day.* The perf. וְהוֹכִחַ, 25a, relates in a preparatory manner to this declaration of Abimelech (in which the correlatives, *neque . . . neque*, are as explicit as *e.g.* at Num. xxiii. 25). This was satisfactory, ver. 27: *And Abraham took sheep and oxen and gave them to Abimelech, and they both made a covenant.* Abraham however causes the acknowledgment of his property in the well, which had been disputed, to be confirmed by a special formality, which forms, as it were, an additional article of the covenant. This formality is symbolical and needs explanation, vv. 28-30: *And Abraham placed seven lambs of the flock apart. Then Abimelech said to Abraham: What mean the seven lambs which thou hast set apart? He said: Because thou shalt take the seven lambs from my hand, that it may be a witness for me that I have digged this well.* "Seven lambs of the flock"—this is one of the cases where, as at 2 Sam. xii. 30, Ps. cxiii. 9, comp. on Cant. i. 11b, the article is connected with the gen. only. In the question: what are (i.e. mean), etc., הֵנָּה is not an adv. of locality as at 23a, but like הֵפֹּה (Zech. i. 9), an expression of the copula (Ew. § 297b). The לְבַדְּנָה, interchanging with לְבִדְיְהָן, is an emphatic form, like כָּלְנָה, xlii. 36; Prov. xxxi. 29 = לְבָדְ, comp. כִּלְהֶן=כִּלְהֵנָה, 1 Kings vii. 37. On the absence of the article in אֶת־שֶׁבַע כְּבָשֹׂת, see Ges. § 117, note 2. The testimony given by Abimelech by his acceptance of the seven lambs is like an oath, for seven is the number of God as manifesting Himself; and to swear נִשְׁבַּע is the same as to seven oneself, i.e. to submit the truth of a statement to the Divine inspection. Hence seven things, as e.g. among the Arabs, seven stones smeared with the blood of the covenant-makers, and lying between them (Herod. iii. 8), are therefore in treaties the symbolical instruments of sanction in the name of God, or take the place of an oath for confirmation. Generally speaking, a gift, which one of the contracting parties accepts from the other, makes the contract the more binding. So in Homer, *Il.* xix. 243–246, where Agamemnon, after swearing reconciliation with Achilles, sends also seven three-footed kettles and seven women to Briseis; and similarly also Gen. xxxiii. 8–15. The name given to the place on account of the occurrence, ver. 31: *Therefore the place was called Beër-'Sébaʽ, for there they both swore.* קָרָא, as at xi. 9, xvi. 14, has the most general subject. The name means the seven-well, or, what is indirectly the same, the well of the oath. After a similar covenant between Isaac and Abimelech, the servants of Isaac find a well, which they call שִׁבְעָה, and from it the name of the city is said to have been also called באר שבע (xxvi. 32 sq.). Robinson actually found there not one but two deep wells of clear, excellent water, still called بِيْر السبع (i. 337–341), which means, in Arabic custom of language, either the lion's well or also the well of imprecation, for السَّبع is a synonym of اللَّعْنَة, "the curse" (*DMZ.*

xxii. 177). The extra שְׁבַע (Josh. xix. 2) has perhaps a similar relation to בְּאֵר־שֶׁבַע as סוּכָר, Συχάρ, has to שְׁכֶם (Neapolis), and is thus the locality of Isaac's well, named as the annex of Beersheba, as Sychar is of Jacob's well. Conclusion of the narrative, vv. 32–34: *And they made a covenant in Beër-ʾSébaʿ; and Abimelech and Phicol, the captain of his host, rose up and returned to the land of the Philistines. And he planted a tamarisk tree in Beër-ʾSébaʿ, and there called upon the name of Jahveh the eternal God. And Abraham sojourned a long time in the land of the Philistines.* Matter not appertaining to the narrative of *E* is here blended with it. According to *J* it is assumed, ver. 34 (xxvi. 1, 26), that Gerar was in Philistia and Beersheba, beyond the Philistine district. Both the treaties were without effect upon subsequent history. We nowhere find a trace that the Philistine nation remembered them, and Israel was directed to expel the Philistines from the land of promise,—a direction indeed which they did not carry into effect. But what is related, ver. 33 and xxvi. 25, from *J* made Beersheba, for all future time, a place of sacred remembrance which false worship turned to profit (Amos v. 5, viii. 14). Abraham there planted אֵשֶׁל (as the *Tamarix orientalis*, abundant in Egypt, Petræa and Palestine, is called), comp. those in Gibeah, 1 Sam. xxii. 6, and Jabesh, 1 Sam. xxxi. 13. The statement that he there called upon and proclaimed the name of Jahveh belongs to the series, iv. 26, xii. 8, xiii. 4, xxi. 33, xxvi. 25; comp. viii. 20, xii. 7, xiii. 18, xxxiii. 20, xxxv. 7. The additional name אֵל עוֹלָם developes what the name יְהוָה declares, which hence designates, not Him who brings into existence, but the existing One, or Him to whom absolute existence belongs. Jahveh as such is אֵל עוֹלָם, who in His power is always equal to Himself. Such He proved Himself to Abraham, ever and again meeting his weakness by His own faithfulness. Hence Abraham dedicates to Him a tamarisk. Its durable wood and evergeen foliage is a symbol of His eternity.[1]

[1] Trumbull in his *Blod Covenant* (New York 1885) takes this tamarisk, as

But hardly had the countenance of the Eternal been thus favourable to the patriarch than it was again overcast with clouds, and this time of the very darkest. For it seemed as though he were to lose the son of promise who, as ver. 34 gives us to understand by way of transition, had grown up in Philistia.

THE SACRIFICE UPON MORIAH, CH. XXII. 1–19.

This first portion of the fourth section of the life of Abraham corresponds with those of the call, of the covenant sacrifice, of the institution of circumcision, which open the three preceding sections. The father of the faithful is now perfected. The obedience of faith drew Abraham into a strange land; by the humility of faith he gave way to his nephew Lot; strong in faith, he fought four kings of the heathen with three hundred and eighteen men; firm in faith, he rested in the word of promise, notwithstanding all the opposition of reason and nature; bold in faith, he entreated the preservation of Sodom under increasingly lowered conditions; joyful in faith, he received, named and circumcised the son of promise; with the loyalty of faith he submitted at the bidding of God to the will of Sarah and expelled Hagar and Ishmael; and with the gratitude of faith he planted a tamarisk to the ever faithful God in the place where Abimelech had sued for his friendship and accepted his present,—now his faith was to be put to the severest test to prove itself victorious, and to be rewarded accordingly. Analysis leads to the incontestable results, that the narrative as to the warp of its fabric is from *E* with insertions from *J*, but that it was not *J* who worked up the account of *E*, but *R* who completed it from *J*, especially by taking from *J* the second angelic voice (vv. 15–18), the naming of the place with its explanation

also the terebinths of Mamre, as covenant trees, and, starting from the assumption that the fundamental rite of ancient covenanting (כרת ברית) consisted in a mutual mingling of blood, thinks besides that they were smeared with the blood of the covenant.

(ver. 14), and calling the angel of God (who could not well be called at one time מַלְאַךְ אֱלֹהִים and at another מַלְאַךְ יהוה), both at vv. 11 and 15, מַלְאַךְ יהוה. It cannot however be maintained that the goal of the journey was not already called אֶרֶץ הַמֹּרִיָּה in *E*, especially as it is not necessary to regard Moriah as containing the Divine name יה. Not only does the Divine name (ה)אלהים point to *E* as the original narrator, but also the mode of statement (וַיַּשְׁכֵּם) after a Divine revelation by night, xxii. 1–3, comp. xxi. 12–14; the voice of the angel from heaven, xxii. 11, comp. xxi. 17; the ram seen upon looking up, xxii. 13, comp. xxi. 19) and also the mode of expression in nowise to be verified in *Q*, but in many instances found elsewhere in *E* (*e.g.* the local פֹּה, xxii. 5, xxxi. 37) or akin to *J* (comp. מְאוּמָה, xxii. 12, with xxxix. 6, 9, 23).

The narrative begins with the same acolouthic formula as xv. 1: *It came to pass after these events, God, testing Abraham, said unto him: Abraham! And he said: Behold, here I am.* The sentence וְהָאֱלֹהִים נִסָּה is not an apodosis proper, but a statement of the circumstances of the apodosis which follows with וַיֹּאמֶר (comp. without ו, xl. 1). Abraham had in the midst of his Canaanite surrounding the practice of sacrificing children before his eyes. He saw how the heathen surrendered their dearest to appease the deity and render him propitious. Hence the question might easily arise within: Wouldst thou be able to do the like to please thy God? Justice is done to the words "God tested him" when we thus psychologically account for the testing becoming a temptation. The temptation had its origin in him, and it became a test when God received it into His plan and gave it a pre-descried goal. God desired thus to try him that he might stand the test. He calls Abraham by name, who answers with willing attention, הִנֵּנִי. Now follows the hard demand, ver. 2: *He said: Take thy son, thine only one whom thou lovest, Isaac, and go to the land of Moriah and offer him there as a burnt-offering upon one of the mountains that I will tell thee.* The obj. is made prominent by a threefold אֶת. Isaac is called his only son not as the only one after the expulsion of Ishmael, but as the only one of his one proper marriage (Prov. iv. 3, Cant. vi. 9). LXX. τὸν ἀγαπητόν (i.e. יְדִידְךָ), but this is stated by אֲשֶׁר־אָהַבְתָּ, whom thou lovest as the long desired, the gift of God, endowed with the glorious promises of God. Of the inward conflict, which this command called forth in Abraham, we read not a word. He fought it out to victory, he remained firm in faith, of which Luther says: *fides conciliat contraria nec est otiosa qualitas, sed virtus ejus est mortem occidere, infernum damnare, esse peccato peccatum, diabolo diabolum, adeo ut mors non sit mors, etiamsi omnium sensus testetur adesse mortem.* The "Land of Moriah" occurs only here, but "Mount Moriah" (הַר הַמּוֹרִיָּה) is, as the testimony of 2 Chron. iii. 1 confirmed upon internal grounds says, the height upon which was the threshing-floor of Ornan, the subsequent temple mount.[1] Prepared for the worst, Abraham starts with Isaac on the morning after this revelation at night, ver. 3. *Then Abraham arose early in the morning, and saddled his ass and took his two young men with him and Isaac his son, and clave wood for the burnt-offering and arose and went to the place that God had told him.* By the two נְעָרִים whom he took with him are said, by the Targ. Jer. *Pirke de-Rabbi Eliezer*, ch. 31, and by the Midrash in general, to be meant Ishmael and Eliezer; but we are not justified in assuming Ishmael's return to his father's house after ch. xxi., without such express testimony as xxv. 9, and Eliezer's age (comp. xxiv. 2 with xv. 2) and Ishmael's position in the family would prevent either of them being called נַעַר. The distance from Beersheba to Jerusalem by way of Hebron amounts to about 38 miles, and still when the traveller arrives on the third day at Mar Elias he is all at once sur-

---

[1] Kuenen (*Einl.* § 13, note 29) thinks, with Wellh. and Dillm., that JE (who worked up the two into a whole) put Moriah in the place of another Ephrainite local name for the sake of transposing Abraham's act of faith to Jerusalem; but to what purpose is this roundabout way, why not rather suppose that the chronicler erroneously indicated the name Moriah?

prised by the sight of the temple-mount; hence it is with topographical fidelity that we are further told, vv. 4, 5: *On the third day Abraham lifted up his eyes, and saw the place afar off. Then Abraham said to his young men: Stay here with the ass, and I and the lad will go yonder and worship and return to you.* Worship—he is certainly going to perform in a devout, submissive frame of mind an act of worship to God; return —so say in him both nature and faith, but with very different meanings, ver. 6 : *Then Abraham took the wood for the burnt-offering, and laid it on Isaac his son, and took in his hand the fire and the knife, and they went both together.* Upon this hardest path that ever father went with his child, Isaac at last breaks the long silence, vv. 7, 8 : *Then Isaac spake to Abraham his father, and said: My father! and he said: Here am I, my son. And he said: Behold the fire and the wood; but where is the lamb for the burnt-offering? Abraham said: Elohim will provide Himself the lamb for the burnt-offering, and they went both together.* Isaac, by way of gradually venturing upon a question, says: אָבִי. To this now heartrending word Abraham replies: הִנֶּנִּי בְנִי. After the deeply stirred father had uttered this word of affection, Isaac further asks about the lamb for the sacrifice. This question agitates his paternal heart to its inmost depth; but master through faith of even the strongest emotions of nature, he finds the right answer, an answer inspired by forbearing love and foreboding hope: God will provide Himself the sacrificial lamb (רָאָה like צָפָה, Job xv. 22), and they went both together—the third stage of the journey, upon which each step was a fresh martyrdom for Abraham, and required a fresh victory. The simply yet deeply-felt and touching delineation recalls the last journey of Elijah and Elisha, 2 Kings ii. 1-8. Arrival at the mountain, vv. 9, 10 : *And they came to the place which God had told him, and Abraham built there the altar, and laid the wood in order, and bound Isaac his son, and laid him on the altar upon the wood. And Abraham stretched out his hand, and took the knife to slay his son.* The narrative accompanies Abraham's victoriously advancing act of obedient faith step by step to the climax of the fatal moment. Isaac, whose fundamental characteristic is quiet endurance, lies without resistance like a lamb upon the pile of wood, and Abraham has already raised the knife for the deadly stroke. Then suddenly the angel of Jahveh lights up the thick darkness that has gathered over the enigma of this history, vv. 11, 12: *Then the angel of Jahveh called to him from heaven, and said: Abraham, Abraham! And he said. Here am I. And he said: Stretch not out thy hand against the lad, and do nothing to him; for now I know that thou fearest Elohim, and hast not withheld thy son, thy only one, from me.* Isaac, after Abraham had not spared him (חָשַׂךְ, to keep back = φείδεσθαι, Rom. viii. 32), was as good as already sacrificed. Abraham is proved to be one who fears God above all things, and obeys Him absolutely (Jas. ii. 21–23, comp. Heb. xi. 17–19). The animal provided by God for sacrifice, ver. 13: *And Abraham lifted up his eyes, and saw, and behold, a ram in the rear had entangled itself in the thicket with its horns; then Abraham went and took the ram and offered him as a burnt-offering in the place of his son.* Ganneau tries to make the ram אַיִל into a stag אַיָּל; but it is not Isaac but Jephthah's daughter who resembles Iphigenia, of whom a stag takes the place. The reading אַיִל אֶחָד, κριὸς εἷς (LXX. Samar. Syr. Targums, Book of Jubilees, Gr. Ven.), preferred by Olshausen and Ewald, tells nothing, while the local אַחַר (here as at Ps. lxviii. 26, an adverb, and of like meaning as when used as a preposition, Ex. iii. 1) states why the animal had hitherto remained unperceived. The MSS. vacillate between the finite נֶאֱחַז and the part. נֶאֱחָז; the noun sentence is more graphic. They also vacillate between בְּקַרְנָיו or (which better suits the plur. סְבָכִי) בִּסְבַךְ. Naming of the memorable place, ver. 14: *Then Abraham called the name of that place Jahveh sees, so that it is said to this day: Upon the mountain Jahveh is seen,* not as it is accented, upon the mountain of

Jahveh (with the genitive attraction of the subject, as at v. 1*b*) there is He seen (a kind of elliptical relative sentence scarcely to be authenticated). "Jahveh sees" is meant like xvi. 13 and like "Jahveh hears" in יִשְׁמָעֵאל (xxi. 17): He sees to it, interposing in extreme necessity. But יִרְאֶה cannot be the passive of ראה in this meaning, for the *Niph.* in the sense of *provideri* is unauthenticated, and when in the course of the history this mountain is spoken of, נִרְאָה always means either the appearing (self-manifestation) of God or the appearing of men before Him. Nevertheless אֲשֶׁר, "so that" (as at xiii. 16, comp. x. 9), presupposes an internal connection of the words customary to this day (which besides form only a fragment of a sentence; comp. x. 9; Num. xxi. 14 sq.) with the saying of Abraham. Nor is this connection difficult to discover; the רְאוֹת of Jahveh coincided in the case of Abraham as in that of Hagar, xvi. 13, xxi. 17, with הֵרָאוֹת: He saw to it by taking upon Himself to see, *i.e.* to interpose. This ver. 14 sounds like a voice from very ancient times, and not as if the word מֹרִיָּה were to be explained by it, which moreover cannot be explained from יָהּ מָרְאֶה, something given to see (Ex. xxv. 40) = appearing of Jah, without phonetic difficulty; we expect מָרְאִיָּה (comp. יְרָאִיָּה) and the article הַמֹּרִיָּה, which also the chronicler, 2 Chron. iii. 1, still maintains is strange (for the case is different in Ps. cxviii. 5); the word seems rather to rank with הַיְחָדִיָה, 1 Chron. iv. 18, than with מַאֲפֵלְיָה, Jer. ii. 31. In any case ver. 14 does not read as if the naming, ver. 2, could be regarded as conscious anticipation. Nor do any of the ancient translators express the Divine name in מריה, not even Symmachus, who translates τῆς ὀπτασίας; the Jewish Targums translate ארעא דפולחנא, Land of worship, the Samaritan Targum ארע חזיתה, and the Samar. Arab.: the chosen land. Differently again, and not worth mentioning, the LXX. and Syriac.

The narrative apparently terminates with ver. 14. Whatever may be the case with this ver. 14, it is evident why it seems to stand more appropriately here (nearer to vv. 8 and 13) than after the repeated promise which now follows, vv. 15–18 : *And the angel of Jahveh called to Abraham a second time from heaven, and said : By myself have I sworn, a saying of Jahveh, that because thou hast done this and not withheld thy son, thine only one—that I will bless, yea bless thee, and increase, yea increase thy posterity like the stars of heaven, and like the sand which is on the sea-shore ; and thy seed shall take possession of the gate of their enemies : And in thy seed shall all the nations of the earth be blessed, because thou hast obeyed my voice.* Not an addition by R, but from J (comp. xii. 1–3, xxiv. 60, also on עֵקֶב אֲשֶׁר, xxvi. 5)—a point of unprecedented lustre in the Old Testament, for Jahveh here swears what He promises, as He does nowhere else in His intercourse with the patriarchs (comp. the passages referring to it, xxiv. 7, Ex. xxxii. 13, Luke i. 73, Acts vii. 17) and for the first time in the sacred history; for His promise that there should no more be so universal a deluge is indeed like an oath in value, Isa. liv. 9, but is not one in words. He swears by Himself, because He can swear by no greater, Heb. vi. 13, engages Himself by means of His own Person (בְּ used in swearing of the means of corroboration). The exalted נְאֻם־יְהֹוָה, unusual as introducing Divine declarations in the primitive history, is the subsequent formula of attestation in prophecy (in the Pentateuch it occurs again only Num. xiv. 28, not even Deut. xxxii.). The resumption too of כִּי (that) at ver. 17 is very emphatic. Thus the form as well as the contents is exuberant, for the victor of Moriah is higher than the victor of Dan. Abraham conquered himself and offered up Isaac. He won him back as ancestor of an innumerable world, subduing people, possessing the gate of their enemies, and a seed blessed to be a blessing to all nations. Thus gloriously recompensed does the patriarch depart, ver. 19 : *And Abraham returned to his young men, and they arose and went together to Beēr-ʿSéba'.*

The change of the Divine name is occasioned by the account being composed from E and J, and is in its present state (which it has not attained without the interposition of R in ver. 11) significant. The God who commands Abraham to sacrifice Isaac is called (ה)אלהים, and the Divine appearance, which forbids the sacrifice, מלאך יהוה. He who requires from Abraham the surrender of Isaac is God the Creator, who has power over life and death, and hence power also to take back what He has given; but it is Jahveh in His angel who forbids the fulfilment of the extreme act, for the son of promise cannot perish without the promise, and therewith God's truthfulness and His counsel of salvation also coming to nought. In fact, the God who requires Abraham to sacrifice his only son after the manner of the Canaanites (2 Kings iii. 27; Jer. xix. 5), is only apparently the true God. The demand was indeed only made to prove that Abraham was not behind the heathen in the self-denying surrender of his dearest to his God, and that when the demand had been complied with in spirit, the external fulfilment might be rejected. Schelling exaggerates the contrast when he thinks that the same evil principle, which misled other nations to human sacrifices, is here called אלהים. The Thorah knows of human sacrifice, and indeed of the sacrifice of a man's own children (sons or daughters, and especially the first-born), only as an abomination of Moloch-worship (Lev. xviii. 21, xx. 1–5; comp. Baudissin's *Jahveh et Moloch*, 1874, and Schlottmann's article, "Moloch," in Rhiem). Jephthah's vow was like that of Idomeneus on his return from Troy, heathen, Israelite and Canaanite popular notions coinciding at that period. The true Israel possessed in the transaction with Abraham an ever valid Divine protest against human sacrifice, and abhorred it. The ram in the thicket, which Abraham offered in the place of Isaac, is the prototype of animal sacrifice, which is here sanctioned upon the same mountain on which, during the entire Old Testament period, the typical blood of animal sacrifice was to be shed, while in the times of apostasy the abomination of human sacrifice, branded by the prophets, was continued in the valley of Benê-Hinnom below. The prototype is however at the same time a type: *quis illo (ariete) figurabatur*—asks Augustine (*Civ.* xvi. 32)—*nisi Christus Jesus, antequam immolaretur, spinis Judaicis coronatus ?* Isaac was only offered up ἐν παραβολῇ (Heb. xi. 17-19), is pre-eminently the abiding parable of the son of Abraham and Son of God, who bore His cross of wood and was really sacrificed thereon, *Christi in victimam concessi a patre, lignum passionis suæ bajulantis* (Tertullian, *adv. Judœos*, c. 10). Isaac carried the wood, says also the Midrash (*Pesikta rabbathi*, 54*a*), like a man who takes up his cross (צלוב). The love of Abraham, loving God above all else and depriving himself of what was dearest for Him, serves the Church as a figure of the super-abundant love of God, who spared not His only-begotten Son, but, Rom. viii. 32, so loved the world that He gave Him up to death, John iii. 16. Hence ancient ecclesiastical art took delight in representing the sacrifice of Isaac especially upon sarcophagi. *Quis picturam Abrahæ cernens et gladium pueri cervicibus imminentem*—asks Gregory the Great in a letter to the Emperor Leo the Isaurian—*non compungitur et collacrimatur ?*

THE NEWS OF NAHOR'S FAMILY, CH. XXII. 20-24.

The special object of the second portion of the fourth section of Abraham's life, xxii. 20 sqq., is Rebecca; she is therein as "the rose among thorns." For it contains intelligence concerning the progeny of Nahor, his brother, which in the difficulties of intercourse then existing arrived thus opportunely. It is *J* who, in the genealogy of the Cainites, and in that part of the ethnographical table which is to be referred to him, uses ילי of the father; the נם־הוא too of vv. 20 and 24 is like iv. 4, 22, 26, x. 21; and though the derivation of עוץ and ארם here is not necessarily in opposition to x. 22 sq., yet it is more probable that intelligence which sounds so differently should be from a different than from the same hand. Hence Budde (pp. 220–226) will be right when he says that it is *J*, who here follows up the history of the temptation related by him, by what prepares for the history of Isaac's marriage which he is about to relate.

A connecting verse, ver. 20 : *And it came to pass after these occurrences that it was told to Abraham thus : Behold Milcah, she also has borne sons to thy brother Nahor.* Eight sons of Nahor, the brother of Abraham, by Milcah, are now enumerated and finally summed up with אֵלֶּה שְׁמֹנָה (אֵלֶּה וגו' for הָאֵלֶּה, as fixed as זֶה, Judg. vi. 14, comp. Josh. ix. 13). 1. עוּץ, the first-born, who, according to x. 23 (which see), was the son of Aram and, according to xxxvi. 28, the grandson of Seir the Horite. Combining thus, we must distinguish within the old Aramæan עוץ a younger Nahorite branch, and perhaps also a Seirite ingredient. 2. בּוּז. In the book of Job a fourth opponent appears in the person of Elihu the Buzite (xxxii. 1). Jeremiah seems, xxv. 23, to reckon the Buzites among the shorn Arabic wandering tribes ; and the Asarhaddon-Prisms mention, after the section treating of Arabia, a land *Bâzu* and a land *Hazû*, coinciding in sound with the חֲזוֹ here named, 22*a* (*Paradies*, p. 306 sq.). 3. קְמוּאֵל אֲבִי אֲרָם, *i.e.* certainly : the ancestor of a younger branch of the Aramæan people, x. 22. 4. כֶּשֶׂד, by no means the ancestor of the ancient Chaldæans, after whom אוּר כַּשְׂדִּים is named, xi. 28, but of a Nahorite tribe mingled with them. 5. חֲזוֹ, the cuneiform *Hazû*, perhaps Χαζήνη, according to Arrian in Steph. Byz., a satrapy on the Euphrates in Mesopotamia. In Strabo, xvi. 736, a satrapy of Assyria between Kalachene and Adiabene bears this name ; perhaps these two Χαζήνη are one and the same. 6. פִּלְדָּשׁ. As a masculine name, פלדשו is Nabatæan, *DMZ.* xiv. 440. 7. יִדְלָף. 8. בְּתוּאֵל, which has always been a personal, and not a tribal or a local name. This Bethuel, called besides, as well as Laban, הָאֲרַמִּי in *E* and *Q*, begat (יָלַד) רִבְקָה, the future wife of the son of promise. To these eight sons of Nahor, four more are added, ver. 24 : *And his concubine, and her name*

94   GENESIS XXIII.

was Reûmah, she also bare . . . The ו of לִשְׂמָה is not that of the apodosis: and his concubine, whose name was Reûmah (which cannot be proved as syntactically possible from Ps. cxv. 7; Prov. xxiii. 24), but the relation is as follows: As to his concubine (xxiv. 29) of the name of Reûmah, she also bare, Ges. § 129, note 1. The children of Nahor by Reûmah: 1. טֶבַח. Places according in sound with this name, and geographically appropriate, are טִבְחַת, one of the cities of Hadadezer, 1 Chron. xviii. 8 (for which 2 Sam. viii. 8, בֶּטַח), and Thœbata in north-western Mesopotamia, in Plin. vi. 30, compared by Kn., also Θεβηθά, according to Arrian in Steph. Byz.; but according to Tab. Peut. xi., south of Nisibis. 2. גַּחַם. 3. תַּחַשׁ. Kn. mentions Ἀταρχάς, north-west of Nisibis, in Procopius, *de œdif.* ii. 4, but as not quite geographically appropriate. The name means the sea-dog (*phoca*), in Assyr. the wether (see Friedr. Delitzsch, *Proleg.* 77). 4. מַעֲכָה, the ancestor of אֲרַם מַעֲכָה, 1 Chron. xix. 6, of an Aramæan tribe settled πλησίον ὄρους Ἀερμών, Euseb. and Jerome in the *Onomasticon* under Μαχαθί. אָבֵל בֵּית הַמַּעֲכָה (2 Sam. xx. 15 and frequently without an article), *i.e.* Abel in Beth-Ma'acha is *Abil*, a little to the south-west of Banias. There are together twelve sons of Nahor, and their relative numbers are the same as in the case of the twelve sons of Jacob: eight by the wife Milcah, as in Jacob's eight by Leah and Rachel; four by the concubine Reûmah, as in Jacob's four by Bilhah and Zilpah. Another parallel to the twelve sons of Jacob are the twelve נְשִׂיאִים of Ishmael. To find at once an artificial schematism in such circumstances would be rashness; accidental coincidences are often curious, and history itself brings much surprising schematism to pass.

DEATH OF SARAH, AND PURCHASE OF THE CAVE OF MACHPELAH,
CH. XXIII.

From this point onwards there follow only the last experiences, testamentary dispositions and arrangements of

Abraham, and first in the third part of the section, the account, ch. xxiii., of Sarah's death, and of the acquisition of a family grave in the cave of Machpelah. *Q*, who delights in formulas and schemes, who is fond of an almost strophic arrangement, even when the matter is not of a nature to be tabulated, and who, in order to inculcate firmly what he testifies, does not shun tautological repetitions, is immediately recognisable as the narrator. Here in ch. xxiii. he works up matter especially adapted to his style of historical composition, not only with legal accuracy, but at the same time with such vivid directness, that we are transposed into the life of the period with its forms of courtesy and mode of dealing. It is to him that we are indebted for this authentic narrative concerning the acquisition of the cave of Machpelah (comp. his intentional references thereto, xxv. 9 sq., xlix. 29–32, l. 13), which is characteristic of his mode of statement, not only by the use of certain favourite words (such as תּוֹשָׁב, מִקְנָה, אֲחֻזָּה) and turns (such as the distributive לְ, ver. 10, and בְּ, ver. 18), but also by a peculiar kind of historiographic art, which knows how to produce great pictures and impressions with the simplest means.

The portion is divided into two parts. The first two verses relate the death of Sarah and the mourning of Abraham, vv. 1, 2: *And the life of Sarah amounted to a hundred and twenty-seven years—the years of the life of Sarah. And Sarah died in Kirjath Arba', which is Hebron, in the land of Canaan, and Abraham came to mourn for Sarah and to weep for her.* As Sarah was ninety (xvii. 17) at the birth of Isaac, he must have been thirty-seven when his mother died (comp. xxv. 20), so that at least twenty years elapsed between the occurrence on Moriah and the death of Sarah. Hence we cannot be surprised to find Abraham, whom we left, xxii. 19, in Beersheba, again in Hebron. Hebron lay to the north-east of Beersheba, about two-thirds of the distance thence to Jerusalem. The narrator first calls the town

קִרְיַת אַרְבַּע, and then explains this by חֶבְרוֹן, just as at xxxv. 27; while, on the other hand, it is found without the older name at xiii. 18, xxxvii. 11. The name Kirjath-arba' is the more ancient. Arba', according to Josh. xiv. 15, xv. 13, xxi. 11 comp. Judg. i. 10, was the name of a ruler of the ancient city who belonged to the primitive gigantic population. The city was, according to Num. xiii. 22, built seven years before Zoan (Tanis) in Egypt. The name might also mean the four-town, *i.e.* the town of four quarters, which to this day would be a suitable one (see Furrer's art. "Hebron," in the *Bibellexicon*); and when it is called, xxv. 27, קרית הארבע, this meaning seems really to be combined with it. Since Caleb, in order to get possession of it, had to drive out this race of Anakim (Josh. xiv. 12 sqq.), while in Abraham's time these anything but barbarous Hethites, who, with other Phenician tribes dwelt in a wider circuit upon the mountains of Judah, were lords of the city,[1] it must have often changed both masters and names. Sarah died here in Hebron, and Abraham went into the inner part of the tent, to the corpse of his wife, to mourn for her (סָפַד, Lat. *plangere aliquem*, Heb. with לְ of him to whom the *planctus* or θρῆνος applies, once לִפְנֵי, 2 Sam. iii. 31: before the dead, when carried to the grave) and to weep for her (לִבְכֹּתָהּ, with small dageshed כ, as also the פ, Ps. xl. 15, and generally the aspirate after לְ are mostly dageshed, but with exceptions such as

---

[1] It need not be brought to bear against credibility of the Hethites of Hebron, that Q is the most recent of the Pentateuchal sources, for in the Jehovistic history also (JE) החתי is everywhere an element of the population of the Holy Land, whether ten nations (xv. 19–21) or six (Ex. iii. 8, 17, xxiii. 23, xxxiv. 11) or five (Ex. xiii. 15), or not reckoning Amalek, four (Num. xiii. 29) are named. And where in Deuteronomy seven nations are named, vii. 1 (comp. Josh. xxiv. 11), or six, xx. 17, החתי stand first. The historical authenticity of a southern branch of the Hethites is justly maintained by W. Wright, *The Empire of the Hittites* (1884, 2nd edit. 1886), by Frederick Brown in his article the "Hittites," in the *Presbyterian Review*, 1886, pp. 277–303, as well as by Sayce, *Alte Denkmäler*, p. 110. An allusion to the northern Hittite land (Josh. i. 4) is found Judg. i. 26 (comp. xi. 3, where LXX. *S* reads in the first passage החוי, and in the second החתי). In Egyptian documents, Kadesh on the Orontes, and in Assyrian, Carchemish, is the Hethite centre.

Jer. i. 10, xlvii. 4). It is purposely that the narrator adds בְּאֶרֶץ כְּנַעַן. It was in the Land of Promise that Sarah the ancestress of Israel died. The Old Testament does not relate with such intensity of purpose the termination of any other woman's life — for Sarah is historically the most important woman of the ancient covenant, she is the mother of the seed of promise, and in him of all believers, 1 Pet. iii. 6, ἧς ἐγενήθητε τέκνα, she is the Old Testament Mary. In her unclouded faith Mary stands far above Sarah, and yet Scripture is silent concerning her age and death. This happens because he whom Sarah bore is not greater than herself, but Mary bore a son, before whose glory her own personality vanishes.

After Sarah's death, Abraham applies to the Hethites for a burying-place, vv. 3, 4: *And Abraham lifted up himself from the face of his dead and spoke thus to the sons of Heth: A stranger and a sojourner am I among you, give me a burying-place with you, that I may bury my dead out of my sight.* What now takes place is, as F. C. v. Moser remarks, a delightful scene of courtesy, simplicity, kind-heartedness, naïveté, humility, modesty, magnanimity, not without some shadow of ambition and of the kind of expectation entertained, when in a bargain everything is ventured upon the kind-heartedness of the buyer. To bury is called קָבַר, which, as the Syriac shows, means as a synonym of צָבַר *cumulare, tumulare,* and hence points to *humatio* not *crematio* as the most ancient mode of burying. Abraham calls his dead מֵת not מֵתָה, because in the case of a corpse the distinction of sex is, as henceforth without importance, in the background. Answer of the Hethites, vv. 5, 6: *Then the sons of Heth answered Abraham, saying to him: Hear us, my lord, a prince of God art thou among us, in the choicest of our sepulchres bury thy dead, none of us will withhold from thee his burying-place to bury thy dead.* Here, as also ver. 14, the לֹא after לֵאמֹר seems with the LXX. drawn to the next verse, and to need to be read there according to

VOL. II. G

ver. 13, לִי שְׁמָעֵנוּ, "hear us, we pray," though the combination לֵאמֹר לִי is according to Lev. xi. 1 allowable, and on the other side לִי with the imp. unusual (comp. on the contrary xvii. 18, xxx. 34). This construction is escaped by correcting with LXX. Samar. לִי into לֹא after 11a (nay, my lord, hear us); but this לִי with the imp. is defended by ver. 13, it gives to the invitation a touch of desire, as the enclitic נָא does to the petition. Instead of the first מִתְּךָ, *Bereshith rabba* c. 58 assumes the reading מָתַי. Touched and encouraged by so respectful and kind a reception, Abraham combines with his thanks a definite request, vv. 7–9 : *Then Abraham rose and bowed himself down before the people of the land, the sons of Heth. And he talked with them, saying : If it is your will to receive my dead into a grave out of my sight, hear me, and entreat for me Ephron the son of Sohar, that he may give me the cave of Machpelah, which belongs to him, which is in the end of his field; for its full money let him give it me in the midst of you for a possession of a burying-place.* The Hethites, as the prevailing population of Hebron and its neighbourhood are called, "the people of the land," just as at Josh. i. 4 all Canaan is called *per synecdochen* אֶרֶץ הַחִתִּים. "Full money" is equivalent to the sum corresponding to the value of the piece of land, 1 Chr. xxi. 22. To express without saying so how readily and quickly this was done, the narrator at once introduces Ephron himself as speaking, vv. 10, 11: *And Ephron was sitting in the midst of the children of Heth, and Ephron the Hethite answered aloud before the sons of Heth, so many of them as went in to the gate of his town, saying : Nay, my lord, hear me, the field give I thee and the cave that is in it, to thee I give it before the eyes of my fellow-countrymen, I give it thee to bury thy dead.* To read לֹא for the first word of ver. 11 (2 Sam. xviii. 12 comp. 1 Sam. xiv. 30) is not so necessary as at 1 Sam. xiii. 13;[1] for Maurer's

---

[1] See K. Kohler's art. on לִי in Geiger's *Jüd. Zeitschrift*, vi. (1868) 21 sqq.

rema:k that לֹא *rustici quid habet* is refuted by the fact, that the refusal of the purchase money is in itself a courtesy great in proportion as the refusal is a decided one. It is a solemn deed of gift which Ephron performs, but which Abraham declines, vv. 12, 13 : *Then Abraham bowed himself down in the presence of the people of the land, and spoke to Ephron in the hearing of the people of the land, saying: If thou on thy part wouldst only hear me! I give the price of the field, take it of me, and I will bury my dead there.* Showing reverence before all the people to the chief of the city, and even exceeding him in expressions of courteous urgency, he answers that he will accept his offer, yet אַךְ with the earnest desire and only under the condition, that he will allow himself to be duly requited. אִם is the optative and לֹא its intensifying permutative. Hitzig's explanation of the אִם־אָתָּה " if thou agreest " is tempting, but the usage of the language nowhere shows the *Kal* of אות (to agree), but only the *Niph*. The combination of the two optative particles with the imperative is indeed rare, on which account LXX., Samar., Onkelos read אִם אַתָּה לִי (if thou wishest me well). It cannot be supported by Job xxxiv. 16 (where בִּינָה is to be accented as a subst.), still we think that it must be regarded as possible on the ground of our passage. Ephron now delicately gives Abraham to understand at what rate he values the land, while apparently persisting in his refusal, vv. 14, 15 : *Then Ephron answere'* \ *saying to him : My lord, hear me—a piece of land of four hundred shekels of silver between me and thee, what is it? And bury thy dead!* The bargain which is here made between Ephron and Abraham, is to this very day repeated in that country. In Damascus, when a purchaser makes a lower offer than can be accepted, he is answered : What, is it a matter of money between us ? Take it for nothing, friend, as a present from me (*hedije minni*); don't feel under any kind of constraint! (*DMZ.* xi. 505). Dieterici (*Reisebilder*, 2.

168 sq.) had a similar experience in Hebron: "In our excursions we had noticed a fine grey horse belonging to the Quarantine inspector. Mr. Blaine, my fellow-traveller, had appeared to wish to buy the animal. It now made its appearance at our tents. We inquired the price, and our astonishment may be conceived, when the dirty Turk offered us the animal as a present. Mr. Blaine declared that he by no means intended to take it as a present, when the Turk replied: What then are five purses (£25 sterling) to thee?" Similar experiences take place every day in Egypt (Lane, ii. 150). Abraham well understood the meaning of this figurative turn of speech, ver. 16: *But Abraham understood Ephron, and Abraham weighed to Ephron the money, which he had stated in the audience of the sons of Heth: four hundred shekels of silver current with the merchant.* The mercantile expression עֹבֵר לַסֹּחֵר exactly corresponds with جايز qui peut passer, bonne à recevoir frequent upon coins, *DMZ.* xxxiii. 356 (comp. also

معاملة current coins, from عامل to trade together, to do business). Jerome translates, *probatæ monetæ publicæ.* Money coined and certified by authority did not as yet exist, but even then merchants may have furnished the bars of gold and silver with a mark to signify that they were of full weight, as we are told of the Phenicians (*Rhetor. Gr.* xiii. p. 180, ed. Ald.), that they πρῶτοι χαρακτῆρα ἔβαλλον upon weighed metal. The normal weight of the heavy (sacred or royal) shekel (שֶׁקֶל from שָׁקַל *pendere*) amounted according to Jewish tradition to 320 medium barleycorns, with which the weight of the Maccabæan shekel (about 218 English grains, and so a little short of the half-ounce avoirdupois) tolerably agrees. If with Cavedoni, *Numismatica biblica* 1850, we admit that the shekel is to be reckoned as in the Mosaic law and in subsequent commerce, the price would be high (nearly £525), which the Rabbis explain as the result of Ephron's covetousness (see Zunz, *Zur Literatur,* p. 138), but still not be incredible. For Jacob's piece of ground at Shechem cost one hundred קְשִׂיטָה, xxxiii. 19, and the site upon which Samaria was built two בִּכַּר of silver, 1 Kings xvi. 24, *i.e.* six hundred heavy shekels. Close of the transaction, vv. 17—20 : *So the field of Ephron which was in Machpelah, which was before Mamre, the field and the cave therein and all the trees that were in the field, that were in its border round about, remained to Abraham as a purchased possession in the presence of the sons of Heth, according as each went into the gate of his city. And after this Abraham buried Sarah his wife in the cave of the field of Machpelah, which is before Mamre: the same is Hebron, in the land of Canaan. And so the field and the cave therein remained to Abraham as a burying place on the part of the sons of Heth.* The *Silluk* divides the one connected sentence vv. 17, 18, into two, as *e.g.* also Ex. vi. 28, 29, Num. xxxii. 3, 4 (see Arnheim, *Hebr. Grammatik*, § 254, because it would have been too long if interpunctuated as one). וַיָּקָם of remaining as a lawful possession, as at Lev. xxv. 30, xxvii. 19. מַכְפֵּלָה is throughout not the name of the cave, but of the district in which was the field with the cave in it. The occasion of its being so called is obscure. A *Cod. Pocock.* in Kennicott and a Spanish one offered for sale at the Viennese Universal Exhibition 1882 by Prof. Garcia Blanco of Madrid, have at ver. 9 the reading מערת המפלה, certainly an error of transcription, but nevertheless a remarkable curiosity.

The first landed property of the patriarchs was a grave. Such was the sole possession which they purchased from the world, and the only permanent one they found here below. Abraham buys a grave in Canaan; he buys and will not accept it as a gift, that he may not appear to take from man what God has promised to give him (Iren. xxxii. 2). And what he purchases is a grave, just because he will rest when dead in the land in which as a living man he as yet has no possession, because he is certain through faith that the promise cannot deceive. In virtue of that promise, which will be fulfilled to his posterity, the land of Canaan is holy ground. In this grave were Abraham and Sarah, Isaac and Rebekah buried, there Jacob buried Leah, there did Jacob desire to rest after death, and there was his corpse actually laid. There rested the ancestors and ancestresses of the tribes of Israel,[1] confessors even in death of faith in the promise. This burying place became the *punctum saliens* of the promised possession of the land. It is with a purpose that its honourable acquisition for the ancestors of Israel is so accurately described. It was the tie which continued to bind the descendants of Abraham in Egypt to the Land of Promise: it magnetically attracted their aspirations thither, and when they entered Canaan they were to know where the ashes of their fathers were reposing, and that they were themselves called to inherit the promise, trusting in which their fathers had been buried in Canaan.

When the city of Hebron is now approached from the north by the high road, the supposed district of Mamre passed, and the last mountain peak gone round, the view suddenly opens of the deep-lying valley of Hebron (*Wady-el-Chalîl*), in the foreground of which the city spreads out to the right, and the fortified and palatial buildings of the mosque of Ibrahim with its two minarets to the left. This Harâm (sanctuary) with its lofty external walls of not less than from fifty to sixty feet high, the lower part of which, built in peculiar pilaster style of colossal blocks of stone, belongs to the most ancient remains of buildings in Palestine, conceals beneath the floor of its interior and beneath its court the cave of Machpelah. The visit paid by the Prince of Wales and his suite to the Harâm April 7, 1862, placed it beyond doubt that the shrines of the patriarchs, which are found variously adorned in recesses in the walls, are only Cenotaphs. At the corner of the shrine of Abraham however is a circular opening, about 8 inches in

[1] According to Josephus (*Ant.* ii. 8. 2, *Bell.* iv. 9. 7), the eleven patriarchs of the tribes, whose graves (including Joseph's) another legend transports to Sichem. On Acts vii. 16, see my Hebr. N. T.

diameter, with an edge built up a foot high ending in a deep
obscure space, and through which a burning lamp is usually let
down into the burying place by means of a chain. The Crown
Prince of Prussia and Capt. v. Jasmund looked down into it
Nov. 1869, long enough to let them perceive all the details
of this space measuring 40 feet square. It appeared empty,
the floor polished by hand, the walls formed from the rock
itself without masonry, and at the one end of the cave was
seen a low grated opening, which seemed to lead to a second
cave (LXX. מכפלה τὸ σπήλαιον τὸ διπλοῦν). The Harâm, a
building consisting of parts of very different dates (see
Baedeker's *Palestine*, 2nd edit. p. 172 sq.), lies on the south-
western slope of the mountain *Ge'âbire*. But the cave, according to vv. 17–19, lay לפני or על־פני of Mamre, *i.e.* opposite
Mamre, and indeed in a southerly direction (comp. Josh.
xviii. 14). Hence, as Consul Rosen rightly infers, Mamre
must have lain on the eastern declivity of the height *Rumeidi*,
a spur of the Kuppe *Na'ir* (recalling עָנֵר) near to the remarkable well *'Ain el-'Gedid*. The terebinths of the patriarchal
time have indeed disappeared, but these were בחברן xiii. 18;
and though the town was formerly of greater extent than at
present, yet its situation must not be transposed to such a
distance as by the tradition concerning Mamre (see on
ch. xiii. towards the end).

THE MARRIAGE OF ISAAC, CH. XXIV.

The fourth portion (ch. xxiv.) relates a further arrangement
on the part of Abraham, in view of his own death, viz. the
marriage of Isaac, which was prepared for both by the glance
at the Nahorite descent of Rebekah, xxii. 20–24 (*J*), and the
blank left in Abraham's family by the departure of Sarah,
ch. xxiii. (*Q*). It is self-intelligible that the statement, that
Isaac married a wife of his father's Aramaic kindred, would
not be omitted in either of the three chief sources of Genesis.

It is evidently *Q* who expressly makes it xxv. 20, and probably *E* who mentions Rebekah's nurse by name and honours her memory, xxxv. 8. But nowhere did the history of this marriage offer itself in such detail to the redactor as in *J;* for it is to him that we are indebted for the charming idyll, the captivating picture of the wooing and bringing home of Rebekah in ch. xxiv. Everything here bears the mark of his pen: God is called יהוה, the birthplace of Rebekah אֲרַם נַהֲרָיִם (not פַּדַּן אֲרָם as in *Q*, *e.g.* xxv. 20), the sum of all good, חֶסֶד וֶאֱמֶת (vv. 27, 49, comp. xxxii. 11, xlvii. 29). Towards the end are found a few words which seem to lead to *E*, such as ארץ הנגב ver. 62 (comp. xx. 1, elsewhere only Num. xiii. 29, Josh. xv. 19, Judg. i. 15), and הַלָּזֶה ver. 65 (comp. only again xxxvii. 19); but vv. 62–65 cannot be referred to *E*, without admitting that *E* relates the story as fully as *J*, which is improbable. We take ch. xxiv. as the sole work of *J*. The recapitulation of the servant falls under the same point of sight as Pharaoh's recapitulation of his two dreams—ancient epic delights in such repetitions. The ethic and psychologic sentiment of this history has been appreciated by no one so much as by F. C. v. Moser in his *Doctor Leidemit*.

It begins, ver. 1: *Abraham was now an old man, well stricken in age, and Jahveh had blessed Abraham in everything.* His great age (the same expression as xviii. 11, *J*) obliged him, and his prosperity encouraged him, to think of Isaac's marrying and of the transmission of his blessing to his remoter descendants, vv. 2–8: *Then Abraham said to his servant, the eldest of his house, who ruled over all that was his: Put thy hand, I pray thee, under my thigh. And I will make thee swear by Jahveh, the God of heaven and the God of earth, that thou take not a wife for my son of the daughters of the Canaanite, in whose neighbourhood I dwell. But to my country and to my home shalt thou go and take a wife for my son Isaac. And his servant said to him: Perhaps the woman will not be willing to follow me into this land—must I then take back thy son into the land whence thou camest? And Abraham said unto him: Beware that thou take not back my son thither. Jahveh, the God of heaven, who took me away from my father's house and from my own country, and who spake to me and swore to me, saying: To thy seed will I give this land, He will send His angel before thee, and thou shalt take a wife for m ' son from thence. But if the woman be not willing to follow thee, then art thou free of this my oath, only thou shalt not take back my son thither.* Parallels to this in both style and matter from *J*, are the mode of swearing, xlix. 29; the reference to God as God of heaven and earth, xiv. 19, 22, בנות הכנעני vv. 3, 37 (not בנען כנען xxviii. 1, 6, 8, xxxvi. 2, *Q*); ארצי and מולדתי vv. 4, 7, like xii. 1, xxxi. 3, xxxii. 10. Isaac's wife must be one corresponding with his Divine calling, and therefore not one of the daughters of the Canaanite (comp. on the matter, Ex. xxiv. 16, Deut. vii. 3 sq.), though such a marriage, externally regarded, opened up all manner of favourable prospects. Nor must Isaac return to Aramæa, whence the God of redemption brought Abraham, he is not to leave the district into which God has transposed his father and himself; on the contrary, his future wife must come to it. But if none can be found, or if the one found is unwilling to leave her home? About this Abraham is not anxious. He leaves the future of his son absolutely to the direction of Jahveh, and appoints the eldest retainer of his house to be the wooer—certainly the Eliezer mentioned xv. 2 (*E*), who, since sixty years have now elapsed, was himself an old man. He is to take a so-called bodily oath, by putting his hand under Abraham's thigh. By placing his hand תחת ירך of Abraham, he binds himself upon the basis of the covenant of circumcision. If the woman will not follow him, the wooer, to the land of promise, he shall be released (נִקָּה *Niph.*), free or quit (נָקִי) like نَقِيَ *DMZ.* xxii. 129) from the obligation imposed on him by his oath (שְׁבֻעָה, for which ver. 41 אָלָה = Arab. *alwa*, with unchangeable *á*, comp. اِلَى conj. iv. from الِى to swear). The servant swears, sets out upon his journey, and on his arrival prays for God's decision, vv. 9–14: *Then the servant put his hand under the thigh of his master Abraham and swore to him concerning this thing. And the servant took ten camels of the camels of his master, and departed with all kinds of precious things of his master's in his hand—he arose and went to Aram of the two rivers, to the city of Nahor. And he made his camels kneel down outside the city by the well of water at evening time, at the time when the water-drawers come out. And he said: Jahveh, God of my master Abraham, let it happen favourably for me this day, and show kindness to my master Abraham! Behold, I stand at the fountain of water, and the daughters of the inhabitants of the city are coming out to draw water. Let it then thus happen; the damsel to whom I shall say: Let down, I pray thee, thy pitcher that I may drink, and she shall say: Drink, and I will also water thy camels—this one Thou hast appointed for Thy servant, for Isaac, and thereby shall I know that Thou hast showed kindness to my master.* The journey of Hazael, 2 Kings viii. 9, was similarly supplied. אֲרַם נַהֲרַיִם (ancient Egyp. *Neheren, Neherina, Naharina*) is the country between the Euphrates and Tigris (in the strict sense exclusive of Babylonia), called since Alexander ἡ Μεσοποταμία, that is, Συρία, the land north of the great desert, which the Arabians call the جَزِيرَة. הַקְרֵה means here, as at xxvii. 20, to cause to meet, to let happen, viz. what one has in mind. הַנַּעַר (from נָעַר, to shoot forth, to shake out, of the fruit of the body, therefore one not long since born) is in the Pentateuch and in this exclusively, double-gendered. הַנַּעֲרָה is written only Deut. xxii. 19, everywhere else it is the Keri to הנער, which is pointed as fem. הוֹבִיחַ, 14*b* (LXX. ἡτοίμασας), is meant of pointing out by means of an act, here with לְ as appointed for the son of Abraham. בָּהּ does not refer to the maiden, but is a neutral fem. as at xv. 6, 8. Guidance of her who had been prayed for, vv. 15-21: *And it came to pass: he had not yet ceased speaking, lo, Rebekah came forth, who was born to Bethuel the son of Milcah, the wife of Nahor, with her pitcher on her shoulder. And the damsel was very fair to look on, a virgin, and no man had known her—she went down to the fountain, filled her pitcher and came up. And the servant ran to meet her and said: Let me, I pray thee, drink a little water from thy pitcher. And she said: Drink, my lord, and let down quickly the pitcher upon her hand, and gave him to drink. And when she had given him enough to drink, she said: I will draw also for thy camels, till they have drunk enough. And she quickly emptied her pitcher into the trough and ran again to the well to draw, and drew for all his camels. And the man looked wonderingly at her, holding his peace, to know whether Jahveh had prospered his journey or not.* The name רִבְקָה means a tie, a band (Lat. *copula*), i.e. a collar for coupling to and coupling together. A maiden is called בְּתוּלָה (Assyr. *batûltu*, fem. of *batûlu*, a youth), certainly from בָּתַל بتل to separate, reflective *tabattala*, to keep oneself in modest consecrated retirement, from her characteristic of maidenly remoteness from marriage, and עַלְמָה (ver. 43), from עלם = غُلْم to be marriageable, √ غل to swell, from the characteristic of nearness to marriage by reason of maturity. The Talmud (*Jebamoth* 61b) is correct in inferring from the addition וְאִישׁ לֹא יְדָעָהּ, 16a, that בתולה does not in itself imply the characteristic of virgin purity, but only states age and condition (אין בתולה אלא נערה). The servant beholds with astonishment, and regards with investigation the quick and welcome alacrity of the maiden to serve him and to anticipate his wants. Knobel and Dillmann take הִשְׁתָּאֵה as equivalent in meaning to הִשְׁתָּעָה, but the analogy of הִשְׁתּוֹמֵם and הִתַּמֵּהּ rather favours the derivation from שָׁאָה desolate, then also like the Aramaic שְׁתָה, תְּהָא, תִּוַּהּ, to be confused, to wonder; on the connective form of the participle before לְ comp. Ps. lxiv. 9. The maiden answers perfectly to the moral test, she indefatigably fetches water from the deep well, to which, according to ver. 16, she went down and fetched water for the man and his cattle; hence it was a spring enclosed by a wall with steps leading down to it (Burckhardt, *Syrien*, p. 232), and is therefore alternately called בְּאֵר הַמַּיִם and עֵין הַמַּיִם; note how שׁחה, which has itself no *Hiphil*, borrows one from שׁקה. Preliminary requital and inquiry, vv. 22, 23: *And it came to pass after the camels had drunk enough, then the man took a gold nose-ring, a half shekel in weight; and two bracelets for her hands ten shekels of gold in weight. Then he said: Whose daughter art thou? tell me, I pray thee! Is there room in thy father's house to lodge us in?* He makes her a present of a nose-ring (ver. 22, comp. 47, Ezek. xvi. 12, and on the other hand Gen. xxxv. 4, where נֶזֶם means an ear-ring) weighing a בֶּקַע, *i.e.* half a shekel of gold, no very great weight in itself, but great for this ornament, which was fastened to one of the nostrils. The nose-ring was in use from Egypt to India, and is still so among the Arabs as a betrothal gift. He also gave her a pair of bracelets of ten shekels of gold. זָהָב is the acc. of nearer definition to עֲשָׂרָה (*erg.* שֶׁקֶל), like שָׁנָה in מֵאָה שָׁנָה, xvii. 17, xxiii. 1. Answer of the maiden, vv. 24, 25: *And she said to him: I am the daughter of Bethuel, the son of Milcah, whom she bore to Nahor. And she said farther to him: We have both straw and provender enough, also room to lodge in.* She calls herself, with a circumstantiality which betrays self-consciousness, the daughter of Bethuel, the son of Milcah (comp. on the inverted position of the genit. apposition, ii. 19b, xiv. 12) the wife of Nahor, and represents her home in as hospitable a light as possible. The pious servant first of all gives thanks to God, vv. 26, 27: *And the man bowed and fell down before Jahveh. And he said: Blessed be Jahveh, the God of my master Abraham, who has not withdrawn His mercy and truth from my master—me, yea me has Jahveh led by the right way to the house of my master's brother.* Bowing (viz. of the head, קָדַד) and falling down appear in combination at xliii. 28 (J) also. חֶסֶד is free love, and אֱמֶת truth, sincerity, faithfulness, binding itself to what love has promised. אָנֹכִי stands as *nom. abs.* emphatically, first like אַתָּה xlix. 8, Deut. xviii. 14. בְּדֶרֶךְ is, as ver. 48 shows (comp. on Job xxxi. 7), equal to, by the right way. Rebekah's intelligence and its impression upon Laban, vv. 28–31 : *And the maiden ran and told her mother's house according to these things. And Rebekah had a brother, of the name of Laban, and Laban ran to the man outside at the fountain. And it came to pass, when he saw the nose-ring and the bracelets on the hands of his sister, and when he heard the words of Rebekah his sister saying: Thus spake the man to me, then he came to the man, and lo, he was standing by the camels at the fountain. And he said: Come in, thou blessed of Jahveh, wherefore standest thou without?* and *I, I have made room in the house, and a place for the camels.* As the text stands, the mood of the sequence וַיְהִי, 30b, declares the effect from the cause by a retrogressive movement of thought, but probably the sentence : and Laban ran to the man outside at the fountain, has been removed from its original place before וַיָּבֹא, 30b (Ilg. Dillm.). Instead of בְּרֹאֹת the Samaritan has כראותו ; this is not necessary as far as the style is concerned. עֹמֵד stands briefly for הוּא עֹמֵד, see on Ps. vii. 10. The entrance and zeal of the servant, vv. 32, 33 : *And the man came into the house, and he unloaded the camels and gave straw and provender to the camels, and water to wash his feet and the men's feet that were with him. And meat was set before him to eat, but he said: I will not eat till I have said what is incumbent on me. And he said: Speak on!* In ver. 32 Laban is the subject to וַיְפַתַּח and וַיִּתֵּן, the change of subject disappears if we read וַיָּבֵא (Jerome *introduxit*), but then אֶת־הָאִישׁ might be expected. The object of his journey is asked by no one, for this would be contrary to Eastern hospitality, which does not permit such a question at least till after a meal. The *Keri* runs passively וַיּוּשַׂם (there was placed), not וַיִּשֶׂם, as mistakenly in recent editions—the *Chethib* is וַיִישֶׂם (one placed, like 1. 26, comp. Isa. viii. 4), to be read as written, 1. 26, from יָשַׂם, which is not authenticated elsewhere, but verbs פּ׳ like יָטַב, יָלַךְ, יָבֵשׁ (=בּוֹשׁ, to be ashamed), offer metaplastic forms. The servant will eat nothing till he has said what is incumbent on him to say. The subject to וַיֹּאמֶר 33*b* is Laban, who represents the family of Bethuel. The two verses 32, 33 are a specimen of the carelessness of the Oriental style, which leaves only too much to be supplied by the reader, vv. 34-49: *And he said: I am the servant of Abraham. And Jahveh has abundantly blessed my master, so that he has become great, and has given him sheep and oxen, and silver and gold, and servants and maidens, and camels and asses. And Sarah, my master's wife, bare my master a son after she was old, and he has given him all that was his. And my master made me swear thus: Thou shalt not take a wife for my son of the daughters of the Canaanite, in whose land I dwell. Nay, to my father's house shalt thou go, and to my kindred, and take a wife for my son. And I said to my master: Perhaps the woman will not follow me. Then he said to me: Jahveh, before whom I have walked, will send His angel with thee, and will prosper thy way, that thou mayest take a wife for my son from my kindred and from my father's house. Then shalt thou be clear of my oath, if thou go hence to my kindred; and if they will not give thee, thou shalt be clear of my oath. So I came this day to the fountain and said: Oh Jahveh, God of my master Abraham: Oh that thou now mayest prosper the way that I go. Behold, I stand by the fountain of water, and let it happen: the maiden who comes out to draw, and I say to her: Give me, I pray thee, a little water to drink from thy pitcher, and she says to me, Both drink thou and I will draw for thy camels—let her be the wife whom Jahveh has appointed for my master's son. I had not yet ceased to speak in my heart, when* *lo, Rebekah came out with the pitcher upon her shoulder and went down to the well and drew, and I said to her: Give me, I pray thee, to drink! Then she hastened and took her pitcher down from her, and said: Drink, and I will give drink to thy camels also; and I drank, and she gave drink to the camels also. Then I asked her and said: Whose daughter art thou? She said: The daughter of Bethuel, the son of Nahor, whom Milcah bare to him. Then I put the ring upon her nose, and the bracelets upon her hands. And I bowed myself and fell down before Jahveh, and blessed Jahveh the God of my master Abraham, who had led me by the right way, to take the daughter of my master's brother for his son. And now, if ye be willing to show kindness and truth to my master, tell me; but if not, tell me, that I may turn to the right hand or to the left.* The form of the oath is purposely omitted at ver. 37. When the servant says, 36*b*, that Abraham has given all that he has to Isaac, this is meant of his resolution to do so (comp. Isa. liii. 9), which is carried into execution, xxv. 5. The אִם־לֹא 38*a* is that of the oath (Ps. cxxxi. 2, Jer. xxii. 6), which thence after a previous denial means, "no, but," Ezek. iii. 6 (comp. Mark iv. 22, according to the reading ἐὰν μὴ φανερωθῇ), stronger than אִם כִּי (the reading of the Samar.). אִם־יֶשְׁךָ נָא 42*b*, means "if thou really art, as I wish," etc., comp. אִם־נָא xviii. 3 (see there). אֱלֵי־לְבוֹ 45*a*, as at viii. 21—he had then brought his desire before God with the silent voice of the heart. "Brother," 48*b*, is more accurately brother's son, as at xiv. 16, xxix. 12. In ver. 49, חֶסֶד וֶאֱמֶת stands for the manifestation of kindness and the faithful undissimulating dealing of men with each other. The consent, vv. 50, 51: *Then answered Laban and Bethuel, and said: From Jahveh does this thing proceed, we cannot say unto thee evil or good. Behold, Rebekah is at thy disposal, take her and go, and let her be a wife to thy master's son, as Jahveh has spoken.* Rebekah had not yet seen the man for whom she was wooed, neither is she asked whether she is willing to be his. Nor is it even her father, but her brother, who has the first word respecting her. This is the result of polygamy; in the history of Dinah also, it is the brothers who act independently of the father; "not evil or good" (here as at xxxi. 24) is equivalent to "absolutely nothing," and לִפְנֵי, to be some one's (here as at xiii. 9, xx. 15), is equal to being at his free disposal. They give Rebekah to him, with the acknowledgment that *Dominus locutus est*. The servant then thanks God for the issue of his wooing, and now empties before them the far from exhausted store of presents which he had brought with him, vv. 52, 53: *And it came to pass, when the servant of Abraham heard their words, he fell on the earth before Jahveh. And the servant brought forth silver vessels and gold vessels and garments, and gave them to Rebekah, and he gave costly presents to her brother and to her mother.* The first gifts are מֹהַר (xxxiv. 12) of the bridegroom for the confirmation of the betrothal, the so-called ἕδνα or ἔεδνα in Homer, and the others (מִגְדָּנוֹת) from מגד مَجَدَ to be precious, costly, Lth.: jewels, which is not unfitting, especially 2 Chron. xxi. 3) come under the point of view of the מֹהַר to be paid to the relatives of the bride (xxxiv. 12), see Riehm's *HW*. under *Ehe*, § 4. The servant presses for departure, vv. 54–58: *Then they ate and drank, he and the men who were with him, and spent the night, and when he rose up in the morning he said: Send me away to my master. And her brother and her mother said: Let the maiden stay with us a few days, perhaps ten, then let her depart. But he said to them: Detain me not, since Jahveh has prospered my way, send me away that I may go to my master. They said: We will call the maiden and inquire at her mouth. And they called Rebekah and said to her: Wilt thou go with this man? And she said: I will go.* The statement of time יָמִים אוֹ עָשׂוֹר means some days (as at Isa. lxv. 20, elsewhere: a long time, iv. 3, xl. 4), or even (or rather) ten (a decade of days). The Samar. has ימים או חדש. Rebekah's bashful but decided brief answer אֵלֵךְ settles the immediate commencement of the journey. The dismissal, vv. 59-61: *Then they sent away Rebekah their sister and her nurse, and Abraham's servant and his people. And they blessed Rebekah and said to her: Our sister, become thou thousands of myriads, and may thy seed possess the gate of their enemies! And Rebekah arose and her maids, and rode upon the camels and followed the man; so the servant took Rebekah and went away.* אֲחֹתָם את־רבקה is said according to the rule *a potiori*, the relation to Laban being generalized. The nurse (Deborah, xxxv. 8) remained, according to ancient custom (in Homer also), a member of the family and the immediate attendant upon her former nursling. The blessing, with which Rebekah is dismissed, proceeds from the frame of mind to which the family of Nahor had been raised by intercourse with the servant of Abraham. The Talmudic tractate כלה begins by drawing from our passage, in agreement with Ruth iv. 11 sq., the conclusion, that " a bride, whether a virgin or a widow, without a previous blessing is interdicted to her husband like one unclean." אֲחֹתֵינוּ has *Zakeph gadol*, which always stands alone without a servant, and is less separative than the preceding *Zakeph katon* (לָהּ). The imperative הֲיִי is vocalized like חֲיִי Ezek. xvi. 6. The combination אַלְפֵי רְבָבָה is like אַלְפֵי אִישׁ Ex. xxxii. 28, and עָם רִבְבוֹת Ps. iii. 7 (Ges. § 120. 2); the genitive is a generic designation of what is enumerated. With אַתְּ between the vocative and imperative, comp. Jer. ii. 31; the pronoun is intended with the distinctness which is expressed in the vocative. The wish 60*b* is almost identical with xxii. 17 (*J*). There we have אֹיְבָיו, here the poetical שֹׂנְאָיו, as also רְבָבָה is the older and more refined word for רִבּוֹ (=רִבּוֹת = רִבּוּת). The arrival of the travelling company and the first meeting of the betrothed, vv. 62-65: *And Isaac was just coming from the way to the well Lahaj Roi, for he dwelt in the land of the south,—for Isaac had gone out into the field towards evening to indulge in his thoughts,*

—*and he lifted up his eyes, and behold, there were camels coming. And Rebekah lifted up her eyes and saw Isaac, and she alighted from the camel. And she said to the servant: Who is that man who is coming to meet us in the field? The servant said: It is my master; then she took the veil and covered herself.* The structure of the sentence vv. 62, 63 is clumsy: first a sentence preparatory to the main fact with the perfect בָּא, then an explanatory sentence of condition with וְהוּא יֹשֵׁב, then following this sentence of condition a parenthetical sentence more nearly explaining this accessory fact בָּא, and now the main fact with וַיִּשָּׂא עֵינָיו. It is assumed that Abraham was then still dwelling at Beersheba, xxii. 19, south of which lay Hagar's well in the well-watered *Wadi el-Muweilih*, where Isaac dwelt after the death of Abraham, xxv. 11. Maimonides already remarks, that it is here purposely not said בָּא מִבְּאֵר,[1] because it would then appear as though he already had his dwelling there. It cannot however be meant that he was just returning from a visit to Hagar's well, for this was too far distant from Beersheba for an evening walk (63*a*), but that he was coming from an evening walk in the direction of this his favourite place, a place hallowed as it had been by a manifestation of God: כִּלְבוֹא=מִבּוֹא 1 Kings viii. 65, comp. לָבוֹא xxxv. 16, לְבֹא Num. xiii. 21. It was in the twilight (לִפְנוֹת עֶרֶב, as it began to be evening, comp. Deut. xxiii. 12, Ex. xiv. 27) that he went into the open air לָשׂוּחַ, *to meditate*. So most ancient translators, taking לְשִׂיחָה=לָשׂוּחַ Ps. cxix. 148, either in the meaning *meditari* (LXX. Aq. Symm. Vulg.) or directly (comp. Ps. cii. 1) *orare* (Talmud, Targums Sam. Saad. Luth. Kimchi, Gr. Ven.), in opposition to which Syr. translates ܠܡܫܬܥܝܘ to take exercise, as though it were לָנוּט, as Gesenius desires to read. This is one of the passages on which the obligation of the Minchah-prayer is based. Isaac is of a quietly enduring, contemplative disposition, and it is in con-

---

[1] To read thus, rejecting the בוא (de Lagarde, Olsh.), is an old proposal; see the *Lemberger Zeitschrift* החלוץ Jahrg. iii. (1856) p. 98.

GENESIS XXIV. 66, 67.   115

formity with this his character that he should go in the direction of Hagar's well (xvi. 13 sq.), to think over the matter of his marriage in silent soliloquy before the Lord. Here the looks of those who were betrothed by God's guidance meet. Rebekah (according to Eastern notions of courtesy in the presence of one who is to be met with reverence) quickly alights from her camel (נָפַל, as at 2 Kings v. 21, of intentionally falling, i.e. swinging oneself down, LXX. κατεπήδησεν, a stronger word for this manifestation of respect than יָרַד 1 Sam. xxv. 23, and עָנָה Josh. xv. 18, Targums אִתְרְכִינַת, she bowed, sank down, let herself slip off), and to make herself certain, asks the name of the man (הַלָּזֶה as only one more, xxxvii. 19) [1] who is coming towards them; and when she hears that it is Isaac, she modestly takes her veil. צָעִיף (from צָעָה ضعف to lay together, to fold, to make double or more) is, according to Abenezra, of like meaning with רָדִיד (by which it is translated in Targ. Jer.), and the latter of like meaning with the Arab. ازار ; the LXX. translates both here and Cant. v. 7 θέριστρον (Jer. *pallium*), a light summer wrap which covers the body and especially the head, the veil or hooded mantle, which is mentioned by Tertullian, *de velandis virg.* ch. 17, Jerome, *ad Eustoch.* ep. 22, and elsewhere, as an Arabic feminine garment (see Lagarde, *Semitica*, p. 24 sq.). It is of similar kind with the white linen wrapping shawl, with which Syrian women cover themselves out of doors (ازار), not the face-veil which forms a separate piece of clothing (برقع); for this muffling of Moslem women is a later custom, which Muhammed borrowed from the court of the Sassanidæ. Rebekah, drawing her mantle over her face, covered herself (*nupsit*), as Sulamith in Canticles, who as a bride wears the bridal veil צַמָּה. Bringing home of the bride, vv. 66, 67: *And the servant told Isaac all the things that he had done. And Isaac brought her into the*

---

[1] In the Samaritan usage of language the sense of brilliant (*illustris*) is combined with הלזה (*DMZ.* xxxix. 196).

tent of Sarah his mother, and he took Rebekah and she became his wife, and he loved her and was comforted for the loss of his mother. The history started at ver. 1 sqq. from Abraham, but does not return to him; we do not however miss this if we look at xxv. 1–11, in which *J* certainly has a share, and if Abraham's remarriage followed the marriage of Isaac. In cases where the widowed father remarries, the affection of the son cleaves the more ardently to the deceased mother. הָאֹהֱלָה שָׂרָה אִמּוֹ is less unusual than הָאֹהֱלִי Josh. vii. 21 (both times with Kateph instead of silent Sheva, comp. נְבֻהּ xiii. 14); for the justification and explanation of this combination of the determinate substantive with the genitivally conceived proper name, see Ges. 22nd ed. § 111. 2. There is no grammatical necessity for regarding שָׂרָה אִמּוֹ as a gloss (Wellh. Dillm. Nöld.), and the assumption that in the mind of the narrator of ch. xxiv. Abraham had meantime died, is not so certain as to make us accept the notion that אַחֲרֵי אָבִיו originally stood in the place of אַחֲרֵי אִמּוֹ (Wellh. Kuen.), or that the whole sentence 67b is a recent addition (Dillm.). With this "after his mother," *i.e.* after he had lost her, comp. לְפָנַי, "before me," *i.e.* before I came, xxx. 30. The grief of Isaac for the loss of his mother was alleviated, when a much loved wife filled up the void made by the death of Sarah.

ABRAHAM'S DESCENDANTS BY KETURAH, AND HIS DEATH,

CH. XXV. 1–11.

(Parallel with 1 Chron. i. 32, 33.)

A fifth portion, xxv. 1–11, relates Abraham's remarriage and death, partly according to *J*, partly according to *Q*. Vv. 1–4 keep to the manner of the Jahvistic element of the ethnographical table (ילד for הוליד, and the summary 4b quite like x. 29b); שְׁבָא and דְּדָן are traced back otherwise than in *Q* x. 7. In 5–7 this genealogical portion is continued. In ver. 5 we recognise the author of xxiv. 36. On the other hand, 7–11a bears as distinctly as possible the impress of *Q*, who also refers in xlix. 31 sq. to what is here related. בְּנֵי חֵת, which occurs eight times in ch. xxiii., and besides in xxv. 10, xlix. 32 (for which J uses the collective וַחִתִּי), is peculiar to him. In 11*b* (the dwelling of Isaac at Lahaj Roi) ver. 6 proceeds in accordance with xxiv. 67. The picture thus composed from two documents is nevertheless a single one. For it is no contradiction, *e.g.*, that according to ver. 6 only Isaac is with Abraham, and that according to ver. 9 Isaac and Ishmael together bury him; Ishmael having hastened thither on the intelligence of his father's death.

Abraham's remarriage, ver. 1 : *And Abraham again took a wife, and her name was Keturah.* According to the statements xxiii. 1, xxv. 7, comp. xvii. 17, Abraham had still a life of about forty years before him. The construction is like xxxviii. 5, and both in matter and diction resembles xvi. 3, where Hagar also is called Abraham's אִשָּׁה. Keturah however is not a secondary wife during the lifetime of his wife. Augustine, *de civ. Dei*, 16. 34, justly lays stress upon this against the opponents of the *secundæ nuptiæ*. She is indeed also called, ver. 6, comp. 1 Chron. i. 32, פִּילֶגֶשׁ; she does not stand on the same level as Sarah, who as the mother of the son of promise stands alone. But in other respects no blot attaches to the second marriage. The relation too to Keturah contributes to the fulfilment of the word of promise, which appointed Abraham, xxii. 4 sq., to be the father of a multitude of nations. The sons and grandsons of Abraham by Keturah form however no special תֹּלְדוֹת; they are but offshoots of the tree whose growth is depicted in Genesis. The list, which in opposition to the account of Kleodemus " the prophet " in Joseph. *Ant.* i. 15 gives an impression of its historical truth, contains in part at least names of Arab tribes still recognisable. These must long ago have become such, when Israel was in course of development at a distance.[1] The Arabic genealogies know indeed

---

[1] See Wetzstein's article on Northern Arabia and the Syrian desert in Kohner's *Zeitschr. für Allgem. Erdkunde*, Annual issue xviii. 1865.

nothing of a great kindred of tribes descended from Keturah, and Sprenger even fathers upon the genealogist the absurdity of making Arabs, with whom he was acquainted as dealers in spices, sons of a Keturah (קטורה = קְטֹרֶת, frankincense). But قطورا is actually alleged to be the name of a tribe in the neighbourhood of Mecca (comp. also قَطَر the present name of the peninsula of Baḥrein). Direct descendants of Abraham by Keturah, ver. 2: *And she bare him* זִמְרָן.[1] Knobel compares Ζαβράμ in Ptol., the royal city of the Kinaedokolpites (الكَنْدَة *DMZ.* xxii. 663), Grotius the Arab tribe of the *Zamareni* in Pliny 6. 32. § 158. The Κασσανῖται, dwelling south of the Kinaedokolpites on the Red Sea, have nothing to do with יָקְשָׁן, for these are the Gassanidæ غسان (*DMZ.* xxii. 668); Arab genealogists give ياقش as the name of a portion of the ancient population of Yemen (*DMZ.* x. 31). The name of the Wadi *Medân* near the ruins of the town Dedan accords with מְדָן, and the name of the town *Madjan* (Μαδιηνή in Joseph. *Ant.* ii. 11. 1), five days' journey south of Aila, with מִדְיָן. مدان and مَدْيَن were the names of an ancient Arabian god (see Hitz. on Prov. vi. 19). Ptolemy mentions a Μαδιάμα in the north of *Arabia felix*, vi. 7. 27, and Μοδίανα (= מדין) in the west of *Arabia felix* on the east coast of the Ælanitic Gulf, vi. 7. 2. شوبك *Sjaubachum* in 'Gebâl, whose name, meaning thicket, *saltus*, became famous in the times of the Crusades, has nothing to do with יִשְׁבָּק (see on xxxvi. 20). שׁוּחַ can scarcely be combined with the tribe السياحى *es-Sejâ'iḥa*, eastward of Aila, and by no means with Σακκαία, Ptol. v. 15. 26, which is on the contrary to be connected with the *'Sakka* سكّا above *Duma* and *Têmâ* in East-Haurân, nor with the two villages of the name of *Siḥân* (with

---

[1] On the phonetic law, according to which the LXX. reads Ζεμβράν for זמרן, Μαμβρη for ממרא, 'Αμβράμ for עמרם, etc., see Flecker, *Scripture Onomatology* (London 1883), pp. 26-28.

(سو), one of which lies in the *Nuḳra* one league north of *Umm Weled*, the other in south *Gôlân*. Friedr. Delitzsch has shown (*Paradies*, p. 297 sq., and the "Essay on the Land of Uz," *Zeitschr. für Keilschriftforschung*, 1885), in cuneiform inscriptions, a land of *Sûḫu*, which lay at all events north of Haurân, and north-eastwards of the great Palmyra road, and also a land *Jasbuḳ*, coinciding phonetically with יִשְׁבָּק. The Jokshanidæ, 3a: *And Joḳsan begat 'Sebâ and Dedân*. The tracing of שְׁבָא and דְּדָן to כּוּשׁ x. 7, is not incompatible with their Semitic derivation here and x. 28 (see on these two passages). The LXX. in Isa. Jer. Ezek. writes for דדן Δαιδάν, similar in sound with the name of the ruins of the town الدّيدان (Jakût ii. p. ۴۱۴, line 3) on the borders of the Belkâ towards Ḥigâz, according to Wetzst. at the eastern foot of the Ḥismâ mountain chain, where is also found a valley of *Medān* sloping towards the east; farther off lies *Dâden*, Syr. *Dídin*, the name of one of the islands of Bahrein. The tribes descending from Dedan, 3b: *And the sons of Dedân were* אַשּׁוּרִם, of whom no trace is elsewhere found, for אַשּׁוּר Ezek. xxvii. 23 is Assyria, and הָאֲשׁוּרִי 2 Sam. ii. 9 probably an error of transcription. The tribes طُسْم and أَمِيم may perhaps be combined with the לְטוּשִׁם and לְאֻמִּים, unless their names are to be regarded, as by Renan, as mutilated from לְטוּשִׁים and לְאֻמִּים (*DMZ*. xx. 175, xxiii. 298). Ramification of Midian, ver. 4: *And the sons of Midian:* עֵיפָה, according to Isa. lx. 6, a trading tribe bringing gold and frankincense from Sheba; עֵפֶר, with which Wetzstein compares عَفَر a district in the *'Alia, i.e.* the highland between the Tihâma range and the Abân, after which this part of Arabia was called بِلَاد عَفَر, the *Nejd* of *'Ofr;* חֲנֹךְ, which harmonizes in sound with the district *Ḥanâkia* compared by Knobel and Wetzstein (Burckhardt, *Arabien*, p. 690 sq., comp. Ritter, *Erdkunde*, xiii. 451), three days' journey north of Medina, where Ibrahim Pasha had a standing camp on account of its abundance of water; אֲבִידָע and אֶלְדָּעָה, about which there is nothing to say but that אבידע and ידעאל occur as Himjaritic personal names (*DMZ.* xxvii. 648), as אשורו and לטשו do as Nabatæan (*DMZ.* xviii. 447). It cannot be wondered that some of these ancient names should, in consequence of the many migrations, intermingling and wars of the Arabic tribes, have been lost without leaving a trace behind.

Abraham makes Isaac heir of all, and gives gifts to the sons of the concubines, vv. 5, 6 : *And Abraham gave all that he had to Isaac. And to the sons of the concubines whom Abraham had, Abraham gave gifts and sent them away from Isaac his son during his lifetime eastward into the east country.* He gave all that he possessed to Isaac, *i.e.* as at xxiv. 36: he promised it to him, and gave it to his management. The concubines are Hagar and Keturah, we know of no others. פִּילֶנֶשׁ (πάλλαξ, *pellex*, or according to an old writing *pælex*) occurred in *J* at xxii. 24. "The east country" is Arabia in the widest sense, in the first place *Arabia deserta* and *petræa*, and then farther southwards the whole Arabian peninsula. It is not without reason that we have here, ver. 6, the apparently superfluous בְּעוֹדֶנּוּ חַי. The Mosaic law and ancient Hebrew custom know only of a so-called intestate hereditary right, *i.e.* one independent of the testamentary disposition of the testator, and regulated according to the degree of lineal hereditary succession. If then Abraham desired not to let the sons of his concubines depart empty, he was obliged to provide for them by gifts during his lifetime. The history of Abraham's life now comes to an end, ver. 7: *And this is the amount of the years of Abraham's life which he lived: a hundred and five and seventy years.* The marriage of Keturah took place in the fourth decade, before the end of this long life (subsequent to the 137th year), which on reckoning up extended to about fifteen years beyond the birth of the twin children, but which, as in the case of Terah, is here anticipatively finished off. His death, ver. 8: *And Abraham expired and died in a good old age, old and full, and was gathered to his people.* The promise xv. 15 was fulfilled. In the case of Isaac, whose death resembled that of his father, we find xxxv. 29 instead of שָׂבֵעַ the fuller expression שְׂבַע יָמִים, like *plenus vitæ* and *satur ac plenus rerum* in Lucretius. On בְּנֵי עָם=עַמִּים see on xvii. 14. וַיֵּאָסֶף has always in this phrase, when it appears in the form of the *imp. consec.*, the tone drawn back (notwithstanding the Tiphcha), ver. 17, xxxv. 29, xlix. 33, Deut. xxxii. 50, comp. on the other hand Num. xx. 24, xxxi. 2. This ויגוע ויאסף is, according to *Bathra* 16b, the special expression for the death of the pious. For as the fulness of life of the patriarchs denotes a desire for another world, where they will be delivered from the tribulations of this, so is union with the fathers not a union merely of corpses but of persons. That death does not, as might appear from iii. 19, put an end to the individual continuity of man, is a notion universally diffused in the world of nations,—a notion originating from and justified by the fact, that not only wrath but mercy was proclaimed to fallen man. Believers however knew more than this, but only by the inference drawn by faith from the premisses of the Divine promise, and breaking through the comfortless notion of Hades. Κατὰ πίστιν ἀπέθανον οὗτοι πάντες, Heb. xi. 13. They were united in faith to Jahveh, as He the ever-living One united Himself to them by His word and placed Himself in a mutual relation to them, which could never cease. Thus also did Abraham depart from this world, after he had already long departed from its history, and had spent in the quiet of his home decades of which history tells us nothing. His burying, vv. 9, 10: *And Isaac and Ishmael his sons buried him in the cave of Machpelah, in the field of Ephron the son of Sohar the Hethite, which is before Mamre, the field which Abraham bought of the sons of Heth. There was Abraham buried, and Sarah his wife.* Isaac and Ishmael, who after Isaac ranks highest among the sons of Abraham, buried him. It is not thence to be inferred that Ishmael was at that time still in his father's house. The blessing of Abraham as regards this world is now transferred to Isaac, ver. 11*a*: *And it came to pass after Abraham's death, that Elohim blessed Isaac his son.* Thus is fulfilled the covenant promise, xvii. 21. Thus far *Q*; 11*b* is added from *J*: *And Isaac dwelt by the well Lahai-roi.* His dwelling by Hagar's well was certainly not without the influence of the answer to prayer there received and never to be forgotten. Beersheba had hitherto been the common residence of himself and his father, xxii. 19. Later on in the evening of his life we find him at Mamre, xxxv. 27 (*Q*). The life of the patriarch was a pilgrimage without a settled dwelling-place.

VII.

THE TOLEDOTH OF ISHMAEL, XXV. 12-18.

(Parallel passage, 1 Chron. i. 28-31.)

BEFORE the history of the seed of promise can go on without interruption, the history of Ishmael must be finished off in accordance with the method of the fundamental document (Q). This is now done, ver. 12: *And these are the generations of Ishmael the son of Abraham, whom Hagar the Egyptian, Sarah's maid, bore to Abraham.* This general title is particularized, ver. 13a: *And these are the names of the sons of Ishmael, by their names, according to their generations.* Before בִּשְׁמוֹתָם, these sons of Ishmael must be supplied in thought. They are now specified according to their names and sequence. There were twelve of them according to the promise xvii. 20, corresponding with the twelve tribes of Israel. The blessing of Ishmael, who was also the seed of Abraham and, differing herein from the sons of Keturah, received Divine promises, made chs. xvii. and xxi. in the name אֱלֹהִים, and ch. xvi. in the name יהוה, is a reflection of the blessing of Israel. The first-born of Ishmael was, according to 13b, נְבָיֹת. Nebajoth and Kedar are mentioned together not only Isa. lx. 7, but also Plin. *h. n.* 6. 32 (*Nabatæi et Cedrei*); *Ḳaidâr* and *Nâbit* (*Nabt*) written with ﺚ are known also to Arabic and Armenian historians (Hübschmann, *Zur Gesch. Armeniens*, 1865, p. 12) as, according to biblical precedent, descendants of Ishmael or also of Madian. Along with this occurs نَبِط (Gentilic

نَبْطِي, plur. of the nation in its manifold totality, اَنْبَاطٌ), genealogically traced back to جم i.e. שֵׁם x. 23, or otherwise, as the name of the Aramæan population of Egypt as far as the Tigris (comp. 1 Macc. v. 24 sq., ix. 35), and especially of the districts between the Euphrates and the Tigris. It is on this account that Quatremère in his *Mémoire sur les Nabatéens*, with the concurrence of Causin, Ritter and Steinschneider (see his additions to Brecher's *Die Beschneidung*, p. 11 sq.), rejects the combination of the Nabatæans with the Ishmaelite נְבָיוֹת. Schrader also (*KAT*. 147, 414) distinguishes the north Arabian *Nabaitai* from the Babylonio-Aramæan *Nabatu*, while Winer, Kless (in Pauli's *RE*. vol. i. 377 sqq.), Krehl (*Religion der vorislam. Arab.* 1863, p. 51), Blau (*DMZ*. xvii. 51) and Nöldeke (*DMZ*. xxxiii. 322 sq.) adhere to the connection of the Nabatæan נבט with the biblical נביות. The manner of writing the name varies; upon the coins of Nabatæan kings נבתו and נבטו are interchanged (see Levy in *DMZ*. xiv. 317), and in the Targum and Talmud the forms נבט, נווט, נוות and even נפט are found together (see Geiger, *id*. xv. 413). The Assyrian inscriptions write the name in all its forms with *t* (*nabaitu*, adj. gentil. *nabaitai*), not with *ṭ* (Friedr. Delitzsch, *Paradies*, 296 sq.). The supposed ancient Nabatæan writings derived from Babylonia, to which Chwolson (1859) gave credence, are, as is now acknowledged, the fabrication of Ibn-Waḥšîja, who says he translated them into Arabic. The name of the Nabatæans is in these writings one of much further reach, including also the Chaldæans, Syrians, and Canaanites, and has hence neither certainty nor outline. It is on the contrary certain that in the first century B.C., and down to the time of Trajan, the Nabatæans were a prominent and civilised people whose realm extended from the Ælanitic Gulf to the land east of Jordan, past Belkâ as far as Haurân, — written memorials of this people are found from Egypt to Babylonia, but Arabia Petræa is the chief mine for them. The supposed ancient Nabatæan writings might, if they contained any ancient germ, coincide with this period of Nabatæan civilisation, with which was combined the flourishing period of Christianity in Arabia Petræa (see my *Kirchliches Chronikon des petr. Arabiens*, Luth. *Zeitschr.* 1840, iv. 41. 1); and whether this civilisation had its starting-point in Babylonia or Arabia, the one is quite as compatible as the other with the Ishmaelite origin of the בני קדם, nor is the Aramaic language of the inscriptions and forms of incantation contrary to this origin. We know indeed but little of pre-Islamite Arabic and its dialects. But the few remains which have been preserved, *e.g.* the cry *Malchan*, with which, according to Laurentius Lydus (*de mensibus*, iv. 75), a Saracen is said to have pierced the Emperor Julian, recognised by the purple, in the Persian War, make it probable that idioms lying midway between the Aramaic and Arabic with which we are acquainted, were in existence. The Aramaic idiom of the Sinaitic inscriptions is moreover of a strongly Arabic tinge (*DMZ.* xiv. 379). The nomadic people mentioned together with Kedar in the times of the Israelite kings must have been as yet politically insignificant, for they are not mentioned in the history of the kings, though this mention might be expected in such connections as 2 Chron. xvii. 11, xxi. 16, Ps. lxxxiii. 7. Petra appears as an Edomite town, and in the Syro - Ephraimitic war Rezin made Ailat an Aramæan colony. But what objection is there to accepting the notion that Ishmaelite wandering tribes may have been subsequently swallowed up in the renowned civilised nation of the *Nabatæi*, who constructed their marvellous buildings upon the ancient Seirite mountains, but were despised by the Arabs as townsmen and pikemen, and not acknowledged as their equals because of their settled habits and industry ?—Ishmael's second son is קֵדָר. This people of north-western Arabia, frequently mentioned in the Old Testament as nomads dwelling in tents and as good bowmen, was already known to Pliny (5. 11) as the *Cedrei*. Kedarenes dwelt eastward of the Nabatæans in the desert beyond Babylonia (Isa. xlii. 11, Ps. cxx. 5). They had disappeared in the first period of Islam. Jefeth on Cant. i. 5 substitutes قُرَيْش the tribe of Muhammed. The third son of Ishmael is אַרְבְּאֵל, according to Friedr. Delitzsch (*Paradies*, 301 sq.) the north Arabian tribe of *Idiba'il*. — The fourth son is מִבְשָׂם, and the fifth מִשְׁמָע, names which occur together also in the genealogy of the tribe of Simeon (1 Chron. iv. 25). The name of the Μαισαιμανεῖς somewhat north-east of Medina, Ptol. vi. 7. 21 (comp. *DMZ.* xxii. 672), and *el-Mismîje* in Leǵâh, the name of the largest town in the mid-Syrian volcanic region, sound like מִשְׁמָע, but actual connection is doubtful in both cases. The sixth son דּוּמָה, probably Δούμαθα, Δούμεθα in Ptolem. and Steph. Byz., *Domatha* in Plin., the present دومة الجندل in the lowest depression of the Syrian land of *Nufûd*, the so-called *Gôf* whence proceeds the question to the prophet, Isa. xxi. 11, is about forty leagues north of *Teimâ*. The seventh son מַשָּׂא sounds like the Μασανοί, Ptol. v. 19. 2, north-east of Duma. An Assyrian inscription in Friedr. Delitzsch (*Paradies*, 302) mentions a *Maš'ai* (from מַשָּׂא?) who surprised the Nabatæans (*Niba'aiti*) after the Assyrians had withdrawn. The name of the country מַשָּׂא is also probably concealed in Prov. xxxi. 1, xxx. 1, which see.—On the eighth son חֲדַד (as according to the Masora 1 Chron. i. 30 is also to be written, with which agree the LXX. Sam. Jos., and according to which Targ. Jer. translates חֲרִיבָא) there is nothing to be said. The ninth son תֵּימָא does not correspond with بنو تيم in the neighbourhood of the Persian Gulf (Θαιμοί in Ptol.), but with the trading tribe of אֶרֶץ תֵּימָא (تَيْمَاء Assyr. *Têm'u*, upon the borders of the Neǵd and the Syrian desert), Job vi. 19, Isa xxi. 14, mentioned in Jer. xxv. 23 between Dedân and Buz, and not to be confused with the Idumæan תֵּימָן, xxxvi. 42, though it almost seems as if תֵּימָא mentioned Jer. xlix. 7 sq., Ezek. xxv. 13, together with Dedân were equivalent to תֵּימָא. Arabian geographers give the name of *Têman* to the southern half of the Neǵd, but are acquainted also with a Petræan Têman in northern '*Alia* called تيمن ذو الطلال the ruins of Têman. Wetzstein has also brought to our knowledge still existing trans-Hauranian localities called *Têmâ* and *Dûma*. There is also found in East Haurân, three and a half leagues south of Têmâ, a still stately town of *Bûzân*. Nevertheless the places here named are more probably to be sought in the Neǵd than in East Haurân.—The tenth and eleventh sons are יְטוּר and נָפִישׁ, both mentioned by the Chronicler, 1 Chron. v. 18–22, in conjunction with נוֹדָב, whose name has been preserved in the Hauranian *Nudêbe* (نديبة) in the *Wadi el-buṭm*, and with the הַגְרִיאִים, *i.e.* 'Αγραῖοι or 'Αγρέες, whose capital was هجر (Ethiop. and Himjar. *hagar* town), in Plin. *h. n.* 6. 32 *Hegra* on the Persian Gulf; they there appear as involved in war with their neighbours the trans-Jordanic tribes of Israel. Of נָפִישׁ we know nothing else. The יְטוּר however, according to Strabo, are the plundering 'Ιτουραῖοι dwelling on Lebanon and the Haurân chain (*Iturœi sagittarii* in Cicero, *Philipp.* 2. 44); the inhabitants of the highest part and of the eastern slope of the Druse mountain chain in Haurân are perhaps their descendants.—The name too of the twelfth son קֵדְמָה is not elsewhere to be pointed out, for בְּנֵי קֶדֶם mentioned with Midian and Amalek Judg. vi. 3, with Moab and Ammon Isa. xi. 14, Ezek. xxv. 4, 10, is a collective name; but Σαρακηνοί, which certainly means the men of the East, appears originally, like קֵדְמָה, as a separate tribe upon the Sinaitic peninsula or elsewhere. We need not be surprised to seek in vain for most of these names in Wüstenfeld's and Sprenger's lists, for even the great tribes, who made a figure in the beginning of the history of Islam, have now disappeared together with their names. Closing summary, ver. 16: *These are the sons of Ishmael, and these are their names in their settlements and their encampments, twelve princes according to their nations.* אֻמֹּת is found also in Q at Num. xxv. 15, where Arabs are spoken of, as the word for nations. Two kinds of dwelling-places are here distinguished, first חֲצֵרִים, the special name for the groups of houses placed within the steppe, and enclosed on every side for fear of surprise,—as described by Burckhardt (translated by Gesenius, p. 1043) among the villages of the *Gôf*—from חָצַר to enclose, comp. حظر, حصر, and especially حضر, to live in a courtyard walled round (*haḍar, haḍâr, haḍâra*); here as at Lev. xxv. 31, and to this day with the obliteration of the characteristic "walled round," the general name for a settled abode (with houses of plaster or stone) in contrast with wandering and tents. Then טִירֹת (from טוּר, comp. طار, طھر) encampment (identical in meaning with صيرات *sîrât* and دوار *duâr*), i.e. circular groups (comp. دور, طور circle, circumference) of pitched tents (haircloth tents, *wabar*). The first appellation of the kind of dwelling designates the stationary, the second the wandering sons of Ishmael. Duration of Ishmael's lifetime, ver. 17: *And this is the amount of the years of Ishmael: a hundred and seven and thirty years, and he departed and died, and was gathered to his people.* Dwelling-places of the Ishmaelites, ver. 18: *They dwelt from Havilah to ʾSûr, which is before Egypt as far as towards Assyria, eastwards of all his brethren came he to dwell.* The topographical עַל־פְּנֵי denotes a position which so covers the front of any place, that it may be seen thence before arriving at it. In itself it tells us nothing of the quarter, comp. Josh. xv. 8 "westwards;" xviii. 4 "southwards," but standing alone it has here, as at xvi. 12, the meaning of eastwards (comp. Deut. xxxii. 49, 1 Sam. xv. 7, 1 Kings xi. 7, Zech. xiv. 4, comp. Num. xxi. 11). The נָפַל usual elsewhere of the territory devolving to any one, means here as at Judg. vii. 12, to settle.

Luther translates after the Vulgate: *coram* (עַל־פְּנֵי as at xi. 28) *cunctis fratribus suis obiit*. But נָפַל is used of falling in war, and not like the Arabic خَرَّ exactly in the meaning of dying; and the prediction xvi. 12, the fulfilment of which is the point in question, shows that it is here synonymous with שָׁכַן. Luther explains it in the *Enarrationes* more correctly: *terram occuparunt*, but with a mistaken interpretation of נָפַל after נְפִלִים (invaders) instead of settlement (comp. xxiv. 64). The חֲוִילָה here coincides locally with the Joktanite Havilah x. 29, the country of the Χαυλοταῖοι mentioned between the Nabatæans and Agræans by Eratosthenes in Strabo, xvi. 4. 2. Between this Havilah on the Persian Gulf and the desert of Shur lying towards Egypt, the Ishmaelites spread themselves over the Sinaitic peninsula and the trans-Jordanic deserts of the Higâz and Negd, as well as further up Mesopotamia בֹּאֲךָ אַשּׁוּרָה in the direction of Assyria, *i.e.* as far as the lands under Assyrian sway. Comparing indeed 1 Sam. xxvii. 8, the suspicion is aroused that בֹּאֲךָ אַשּׁוּרָה is a recent gloss which erroneously interprets the שׁוּר,—what it states is however correct as to matter (Dillm.), and the sentence עַל־פְּנֵי כָל־אֶחָיו נָפָל, to which Wellh. also objects (*Composition*, i. p. 410), is quite unassailable. But it is possible that ver. 18 is an addition from *J*, in which its original place was perhaps after ver. 6.

VIII.

THE TOLEDOTH OF ISAAC, XXV. 19-XXXV. 29.

THE THREE PERIODS OF THE HISTORY OF ISAAC.

WE have already had preliminary information concerning Isaac, but his proper history according to the view and plan of Genesis commences here. It is opened by *R* with matter derived from *Q*, who furnishes its scaffold and framework, vv. 19, 20: *And these are the generations of Isaac, the son of Abraham; Abraham begat Isaac. And Isaac was forty years old when he took to wife Rebekah, the daughter of Bethuel the Aramæan from Paddan Aram, the sister of Laban the Aramæan.* The תּוֹלְדֹת of Isaac assume that he is an independent commencement. And this he became after obtaining a wife in Rebekah from פַּדַּן אֲרָם. Here for the first time we meet with this name of the Aramæan plain, occurring elsewhere only in *Q* and never out of Genesis. It is perhaps (comp. Spiegel, *Eränische Alterthumskunde*, i. 289) of a narrower meaning than the Jahvistic אֲרַם נַהֲרַיִם, and denotes those plains of the immense fruitful *campi Mesopotamiæ* (Curtius, iii. 2. 3, v. 1. 15) in which lay Harran and Edessa (*Urhoi*). The word פַּדָּן (فَدَّان) is of like root with الفَضا the broad desert plain, and properly means the extended level; in Aramaic and Arabic it is transferred to the oxen yoked to the plough and to the plough itself (*DMZ.* xxviii. 623). But even in these tongues its original meaning of plain, field, cultivated land (Gr. πεδίον, which however means trodden ground), whence نَدَى as the designation of the landowner is derived, has been maintained as a local name (*DMZ*. xxix. 433). Hos. xii. 12 has שָׂדֶה for פַּח (comp. *Shabbath* 118*b* שְׂוִרי=שָׂדִי). Isaac's marriage with Rebekah, who came from this Aramæa, remained childless for twenty years; it was not till fifteen years before the death of Abraham (not after that event, as Josephus, confusing the historiographic with the historic sequence, thinks) that Rebekah bore children, and that the new beginning appointed to take place with Isaac made an advance. The Toledoth of Isaac are divided into three sections: the first extends from the birth of the twin children amidst marvellous circumstances to the sending away of Jacob to Harran, xxv. 21 to xxviii. 9; the second begins with Jacob's dream of the heavenly ladder on his way to Harran, and reaches to his final peaceable departure from Laban, xxviii. 10 to xxxii. 1; the third begins with the miraculous experiences of Jacob during his return, at Mahanaim and Peniel, and terminates with the death of Isaac, xxxii. 2 to xxxv. 29. The history of Isaac differs from that of Abraham by the chief personage not being as in the latter the patriarch himself, but his son Jacob. Isaac is the middle, the entirely secondary and rather passive than active member of the patriarchal triad. The usual course of the historical process is, that the middle is weaker than the beginning and end, the fundamental figure of its rhythmic movement is the amphimacer $-\cup-$. And thus also does the patriarchal history advance to its goal. What is told us of Isaac is comparatively little, and we see Abraham's history repeated *in parvo*. Isaac is blessed for Abraham's sake, and he himself blesses with the blessing of Abraham, while in the respect shown him by Abimelech, in the long barrenness of his wife, in her exposure to danger by his faithless policy, in his two dissimilar children, in his domestic vexations—in all these he is the copy of Abraham; even the wells which he digs are those of Abraham which have been stopped up by the Philistines, and the names he

132   GENESIS XXV. 21.

gives them are the old ones renewed. He is the most passive of the three patriarchs.

THE TWIN CHILDREN AND ESAU'S FIRST SALE OF HIS BIRTHRIGHT
TO JACOB, CH. XXV. 21–34.

The patriarchal history began with the separation of Abraham the Shemite from the mass of the nations; it continued with the separation of the son of promise from Abraham's other progeny; it closes with a fresh separation made between the twin sons of Isaac. The birth of these twin sons and their separation by Divine choice and then by their own decision is related in the first section of the life of Isaac, xxv. 21–34, in which vv. 21–23 may be certainly distinguished as derived from *J*, and 26*b* as from *Q*. In the rest the analysis is uncertain, for it is not necessary to assume that 25*a* purposes to give another occasion for the name אֱדוֹם, and xxvii. 35 sq. an explanation of the name יַעֲקֹב in contradiction to ver. 26, both according to *E* in distinction from *J*. Neither is it necessary to regard Rebekah's exposure to danger by reason of her beauty, xxvi. 6–11, as occurring before she became a mother.

Isaac's prayer for the blessing of children, ver. 21: *And Isaac prayed to Jahveh in respect of his wife, for she was barren. And Jahveh was entreated by him: Rebekah his wife conceived.* He prayed לְנֹכַח אִשְׁתּוֹ, *i.e.* as at xxx. 38, with respect to her from נֶכַח نكس *figere oculos in aliqua re.* The verb עָתַר properly means to burn incense (Syr. Arab. עטר=קטר ܩܛܪ), which meaning is favoured by Ezek. viii. 11, where עֲתָר means the scent (of the cloud of incense)—the Arab. عتر retreating from this original meaning, is more generally: to bring sacrifices, not merely with an object (*Jâkût,* iii. p. 912, Z. 13), but also absolutely (*id.* p. 913, line 2), as also עֲתָרַי Zeph. iii. 10 means my worshippers (by sacrifice and prayer)—the transition from *adolere* to *sacrificari* (comp. θύειν) and then to *colere* (comp.

نسك), and farther to *precari*, is natural. The *Niph.* נֶעְתַּר is a synonym of נַעֲנָה, to let oneself be entreated. The Talmud and Midrash combine עתר with חתר in the meaning of to engrave = to penetrate, for which the Arabic is appealed to (see *Pesikta de Rab Cahana* 162b, ed. Buber); another Haggadic meaning is found in Buxtorf, *Lex. Talmud.* col. 1687. Apparent menace to maternal hopes, ver. 22: *And the children thrust each other within her, then she said: If it be thus, for what purpose am I? And she went to inquire of Jahveh.* The thrusts within seem to her indications not of the favour but of the wrath of God. Hence she complains and inquires: Why (comp. xxvii. 46) do I live at all? לָמָּה in its first meaning *ad quid, cui rei*, as *e.g.* at Amos v. 18. Rebekah is of a sensitive, sanguine disposition, as prompt in action as she is easily discouraged; she maintains however amidst all her changes of emotion a direct regard to God and to His promise. So too here: she goes to some holy place consecrated by revelation and by the worship of God לִדְרֹשׁ אֶת־ה' *ad petendum Domini oraculum*, and receives comfort and information, ver. 23: *Jahveh said to her:*

> *Two nations are in thy womb,*
> *And two peoples shall be separated from thy bowels;*
> *And a nation overcomes a nation,*
> *And the elder will serve the younger.*

The poetic form of this tetrastich is unmistakeable. We here see how akin prophecy is to poetry. In xxiv. 60 we had the poetry of the ברכה, here the poetry of the נבואה. The answer corresponds as to its tenour with the paradoxical character of the patriarchal period. After the long barrenness of Rebekah, which made the life of Isaac an enigma, is removed, the mark of an inversion of natural order is impressed upon Rebekah's children even in their mother's womb. God's thoughts, which are far above men's thoughts, are here ordering everything. Birth of the twins, vv. 24–26: *When then her days were fulfilled to be delivered, behold there were twins in her womb. And the first came forth ruddy quite like a hairy garment, and they called his name Esau. Afterwards his brother came forth, his hand holding to Esau's heel, and his name was called Ja'akob, and Isaac was sixty years old at their birth.* The twins are here called תוֹמִם, contracted from תְּאוֹמִים xxxviii. 27, comp. Θωμᾶς = תּוֹמָא. The first-born appeared אַדְמוֹנִי, *i.e.* with flesh of a red-brown colour (comp. 1 Sam. xvi. 12, xvii. 42), and quite כְּאַדֶּרֶת שֵׂעָר (Zech. xiii. 4 comp. Heb. xi. 37), *i.e.* as to his whole body like a mantle (from אָדַר *amplum esse*) covered with hairs (from שֵׂעָר *horrere*, to bristle, comp. *hirtus, hirsutus*, rough), an anomalous luxuriance of hair (Hypertrichosis), which sometimes occurs in the newly born, here, as was also the darker colour of the skin, a prognostic of bodily strength and fierceness. In שֵׂעָר here and xxvii. 11, 23, there may be an allusion to the national name שֵׂעִיר, but no actual line of connection is drawn. The second born made his appearance holding the heel of his brother, with his hand held above his head. We are not told that it was thus in his mother's womb (a position of twins hardly possible), but that he followed his brother with this movement of the hand. They called (וַיִּקְרְאוּ) the one עֵשָׂו, the hairy, the other they called (וַיִּקְרָא as at xxxv. 8, xxxviii. 29 sq.) יַעֲקֹב, the heel-holder, *i.e.* the crafty (comp. Hos. xii. 4). Reifmann, referring to the interchange of ע and כ in Galilean-Samaritan, explains עֵשָׂו as "the covered over," from עָשָׂה = כָּסָה; but the Arabic أعْنَى *hirsutus*,[1] makes the existence of a verb עָשָׂה (עָשַׂו), to be hairy, probable, whence is formed עֵשָׂו after the formation עֵב, like קָדָר and רָכָב. Isaac was sixty years old, and had hence been married twenty years, when they were born (בְּלֶדֶת אֹתָם) without a subject: at their birth, Ew. § 304*a*, comp. בְּהִלֵּד, when one bears, iv. 18). The different characters of the two brothers, ver. 27: *And the boys grew, and Esau was a*

---

[1] Notwithstanding the anomalous change of שׁ and ث (Aramaic ת), see Fleischer on Levy's *Neuhebr. WB.* iii. 732.

man skilled in hunting, a man of the field, but Jacob an amiable man, dwelling in tents. Esau appears also as a sportsman under the name of Οὔσωος in Phœnician legends. אִישׁ תָּם is here not so much the praise of piety, as the designation of natural temperament: a perfect and, because love is the bond of perfectness, a kind and amiable man (comp. the ancient Arab. كَلِفَ, used of loving devotion), not wandering about as a hunter in the open field, but dwelling in tents as a shepherd (iv. 20). Relation of their parents to them, ver. 28: *And Isaac loved Esau, because he relished venison, and Rebekah loved Jacob.* The former was the favourite of Isaac because venison was in his mouth, *i.e.* because he often ate and liked it; the latter was the favourite of Rebekah, who was better pleased with his quiet, gentle and thoughtful disposition, than with the boisterous, wild, clumsy Esau. The fatal lentil pottage, vv. 29, 30: *And Jacob sod pottage, then came Esau from the field and he was faint. And Esau said to Jacob: Oh let me swallow of the red, the red there, for I am faint—therefore his name was called Edôm.* Another motive for the name אֱדוֹם (the red-brown) was perhaps hinted at in אַדְמוֹנִי; the designation is expressly based only upon אָדוֹם, that red, *i.e.* yellow-brown lentil pottage φοινικίδιον. Elsewhere too, *e.g.* among the Arabs (comp. Abulfeda's *hist. anteislamica* and Wetzstein's inscriptions in the *Transactions* of the Berlin Academy, 1863, pp. 335–337), innumerable names have a similarly accidental origin,[1] and he who finds it impossible that the fortunes of a nation should for a thousand years be connected with a dish of lentils, if he will only look into the history of the world, and especially of the East, will not look in vain for parallels. Lentils ('*adas*) are and were a favourite dish in Syria and Egypt; besides Esau was hungry, so that the appetizing meal (נָזִיד), a noun formed from the verb זוּד, *Hiph.* הֵזִיד, with the

---

[1] If a Bedouin girl is born at night, she is called *Lêla*; if when snow is falling, she is called *Thelga*; if her mother's eye encountered at her birth a swarm of ants, she is called *Nimla*, etc.

preformative *na* common in Assyrian, and with the retention of the characteristic middle sound), pleasant to sight and smell, was a trial to his self-denial, to which he was unequal. Jacob profits by his moment of weakness, vv. 31–33: *Then Jacob said: Sell me first of all thy birthright! And Esau said: Behold, I am about to die, and of what use is the birthright to me? And Jacob said: Then first swear to me, and he swore to him, and sold his birthright to Jacob.* The hardly translateable כַּיּוֹם means just now, first of all, before all else, comp. 1 Sam. ii. 16, 1 Kings i. 51, xxii. 5. Esau consents to the bargain, profanely preferring (Heb. xii. 16) the palpable and present to the unseen and future. Jacob's cheap payment, ver. 34: *And Jacob gave Esau bread and lentil pottage, he ate and drank and rose up and went away, and Esau despised his birthright*, i.e. he thought no more about it, till he saw too late how foolishly he had acted. The בְּכֹרָה generally consists in the right to the larger portion of the inheritance, xlviii. 19, xlix. 3, Deut. xxi. 17, but we do not see Jacob afterwards lay claim to anything of the kind. In this instance it is the claim to the בִּרְכַּת אַבְרָהָם in the sense of xxviii. 4, and the princely and priestly prerogative involved in it, for which Jacob is concerned. "Before the tabernacle was erected"— says the Mishna *Sebachim* xiv. 4—" the Bamoth (local sanctuaries) were permitted, and the Abodah (the priestly office) was with the first-born; but after the erection of the tabernacle (the central sanctuary) the Bamoth were forbidden and the Abodah was with the Cohanim." Jerome thus correctly reports as Jewish tradition, *hæc* (viz. the *sacerdotium*) *esse primogenita quæ Esau fratri suo vendiderit Jacob.* In a word: the first-born is the head of the patriarchal family, and the right of the first-born includes the representative privileges derived from this exalted position. Esau's forfeiture of these privileges is, according to Rom. ix. (comp. Mal. i. 2 sq.), a work of free Divine election, but not without being at the same time, as this narrative shows, the result of Esau's voluntary self-degradation. As Ishmael had no claim to the blessing of the first-born, because begotten κατὰ σάρκα, so does Esau, though not begotten κατὰ σάρκα, forfeit the blessing of the first-born, because minded κατὰ σάρκα. The unbrotherly artifice of Jacob is indeed also sinful, and we see this one sin produce first the sin of deceiving his aged father, before whom Jacob did not venture to assert his purchased claim to the blessing, and then penal consequences of every kind. By reason however of the fundamental tendency of his mind towards the promised blessing, Jacob is the more pleasing to God of the two brothers; hence his sin itself must contribute to the realization of the Divine counsel, and his dishonour to the glorification of Divine grace.

VARIED CONFIRMATION OF THE PROMISE TO ISAAC, CH. XXVI.

The second portion, ch. xxvi., tells us of Isaac's joys and sorrows during the period of his Philistine sojourn, and thereby gives us a picture of his life in general—a life bearing the relation of a copy to that of Abraham, but also made illustrious by appearances of God (vv. 2, 24), and thus maintained at the patriarchal level. The narrator is *J*, in whose work this mosaic of matters concerning Isaac perhaps preceded the birth of the twin children. This narrator is announced by the Divine name יהוה, the continuations of the promise that the nations shall be blessed in the seed of the patriarch, 4b, comp. xxii. 18, the series ויקרא בשם ה' in ver. 25, and by other particulars. Both diction and matter however point in many respects to *E*, *e.g.* עַל־אֹדוֹת 32a, and the mention of Phicol with Abimelech ver. 26 comp. xxi. 22, hence the source may more correctly be designated as *JE* (*i.e.* *J* with matter from *E* worked into it). In vv. 1–6 Dillmann thinks he can even separate from each other the elements belonging respectively to *J* and *E*. Undoubtedly ver. 5 in this passage is from the hand of the

Deuteronomist. It has a special connection with the closing portion, xxvi. 34 sq. 1. RENEWAL OF THE PROMISE IN GERAR, xxvi. 1-6 : *And there arose a famine in the land, beside the former one, which arose in the days of Abraham, and Isaac went unto Abimelech, king of Gerar. And Jahveh appeared unto him and said: Go not down into Egypt, remain in the land that I will tell thee. Sojourn in this land, and I will be with thee and bless thee, for to thee and to thy seed will I give all these lands and fulfil the oath which I swore to thy father Abraham, and I will increase thy seed as the stars of heaven, and will give to thy seed all these lands, and in thy seed shall all the nations of the earth bless themselves, for a reward that Abraham obeyed my bidding and observed my precept, my commandments, my statutes and my instructions. Then Isaac dwelt in Gerar.* xii. 10 is referred to by מִלְּבַד וגו׳ (in meaning = לְבַד מִן); the narrator as here is there *J*, the reference however is surely an addition of *R*'s. The facts related resemble each other as to matter. The famine directs Isaac's as well as Abraham's view to Egypt, the granary of the Holy Land in such cases, and he journeys on the road thither first to Gerar (three leagues south of Gaza in the broad and deep *'Gurf el-'Gerâr* where Rowlands discovered ruins). This district was still governed by a king who had been on friendly terms with Abraham, ch. xx. 21, 22 sqq., and who bears here the title מֶלֶךְ פְּלִשְׁתִּים which was missing in the text of *E*. Arrived in Gerar, Isaac receives Divine direction to pursue his journey towards Egypt no farther, but to remain (שָׁכַן) in the land which God points out to him: he is to sojourn in the land where he now is, viz. Philistia (גּוּר, the standing word for the sojourning of the patriarchs in Canaan and Philistia) ; at the same time the fulfilment of the oath by which God confirmed His promises to Abraham upon Moriah is assured to him, and indeed for the sake of Abraham's obedience. The relation both in diction and matter to xxii. 15-18 is unmistakeable. But there is in vv. 2-5 many a token of the interposition of a more recent hand.[1] The expression אֶת־כָּל־הָאֲרָצֹת הָאֵל, i.e. Canaan proper with the neighbouring lands, is peculiar (comp. אַרְצוֹת יִשְׂרָאֵל in 1 Chron. xiii. 2, 2 Chron. xi. 23); הָאֵל is here no archaism, but an abbreviation of the original הָאֵלֶּה (see on xix. 8). The combination מִצְוֹתַי הֻקּוֹתַי וְתוֹרֹתָי has a Deuteronomic ring (the plur. תּוֹרֹת however occurs only Ex. xvi. 28, xviii. 16, 20, Lev. xxvi. 46, and not in Deuteronomy), Abraham's performance of the obedience due to God being thus divided according to the language of subsequent legislation. 2. PRE-SERVATION OF THE PATRIARCH'S WIFE IN GERAR, xxvi. 7–11. It is conceivable that what is here related may have taken place in the period preceding the birth of the twin children, and may be introduced here retrospectively in an appropriate connection. But this is unnecessary, for it is found now as formerly that a woman may be still seductively beautiful, even after she has borne children. Her cowardly exposure, ver. 7: *And the people of the place asked him concerning his wife, and he said: She is my sister, for he feared when he thought: Let not people of this place kill me for the sake of Rebekah, for she is fair to look on.* The לְ after שָׁאַל is that of relation, and therefore of the object of the inquiry, as at xxxii. 30, xliii. 7, comp. אֶל and לְ after אָמַר xx. 2, 13, where also עַל (on account of), ver. 3, is equally used as here and at ver. 9. He who was untruthful through fear of man is put to shame, vv. 8–11: *And it came to pass when a long time had passed there with him, that Abimelech, king of the Philistines, looked through the window, and he saw and behold Isaac was caressing with Rebekah his wife. Then Abimelech called Isaac and said: She is certainly thy wife, and how canst thou say she is thy sister? And Isaac said to him: Because I thought: Let me not die on her account. Then said Abimelech: What hast thou done unto us? In a little one of the people might have lain with thy wife, and thou wouldst have brought guilt upon us. And Abimelech commanded the people*

---

[1] So already Hitzig, *Begriff der Kritik* (1831), p. 169 sq.; comp. Kuenen, *Einl.* (1887) § 13, note 31.

thus: Whosoever toucheth this man or his wife shall die the death. The juxtaposition of יִצְחָק מְצַחֵק sounds like a play upon the words: *Isaac isaacabat cum Rebecca h. e. blandiebatur uxori.* In distinction from one-sided playing with בְּ צָחַק, צָחֵק אֵת means exchanging jests, caresses. Ver. 9 is parallel with xx. 9. אֵיךְ *quomodo* is here equal to *quo jure.* With כִּמְעַט שָׁכַב *pæne concubuisset* comp. Ps. lxxiii. 2, xciv. 17, cxix. 87, Prov. v. 14. וְהֵבֵאתָ has the tone on the *ult.*, like רְבִי 22a and נְחֵה Isa. xi. 2, on account of the else scarcely audible ע which follows. Isaac, in consequence of saying that Rebekah was his sister, has an experience essentially the same as that of Abraham in Egypt and afterwards in this very place Gerar. xxvi. 7–11 also resembles ch. xx. in mode of delineation and tone of language. These events were nevertheless regarded by the ancients as different (comp. Ps. cv. 14 with chs. xii. and xx.; cv. 15 with xxvi. 11), indeed they are also characteristically distinguished from each other by the fact, that Jahveh does not suffer Rebekah's exposure to danger by the fault of Isaac to go so far as in the case of Sarah's by the fault of Abraham. The Philistine king being here as in ch. xx. called אֲבִימֶלֶךְ suggests the conjecture, that this was a general name of Philistine as פַּרְעֹה was of Egyptian, عَبَلَة (plur. عَبَاهِلَة) of Jamanite, and *Lucumo* of Etrurian kings (comp. 1 Sam. xxi. 11 with Ps. xxxiv. 1); nevertheless it may perhaps be the same Abimelech as at ch. xx., though about eighty years had elapsed. The same chaste and God-fearing behaviour speaks for the sameness of person, while the thought that he might himself have appropriated Rebekah being entirely absent from him, speaks for his meantime much advanced old age. 3. ISAAC'S INCREASED POSSESSIONS, WHICH BECOME OBJECTIONABLE IN GERAR, xxvi. 12–17. Success of Isaac's Philistinian agriculture, ver. 12: *And Isaac sowed in that land and gained in the same year a hundredfold, and Jahveh blessed him.* He obtained, gained (as מצא means) in that same year, which followed the year of famine, מֵאָה שְׁעָרִים a hundredfold, *i.e.* according to Luke viii. 8 καρπὸν ἑκατονταπλασίονα, as at present occurs only in the "red earth" (the lava soil) of Haurân. We see from this union of agricultural with nomadic life (comp. xxxvii. 7), not as yet found in the history of Abraham, that Isaac, encouraged by the Divine promise, had set firm foot in the land. It was not till their sojourn in Egypt that tillage and the rearing of cattle became equally pursuits of the Israelites, and not till after the Exodus that the former obtained the upper hand. Isaac's increased prosperity excites envy, vv. 13, 14: *And the man became great and became continually greater, till he became very great. And he possessed herds of small cattle and herds of oxen and a great household, so that the Philistines envied him.* Instead of the *inf. absol.* וְגָדוֹל 2 Sam. v. 10 (comp. above, viii. 3, 5) we have here וְגָדֵל 3rd praet. like 1 Sam. ii. 26 in accordance with Josh. vi. 13, Isa. xxxi. 5, or also the participial adj. in accordance with Judg. iv. 24, 2 Sam. xvi. 5. פְּלִשְׁתִּים is always without an article in the Pentateuch; עֲבֻדָּה besides here occurs only in the imitative passage Job i. 3. Consequences of this envy, vv. 15-17: *And all the wells, which the servants of his father had digged in the days of Abraham his father, the Philistines stopped up and filled them with earth. Then Abimelech said to Isaac: Go forth from us, for thou art become too mighty for us. Then Isaac departed thence and encamped in the valley of Gerar, and dwelt there.* The verbs referring to the fem. plur. בְּאֵרֹת have the suffix *ûm* instead of *ûn*, the former being used for both genders. Ewald 249*b*, 3. The style of expression of ver. 15 places its statement in a circumstantializing relation to ver. 16. The self-help of his people gives occasion to the demand of the king, that Isaac should depart from the district of Gerar. Such well-digging on the part of Abraham is spoken of xxi. 25-31. It is in accordance with the character of the enduring Isaac, that he willingly submits and leaves the district of the town of Gerar, taking up his abode in the valley of Gerar. Here ἐν Γεράροις ἐν τῷ χειμάρρῳ, Constantine, according to Sozomenus, vi. 32, erected a monastery. 4. ISAAC'S RESTORED AND NEWLY DISCOVERED WELLS, xxvi. 18 – 22. Redigging of the stopped up wells, ver. 18 : *And Isaac dug again the wells of water, which they had digged in the days of his father Abraham and the Philistines had stopped up after Abraham's death, and called them by names like the names by which his father had called them.* Thus the self-help of the Philistines had not been limited to the district of Gerar. The conjunctive form of the plural of בְּאֵר was at xiv. 10 בְּאֵרֹת, here and Deut. x. 6 בְּאֵרֹת like the chief form. The subjects of חָפְרוּ are the עַבְדֵי אָבִיו 15a. The newly discovered spring, vv. 19, 20 : *And the servants of Isaac were digging in the valley and found there a spring of living water. Then the herdmen of Gerar strove with the herdmen of Isaac, saying: The water belongs to us; therefore he called the name of the spring* '*Eseḳ, because they had contended with him.* Isaac's people discovered a vein of water, which was not difficult to lead upwards and lay hold on (see my discussion on such desert springs in Luthardt's Zeitschr. 1882, p. 454 sq.). עֵשֶׂק means contention ; the verb עשׂק (post-biblical עסק) seems related to עשׂה as *facessere* to *facere*. A second new well, ver. 21 : *And they dug another well and they strove about that also, then he called its name Siṭna,* i.e. *enmity.* A third new well, ver. 22 : *And he departed thence and dug another well, and about this they strove not, then he called its name Reḥóbóth and said: Truly now hath Jahveh made room for us, and we may increase in the land.* A *Wadi Ruḥaibe* was found by Robinson south-west of Elusa (Chalaṣa) with extensive ruins of a town of like name upon a hill; he came from Ruḥaibe to Chalaṣa and found there also a *Wadi* '*Suṭein* pointing to the well שִׂטְנָה. The name רְחֹבוֹת means distances, spaces for free movement, in opposition to צָרוֹת *augustiae.* כִּי in stating the reason for the name is not merely ὅτι *recitativum,* to which like the Aramaic דִי *e.g.* Dan. ii. 25, it has been certainly diluted, but means, with a transition from the reason-giving meaning to the confirmatory: truly, indeed, like *e.g.*

xxix. 33, Ex. iii. 12, iv. 25, and in the connection כִּי עַתָּה, truly now, xxix. 32, especially in the apodosis of a hypothetical prodosis: truly then, so . . . now, xxxi. 42, xliii. 10, Job iii. 13, with the preterite or with the imperf. as at Job vi. 3, viii. 6, xiii. 19, comp. כִּי־אָז Job xi. 15, according to the nature of the prodosis. 5. ISAAC'S DEPARTURE FROM THE VALLEY OF GERAR AND ABODE AT BEERSHEBA, xxvi. 23-25: *And he went up thence to Beërŝeba. And Jahveh appeared to him that same night and said: I am the God of Abraham, fear not, for I am with thee and will bless thee and multiply thy seed for my servant Abraham's sake. Then he built there an altar and proclaimed the name of Jahveh and pitched his tent there, and there Isaac's servant bored a well.* In Beersheba (12 leagues south-west of Hebron), where, according to the present composition of Genesis, Abraham had dwelt for a long period between his two sojourns in Hebron, ch. xviii.–xix. 23, are the promises made to his father confirmed to Isaac. He there built an altar, held solemn acts of worship and there stretched (וַיֶּט־שָׁם) his tent: his servants also bored a well in the neighbourhood of his new quarters. On the distinction of the synonyms חפר and כרה see my discussion in Luthardt's *Zeitschr.* 1882, p. 452. 6. ABIMELECH'S COVENANT WITH ISAAC, xxvi. 26-33. This event of Isaac's life bears a striking resemblance with what is related in the life of Abraham, xxi. 22 sqq. What is here related by *J* is strikingly like what was there related by *E*. When about to enter into a covenant with Isaac, Abimelech is here as there accompanied by Phicol, vv. 26-29: *And Abimelech went to him from Gerar, and Ahuzzat his friend and Phicol his captain of the host. Then Isaac said to them: Why are ye come to me, since ye hate me and have driven me from you? They said: We saw plainly that Jahveh is with thee, and we thought: Let there now be an oath betwixt us and thee and we will make a covenant with thee, that thou wilt do us no evil, as we have not molested thee and as we have done unto thee nothing but good and have sent thee away in peace—thou art now the blessed of Jahveh.* The king has with him, beside Phicol, Ahuzzath (with the original fem. ending like בְּלִית, בְּשֶׂמֶת 34*b* and the like) his friend, *i.e.* counsellor; the name "friend" may here already designate not merely a personal but an official relation, as subsequently at the Persian and Roman imperial courts (perhaps also in Egypt, if according to A. Geiger Πτολεμαῖος = פ־תלמי the brother, *i.e.* friend, comp. on xli. 43). Here as at xxi. 22 they acknowledge and bear testimony to the patriarch, that Jahveh is with him (רָאֹו 28*a* = רָאֹה, as חֲמוֹ xx. 6 = חֲמָא, see Ges. § 75, note 2). The declaration on oath for which they apply to the patriarch, and the reason for so doing, are similar to xxi. 22 sq. (אָלָה as a syn. of בְּרִית, like Deut. xxix. 11, 13, comp. Ezek. xvi. 59). תֵּעָשֶׂה has here *Tsere* in the final syllable as in only three other passages, Josh. vii. 9 with *Tiphchah* and therefore in half pause, 2 Sam. xiii. 12 and Jer. xl. 16, perhaps to guard against the confusion of the first syllable of the second word with the last of the first, see on Isa. lxiv. 3. The consonance אַתָּה עַתָּה is like וַאֲנִי עָנִי Ps. xl. 18 and frequently. The conclusion of the covenant, vv. 30, 31: *Then he made them a feast and they ate and drank. And they arose up betimes in the morning and swore to one another, and Isaac accompanied them, and they departed from him in peace.* There is nothing said of a covenant repast at xxi. 23, it finds its parallel at xxxi. 54, but here as there the name of the subsequent Beersheba originates on the occasion of the covenant by reason of a well standing in connection with it, vv. 32, 33: *And it came to pass on the same day that Isaac's servants came and made report to him with respect to the well which they had digged, and said to him: We have found water. Then he called it 'Sib'ah, therefore the city is called Beĕrŝeb'a to this day.* The well with the boring of which Isaac's people were occupied (ver. 25) soon after his settlement at Beersheba is here intended. They now announce to him their success, and the covenant just concluded with Abimelech gives occasion to Isaac to name this well שִׁבְעָה. An oath is called a sevening as being an asseveration by seven things, as shown by the narrative concerning the origin of the name of the town of Beersheba, xxi. 28–31, taken from *E*, while the one now before us is from *J*. The similarity of the two histories does not of itself stamp the one as a copy of the other (comp. on the contrary *e.g.* Judg. ix. in relation to Gen. xix.). There are many indications, as we saw on xxi. 31, that Beersheba had its name with relation to two treaties with Abimelech concerning two wells, the one made by Abraham, the other by Isaac, and names with two similar historical connections also occur elsewhere. At ver. 18 also we find Isaac preferring to renew the old names of the wells. It is indeed difficult, *i.e.* chronologically difficult, to separate the two stories, because Phicol again appears with Abimelech, whom one may think of at ch. xxi. as still very young; Jacobus Edessenus takes the king and the captain of the host for grandsons of the same names. 7. ESAU'S MARRIAGES, xxvi. 34 sq.: *And Esau was forty years old, then he took to wife Jehudith the daughter of Beëri the Hittite and Basmath the daughter of Elon the Hittite. And they were a grief of heart to Isaac and Rebekah,* properly a bitterness of spirit (מֹרָה = *morra* Prov. xiv. 10), *i.e.* a cause of bitterness of feeling. In the תּוֹלְדוֹת of Esau ch. xxxvi. their names and those of their fathers, as also that of Esau's third wife, xxviii. 9, are given somewhat differently from those in our present Jehovistic portion, without however their identity being lost. It is striking that יְהוּדִית (a patronymic from יְהוּדָה praise) appears here (against xxxvi. 2) so early as a Canaanite name. The formation בָּשְׂמַת here and xxxvi. 3 (comp. above אֲחָוַת and xxviii. 9 מַחֲלַת) is an ancient principal form of the feminine. The terminations ت, ة, ى represent three successive periods of the language (*DMZ.* xvi. 160). The most obvious explanation of the difference between xxvi. 34 sq., xxviii. 9 and xxxvi. would be to adopt the view that the narrator is here *J* and there *Q*. There is much to favour this: the marriage of Esau in his fortieth year is similar to Isaac's in his fortieth year, the exclamation of Rebekah xxvii. 46b to her exclamation xxv. 22a, and בְּנוֹת חֵת might also have been once written by J, especially as in the passage xxviii. 1–8, which is in any case Q's, בְּנוֹת כְּנַעַן is said for it. But xxviii. 8 cannot be separated from xxviii. 9 of which it is the premiss, and עַל־נָשָׁיו xxviii. 9 points back to xxvi. 34 sq., so that in fact xxvi. 34 sq., xxvii. 46, xxviii. 1–9 must be attributed to the same author and hence to Q. Consequently the wives' names are here given according to the wording of the text of Q, and the fact that they nevertheless run differently in the Toledoth of Esau, which is as to its foundation derived from Q, obliges us to adopt the view that R there inserted them from another source, in accordance with his principle of preserving two differing traditions and not violently reconciling them. In the mosaic ch. xxvi., ver. 34 sq. forms, in the present form of the composition, the concluding portion. Through all these seven short histories from the first forty years of the independent story of Isaac's life, there runs like a thread the purpose of showing how Isaac also, though less great in action than in endurance, nevertheless came under the blessing and protection of Jahveh, honourably through all complications, and rose to more and more wealth and respect. His life is an echo of the life of Abraham. All its vibrations arise from the powerful impulses given in the life of Abraham. Nevertheless the son of promise is not unworthy of his father. He manifests in "elasticity of endurance" (Kurtz) a special greatness, which has been transmitted as an ineradicably tenacious vital faculty to the nation descended from him.

JACOB OBTAINS BY CRAFT THE BLESSING OF THE FIRST-BORN,
CH. XXVII. 1–40.

This third portion also gives us an equally double-sided picture of Isaac: he shows himself weak, passive and pliable

GENESIS XXVII. 1-4.   147

in the hands of men, but elevated and inwardly profound, and at last obedient to God alone and strong in Him. The narrative is composed of the accounts of *J* and *E* worked into each other and completed from each other by *R*. This is seen from the two וַיְבָרֲכֵהוּ, one of which 23*b* follows the testing by touch, the other 27*a* the testing by smell; from the two equivalent ויהי 30*a*; from ver. 34 sq. in relation to vv. 36—38 with the twice told outburst of grief on the part of Esau; from the reiterated " until thy brother's fury turn away," 44*b*, 45*a*. The aged father makes preparations for the blessing of the first-born, vv. 1-4: *And it came to pass, when Isaac was old and his eyes had become dull of sight, that he called Esau his elder son and said to him: My son! And he said: Here am I. He said: Behold I am old, I know not the day of my death. Take then, I pray thee, thy weapons, thy quiver and thy bow, and go out into the field and hunt me venison, and make me a savoury dish such as I love, and bring it me, that I may eat, that my soul may bless thee before I die.* The occurrence falls, according to xxv. 26, xxvi. 34, in a period when Isaac had already passed his 100th and his sons their 40th year. The principal sentence introduced by וַיְהִי is continued with וַיִּקְרָא. The *impf. cons.* designates his dulness of sight as a result of his having grown old. The מִן of מֵרְאוֹת is the negative (away from seeing), like xvi. 2, xxiii. 6. תְּלִי is the quiver (אַשְׁפָּה) with a shoulder-belt, ἅπαξ γεγρ., forming together with the bow the usual hunting equipment (Isa. vii. 24). For צַיִד the *Chethib* has צֵידָה commonly used in the general meaning of diet, but here quite appropriate as a *nomen unitatis*. The weak side of Isaac's preference for Esau is here betrayed, in that he desires the dish of game, which he is fond of (אָהֵב vv. 4, 9, 14), not only for the sake of enjoying it, but that his son may, before he blesses him as a father, show the willing obedience of child-like affection. In Arabic a present is plainly called *tabarruk* as the means of obtaining a blessing. Hereupon Rebekah urges Jacob to obtain his father's blessing, by bringing him a spurious dish of savoury meat, vv. 5–10: *And Rebekah heard when Isaac spake to Esau his son, and Esau went to the field to hunt for venison, to bring it. And Rebekah said to Jacob her son: Behold, I have heard thy father speak unto Esau thus: Bring me venison and make me a savoury dish, that I may eat, and I will bless thee before Jahveh, before my death. And now, my son, hearken to my voice in what I bid thee do. Go now to the flock and fetch me thence two young goat-kids, and I will make of them a savoury dish for thy father such as he loveth. And thou shalt bring it to thy father, that he may eat, and bless thee before his death.* It is not without emphatic meaning that Esau is called Isaac's, and Jacob Rebekah's son. Instead of לְהָבִיא the LXX. has suitably לְאָבִיו (for his father), but the former cannot be criticized either as to matter, see vv. 4, 7, nor as to syntax (on account of the missing suffix, comp. 31a, Jer. xli. 5). לִפְנֵי ה׳ 7a is important and not pleonastic. Rebekah knows that it is done in the presence of Jahveh, and therefore with divine reality, with prophetic power. The לְ of לַאֲשֶׁר 8b is not that of the norm but that of reference, Ges. § 123. 2. גְּדָיֵי from גְּדִי is inflected just like לְחָיֵי from לְחִי (Backe). Jacob's objection appeased, vv. 11–13: *Then Jacob said to Rebekah his mother: Behold, Esau is a hairy man and I am a smooth man, perhaps my father will feel me, and I shall seem to him a mocker and bring upon myself a curse and not a blessing. And his mother said to him: I take thy curse upon me, my son; only hearken to my voice and go fetch* (them) *me.* מְתַעְתֵּעַ does not mean "a deceiver," but contempt is here combined with the deceit, the kind of deceit being like a joke played upon an aged father. Jacob fears, if detected, to bring upon himself a curse and not a blessing. Rebekah however replies decidedly: Let the curse thou meetest lie upon me, I will bear it and its consequences —a proof that, notwithstanding the impure means by which she incurred guilt, she yet leaned upon the word of promise, and now when this was threatened with frustration, was willing at any cost to promote its fulfilment. Preparation for the deception thus planned, vv. 14–17: *Then Rebekah took the garments of Esau her elder son, the costly ones, which she kept in the house, and clothed Jacob her younger son. And the skins of the kids she put upon his hands and upon the smooth of his neck, and gave the savoury dish and the bread which she had prepared into the hand of Jacob her son.* בגדי may, according to 2 Chron. xx. 25, be repeated as the governing word before הַחֲמֻדֹת (garments of the desired one, *i.e.* such as are the object of desire), or we may, according to Lev. vi. 20 (where בֶּגֶד is construed as a fem.), take it as an adj. (Reggio: *gli abiti più preziosi*). בַּבַּיִת means at home, within בָּאֹהֶל, which however is not so usual, as the opposite of בַּשָּׂדֶה (xxxiv. 5) would be more accurate. צַוָּארָיו is the inflected form of the dual which does not occur in the principal form, and means the fore and hind parts of the neck. Jacob begins to carry out the plot, vv. 18–20: *And he came to his father and said: My father, and he said: Here am I, who art thou, my son? Then Jacob said unto his father: I am Esau, thy first-born, I have done as thou saidst unto me; rise up then, sit and eat of my venison, that thy soul may bless me. And Isaac said to his son: How hast thou found it so quickly, my son? And he said: Because Jahveh thy God favoured me.* The construction מִהַרְתָּ לִמְצֹא is like xxvi. 18, xxxi. 27. Ges. § 142. 2. On הִקְרָה לְפָנַי see on xxiv. 12. The test by feeling, vv. 21–23: *Then Isaac said to Jacob: Come near, I pray thee, that I may feel thee, my son, whether thou there be my son Esau or not. Then Jacob came near to Isaac his father, and he felt him and said: The voice is Jacob's voice and the hands Esau's hands, and he discerned him not, for his hands were hairy as his brother Esau's hands, so he blessed him.* The interrogative ה in הַאַתָּה has Pathach, as also Judg. vi. 13 must be pointed. אַתָּה זֶה means, thou whom I have there before me. וַיְבָרְכֵהוּ is in the present connection an anticipation of the result, since we are told farther on how he proceeded to bless him, and in what words. Isaac makes a further trial, takes the offered meat and, confirmed by the smell of the garments that Esau is before him, prepares to bless him, vv. 24—27a: *And he said: Art thou there, my son Esau? And he said: I am. And he said: Bring it here to me, that I may eat of my son's venison, that my soul may bless thee. Then he brought it near to him and he ate, and he brought him wine and he drank. Then his father Isaac said to him, Come near, I pray thee, my son, and kiss me. Then he came near and kissed him, and he smelled the smell of his garments and blessed him and said.* Perplexed by the voice, which was not that of Esau, Isaac asks again whether it is Esau who is standing before him, and Jacob affirms it with emboldened composure. The psychologic acuteness and rigid objectivity of the narrative are admirable. The deceived father eats and drinks, and inaugurates his son for the blessing with a kiss of grateful affection (וַיִּשַּׁק with ־ under a non-guttural after ו as at ii. 12 and frequently, from נָשַׁק with ְ according to an ancient original construction). While kissing him he smells the odour of his garments. They were the garments of Esau the sportsman, saturated with the odour of the luxuriant vegetation of the field. The deception was thus perfect, and Isaac blesses him and says:

> 27b *See: The smell of my son is as the smell of a field*
> *Which Jahveh has blessed,*
> 28 *And GOD will give thee of the dew of heaven*
> *And of the fatness of the earth,*
> *And corn and wine in plenty.*
> 29 *Peoples shall serve thee*
> *And nations bow down to thee.*
> *Be lord over thy brethren,*
> *And thy mother's sons shall bow down to thee.*
> *Cursed be they that curse thee,*
> *And blessed be they that bless thee!*

The odour of the garments gives rise to the first thought of the blessing, it is the God-blessed Paradisaic plains of the Promised Land that appear before the mind's eye of Isaac, and his son seems to him to be scented with the perfume of this his inheritance (Hos. xiv. 7). It is true that God the Creator is also called יהוה (*e.g.* Ps. civ. 16), but here where we find ver. 28 הָאֱלֹהִים used, the reason for the change is, that the plains of Canaan, which are blessed by the God of the history of redemption, are the subject of thought. Heaven and earth are to dispense their mingled powers, the former its dew, the latter the soil of its most fruitful tracts, to produce an abundance of the noblest products, corn (edible grain) and wine. Although מִשְׁמַנֵּי has a non-dageshed Shin, it is nevertheless, as also it is here and there pointed, the same as מִשְׁמַנֵּי, parallel with מִפַּל, comp. מְלֹאִם xxv. 23, מִשְׁתִּים for מִשְׁתִּים Jonah iv. 11, perhaps also מְפֹרָיו=מְמַפְּרָיו Deut. xviii. 8. שְׁמַנֵּי is a plural to be referred not to שֶׁמֶן but to שָׁמֵן=שְׁמֵן (whence שְׁמָנִים *loca pinguia*), and formed like קְטַנִּים—חֲלָקוֹת מִשְׁמַנַּי with a formative Mem would not indeed be inadmissible, but has the parallelism against it both here and ver. 29. After pointing to a land loaded with abundant blessings by Jahveh, the blessing rises to the future position in the world of him whom it concerns. It passes far beyond the limits of the person of Jacob and the immediate future, gives to him who receives it and to his seed supremacy and exaltation above the nations both kindred and remote, and makes the relation of God to them conditional on the relation they take up to him and to his seed. It is the blessing of Abraham transmitted from Abraham to Isaac (xii. 7 and elsewhere xx. 17, xii. 3), which Isaac by the spirit of prophecy and in poetic diction here bestows upon his son. גְּבִיר after the formation of the Aramaic *part. pass.* occurs only here (comp. the ref. 37*a*). The *Chethîb* וישתחו is rightly interpreted by the *Keri*: it is, as at xliii. 28, an incorrectly defective writing. As עַמִּים and לְאֻמִּים are interchangeable words without any difference of conception, so too do אַחֶיךָ and בְּנֵי אִמֶּךָ coincide, comp. Ps. l. 20, lxix. 9, while on the other hand Lev. xviii. 9, Cant. i. 6 speak without parallelism of step-brothers and sisters. The construction of the plural in

29b with the sing. of the predicate is individualizing or distributive; it is repeated Num. xxiv. 9, comp. e.g. Zech. xi. 5, Ges. § 146. 4. The evolution of thought advancing in parallelism, the first smooth then impetuous rhythm, the expressions (the more unusual רְאֵה for הִנֵּה, שְׁמֵי הָאָרֶץ, הָוֵה for הָיָה, like הֱוֵא Job xxxvii. 6 and הֱוִי Isa. xvi. 4, וּבְיִר) and thoughts—everything is here poetical. The aged patriarch once more renews his youth and hovers on the wings of prophecy over the new era which commences with his son.

Esau now arrives, Isaac sees through the deception under which he has suffered, but declares the blessing imparted to be irrevocable, vv. 30–33: *And it came to pass when Isaac had finished blessing Jacob, and it came to pass when Jacob had only just gone out away from Isaac his father, that his brother Esau came from his hunting. And he also prepared a savoury dish and brought it to his father, and said to his father: Let my father arise and eat of his son's venison, that thy soul may bless me. Then Isaac his father said to him: Who art thou? And he said: I am thy son, thy first-born, Esau. Then Isaac was terrified with an exceeding great terror and said: Who then was it that took venison and brought it me, and I have eaten of all before thou camest, and blessed him—blessed also shall he be!* It is unmistakeable that in 30a two different expressions of one and the same thing are joined together, the first from J, who uses with preference the phrase כִּלָּה לְ (xviii. 33, xxiv. 15, 19, xxii. 45, xliii. 2), the other therefore certainly from E (Dillm.), who must also have written 30b, for the two sentences stand in mutual relation according to the scheme of the contemporaneous (comp. on vii. 6), which here (comp. on the contrary 2 Kings xx. 4) strengthens the expression of the exactly coincident to the *inf. intens.* which adds *vix exierat* Ew. 312a (comp. 314d), וַיְהִי introduces the two facts as simultaneous (Driver, § 165). Undeceived to his great terror, Isaac would immediately ask himself, whether what had been done were not a sinful trifling with God's blessing, and the conviction would also forthwith be pressed upon him, that it was the operation of God which had repressed his doubt as to whether he, who was to be blessed, were before him; and as it was now Jacob and not Esau, he would see his love for Esau, who had lost all higher consecration, condemned. To retract the blessing of Jacob seems to him impossible, for while blessing he had surrendered himself as an instrument without will into the hands of the Almighty and All-knowing, and is therefore obliged to acknowledge the indestructible objective power of his blessing: I blessed him (וָאֲבָרֲכֵהוּ), most editions erroneously וָאֲבָרְכֵהוּ), also he will remain blessed; גם (Samar. וגם) stands first, but belongs according to the sense to יהיה (comp. 1 Sam. xxviii. 20 and on Job ii. 10). Isaac remembers the saying of God xxv. 23, which with the intimacy of his marital relation could not have been hidden from him, and perceives that Divine Providence has obliged him against his will to fulfil it to Jacob. Hitzig with the concurrence of Olshausen corrects: וַיְהִי: גַּם בָּרוּךְ, but that would say: I have also truly blessed him, and it is a pity to miss the expression of unchangeableness. It is more possible that ויהי is with LXX. Samar. to be inserted before ver. 34, though it is perhaps omitted for the same reason as at xliv. 3, comp. xv. 17. With a violent outburst of grief Esau entreats his father to give him also a blessing, ver. 34: *When Esau heard the words of his father he raised a cry, exceeding loudly and bitterly, and said to his father: Bless me also, I pray thee, my father!* On גַּם־אָנִי, also me (like אַף־אַתָּה, also thee, Prov. xxii. 19), see Ges. § 121. 3. The בָּרֲכֵנִי גַם־אָנִי is repeated 38*a* after Isaac has more expressly declared the irrevocability of the blessing bestowed, vv. 35–38: *Then he said: Thy brother came with craft and took away thy blessing. And he said: Is it that he is called Jacob (overreacher) and he has now twice overreached me? My birthright he took away, and behold, he has now taken away my blessing, hast thou reserved no blessing for me? Then*

Isaac answered and said: Behold, I have appointed him thy master and have given to him all his brethren for servants, and with corn and wine have I sustained him, and what in all the world shall I do for thee, my son? Esau said to his father: Is this blessing thy only one, my father? Bless me also, I pray thee, my father! And Esau lifted up his voice and wept. He can produce no change of mind in his father, μετανοίας τόπον οὐχ εὗρεν, Heb. xii. 17. The question with הֲכִי (Job vi. 22) stands here, as at xxix. 15, in a paratactic double sentence, which by transposing the period runs thus: Is it because he bears this name now twice come thus to pass? The denominative עקב means to hold the heel in order to get before; the text. rec. followed by Ben-Asher has וַיַּעְקְבֵנִי from יָעֹב Jer. ix. 3, Ben-Naphtali וַיַּעְקְבֵנִי with a helping Pathach. The verb סמך is at 37a combined with a double accusative as at Ps. li. 14, as is also סָעַד at Judg. xix. 5. The writing לְכָה for לְךָ (only here in the Pentateuch) is like the writings iii. 9, Ex. xiii. 16. אֵפוֹא in the interrogative sentence stands either after the interrogative word ver. 33, or after the prominent word of the interrogative sentence, comp. Ex. xxxiii. 16, Job ix. 24, xxiv. 25. The vocalization הַבְרָכָה with Khateph is similar to לְשֶׁקֶת 28b. Isaac, acceding to Esau's impetuous request, bestows upon him also a blessing, which is however only a shadow of Jacob's blessing, and at the same time brings upon this latter blessing a cloud reproving the impurity of the means by which it had been obtained, ver. 39: *And Isaac his father answered and said to him:*

> *Behold, far from the fat plains of the earth shall be thy dwelling,*
> *And far from the dew of heaven above,*
> 40 *And by thy sword shalt thou live*
> *And serve thy brother.*
> *But by restlessly struggling*
> *Thou shalt break his yoke from off thy neck.*

The first question of all is, whether the two מִן have a partitive meaning (Meissner in *Luth. Zeitschr.* 1862) as in the blessing pronounced upon Jacob, ver. 28 (where it is at least assured to the מִן of מִשְׁמַנֵּי), or a privative (Keil, Dillm. and others). For that the מ of מִשְׁמַנֵּי is not a formative letter, as might be thought from the present punctuation (comp. on the contrary 28a and the Targums on our passage), is here shown still more plainly than at ver. 28 by the parallel מִטַּל. It is indeed true that, since Isaac desires to bestow a blessing upon Esau, there is no necessity for his denying him a fruitful land; Esau's servitude in opposition to Jacob's lordship is a dark shadow enough in this supplementary blessing. But there are besides linguistic and actual reasons against the partitive, and for the negative meaning. (1) The mountainous country of the Edomites is, as Seetzen says, perhaps the most barren and desert in the world (on which account שֵׂעִיר can hardly, with reference to its natural condition, be equivalent with the Arab. الاشعر "the overgrown"). Robinson describes the hills in the west of the Arabah as entirely unfruitful, the Arabah itself is the most dreadful stony desert to be met with, the plateau east of Wadi Musa bears the aspect of being hardly worth cultivation. Burckhardt, who passed through this mountainous district from Maân in a south-westerly direction, following the course of the *Wadi Gharundel*, found it entirely barren, and the declivity, which was composed of bare chalk and sandstone, utterly devoid of vegetation. The fact that the mountainous country about Petra and elsewhere has been transformed by skill and industry, especially by means of terrace-building and artificial irrigation, into a land of hanging gardens, cannot be used, as by Pusey (*Minor Prophets*, p. 144), in favour of the partitive sense of the מִן. The land and soil of Idumæa were for the most part unfruitful, and in the blessing the reference to the country concerned not the results of cultivation but the natural conditions. And (2) it is in opposition to ver. 37 that Isaac, after declaring that he has already bestowed upon Jacob the blessing of superabundance of the fruits of the earth, should begin the blessing of Esau in like terms with that of Jacob. But (3) we have also in Mal. i. 3: *Esau have I hated, and made his mountains a desert and his inheritance desolate tracks,* so far as we understand the prophet as St. Paul does Rom. ix. 13 (see Köhler on the passage), an ancient testimony to the privative meaning. Desolation is the lot to which the land of Edom is again and again doomed in virtue of Isaac's history-making word of prophecy, though art may, as we still see by the ruins of the valley of Petra, have transformed it. The more elevated style of writing prefers the pregnant use of מִן in the sense of *absque* (2 Sam. i. 22, Job xi. 15, xix. 26, xxi. 9, Isa. xxii. 3), and with respect to the dilogy (*de* and then *absque*) xl. 13, 19 sq. may be compared. The words: far from the dew of heaven above (מֵעַל elsewhere a prep., here an adv. as at xlix. 25, Ps. l. 4), have their natural truth in the many ravines and depressions of the Idumæan mountains, which are inaccessible to the fertilizing dew. Edom is truly "a dweller in the clefts of the rock," Obad. ver. 3 (Jer. xlix. 16). Thus the land of Esau will be, as Isaac predicts, a sharp contrast to the land of Jacob. For this very reason the peaceful pursuit of agriculture will not be his source of maintenance, but upon his sword (עַל) of the means of support as at Deut. viii. 3, comp. Isa. xxxviii. 16) will he live. Here first does the statement concerning Esau take a favourable turn. כַּאֲשֶׁר compares, like Num. xxvii. 14, the cause and result. The *Hiph.* תָּרִיד (from רוּד כּ,ا) means wandering hither and thither, roaming about, hence: leading an unrestrained, roving, freebooter kind of life. Dillm., according to the Arabico-Ethiopic but (comp. Nöldeke, *DMZ.* xxxviii. 539 sq.) contrary to the Hebrew use of language, renders: when thou shalt strive, exert thyself.[1] The fundamental meaning of the verb פָּרַק is to break, *frangere,* which here has the special meaning to break off, as elsewhere to break loose = to free oneself and to break to pieces = to

[1] The Ethiopic text of the Book of Jubilees vacillates, as Dillmann has shown in his contributions from the Book of Jubilees to the criticism of the text of the Pentateuch (delivered in the Royal Prussian Academy of the West, March 1, 1883), between the Masoretic reading תריד and the Samar. תאדר *si magnus factus fueris.*

crush. It is not freedom from the rule of Israel that is promised to Edom, but restless and not unsuccessful struggles for freedom. Edom became indeed a θορυβῶδες καὶ ἄτακτον ἔθνος ἀεί τε μετέωρον πρὸς τὰ κινήματα καὶ μεταβολαῖς χαῖρον (Joseph. *Bell.* 4. 4. 1), and his relation to Israel was a ceaseless interchange of subjection, rebellion and resubjection. An afterpiece of this change was still shown in the time of the Roman Empire: it continued an ineffaceable obscuration of the blessing of Jacob, that it was an Idumæan dynasty and the admission of the Edomites into Jerusalem when threatened by the Romans, which was the downfall of the Jewish State.

Thus were strictly fulfilled the blessings of Isaac upon Jacob and Esau which he spoke πίστει περὶ μελλόντων, Heb. xi. 20. Modern criticism indeed carps at this, and says the author who wrote xxvii. 40 knew, according to its judgment, not only of David's conquest of the Edomites, but also of their revolt against Solomon and their subjection by Jehoram of Judah. For such criticism denies the truth and reality of prediction, and the entire patriarchal history is according to its notions national history in the form of legendary family history. Our standpoint is fundamentally different; we believe in the power of a believing, prayerful blessing, when the energy of an intellect, which has sunk itself in God's word of promise and counsel of grace, and of a will whose strength is derived from the fulness of God, are therein comprised. There is in Isaac's blessing an efficacy which is far-reaching, a magic which fashions the future, God and his ego are therein one (comp. ver. 37 with Jer. i. 10 and other passages). Isaac himself knows this (see ver. 37), and Rebekah together with Jacob knew it. Both therefore think that they must at the decisive moment take care that God's promise shall not fall to the ground. But God has no need of creature help to make His faithfulness stand. Hence, though Jacob continues to be the possessor of the blessing as, in accordance with the counsel and promise of God, he was to be (Rom. ix. 10–13), yet the Divine judgment falls upon him and upon every member of his family in proportion as they have been sharers in his transgression. Isaac is punished for his preference for Esau, a preference determined not according to the ascertained will of God, but according to natural affection, by the deception which he undergoes. Esau is punished for profanely despising the blessing of the firstborn by its loss. Rebekah is punished for her contrivance of the fraud by separation from her favourite son, whom she never saw again, while the life of Jacob was, from the time when he confirmed himself in the possession of the sinfully purchased birthright by sinfully and surreptitiously acquiring the blessing, one long chain of hardships, disappointments, strifes and anxieties, which made him fully feel how he had sinned against his brother and father. The Fathers down to the Middle Ages see in the part Jacob played in ch. xxvii. an acting according to Divine impulse, and, after mystically importing into ch. xxvii., as already into xxv. 23, all manner of typical references to New Testament matter, pass sentence on Jacob's fraud in accordance with the precedent of Augustine: *non est mendacium sed mysterium.* It was Duns Scotus († 1308), the *Doctor subtilis,* and after him Nicolaus de Lyra, the *Doctor planus,* who first recognised its moral reprehensibleness, but still without a right perception of the Divine side of the occurrence.[1] The scriptural account itself abstains from all comment—but the history of aftertimes passes the severest criticism upon Jacob's conduct. The government of God which can make even sin subserve its purposes, soars so high above this tangled web that, without infringing human freedom, nothing comes to pass but what He has foreseen and predetermined.

[1] See Petrus Hötzl, *Jakob und Esau, Typik und Kasuistik,* 1881, an instructive monograph, which gives the history of opinion on this occurrence and intelligently seeks to find the right medium between the patristic *non est mendacium sed mysterium* and the rationalistic *non est mysterium sed mendacium.*

JACOB'S FLIGHT TO HARAN, CH. XXVII. 41-XXVIII. 9.

The fourth portion, xxvii. 41 to xxviii. 9, relates the flight or dismissal of Jacob to Haran. Esau is meditating assassination, ver. 41: *And Esau laid snares against Jacob, because of the blessing wherewith his father had blessed him, and Esau said in his heart: The days of mourning for my father are near, then will I slay my brother Jacob.* Luther (like Bedarschi in his *Synonymik*) takes אבי as the gen. of the subject: *that my father must bear sorrow* (viz. on account of Jacob when he, Esau, shall have avenged himself on him), but the gen. following upon אֲבֶל (אָבַל) always designates the object. The prudent mother proposes to her favourite to escape the vengeance of his brother by fleeing to his uncle in Haran, vv. 42-45: *And the words of Esau, her elder son, were told to Rebekah, then she sent and called her younger son Jacob and said to him: Behold, Esau thy brother will comfort himself on thee to kill thee. And now, my son, hearken to my voice and arise, flee to Laban my brother to Haran, and tarry with him some time, until thy brother's fury turn away from thee, until thy brother's wrath turn away and he forget what thou hast done to him, then will I send and fetch thee thence—why should I be deprived of you both in one day?* The *Hithpa.* הִתְנַחֵם means here (as a weaker power of הִתְנַקֵּם parallel to the *Niph.* נָחַם Isa. i. 24) to procure oneself comfort, rest, satisfaction; the participial construction declares that Esau is purposing this. Rebekah mitigatingly says ἡμέρας τίνας (LXX. comp. xxix. 20) for the purpose of thus gaining him over to her plan. On שָׁכֹל with the accusative see Ges. § 183. 3. Both would be lost at the same time, Jacob by means of Esau, Esau in accordance with ix. 6 by the execution of the penalty against the murderer, or even that as a murderer he would not at all events be able again to enter the presence of his parents. The varying expression in 44*b*, 45*a* (comp. xxxi. 18) points to extracts from different sources. But that Jacob may not depart unaccompanied by his father's blessing, Rebekah expresses to the latter her vexation at her Hittite daughters-in-law (xxvi. 34, Q), and urges him to send Jacob away, to seek a wife in another country, ver. 46: *And Rebekah said to Isaac: I am weary of my life, because of the daughters of Heth; if Jacob take a wife of the daughters of Heth, like these of the daughters of the land, of what use is my life?* The text is compounded from Q (of whom בְּנוֹת חֵת and בְּנוֹת חֵת are characteristic) and J (comp. xxv. 22). There were certainly good grounds for Rebekah's displeasure at Hittite daughters-in-law, and hence her wish in respect of Jacob was justified. It was therefore from no lack of independence that Isaac felt the same desire, though it showed his natural weakness that he did not in this respect act of his own accord, but on the instigation of his wife, who, with her excessive sensitiveness, understands the art of turning her husband which way she chooses. Isaac calls Jacob and sends him with his blessing to Aramæa, to marry there, xxviii. 1–5: *Then Isaac called Jacob and blessed him, and commanded him and said to him: Thou shalt not take a wife of the daughters of Canaan. Arise, go to Paddan Aram, to the house of Bethuel, thy mother's father, and take thee from thence a wife of the daughters of Laban, thy mother's brother. And God Almighty will bless thee and make thee fruitful and multiply thee, and thou shalt become a company of nations. And He will give thee the blessing of Abraham, to thee and to thy seed with thee, to possess the land of thy sojournings, which God gave to Abraham. Thus Isaac sent Jacob away, and he went to Paddan Aram to Laban, the son of Bethuel the Aramæan, the brother of Rebekah, the mother of Esau and Jacob.* Characteristic tokens of the style of Q are here plentiful: בְּנוֹת כְּנַעַן (like xxxvi. 2, for which J has בְּנוֹת הַכְּנַעֲנִי xxiv. 3, 37), פַּדַּן אֲרָם (see the introduction to the history of Isaac), אֵל שַׁדַּי with אֱלֹהִים, אֶרֶץ מְגֻרִים (xvii. 8) and קְהַל עַמִּים certainly not to be restricted to the tribes of Israel (xxxv. 11, xlviii. 4). The *Segol* of פַּדֶּנָה אֲרָם follows a well-known euphonic law, because the original form פַּדְּנָה and the orthophonic *Gaja* in the

GENESIS XXVIII. 6–9.   161

final syllable ah are intended to prevent this from being lost owing to the אָ following, comp. גְּבִיעַ הַכֶּסֶף xliv. 2, תִּשְׁעִי־עֶשְׂרֵה xi. 25. לְרִשְׁתָּהּ 4b has a subjective suffix as at xix. 21. Bethuel is particularly designated as the father and Laban as the brother of Rebekah, and herself as the mother of Jacob and Esau, to facilitate the survey of the impending extension of family relationship, and at ver. 5 the fact that Jacob willingly obeyed the paternal behest is, according to the present arrangement of the historical matter, summarily anticipated, as at xxvii. 23 the fact that Isaac blessed him. Hosea is referring to what is related xxvii. 43, xxviii. 5, when he says, xii. 13: וַיִּבְרַח יַעֲקֹב שְׂדֵה אֲרָם. Esau now takes example and tries on his part to do what is agreeable to his parents, vv. 6–9: *When Esau saw that Isaac had blessed Jacob and sent him away to Paddan Aram, to take him a wife from thence, and that while blessing him he gave him a charge, saying: Thou shalt not take a wife of the daughters of Canaan, and that Jacob had hearkened to the voice of his father and mother and had gone to Paddan Aram; then Esau saw that the daughters of Canaan were displeasing to his father Isaac, and Esau went to Ishmael and took unto his wives Mahalath, the daughter of Ishmael, the son of Abraham, the sister of Nebajoth, to be his wife.* Esau shows himself good-natured, but with limited perception and through jealousy of Jacob, hence not from pure motives. When it is said that he went אֶל־יִשְׁמָעֵאל, Ishmael himself (like Ephraim himself at 1 Chron. vii. 22) seems intended, and this is possible, if with Dillmann we infer from xxvi. 34 sq., xxvii. 46, that Jacob migrated to Aramæa between his fortieth and fiftieth years, for Ishmael was, according to xxv. 17, 137 years old, and Jacob's forty-fifth year coincides with Ishmael's 119th year (comp. xvii. 24 sq., xxi. 5, xxv. 26). But if, in a lawfully harmonistic manner, we take xlvii. 9, xli. 46, xlv. 6, xxx. 22–26, xxix. 27 into the reckoning, Jacob was seventy-seven at his migration into Syria (Köhler, *Gesch.* i. 135), and this leads us beyond the limits of Ishmael's life, so that יִשְׁמָעֵאל

VOL. II.   L here, like e.g. כלב Josh. xiv. 14, can only be meant of the family of Ishmael. Esau's third wife was called Mahalath (for which we have, xxxvi. 2, Bāsmath). She is said to be the sister of the first-born of her brothers, who is named instead of all the rest, xxv. 13, as Miriam is always called the sister of Aaron.

JACOB'S DREAM ON THE ROAD TO MESOPOTAMIA, CH. XXVIII. 10—22.

Jacob's journey, which he had already begun xxviii. 5, is now more particularly described with a retrospective glance at its commencement. There its goal was called פדנה ארם, here חָרָנָה. Mosaic stones from J and E are added to the narrative of Q. Jacob becomes from henceforth the motive-principle of the history of Isaac, the second section of which begins at xxviii. 10. The portion xxviii. 10 sqq. relates the divine manifestation, which Jacob experienced on the soil of Luz, afterwards Bethel, after some few days' journey, and by which the blessing bestowed was solemnly confirmed to him by God Himself. We have here the first dream revelation in the life of the patriarchs (not reckoning the dream of Abimelech, ch. xx., nor that of Laban afterwards). Henceforward this mode of revelation becomes more frequent. Such experiences were however no everyday matter in their lives. Jacob was now far past forty years old, and the whole history of his life has only five Divine revelations to show, two בַּחֲלוֹם xxviii. 12 and xlvi. 2, two with וַיֹּאמֶר xxxi. 3, xxxv. 1, one with וַיֵּרָא xxxv. 9. It is E who delights in narrating Divine manifestations in the night. Those portions in xxviii. 10 sqq., in which God is called אלהים, belong with their contexts to him; hence ver. 12, with 11, vv. 17—22 are his, while on the contrary vv. 13—16 show themselves to be J's by the Divine name יהוה, the promise of the blessing of the nations in the seed of the patriarch and other particulars. Both narrators give accounts of a Divine manifestation by night at Luz-

Bethel (so that both must have furnished what is said at
ver. 19): *E* giving prominence to the dream, *J* (whom in
opposition to Dillm. Kuen. and others we recognise also
at xxii. 14–18) to the words of God; *R* has combined
these two accounts as supplementing each other. Starting-
point and goal of Jacob's journey, ver. 10: *And Jacob
departed from Beersheba and went to Haran.* A counterpart
to xxviii. 5. Beersheba had been since xxvi. 23 his father's
place of abode. This verse joins on to xxvii. 44, and is
there followed by completions from *Q*. Now begins the text
from *E*, vv. 11, 12: *Then he lighted upon a place and passed the
night there, for the sun was set, and he took one of the stones of
the place, made it his pillow, and lay down to sleep in that place.
Then he dreamed, and behold, a ladder was set up upon the earth
and its top reached to heaven, and behold angels of Elohim
ascending and descending upon it.* He lighted upon a certain
place (בַּמָּקוֹם, comp. *certi homines, i.e.* certain in the abstract but
not to be more particularly designated), probably a hill-top
inviting for its pleasantness and safety, and then prepared his
night's quarters by making one (ver. 18) of the stones of
the place his pillow. מְרַאֲשֹׁתָיו for מְרַאֲשֹׁתָיו (comp. מְהַלְעוֹת for
מַלְתְּעוֹת) is the usual extensive plural for parts of body and
space, the principal form to be accepted for which is מְרַאֲשָׁה,
מְרַאֲשָׁה (comp. מְרַאֲשֹׁתֵיכֶם Jer. xiii. 18, from מְרַאֲשָׁה, Böttch. § 695).
There upon his hard pillow sleeps Jacob, banished from his
home, about to encounter an uncertain future, purposely fleeing
from the company of mankind in a foreign land, solitary and
without a roof over his head. He is there comforted by a
divinely-effected dream. The הִנֵּה (three including 13*a*) are
finger-posts of childlike astonishment at the glorious appearance which the participles describe, as from a post of
observation. The ladder is an image of the invisible, but
actual and unceasing connection in which God, by the ministry
of His angels, stands with the earth, in this instance with
Jacob, who is now where the ladder has its earthly standing

place; in his behalf are the angels of God "ascending and descending upon it" (the same expression as Prov. xxx. 4, John i. 52), to fetch and receive commands, to bring them down and execute them. Before the happy dreamer can inquire of one of the angels, he hears the word of Jahveh, and thereupon awakes, vv. 13–16: *And behold Jahveh stood beside him and said: I am Jahveh, the God of Abraham thy father and the God of Isaac; the land whereon thou liest, to thee will I give it and to thy seed. And thy seed shall be as the dust of the earth, and thou shalt spread to west and east and north and south, and all the families of the earth shall be blessed in thee. And behold, I am with thee and will keep thee whithersoever thou goest, and will bring thee back to this land, for I will not leave thee, till I have performed what I have told thee. Then Jacob awoke from his sleep and said: Surely Jahveh is present in this place and I knew it not.* In the present connection it seems as if עָלָיו 13a must be referred to the ladder (LXX. Targums, Jerome): there, where the ladder reached to heaven, God Himself was present to the dreamer; but נִצָּב עַל means everywhere in *J* standing beside, xviii. 2, xlv. 1, and this is also its meaning Amos ix. 1. Jahveh there stood at his side (Rashi: לְשִׁמְרוֹ), and His word is added to the silent image. The God, whom angels and all powers serve, will fulfil to Jacob the great promises, xii. 3b, xiii. 14–17, and not take from him His special protection until He has first (עַד אֲשֶׁר אִם without obliteration of the conditional meaning of אִם as at Num. xxxii. 17, Isa. vi. 11, comp. עַד אִם xxiv. 19, Ruth ii. 21, and see on xxxviii. 9) fulfilled what He has promised to him. When Jacob awakes from sleep he says: Truly (אָכֵן only again in the Pent. Ex. ii. 14) Jahveh is in this place; contrary to expectation, he has learned that this too, far from the holy places of his family, is a place of Jahveh's gracious presence, that He has gone with him into this strange land, that he may not be, like Ishmael, a broken-off branch. Now follows the exclamation of Jacob on what he beheld, from

E, ver. 17: *And he was afraid and said: How awful is this place! this is none other than a house of God, and this is the gate of heaven.* He has here had a glimpse of the government of God and of the supersensuous world (Wisd. x. 10); it is as though this were the abode of God and of His good spirits, as though this were the gate of heaven, by which they enter and depart. It is now related what Jacob did the next morning, ver. 18: *And Jacob rose up early in the morning, and took the stone which he had made his pillow, and set it up for a memorial pillar, and poured oil upon it.* He consecrates the stone as a memorial, as the foundation of a sanctuary; for the pure, golden, gently penetrating oil is a symbol of consecration. This setting up and consecration of memorial stones (comp. xxxi. 45, Ex. xxiv. 4, 1 Sam. vii. 11) recalls the heathen worship of anointed stones and baetylia (λίθοι λιπαροί, ἀληλιμμένοι, *lapides uncti, lubricati, unguine delibuti*) which had spread from India throughout the whole East as far as Greece and Rome, where Cybele was worshipped in the black stone from Pessinus; this heathen custom is the idolatrous form of the patriarchal custom which exists to this very day (August. *Civ.* xvi. 39).[1] The baetylia were especially meteoric stones, which were traced to this or that god, and held to be pervaded by deity, at least those which chiefly received the names βαίτυλοι, βαιτύλια, *betyli* were such (*Photii Bibl.* i. p. 348, ed. Bekker; *Plinii h. n.* xxxvii. 9, comp. Orelli on *Sanchun.* p. 30 sq.), a name which may have been occasioned by the fetish-like degenerate veneration of the memorial stone at Bethel (comp. the fate of Gideon's ephod, Judg. viii. 27). Dietrich however (in Grimmel's article, *de lapidum cultu apud Patriarchas quæsito*, Marburg 1853) refers it, in the meaning of amulet, to the verb בָּטֵל to make ineffectual. In Carthage they were called, according to Pausanias, x. 24, and Priscian,

[1] Dr. Alex. Robb (now of Jamaica) told me of such a stone in *U-wét* on the Old Calabar river in Western Africa, worshipped by the negro tribe there as fallen from heaven and bestowed upon their ancestors by the God of heaven (whom they called *A-bá-si*), to be their tutelary deity.

v. 3, 18, *abbadires* = אָבֶן אַדִּיר. The Thorah forbids, because of their heathen abuse, any erection of מַצֵּבוֹת Lev. xxvi. 1, Deut. xvi. 22, and commands the overthrow of such as exist, Ex. xxiii. 24, xxxiv. 13, Deut. xii. 3. The prophets rebuke the degeneration of the custom (Hos. x. 1 sq. comp. iii. 4), without finding it reprehensible in itself (Isa. xix. 19). Change of name of this patriarchal place of revelation, ver. 19: *And he called the name of that place Bethel, on the contrary Lûz was its name formerly*. Jacob called the place where he had set up the מצבה, בֵּיתְאֵל (written in the MSS. sometimes as one word, sometimes as two); whereas the town was called לֹח formerly (וְאוּלָם) elsewhere xlviii. 19, Ex. ix. 6, Num. xiv. 21 in a rhetorical, here in a historical connection, originally a noun, Assyr. *élamu*, in which the meaning: before, opposite, shows the radical meaning, comp. נֶגֶד). This is not however to be so understood, as though the ancient Luz and the more recent Bethel were absolutely the same, but so that the ancient Luz (xlviii. 3) gradually retreated and disappeared before Bethel, which lay near it, Josh. xvi. 2. The appellation בֵיתאֵל xii. 8, xiii. 3 is anticipative. The ruins still bear the name of *Beitîn*. It lies forty-five minutes from el-Bireh (Beëroth) and three hours by horse from Jerusalem, on the declivity of a hill between two valleys, which still, as in the days of Abraham, affords the most excellent pasturage, but belongs to the holy places which have fallen into oblivion. Jacob's vow, vv. 20–22: *And Jacob made a vow and said: If Elohim will be with me and keep me upon this way that I go, and give me bread to eat and clothing to put on, and I come back in safety to my father's house, then shall Jahveh be my God, and this stone which I have set up as a memorial pillar shall be a house of Elohim, and of all which thou shalt give me I will give a tithe to thee*. The apodosis begins at 21*b*: then will he have Jahveh, and him alone, for his God, without turning to other gods. This fundamental oath sounds like an echo of the promise xvii. 8, comp. Ex. vi. 7 and frequently. The words of God flow forth 22*b* in an address to God. We here meet for the second time since xiv. 20 in the primitive history with the custom of giving a tithe to God ; it is common to almost all antiquity, the legislation Lev. xxvii. 30–33 and farther on does but regulate what already existed. How ver. 22 was fulfilled, we partly learn in ch. xxxv. Bethel became already in patriarchal times a place of sacrifice, and in the times of the Judges the sanctuary, Judg. xx. 18, 1 Sam. x. 3, with the ark of the covenant, Judg. xx. 18, stood here for a long period upon Mount Ephraim. The Divine name אלהים in vv. 12, 17 is of itself no certain token of a source: the matter there in question is indeed a glance into the world of spirits, and also the origin of the local name ביתאל. But the case is different with אלהים 20*b* and with והיה יהוה לי לאלהים 21*b*. In the report of the vow *J* seems to be blended with *E*, or it may have been taken as it stands from *JE*. Jacob will on his return to his home be determined by his experience of Divine assistance to choose Jahveh for his God for ever, to make the stone which he has set up the foundation-stone of a house of God, and to tithe, *i.e.* to apply to the purpose of Divine worship, every blessing bestowed on him.

JACOB'S TWO MARRIAGES IN HARAN, CH. XXIX. 1–30.

The second portion, xxix. 1–30, which continues Jacob's experiences in a strange country and first his involuntary double marriage in Haran, is compounded, like ch. xxvii., from *J* and *E* worked into each other. In the first half *J*, in the second *E* predominates, in ver. 15 the transition is made from *J* to *E* (Dillm.). But no Divine name occurs, and striking characteristics are lacking. In the second half שפחה is found, where according to the usual diction of *E* we should expect אמה, and the distinction of age by בכירה and צעירה is elsewhere only found in *J* (xix. 30–38).

Ver. 1 is peculiar: *And Jacob lifted up his feet and went to the land of the sons of the East.* Encouraged by what he had heard and seen in his night dream, he continues his journey refreshed and cheered אַרְצָה בְנֵי־קֶדֶם, *i.e.* to *Arabia deserta*, which reached as far as Euphrates including Mesopotamia lying beyond that river. In *J* xxviii. 10 his destination was called חָרָנָה, in *Q* xxviii. 2 פַּדֶּנָה אֲרָם, here we have the third and most general designation, as Dillmann conjectures from *E*, but according to xxv. 6 more probably from *J*, to whom what follows, at least as far as ver. 15, belongs. The meeting with Rachel, vv. 2-12: *And he looked and behold a well was in the field, and, lo, three flocks of sheep lying beside it, for out of that well they used to water the flocks, and the stone at the mouth of the well was great. And thither were all the flocks gathered, and they rolled the stone from the mouth of the well and watered the flocks, and brought the stone again to the mouth of the well, to its place. Then said Jacob to them: My brethren, whence are ye? And they said: Of Haran are we. And he said to them: Know ye Laban, Nahor's son? And they said: We know him. Then he said to them: Is it well with him? And they said: It is well, and behold, Rachel his daughter is coming even now with the sheep. And he said: It is indeed still high in the day, nor is it yet time to drive in the cattle; water the sheep and go hence and feed them! And they said: We cannot, till all the flocks are gathered together, then they roll away the stone from the mouth of the well and water the sheep. While he was yet speaking with them, Rachel came with the sheep, which belonged to her father, for she was a shepherdess. And it came to pass, when Jacob saw Rachel, the daughter of Laban his mother's brother, and the sheep of Laban his mother's brother, that Jacob went near and rolled away the stone from the mouth of the well and watered the sheep of Laban his mother's brother. And Jacob kissed Rachel and lifted up his voice and wept. And Jacob told Rachel that he was her father's relative, and that he was Rebekah's son*—*and she ran and told her father.* The imperf. יַשְׁקוּ 2*a* is, like ii. 6, meant of custom in the past, and continues here as there in the perfect, Ges. § 127. 4*b*, Driver § 113. 4*β*.

גְּדוֹלָה is the predicate and עַל־פִּי הַבְּאֵר a completion of the subject, comp. Job xxxvii. 22b, Micah vi. 12b; for it is the greatness, not the position that is emphasized. Laban is called by Jacob 5a בֶּן־נָחוֹר. Bethuel, of whom Laban was directly the son, is strikingly kept in the background in the history of Isaac's marriage also, ch. xxiv. Jacob inquires concerning the welfare of Laban: הֲשָׁלוֹם לוֹ (comp. xliii. 27 sq.); they are able to give him the information desired, and point to Rachel, who was just approaching with her flock (בָּאָה participle); and when he invites them, the day being yet great, *i.e.* still far from passing into the evening, when the cattle have to be put in the stall, to water the flock, they excuse themselves by saying that the rolling away of the stone requires the united strength of all the shepherds. While he is thus talking with them Rachel arrives (בָּאָה preterite like xxvii. 30), bringing the flock which is her father's (אֲשֶׁר לְ like xl. 5), that it may be watered with the other flocks; and Jacob then rolls away alone the great stone from the mouth of the well. Such gigantic strength was given him by the affection of blood relationship (as is prominently shown by the threefold אֲחִי אִמּוֹ), and at the same time by a presentiment of love, for his father's words xxviii. 2 were ever ringing in his ears. Hence various feelings were combined in the kiss and in the tears that followed, ver. 11. Laban also now hastens to the scene and gladly welcomes his nephew, vv. 13, 14: *And it came to pass when Laban heard the tidings of Jacob, his sister's son, that he ran to meet him and embraced him and kissed him and brought him into his house, and he told Laban all these things. Then Laban said to him: Surely thou art my flesh and bone, and he abode with him a month of days.* The genitive after שֵׁמַע (*e.g.* Isa. xxiii. 5) and שְׁמוּעָה (*e.g.* 2 Sam. iv. 4) is (except perhaps Isa. liii. 1) always objective. Laban, when he hears the news of Jacob's arrival, runs to meet his brother, *i.e.* nephew (אָח like ver. 12), spreads out his hands to embrace him (חִבֵּק לְ as at xlviii. 10), overwhelms him with kisses (as is meant by לְנַשֵּׁק as distinguished from לִשֹּׁק ver. 11), and brings him, as being indeed his flesh and bone (as at ii. 23), into his house, where Jacob relates to him "all these things," *i.e.* his arrival at his journey's end and the providential meeting at the well. It is affection which makes Laban so speedy and so kindly, but also, no less than at xxiv. 29, a selfish and calculating eye to the future. He knows however how to hide his intentions under the appearance of the greatest unselfishness. So Jacob remains חֹדֶשׁ יָמִים (xli. 1, Num. xi. 20 sq. and frequently) a month of days, *i.e.* a full month, during which Laban perceives of what service Jacob, the experienced shepherd, can be to him. His compact with Jacob, who serves him seven years for Rachel, vv. 15–20: *Then said Laban to Jacob: Is it because thou art my kinsman that thou shouldest serve me for nought? Tell me, what shall be thy wages? And Laban had two daughters, the name of the elder was Léah and the name of the younger Raḥel. And the eyes of Leah were weak, but Rachel was beautiful of form and fair to look on. And Jacob loved Rachel and said: I will serve thee seven years for Rachel thy younger daughter. Then said Laban: It is better that I should give her to thee, than that I should give her to another man; abide with me. Then Jacob served seven years for Rachel, and they were in his eyes as a few days, because of his love for her.* The sentence beginning with הֲכִי (as at xxvii. 36) as inwardly organized runs thus: Should I, because thou art my kinsman, require from thee gratuitous service? Laban had two daughters (two, and not one only, as we here learn for the first time), of whom the younger Rachel (רָחֵל, رَخِل, ewe lamb) was beautiful in face and figure; the elder, Leah (לֵאָה, علٰى wild cow, a kind of antelope[1]), had on the contrary weak eyes (LXX. rightly: ἀσθενεῖς, Vulgate wrongly: *lippis oculis*), hence she lacked an important feature of female beauty. Jacob offers to

[1] See *Job*, 2nd edit. p. 507, comp. Zimmern, *Babyl. Busspsalmen*, p. 20.

serve seven years for Rachel; Laban plays the agreeable and accepts the offer. The hand of a cousin is to this very day among the Arabs due to her cousin in preference to any other wooer, and husband and wife generally address each other, *já bint 'ammî* and *jû ibn 'ammî, i.e.* oh my female cousin, my male cousin. The seven years passed by to Jacob like a few days, "the other days lighted by hope disappeared as one day," as Camoens paraphrases it in his 29th Sonnet. One might have thought that they would rather have appeared long to him. Both are true: *amor paucos dies æstimat plurimos affective, non autem appreciative* (Calov.). Laban's deception and excuse, and Jacob's second seven years' service, vv. 21-30: *Then Jacob said to Laban: Give me my wife, for my time is fulfilled, that I may go in unto her. And Laban assembled all the people of the place and gave a feast. And it came to pass in the evening, that he took Leah his daughter and brought her to him, and he went in unto her. And Laban gave Zilpah, his handmaid, to his daughter Leah for her handmaid. And it came to pass in the morning, behold it was Leah, and he said to Laban: What hast thou done to me? Did not I serve with thee for Rachel? And why hast thou deceived me? Then Laban said: It is not the custom so to do in our place, to give the younger before the first-born. Stay out the week of this one, and we will give thee this also for a service which thou shalt serve with me seven other years. And Jacob did so and fulfilled his week, then he gave him his daughter Rachel to wife. And Laban gave to his daughter Rachel, Bilhah, his handmaid, to be her handmaid. And he went in also unto Rachel, and he loved Rachel more than Leah, and he served with him seven more years.* When the seven years were over, Jacob demands his wife (הָבָה before a following א with the tone upon the *ult.*), for such she is already in virtue of the marriage contract, and when the marriage feast (מִשְׁתֶּה), *i.e.* the first and special day of the marriage festivities, is over, he experiences, while intoxicated and blinded by love, a deception similar to that which he had played upon his father. Instead of Rachel, Leah (veiled, comp. xxiv. 65) is brought to him. Laban gives her Zilpah for her handmaid, which particular, as well as his giving Bilhah to Rachel, ver. 29, added in a manner which interrupts the connection, seems inserted from Q. When he reproaches Laban with this fraud, which was no less shameful an injustice to Rachel than to himself, Laban excuses himself by appealing to a custom of the country (לֹא־יֵעָשֶׂה comp. xxxiv. 7) not to marry the younger daughter before the elder—a custom stubbornly adhered to also in India and in the old imperial towns of Germany. He offers however to give him Rachel also after the lapse of the seven days' (שְׁבֻעַ זֹאת) marriage festivities, viz. Leah's (Judg. xiv. 12, Tobit xi. 18, the duration down to the present time of a marriage among the Syro-Palestinian peasants, the Nestorians, etc.), if he will promise to serve him seven years more. It was the custom only to give a daughter in marriage for a price (מֹהַר), but Laban bargains with his daughters like wares, without any regard to relationship, and it is of this that they complain, xxxi. 15. Jacob agrees and receives Rachel also. Both daughters have only one handmaid each, Rebekah had more, xxiv. 61, but Laban was avaricious. Jacob has now two wives instead of one, one more, one less beloved. Of the two גם ver. 30 the second in conjunction with מן means *adeo magis quam*, but no other example for this use of גם with מן can be adduced, LXX. Jerome leave it unexpressed, Dillm. expunges it. Thus is Jacob the deceiver deceived by Laban. And this same Jacob, who, as Hosea says xii. 13, served for a wife and for a wife (בְּאִשָּׁה with ב of the reward as at ver. 18), kept sheep, became the ancestor of the nation which, as Hosea goes on to say, was led by a prophet out of Egypt and by a prophet was preserved. It is to this double, and, according to the subsequent law (Lev. xviii. 18), detestable double marriage, that the people of the law owed their origin. The Thorah relates it without concealment and without palliation.

BIRTH OF THE ELEVEN SONS OF JACOB, CH. XXIX. 31–XXX. 24.

The third portion, xxix. 31–xxx. 24, leads us straight to the origins of Israel, and transports us, so to speak, into the midst of Israel's natal hours. The birth of these ancestors of Israel was found in both *J* and *E*, related in the respective manner of each; the narrative as we now have it is a combination of these two sources. They may be distinguished by the change of the Divine names both in the mouth of the women, *e.g.* xxix. 32, xxx. 6, and of the narrator himself, *e.g.* xxix. 31, xxx. 17. Here and there two explanations of a name stand side by side, xxx. 20, and we see from the change of the Divine names, that one is taken from *J* and the other from *E*, xxx. 23, 24. The statements concerning the handmaids, xxx. 4*a*, 9*b*, join on to xxix. 24, 29, and look like woof-threads from *Q*. Rachel is the more youthful and blooming of the two sisters, and the best beloved of Jacob; but Rachel remains childless, whereas Leah, the less beloved (ver. 30) and comparatively hated (שְׂנוּאָה as at Deut. xxi. 15), is blessed with children. פָּתַח רֶחֶם LXX. ἀνοίγειν τὴν μήτραν is the opposite of סְגֹר רֶחֶם 1 Sam. i. 5, Job iii. 10. Jacob's first son Reuben, by Leah, ver. 32: *Leah conceived and bare a son and called his name Reûben, for she said: Surely Jahveh hath beheld my affliction, for now will my husband love me.* The name means: See, a son! It is an exclamation of joyful surprise. כִּי is, as at xxvi. 22, explicative, confirmative, assertive. רָאָה בְ means to behold with heartfelt interest, as at 1 Sam. i. 11, Ps. cvi. 44, comp. above xxi. 16. The impf. יֶאֱהָבַנִי has the connecting vowel *a* as at xix. 19. Jacob's second son Simeon, by Leah, ver. 33: *And she conceived again and bare a son, and said: Surely Jahveh has heard that I am hated and hath given me this also, therefore she called him 'Sim'ôn.* The transition from the explicative to the assertive, from the confirmative to the affirmative meaning of כי is here evident, the name means: hearing. Jacob's third son Levi, by

Leah, ver. 34 : *And she again conceived and bare a son, and said: Now this time will my husband be attached to me, for I have borne him three sons, therefore she called his name Levi.* For קָרָא (they called, like xi. 9, xix. 22, xxv. 30) LXX. Samar. Syriac reproduce the expected קָרְאָה. The name means the attached, from an assumed לָוָה annexation *societas* formed according to the formation גֵּו. Jacob's fourth son Judah by Leah, ver. 35 : *And she conceived again and bare a son, and said: This time I praise Jahveh.* Instead of עַתָּה 32b and הַפַּעַם 34a (like עַתָּה חַן 1 Kings xvii. 24), we have here, as also in *J* ii. 24, הַפַּעַם. The name יְהוּדָה is formed after the analogy of the passive to יְהוּדָה Neh. xi. 17 (comp. the forms Ps. xxviii. 7, xlv. 18), and means (since ה ֶ as a masculine termination arising from ה ָ cannot be proved) the being praised (Joseph. εὐχαριστία, Jerome *confessio*), hence as a proper name one who is the subject of praise. After these four births a pause takes place with Leah. Rachel is vexed to death that she has no children—the modest desire of husband and wife for the blessing of children is a characteristic of virtuous marriage. Her grief was just, but it made her unjust towards her husband, xxx. 1, 2 : *When Rachel saw that she bare Jacob no children, Rachel was envious of her sister and said to Jacob: Give me children, or I die. Then was Jacob wroth with Rachel and said: Am I instead of Elohim, who has denied thee the fruit of the womb?* It is a childish demand which she makes of her husband (comp. with this הָבָה the הַב הַב with reference to עֲלוּקָה רַחַם Prov. xxx. 15 sq.), to which he cannot but answer indignantly: Am I in the place of God? (to be explained as l. 19 must, according to 2 Kings v. 7). Jacob's fifth son Dan by Bilhah, Rachel's handmaid, vv. 3-6 : *And she said: Behold my handmaid Bilhah, go in unto her, that she may bear children upon my knees, and I also may obtain children by her. And she gave to him Bilhah her handmaid to wife, and Jacob went in unto her. And Bilhah conceived and bare Jacob a son. Then Rachel said: Elohim has done me justice and also hearkened to my voice and hath given me a son, therefore she called his name Dan.* The Divine name אלהים leads to *E*, and so also does אָמָה which is characteristic of this writer. It is here however interchanged with שִׁפְחָה, perhaps through the regard of *R* to the text of other sources. The person upon whose knees a new-born babe is laid (1. 23, comp. Job iii. 12) owns it as his own child. On בָּנָה to be built up (not a denominative: to become possessed of children) see xvi. 2. The name דָּן corresponds to the Latin *vindex*, defender, advocate. She calls him thus, because Elohim has taken her under His protection, has heard her prayer and taken from her the undeserved reproach of childlessness. Jacob's sixth son Naphtali, the second by Bilhah, Rachel's handmaid, vv. 7, 8 : *And Bilhah, Rachel's maid, again conceived and bare Jacob a second son. Then Rachel said : Wrestlings of Elohim have I wrestled with my sister and have also prevailed ; so she called his name Naphtali.* The name signifies that which has been the object of the struggle, that which has been obtained by wrestling. The נַפְתּוּלֵי אֱלֹהִים are the prayerful wrestlings of tempted faith. A wrestling with Leah, but in truth with God Himself, who seemed to have bestowed His favour upon her only, or perhaps more generally: struggles such as only a higher Being is able to sustain, superhuman struggles, אלהים being thus not *gen. objecti* but *subjecti*. Hengstenberg and Drechsler define the notion yet differently : struggles whose issue bears the character of a sentence of God ; the idea of a Divine sentence of the *concursus specialissimi* prevailing from xxx. 1–23 being also the reason for the use of אלהים here instead of יהוה. The change of the Divine name is however caused by that of the source of the extracts. It was intentionally that the author of Genesis interwove both Divine names into the origins of Israel, and it is certainly not accidental that the name יהוה is impressed upon the first four births, and the name אלהים upon the seven others. We are to be impressed with the fact, that the covenant faithfulness of Jahveh and the wonder-working power of Elohim concurred in laying the foundation of Israel. Jacob's seventh son Gad, by Zilpah, Leah's handmaid, vv. 9–11: *When Leah saw that she had ceased from bearing, she took Zilpah, her handmaid, and gave her to Jacob to wife. And Zilpah, Leah's handmaid, bare Jacob a son. Then Leah said: Good fortune! and called his name Gad.* She called him גָּד propitious star, saying (according to the *Chethîb*): בְּגָד with fortune! (LXX. ἐν τύχῃ), *i.e.* for my happiness, or (according to the *Kerî* which takes ב as an abbreviation of בָּא): בָּא גָד which the Targums and Syr. explain: fortune is come. It is true that the Keri may be also explained (according to xlix. 19): *there come troops* (Venet. ἥκει στράτευμα), viz. troops of children. But גְּדוּד=גָּד is not to be authenticated in this unwarlike meaning, and the mythological appellation of fortune (Arab. *ǵedd*), in accordance with בַּעַל גָּד (Josh. xi. 17, xii. 7, comp. Isa. lxv. 11), cannot seem strange in the mouth of an Aramæan woman. In later times, the commencement of which cannot be determined, the notion of the בעל גד was united to the planet Jupiter, as that of the גד עשתרת (on Carthag. III. in Gesenius' *Monumenta*) to the planet Venus. The Turanian name of Jupiter on inscriptions is *Lubat guttav* (*guttam*). Jacob's eighth son Asher, his second son by Zilpah, Leah's handmaid, vv. 12, 13: *And Zilpah, Leah's handmaid, bare a second son to Jacob. Then Leah said: Happy me! for the daughters will call out Happy art thou! so she called his name Aśer.* The name means the happy one (from יָשַׁר=אָשַׁר يسر whence *jusr*, happiness)—thus Leah called him saying בְּאָשְׁרִי Happy me! (which by altering this strange בְּ in accordance with the preceding בָּנֵי may also be read אָשְׁרִי=בָּאָשְׁרִי (בָּא). כִּי is followed, as frequently, *e.g.* Isa. lx. 1, by the perf. of certainty, and בָּנוֹת is in poetic fashion without the article (LXX. αἱ γυναῖκες, comp. Mary's *magnificat*, Luke i. 48). It now again becomes Leah's turn to bear, notwithstanding the love-apples obtained by Rachel, vv. 14–16: *And Reuben went*

*in the days of wheat harvest and found mandrakes in the field
and brought them to Leah, his mother; then Rachel said to
Leah: Give me, I pray thee, of thy son's mandrakes. And she
said to her: Is it too little that thou hast taken my husband from
me, to take also my son's mandrakes? Then Rachel said: Let
him then lie with thee this night for thy son's mandrakes. When
then Jacob came home from the field at even, Leah went to meet
him and said: Thou must come in unto me, for I have hired
thee, yea hired thee, for my son's mandrakes.* The LXX. correctly
translates דּוּדָאִים μῆλα μανδραγορῶν; דּוּדַי (in accordance with
the formation לְגַי) from דּוֹד (דּוּדִים), ancient Egyptian *duda, dudua,
dudu* (see Brugsch, *Die neue Weltordnung*, etc. 1881, p. 38), is
the *mandragora autumnalis* which blossoms in November at the
commencement of the winter rain. It comes from the Persian
merdum gidh, man-plant, Aram. and Arab. *jabrûḥ*, by which
the Targums (comp. *Sanhedrin* 99b) and the Syriac translate
it, or also *luffâḥ*, by which Saad. renders it. Its flowers of
purple inclining to dark blue become in May and June
(Cant. vii. 14), or what is the same, in the days of wheat
harvest, yellowish green apples, about the size of a nutmeg, of
a particularly pungent odour (Arab. *tuffâḥ esseitân* or *tuffaḥ
el-meǵnûn* or *baid el-ǵinn*, dæmons' eggs). The mandragora is
a plant frequently found in Palestine and also in Aramæa, its
fruit and root are esteemed as a means of promoting fertility
and as an Aphrodisiacum in general, on which account it is
figuratively called عبد السلام (servant of love's salute), and
is glossed by عشاق أوتى (lovers' herb).[1] Circe used the
root in her charmed potions, and Hamilcar brought upon
his adversaries the Libyans the sleep of intoxication, by
means of wine in which this root was mingled. But the
perfect plant, drawn out uninjured, with its root reaching from

---

[1] See Wetzstein's Excursus on the Dudaim in *Comm. zum Hohenliede*, pp.
439–445, and James Neil's (formerly pastor of Christ Church, Jerusalem) article
on the same subject (with an illustration) in the *Jewish Intelligence*, 1886, pp.
194–196.

three to four feet and sometimes deeper, with its egg-like fruits in their leafy nests, was reckoned particularly valuable and effectual. Of such kind were the Dudaïm which Reuben brought with him from the field. When Rachel begs for them, with a purpose which she has no need to express, Leah gives her an indignant refusal. לָקַחַת (not לְקַחְתְּ or לְקִחְתְּ) is, as the Targums also take it, *inf. constr.: ut præreptura sis.* Rachel however obtains the mandrakes by renouncing her husband for the next night. בַּלַּיְלָה הוּא (instead of הַהוּא) as at xix. 33. Since Rachel however remains barren notwithstanding the mandrakes, it is again shown that an incalculable power presides over the history of the patriarchs. Jacob's ninth and Leah's fifth son, Issachar, vv. 17, 18: *Then Elohim hearkened unto Leah, and she conceived and bore Jacob a fifth son. And Leah said: Elohim hath given me my hire, because I have given my handmaid unto my husband, and she called his name Jissachar.* The *Textus rec.* points יִשָּׂשכָר, while according to Ben-Asher יִשָּׂשכָר, its *Keri*, is *perpetuum*, against which Ben-Naphtali read יִשָּׂשכָר *affert præmium*, or according to Baer read just like Ben-Asher, but wrote יִשָּׂשכָר; Moses b. Mochah read, according to Jer. xxxi. 16, 2 Chron. xv. 7, יֵשׁ שָׂכָר *est præmium*, see Pinsker, *Zur Gesch. des Karaismus*, p. 98 sq. Leah regards this son as a reward (בַּעֲבוּר אֲשֶׁר or תַּחַת אֲשֶׁר=אֲשֶׁר like xxxiv. 27, xxxi. 49) of her self-denial, not, as Josephus takes it (= ἐκ μίσθου γενόμενος), as a compensation for the mandrakes. Jacob's tenth and Leah's sixth son, Zebulun, vv. 19-20: *And Leah conceived again and bore a sixth son to Jacob. Then Leah said: Elohim hath endowed me with a good dowry; this time my husband will esteem me, for I have borne him six sons, so she called his name Zebulun.* The meaning, to present, is assured to the verb זבד by the Aram. and Arab.; it occurs only here, but all the more numerous are the proper names formed from it (see the Lexicon). Can there be here two interpretations by different narrators, one of whom assumes that זְבֻלֹן is formed from זבד? Scarcely, for he would see in the name only an allusion to זבד, and would then be responsible for the interpretation. At all events, the name is explained first from its consonance with זבד and then from זבל as its stem-word. Certainly זבל has been understood in the meaning to dwell, which is by no means assured to it; verbs of dwelling (inhabiting) of course take the accus. (*e.g.* also גור Ps. v. 5), but "he will inhabit me," for "he will hold to me" (Jerome *mecum erit*), is an improbable expression. The Assyrian offers for זבל the more suitable meaning to raise up, to elevate, with which the LXX. αἱρετιεῖ με, *i.e.* according to Hesychius προτιμοτέραν με ἡγήσεται, may be brought into connection and to which זְבֻל (a thing erected = dwelling-place) may fitly be referred (Guyard, Friedr. Del.); the opposition of Halévy is here of no avail. Birth of a daughter to Jacob by Leah, ver. 21 : *And afterwards she bore a daughter and called her name Dinah.* Dinah, who was not Jacob's only daughter, xxxvii. 35, xlvi. 7, could not be left unmentioned because of ch. xxxiv., but is, as being a daughter, dismissed in few words (comp. iv. 22, Num. xxvi. 46). Jacob's eleventh and Rachel's first son, Joseph, vv. 22-24 : *Then Elohim remembered Rachel, and Elohim hearkened unto her and opened her womb. And she conceived and bore a son, and said: Elohim hath taken away my reproach. And she called his name Joseph, saying: May Jahveh add unto me another son.* At last God remembered Rachel also (like 1 Sam. i. 19), and granted her so long seemingly unheard petition. The name of her first own son is interpreted by *E* "Taker away" (viz. of the reproach) of childlessness (like Isa. iv. 1 of celibacy), by *J* "increaser," as the first who is the precursor of a second. The addition is characterized by לאמר, which occurs nowhere else in the giving of names.

The passing notice of Dinah, Leah's daughter, has its appropriate place after the six sons of Leah, without our having to infer therefrom that her birth took place before that of Joseph. The first four births of sons (Reuben, Simeon,

Levi and Judah) by Leah happen in the first four years of the second seven years, the two by Bilhah, Rachel's handmaid, in the fourth to the fifth. During the fifth year Leah is in vain expecting the blessing of children, and at last, after the example of Rachel, gives Zilpah to her husband, and she bears to him Gad and Asher from the sixth to the middle of the seventh year. Meantime Leah is again blessed with children, and brings forth Issachar at the end of the seventh year of the now elapsed second seven years, Zebulun in the first of the last six years (of the twenty, xxxi. 38), and Dinah in the second of the six. Rachel however bore a son, as is evident from ver. 25, at the end of the second seven years; hence the birth of Joseph took place between the births of Issachar and Zebulun (not before that of Issachar, as Astruc, *Conjectures*, p. 396 sq., thinks), and probably in the last month of this seventh year (comp. Demetrius in Euseb. *Præp.* ix. 21). Unless we place two of Leah's births in the six years (xxxi. 41) after the two seven years, Leah must have borne seven children within the seven years, during which a considerable interval of vain expectation elapsed. Kurtz accepts this, limiting the period during which Leah was certain that a cessation had taken place to "a few months." But at xxxvii. 35, xlvi. 7, daughters of Jacob are mentioned, concerning whose births nothing is said, and elsewhere in Genesis homogeneous events are, as here in the case of the children with which Jacob's two marriages were blessed in Arammæa, taken together as though continuous, the distribution of the succession of time, as here of the 7 + 7 + 6 years, being left to the reader.

NEW COMPACT FOR SERVICE BETWEEN JACOB AND LABAN, XXX. 25–XXXI. 3.

When Rachel after long yearning became a mother, the second seven years of service had elapsed; the fourth portion, xxx. 25 to xxxi. 3 (from *J*, though with here and there a glance at *E*), now relates how a new compact for service between Jacob and Laban came to pass, and how Jacob, during this new service, attained great wealth in cattle through an artifice blessed by God. Jacob presses for his dismissal, and Laban for Jacob's stay, 25—30 : *And it came to pass when Rachel had borne Joseph, that Jacob said to Laban: Send me away, that I may go to my own place and to my country. Give me my wives and children, for whom I have served thee, that I may go; for thou knowest my service which I have done for thee. Then Laban said to him: Oh, if I have found favour in thine eyes—! I have well marked that Jahveh hath blessed me for thy sake. Then he said: Decide thy wages, and I will give it. And he said to him: Thou knowest how I have served thee, and what thy cattle have become with me. For a little, which thou hadst before my time, has spread into a multitude, and Jahveh hath blessed thee where I turned my foot, and now, when shall I work also for my own house?* The apodosis to אָם־נָא 27*a* must be completed according to xviii. 3 : so let thy purpose be—a courteous oh not so ! (comp. xix. 18 sq.). נִחֵשׁ is a heathen expression for inquiring into the future by means of magic, and then means in general *divinare*, to perceive, to remark (xliv. 15). The two וַיֹּאמֶר with the same subject (Laban) in vv. 27, 28 show that *R*, wherever it is possible, reproduces the words of his authorities unaltered. We translate מְעַט 30*a* "a little," for "the little" is called הַמְעָט, *e.g.* Deut. vii. 7. We have already had פָּרַץ, to spread, in *J* xxviii. 14. לְרַגְלִי, at my foot, is equivalent to: blessing followed wherever I went (comp. Job xviii. 11 ; Isa. xli. 2 ; Hab. iii. 5). עשׂה לְ a pregnant expression : to act, to work, to take trouble for any one. New compact between Jacob and Laban, vv. 31—34: *Then he said: What shall I give thee? And Jacob said: Thou shalt give me nothing, if thou wilt grant me this thing: I will again tend thy flock and take it under my care. I will to-day go through all thy flock, taking out from it every speckled and spotted one and every black one among the* *lambs, and the speckled and spotted among the goats, and that shall be my hire. And on the morrow, when thou shalt inspect my hire, my own righteousness shall testify against me before thee: every one that is not speckled and spotted among the goats and black among the lambs, let that with me be reckoned stolen. Then Laban said: Well, let it be according to thy word!* Jacob lets himself be prevailed upon again to tend and keep Laban's flock under a certain condition (שָׂכָר as at Hos. xii. 13. Comp. on the explanatory, surpassing compensation of the one notion by the other, Ps. xv. 4). The transaction is carried on with the same conventional forms of Oriental courtesy, as that in ch. xxiii. between Abraham and the Hethites. The sheep are in that country almost all white (Cant. iv. 2), only a few, chiefly rams, black, the goats for the most part if not black (Cant. iv. 1*b*) of a dark colour, and only very seldom white or spotted with white. Hence it is apparently a very small wage for which Jacob stipulates, when he claims all the speckled, spotted and black among the sheep (כְּשָׂבִים for the later כְּבָשִׂים, a Pentateuchal form occurring also in Lev. Num. and Deut.), and all the speckled and spotted among the goats, which are now and henceforth may be produced in Laban's flock. This is the sense of ver. 32 sq. After the preceding הָסֵר, אֶעֱבֹר cannot, as Tuch, Baumg., Kn. understand it, be *imperative*, it is *infin. absol.* Consequently וְהָיָה שְׂכָרִי cannot, as Tuch, Baumg., Kurtz and already Luther take it, mean: and all that in future happens to be of an abnormal colour in the now normal coloured flock shall be my hire; והיה שכרי aims at the present, but in such wise that all that may in the future happen to be of abnormal colour is at the same time stipulated for. It is in accordance with this that ver. 33 must be explained: my own rectitude shall, when thou shalt to-morrow and henceforth make investigation concerning that which is claimed by me, testify against me (עָנָה בְּ everywhere else, also 1 Sam. xii. 3, and therefore certainly here too used of witness against or accusation). Luther 1545 with the LXX. and

Jerome rightly understands the וְהָיוּ in the sense of וְאִשֶׁר־, אֵינֶנּוּ חוּם, for Jacob claims for himself the black sheep as those of abnormal colour; hence it is not the black, but those that are not black, that are to be regarded as stolen by him. Laban gladly consents, ver. 34 : *Yea* (הֵן as in the Mishna diction) *let it be* (לוּ as at xvii. 18) *according to thy word*. It might now be thought that Jacob would undertake the separation, instead of which Laban undertakes it himself, vv. 35, 36: *Then on the same day he removed the striped and spotted rams, and all the speckled and spotted goats, all upon which was any white, and every black one among the lambs, and gave them into the hands of his sons. And he put a distance of three days' journey between himself and Jacob, and Jacob fed the rest of Laban's flocks.* Laban himself separates the unusual coloured cattle, especially the rams תְּיָשִׁים (which is certainly not made prominent without intention), and delivers these separated and unusually coloured cattle to his sons (comp. xxxi. 1), for Laban's own flock, consisting now of only normal coloured cattle, was pastured by Jacob. He then orders a separation of three days' journey (*i.e.* about 3 × 7 hours) between the two flocks, in order to prevent any copulation between the normal and abnormal coloured cattle. We cannot here escape the impression, that the accounts of two authorities are here worked into each other; nevertheless, the narrative, as we have it, must be capable in the mind of *R* of being drawn together into one harmonious picture. Hence we shall have to conceive that Laban, in order to guard against any diminution, himself undertook the separation, and for the same reason delivered what belonged to Jacob to his (Laban's) sons, and entrusted what was his to Jacob. It is strange indeed that ver. 32 is left in the wording which leaves unexpressed Jacob's meaning, that what is produced of an abnormal colour in the future is also to belong to him. But that this is Jacob's meaning is presupposed, as the further course of the narrative shows.

In order to obtain within the one coloured flock of Laban the greatest possible number of abnormal coloured births, Jacob in his inventive policy makes use of two artifices. The first stratagem, vv. 37–40: *Then Jacob took fresh rods of storax, almond and plane trees, and peeled thereon white stripes, laying bare the white that was on the rods. And he placed the rods, which he had peeled, in the gutters, in the water troughs, where the cattle came to drink, over against the cattle, and it was pairing time when they came to drink. And the cattle mated among the rods, and the cattle brought forth striped, speckled, and spotted. And Jacob separated the lambs and turned the faces of the flocks toward the striped and all the black among Laban's flocks, and made droves apart, and put them not to Laban's cattle.* Of the three kinds of trees לִבְנֶה is the storax tree (*styrax officinalis*, from לָבָן in accordance with the formation לִבְנֵי=אִשָּׁה لبنى on account of the fragrant milk *leben* thickening to a gum which flows from its wounded bark)—not the white poplar, which is called حَوَر ضَنَوْبَل (*DMZ.* xvi. 588); לוּז the almond tree (the more Aramaico-Arabic name for שָׁקֵד *amygdala*, whose fruit is called almonds, or almond nuts, *nuces*, Arab. لَوْز *lôz*), and עֶרְמוֹן the plane (*platanus orientalis*, from עָרַם *denudare*, because the smooth bark of the tree comes off every year and leaves it bare). In the fresh sticks of these trees he peeled white stripes (פְּצָלוֹת peeled places) by exposing the white (מַחְשֹׂף adv. Acc. for חָשׂף *decorticando*), and placed (הַצִּיג in distinction from הִצִּיב of temporary placing) the parti-coloured sticks in or near the troughs רְהָטִים (perhaps from J xxiv. 20), which is explained by שִׁקְתוֹת חַמִּים (plur. of שֹׁקֶת with the ת taken rootwise as in בְּסָתוֹת). לְנֹכַח הַצֹּאן belongs to the remote וַיַּצֵּג as לְפָנֶיךָ 33*a* to the remote תְּעַנֶּה־בִּי, unless the meaning is, that the animals stood while drinking on both sides of the trough opposite each other, so that וַיֶּחֱמְנָה is meant of the instinct excited by the help of this position. This וַיֶּחֱמְנָה instead of

וַתְּחַמְנָה (from חָמַם, as at 1 Sam. vi. 12, Dan. viii. 22) is one of the three forms designated by the Masora as מלין אדרונים, hybrid words. Thus they mated (וַיֵּחַמּוּ=וַיַּחְמוּ) from חָמַם, though it also might be *impf. Kal* from יָחַם for וַיֵּחָמוּ, according to a similar change of sound, as at Ps. li. 7, comp. Judg. v. 28, for וַיֵּחָמוּ) among the rods, and this produced unusual coloured animals among the lambs. Then Jacob separated these unusual coloured lambs and kids from the normal coloured animals belonging to Laban, and so led the latter that their faces were turned to the parti-coloured, so as to obtain continually fresh additions from the flock of Laban. Hence it must have been arranged, at least at the first, that from the first separation (ver. 35 sq.) to a second and final one, the flocks of Laban should remain together under the care of Jacob. For otherwise it cannot be explained that Laban should so easily have connived at the normal and abnormal coloured cattle remaining together and not from time to time have continued the separation made at the beginning, that he should even have looked on quietly, when Jacob formed separate flocks of the parti-coloured cattle obtained by stratagem, for the purpose of overlooking his property, and at the same time of obtaining continually fresh increase by turning the faces of the one-coloured animals towards the numerous parti-coloured ones. If instead of אֶל we are with Kn. to read כָּל, according to the Targums and Saad., it is to be explained: he placed in the sight of the sheep all the striped and dark-coloured animals (so that they had always had the latter in their sight). But this is of no avail. It cannot be mistaken that the words ויתן to בצאן לבן in ver. 40 import an alien element into the narrative; they give the impression of being an insertion, the contents of which are opposed to what precedes (the separation) and follows (the formation of separate parti-coloured flocks). The second stratagem, vv. 41, 42: *And it came to pass, whenever the strong sheep conceived, then Jacob used to lay the rods in the gutters before the eyes of the sheep, that they might mate among the rods. And when the sheep were feeble he laid them not therein, and thus the feeble became Laban's and the strong Jacob's.* The apodosis begins with וְשָׂם not וַיָּשֶׂם, because it was not a single but a repeated act. The strong animals are called הַמְקֻשָּׁרוֹת (42b הַקְּשֻׁרִים), the compact, *i.e.* the full, the sturdy (comp. חַיִל, גָּדוֹל, גֶּבֶר = Engl. strength), and the feeble הָעֲטֻפִים, from עטף, to wrap and to weaken; the *Hiph.* הֶעֱטִיף means, as intrinsically transitive, to show weakness. The form לְיַחְמֵנָּה is *Piel* (xxxi. 10) from יחם, with the suffix *enna* instead of *ān = ahun*. Only during the mating of the strong sheep did he put in the sticks, that they might conceive among them, and not when, on the contrary, the sheep were in a feeble condition, *i.e.* when in consequence of bad pasture the rams and ewes were less strong. This means, perhaps, that he laid them there in summer (according to Varro and Pliny: *a tertio Idus Majas in X Calend. Aug.*, with us in July and the first half of August), so that the strong (unusual coloured) winter lambs became his, but not in autumn (Pliny: *postea concepti invalidi*), so that the weaker (usual coloured) spring lambs were left to Laban. Luther on the contrary: *Also wurden die Spetlinge Labans, aber die Fruelinge Jacobs*, according to which Jacob must have carried out his artifice from towards the end of September till October, when the lambs would be brought forth in March and April. The text itself gives no kind of indication as to whether Jacob had in view the winter or the spring lambing. For the rest it is a well-known fact that what is presented to the senses of the pregnant animal is imitated in the formation of the offspring, and that in no animal has the imagination of the mother such influence upon the offspring as in the sheep; on which account sheep-breeders, to obtain white sheep, make use of a like means with Jacob, by placing something white in the drinking troughs of the sheep, giving them troughs made of quite white stone, or hanging up white cloths in their stalls, just as horse-breeders, to obtain a fine breed, hang up representations of fine horses before their foaling mares (Friedreich, *Zur Bibel*, 1. 36-41). Jacob's increasing prosperity, ver. 43: *Thus the man increased exceedingly, and obtained many sheep, and maid-servants and men-servants, and camels and asses.* At ver. 30, and at xxviii. 14, also פרץ of the person is found in *J;* comp. notwithstanding the מְאֹד מְאֹד (elsewhere only in *Q*, vii. 19), the Jahvistic parallels in matter and style, xii. 16. צֹאן רַבּוֹת does not mean: many flocks, but many heads of sheep and goats, comp. *e.g.* Num. xxxi. 32. Jacob's prosperity increased immensely, but (as is further narrated according to *J*) it was now also time that he should quit the place, xxxi. 1-3: *And he heard the words of Laban's sons, that they said: Jacob has taken to himself all that was our father's, and of our father's property has got for himself all this wealth. And Jacob beheld the countenance of Laban, and it was no more towards him as yesterday and before yesterday. And Jahveh said to Jacob: Return to the land of thy fathers and to thy home, and I will be with thee.* Jacob's brothers-in-law having been, contrary to Oriental custom, still silent individuals at their sisters' marriages, were still quite little fourteen years ago, and perhaps not born twenty years ago; now however they are grown up (xxx. 35) and of age. כָּבוֹד weight, means both a great quantity (of wealth only here in the Pent., but comp. xiii. 2) and an imposing appearance (*gravitas, gloria*). עשׂה to obtain, to gain, as at xii. 5. אֵינֶנּוּ after פְּנֵי, as at Lam. iv. 16. On מוֹלֶדֶת see on xii. 1, and compare the reference to it xxxii. 10.

JACOB'S FLIGHT AND FINAL PEACEABLE DEPARTURE FROM LABAN, CH. XXXI. 4-XXXII. 1.

The fifth and last portion of the first section of Isaac's life now follows, not of Jacob's, for Isaac is still alive and rules the history, which Jacob only stirs. The close of the former portion, xxx. 43-xxxi. 1-3, bore the stamp of *J*, but now the text of E is resumed and prevails, xxxi. 4–xxxii. 1, though other elements, especially parallels in matter from J and in ver. 18 from Q, are perceived to be worked into it. The different source is already betrayed by the behaviour of Laban, and Jacob's prosperity, notwithstanding, being somewhat differently represented here and in ch. xxx.

Jacob summons Rachel and Leah to the field and lays before them the motives of his resolution to return home, vv. 4–9: *Then Jacob sent and called Rachel and Leah to the field unto his flock, and said unto them: I see the countenance of your father, that it is not towards me as yesterday and before yesterday, but the God of my fathers was with me. And you know that with my whole power I have served your father. But your father has deceived me and changed my hire ten times; but Elohim has not allowed him to do me harm. If he said: The speckled shall be thy hire, then the whole flock bare speckled; and if he said: The striped shall be thy hire, then all the flock bare striped. And so Elohim has taken away the flocks of your father and has given them unto me.* Expressions peculiar to E are מַשְׂכֹּרֶת (=שָׂכָר) here and ver. 41, xxix. 15, and עֲשֶׂרֶת מֹנִים here and ver. 41, ten (= many) times, instead of the synonymous עֲשֶׂרֶת פְּעָמִים. וָאַתֶּנָה instead of וָאֶתֵּן, which occurs besides only three times in Ezekiel, is also worthy of notice (Assyr. *attina*). The use of gender is here also shown to be imperfectly developed: אֲבִיכֶן with respect to the wives being exchanged 9b for אֲבִיכֶם. It is from E that it is here told that Laban did not keep to his agreement with Jacob, but fooled him (הֵתֶל Hiphil of תָּלַל, Ew. § 127d) by ever and again changing the hire allotted him, but without profiting thereby, because God frustrated his selfish intention. Continuation of Jacob's address to his wives, vv. 10–13: *And it came to pass at the pairing time of the cattle, that I lifted up mine eyes and saw in a dream, and behold, the rams which leaped upon the sheep were striped, speckled and dappled. And the angel of God said to me in a dream: Jacob! And I said: Here am I. And he said: Lift up thine eyes and see: All the rams which leap on the sheep are striped, speckled and dappled; for I have seen all that Laban doeth to thee. I am the God of Bethel, where thou anointedst a pillar, where thou vowedst a vow unto me—now arise go out of this land and return to the land of thy home.* What appeared in the former portion to have been obtained by Jacob's artifice, is here represented as the blessing of Elohim. That the Divine direction, now to return home, closely follows in the dream-vision upon the image of the leaping upon the cattle of unusual coloured rams, and thus took place at the end of the six years (Dillm.), is perhaps based only on the circumstance, that what was objectively related in *E* is here taken up retrospectively in Jacob's address. Jacob should and must at last have been inwardly conscious, that after all it had been God's providence and not his own artifice which had protected him against Laban and made him so wealthy, that, as Antonio says in Shakespeare, it was "a thing not in his power to bring to pass, but swayed and fashioned by the hand of Heaven." The variegated animals are here called, ver. 12, עֲקֻדִּים banded—which appeared already xxx. 35 נְקֻדִּים spotted and בְּרֻדִּים dappled (here for the first time), from בָּרַד = برش *variegare*, syn. with טְלָאִים xxx. 32, 33, 35 in *J*. The manifestation at Bethel to which ver. 13 refers is that related xxviii. 12, 17-19. The demonstrative prominence of the first member of the *st. constr.* in הָאֵל בֵּיתְאֵל is like הַמֶּלֶךְ אַשּׁוּר Isa. xxxvi. 8, and in cases like 2 Kings xxiii. 17, where apposition cannot be supposed instead of annexation; comp. הבעלת גבל upon the pillar of the Jehavmelek of Gebal, "the Ba'alat of Byblos." The two wives approve of Jacob's proposal; their father has alienated their hearts also by his unkindness and covetousness, vv. 14-16: *Then Rachel with Leah answered, and they said to him: Have we yet a portion and inheritance in the house of our father? Are we not esteemed by him as strangers? for he has sold us, and has even quite devoured the price paid for us. Nay, all the wealth which Elohim has taken from our father belongs to us and our children; now then, whatever Elohim has told thee, do!* Laban sold his daughters for the price of fourteen years' service, without giving them, as a marriage portion, anything that Jacob's services had procured for him. He has abundantly profited by this כֶּסֶף paid to him as מֹהַר; גַּם with the *inf. absol.* like xlvi. 4 (and 1 Sam. xxiv. 12, if we are to read there with Hupfeld רָאֹה) increases the emphasis. כִּי 16*a* confirms and strengthens, see xxix. 32 sq. They can with a good conscience look upon what Jacob has, by the blessing of God, obtained for himself during his time of service, as their marriage portions, which have been extorted from him. They are contented that he should prepare for departure. The return home, vv. 17–21: *Then Jacob arose and set his sons and his wives upon the camels, and carried away all his cattle and all his property which he had made his own, the cattle of his getting, which he had made his own in Paddan Aram, to go back to Isaac his father in the land of Canaan. And Laban was gone to shear his flock, then Rachel stole the teraphim of her father. And Jacob stole the heart of Laban the Aramaean, in that he made no communication to him, for he meant to flee. So he fled, and all that belonged to him; he arose and passed over the river, and set his face toward the mountains of Gil'ad.* In ver. 18 the text of *E* from וְאֶת־רְכֻשׁוֹ onwards is illustrated from *Q*, comp. xii. 5, xxxvi. 6, xlvi. 6. When this happened Laban had gone sheep-shearing, which, as must be inferred from ver. 27, was then as later (xxxviii. 12 sq., 2 Sam. xiii. 23 sq.) celebrated as a rustic festival, and would with such large flocks as Laban's last above a week. Rachel made use of her father's absence to steal his תְּרָפִים (a *Pluraletantum* like *penates*, sometimes an actual plural as here, comp. xxxv. 2, sometimes an intensive one, as at 1 Sam. xix. 13, like בְּעָלִים, אֲדֹנִים: the tutelary gods or god of his house, properly dispenser of prosperity, from תרף, تَرِفَ, تَتَرَّفَ to be opulent, to live well, whence رَنَج, prosperity, superfluity, as the Penates have their name from the *penus*, the domestic store-chambers, as protecting and filling them).[1] Rachel, like Æneas, took the teraphim *penatiger* (Ovid, *Met.* xv. 450) with her, but in an unlawful manner, not for the purpose of withdrawing her father from these idols (Ephrem and others), but to take with her the fortune of the house. For Laban was, as he is called xxxi. 20 and also elsewhere in *E* and *Q*, אֲרַמִּי, and therefore, as thus hinted, if not wholly, still half a heathen. The verb גנב with לֵב, or just the Acc. of the person, ver. 27, means, like κλέπτειν νόον and κλέπτειν τινά, to deprive any one of the knowledge of anything, to delude him; the original meaning of גנב is to bring aside, which acquires the more special meaning of removing (purloining), or also, as at 2 Sam. xv. 6, of tempting. Jacob deceived Laban in that (עַל, Samar. ער) he did not tell him beforehand that he was about to depart (בְּלִי with the *verb. fin.* as at Job xli. 18, Hos. viii. 7, ix. 16, *Chethib* Isa. xiv. 6; Ew. § 322*a*); he let nothing be perceived, for he intended to depart secretly (*clam se subducturus erat*, for נוס properly means to flee, ברח, on the contrary, to depart, to withdraw). So Jacob with all that was his passed over the river (which can only mean the Euphrates), and thence proceeded in the direction of the mountains of Gilead. Pursuit, warning and overtaking, vv. 22-25: *And it was told Laban on the third day that Jacob had departed. And he took his brethren with him and pursued after him seven days' journey, and overtook him in the mountain of Gilead. And Elohim came to Laban the Aramaean in a dream at night, and said to him: Take heed that thou speak not to Jacob either good or bad. And Laban came up with Jacob; and Jacob had pitched his tent in the mountain, and Laban with his brethren pitched in the mountain of*

---

[1] Ad. Neubauer in *The Academy*, 1886, No. 756, conjectures a connection between רפאים and תרפים; but the teraphim do not appear to be adored manes (ancestral spirits), and the existent verbal stem תרף excludes the derivation from רפה.

Gil'ad. The point of departure was according to all informants Haran. If Gilead could not be thence reached in a seven days' march, and not by a nomad with his flocks in from ten to twelve, *E* and *J* must bear the responsibility; the conjecture that *E* placed Laban's dwelling nearer to Gilead (Dillm.) being unjustified. Since however 23*b* (וַיַּדְבֵּק וגו׳) belongs in all probability to *E* and ver. 25 (וַיַּשֵּׂג וגו׳) to *J*, the conjecture is suggested that there was in the text of *J* a more particular designation of Jacob's halting-place than בָּהָר, which was left out by *R* because of 23*b* (Dillm.). The mountain chain of Gilead is divided into a northern and southern half, separated by the ravine of the Jabbok. The meeting took place before the subsequent passage of the Jabbok by Jacob, hence somewhere in the hill country *'Aǵlûn* between the Jarmuk and the Jabbok. The kindred of Laban are called his brethren, as *e.g.* 2 Sam. xix. 13. Laban is directed to behave to Jacob in an entirely passive manner, *i.e.* not to meet him in a hostile spirit. What now follows is not meant to be regarded as a transgression of the Divine admonition on the part of Laban.

The eloquent reproof, vv. 26-30, is limited to bitter reproaches, in which paternal affection and hypocrisy are intermingled: *Then Laban said to Jacob: What hast thou done? that thou hast stolen my heart and carried away my daughters as captives of the sword. Why didst thou depart so secretly and deceive me and hast told me nothing, so I might have sent thee away with mirth and with songs, with tabret and with harp, and hast not let me kiss my sons and my daughters— thus hast thou done foolishly. It was in my power to do thee harm, but the God of your father spake to me in the past night saying: Take heed that thou speak not to Jacob either good or ill. And now thou wentest forth uncontrollably because thou sorely longest for thy father's house—why hast thou stolen my gods?* The apodosis to וְלֹא־הִגַּדְתָּ לִּי logically begins with וָאֲשַׁלֵּחֲךָ 27*b*. The LXX. apparently read וְלוּ *καὶ εἰ*, but comp. a similar apodosis after

לֹא at Ps. lv. 13, Job ix. 32 sq., xxxii. 22. On בְּשִׂמְחָה וגו׳, comp. 1 Sam. xviii. 6 and LXX. 2 Sam. vi. 5. לַעֲשׂוֹת or even the *inf. abs.* עָשֹׂה might (according to the beginning of ver. 27) follow הִסְכַּלְתָּ; we find however the *inf. constr.* without לְ (Ges. § 131. 4, note 2), which in *E* is written also l. 20 and even with a suffix Ex. xviii. 18 עֲשֹׂו (comp. רְאֹה xlviii. 11). אֵל in the phrase: it is, or: it is not לְאֵל יָדִי, means power (from אול, whence also אֱיָלוּת Ps. xxii. 20), properly the powerful matter, or (since אֵל, Assyr. *ilu*, seems to have only a tone-long *ê* and originally a short *i*) perhaps reach, especially reach of power (according to Lagarde, from אָלָה, like קֵט from קטה). He could avenge himself, but "the God of your father," he says, *i.e.* the God of Isaac, who is now the head of the family to Jacob's wives also, warned me אֶמֶשׁ in the preceding night; we already read this word conceived of adverbially as an Acc. xix. 34 (where see), and it occurs again only here in ver. 42 and Job xxx. 3, 2 Kings ix. 26, while the Assyr. freely uses *mûšu* (plur. *mûšâti*), late evening, night, as a noun. The strengthening *inf. intens.* הָלֹף and נִכְסֹף (to long for, here: to long back, as in the Bedouin حَسَفَ, *DMZ*. xxii. 158) are psychologically significant. The וְעַתָּה looks towards the inquiring לָמָּה; we should say, transposing the sentence: now then, why, if sore home-sickness irresistibly impelled thee, hast thou stolen my gods? Jacob's excuse and protest, vv. 31, 32: *Then Jacob answered and said: Because I was afraid; for I thought, lest thou shouldst perhaps even rob from me thy daughters. With whom thou shalt find thy gods, he shall not live; in the presence of our brethren, look strictly to what is found with me and take it to thee!—Jacob knew not that Rachel had stolen them.* Instead of עִמּוֹ ⋯ אֲשֶׁר (xliv. 9 sq.), *is apud quem*, we here read עִם אֲשֶׁר, *apud quem* (*is vivere desinat*). יִחְיֶה has rightly *segolta*; for נֶגֶד אַחֵינוּ refers not to the execution, but to the inspection, which is to be made before the eyes of all the persons belonging to them both. Rachel's stratagem prevents the discovery of her theft, vv. 33–35: *Then Laban went into Jacob's tent and into Leah's tent and into the tent of the two handmaids and found nothing, and having come out of Leah's tent he went into Rachel's tent. Now Rachel had taken the teraphim and put them into the saddle of the camel and was sitting upon them, and Laban felt about all the tent and found nothing. And she said to her father: Let not my lord be angry that I cannot rise up before thee, for it is with me according to the manner of women*—so he sought but found not the teraphim. Thus Rachel, whose turn came next to Leah, and with whom the narrative now tarries longer (the handmaids being here, where the historic course of Genesis is reflected *in parvo*, despatched *extra ordinem*), was able to deceive her father, by putting the teraphim into the saddle of the camel and then sitting upon it. On אֲמָהוֹת, plur. of אָמָה, see on xx. 17. The saddle is called כַּר from its (basket-shaped) roundness. Luther, misunderstanding the *stramenta* of Jerome (after σάγματα of the LXX.), translates *die strew der Kamel*. She excuses herself from rising before her father (מִפְּנֵי, like Lev. xix. 32) because of her condition. The stratagem was cunningly devised, for even though Laban might not have esteemed it unclean and unfitting to touch the seat on which she sat (see Lev. xv. 22), how could he have thought it possible that a woman in her circumstances should be sitting upon his gods! Thus Laban stands discomfited, and the right of casting reproach is all at once transferred to Jacob, who upbraids him with the injustice of this hostile pursuit, and with all the faithful, unselfish and hard service which he has rendered him, vv. 36-42: *Then Jacob was angry and chode with Laban; Jacob answered and said to Laban: What is my offence, what is my sin, that thou hast pursued after me? Thou hast felt about all my stuff, what hast thou found of all thy household stuff? Set it here in the presence of thy and of my brethren, let them judge between us two. In the twenty years that I have been with thee, thy ewes and thy she-goats have not cast their young, and the rams*

*of thy flock have I not eaten. That which was torn I brought
not home to thee, I myself replaced it, of my hand thou didst
require it, that which was stolen by day and stolen by night.
Where I was by day, the heat consumed me and the frost by
night, and sleep fled from my eyes. Twenty years have I spent
in thine house; fourteen years I served thee for thy two daughters
and six years for thy flock, and ten times hast thou changed my
hire. Unless the God of my father, the God of Abraham and
the fear of Isaac, had been for me, surely then thou wouldest
have sent me away empty—my affliction and the labour of my
hands hath Elohim seen and decided yesternight.* In ver. 36
מַה חַטָּאתִי is to be written with Pathach before ח, as at Job
xxi. 21. The phrase דָּלַק אַחֲרֵי to pursue violently, is repeated
1 Sam. xvii. 53. That the mother sheep did not drop their
lambs (miscarry שִׁכֵּלוּ 38a), shows that he had treated them
gently (comp. xxxiii. 13), and that God had blessed his carefulness. In ver. 39 חֲטָאָה, LXX. ἀποτιννύειν, has the same
meaning as שִׁלֵּם Ex. xxii. 12; אֲחַטֶּנָּה for אֲחַטְּאֶנָּה is formed as
from חָטָא=חָטָה. The twice repeated גְּנֻבְתִי has the connective
i, which here as everywhere, with the exception of Lam. i. 1,
Hos. x. 11, has the tone on the *ult.;* the ־ָ ought to stand
at אחטנה, for מִידִי תְבַקְשֶׁנָּה points onward to what was lost and
Jacob had to answer for. The verb נָדַד (related to נוד iv. 12)
appears only here, ver. 40, in the Pentateuch. "My sleep"
שְׁנָתִי is that which is fitting and should be allowed me
(Isa. xxi. 4). According to the statement of time in ver. 41,
the births of Jacob's eleven sons, with that of Dinah and
certain other daughters, takes place in the last 7 + 6 years of
his Aramæan sojourn, see above xxx. 24. The speech of Jacob
has, by reason of the strong emotion and self-conscious elevation expressed therein, both rhythmic movement and poetic
form. Its truth, and especially its close, cuts Laban to the
heart. פַּחַד fear is here equal to the object of fear (σέβας =
σέβασμα). כִּי־עַתָּה with the praet. begins the apodosis of a
hypothetical prodosis referring to the past, as at Num. xxii.

29, 33, 1 Sam. xiv. 30, comp. פִּי 1 Sam. xxv. 34, 2 Sam. ii. 27. Laban disarmed offers reconciliation and to enter into an agreement, vv. 43, 44 : *Then Laban answered and said to Jacob: The daughters are my daughters and the children are my children, and the flocks my flocks, and all that thou seest is mine ; but for my daughters, — what shall I this day do, or for their children whom they have borne ? Come then, we will make a covenant, I and thou, and it shall be for a witness between me and thee.* The subject to וְהָיָה cannot be בְּרִית, which is fem., but a neuter, " it," viz. the present occurrence. Jacob incorporates and fixes this עֵד in a monumental form, ver. 45 : *Then Jacob took a stone and set it up for a memorial pillar.* Thus it stood in *E*, but now *J* is further added to *E*, vv. 46–48 : *And Jacob said to his brethren : Gather stones ; and they took stones and made a heap, and ate there upon the heap. Laban called it Jegar sahadûtha, and Jacob called it Gal'ēd. And Laban said : This heap is witness between me and thee this day, therefore he called its name Gal'ēd.* The heap served, as is summarily remarked beforehand 46*b* (comp. the anticipations xxvii. 33, xxviii. 5), as a table for a common covenant repast (comp. xxvi. 30), and is called by Laban יְגַר שָׂהֲדוּתָא (which is both East and West Aramaic), by Jacob גַּלְעֵד, the heap of witness. These are the only two דברים תרגום in the Thorah, as the tractate *Soferim* i. 10 expresses it. In the Jerus. Talmud (*Sota* vii. 2) and elsewhere this language is called סורסי, συριστί (*DMZ.* xxv. 128 sq.). The verbs סָהַד שְׁהַד, شهد and עוּד have the fundamental meaning of making firm, the verb יָגַר that of heaping together, גָּלַל that of rolling. Thus the appellations are pretty nearly identical. It was formerly inferred (Bochart, Huet, le Clerc, Astruc and others) from this passage that Abraham brought with him from Ur Casdim the Aramaic language and exchanged it in Canaan for the שפת כנען (Isa. xix. 18). The case, on the contrary, is that the Terahites, who remained in Mesopotamia, there became acquainted, during the

180 years which elapsed from between Abraham's migration into Canaan and this occurrence on the mountain of Gilead, with the Aramaic speech of the country, but that in the family of Terah the Babylonio-Assyrian, which differed less than the Aramaic from the tongue of the Canaanites who had migrated thence (from the Erythræan Sea), was spoken. Hence a change of language cannot be spoken of in the same manner in the case of Abraham as in that of his kindred in Haran (König, *Lehrgeb.* § 4. 2).—In 48*b* the style betokens the hand of *J;* the same formula xi. 9, xix. 22, xxv. 30 (xxix. 34, where however the reading may be קָרְאָה), shows that קָרָא is to be understood with the most general subject (they called), and at the same time indicates that ver. 47, where Jacob is said to have given the name, was written by another hand, viz. *E.* That we have here materials offered by different sources worked up together, is also shown by the connection, ver. 49, not fitting in with what preceded: *And Mispah, for he said: May Jahveh watch between me and thee, when we are out of sight of one another.* וְהַמִּצְפָּה has no other connection than with the preceding: therefore he called the heap of stones גַּלְעֵד, and this place of the meeting of Jacob and Laban was called המצפה, because (אֲשֶׁר, as at xxx. 18, Deut. iii. 24) he (Laban) said— the words of Laban are taken from his speech in *J*, and והמצפה אשר אמר seems to be an addition by *R.* The well-known Mizpah in the mountains of Gilead, the residence of Jephtha (Judg. xi. 34), the subsequent Gadite city of refuge, cannot here be intended, for the Mizpah in question lay in the neighbourhood of the Jabbok (see Mühlau under Mizpah-Mizpeh in Riehm's *HW.*), which Jacob did not pass over till after the reconciliation with Laban. The Samar. reads והמצבה (in the Samar. Targ. וקעמתה), which Wellh. turns to account for the analysis of sources; but the explanation אשר אמר ונו' and והמצפה are surely derived from the same hand, and והמצבה cannot be equivalent with והמצפה, these words having different verbal stems and expressing different notions. The exclamation

of Laban וגו׳ יֵצֶר, with which iv. 14 can hardly be compared, because dissimilar, is continued, ver. 50, in words from *E*: *If thou shalt ill-use my daughters, and if thou shalt take wives beside my daughters, it is not a man that is with us—behold. Elohim is witness between me and thee.* In order not to be betrayed into a false analysis, it must be observed that the covenant obligation, which Laban here imposes upon Jacob, is a different one from that in ver. 51 sq. Here the only matter is that Jacob shall be a faithful and considerate husband to Laban's daughters. With regard to the Divine names in ver. 49 sq., they testify to both *J* and *E*. The appeal to God, as surety of the covenant, does not come into collision with the memorial of the covenant. Another covenant obligation, whose acceptance the memorial is to recall to future ages, consists in this, that the boundary of which it is the mark is not to be passed with hostile intention, 51–53a: *And Laban said unto Jacob: Behold this heap of stones and behold this pillar, which I have set up between me and thee. Let this heap be witness, and let this pillar be witness: neither will I pass over this heap unto thee, neither shalt thou pass over this heap nor this pillar unto me, for ill. The God of Abraham and the God of Nahor judge between us, the God of their father!* The express threefold juxtaposition of the two monuments looks like the comprising together of two accounts, in one of which the מצבה and in the other the גל was prominent. אִם־אָנִי— אִם־אַתָּה answer to the correlative *sive . . . sive*, as at Ex. xix. 13; the אִם of the oath is not intended, for אִם לֹא is an affirmative oath. יָרִיתִי is to be understood according to Job xxxviii. 6 and ירו in the name of Jerusalem. The אֱלֹהֵי אֲבִיהֶם coming in afterwards in a supplementary manner, and hence as a later addition, is not meant to signify "the gods of their father," but, on the contrary, makes the God of Terah, as a higher unity and as a bond of union between the two parties, predominant to the God of Abraham and Nahor. Jacob however does not enter into this syncretistic view of Laban, ver. 53b: *Then*

Jacob swore by the fear of his father Isaac. He swears by the God reverently adored by his father. The narrator, as at ver. 42, is *E*. What was anticipatively related from *J*, ver. 46, now follows in the more detailed form in which it is found in *E*, ver. 54: *And Jacob offered a sacrifice upon the mountain and called his brethren to eat bread, and they ate bread and remained all night in the mountain.* This was the covenant-repast as at xxvi. 30, where however we are not told, as here and xlvi. 1, that there was an offering of the flesh. Elsewhere on the contrary we meet indeed with altars in the patriarchal history, but, except in the sacrifice at Moriah, without mention of sacrifices offered thereon. Next morning a peaceful departure takes place, xxxii. 1: *Early in the morning Laban rose up and kissed his sons and daughters and blessed them, and Laban returned to his place.* Though 1*b* sounds like xviii. 33 (but comp. also Num. xxiv. 25), the account of *E* still continues. Laban in caressing his children does what, according to xxxi. 28, he had desired to do.

THE ANGELIC VISION, THE NIGHT AT PENIEL, AND THE UNEXPECTEDLY KIND BEHAVIOUR OF ESAU, XXXII. 2–XXXIII. 17.

The third section of the Toledoth of Isaac, derived from *E* and *J*, begins with xxxii. 2. A narrative portion from *J* closes with וַיֵּלֶךְ xxxii. 14*a*, and one from *E* with וַיְהִי לוֹ xxxii. 22*b*. What was first related in the words of *J* is repeated ver. 23 sq. in the words of *E*, to whom we are indebted for the narrative of the conflict at the Jabbok. The Divine name אֱלֹהִים however appears both at xxxii. 29 (where the subject gives occasion for it) and at xxxiii. 5, 11 in a Jahvistic context (comp. *e.g.* also xxviii. 21), it is of itself no decisive criterion against *J*, to whom Wellh. ascribes vv. 23–33. Driver also (*Critical Notes*, 1887, p. 41) thinks it probable that 24–32 is derived from *J*. So too Kuenen, to whom the history of Jacob's conflict at Jabbok seems to bear the stamp of the " pre-prophetic" traditions of the Hexateuch (*Einl.* § 13, note 23). It is evident that the answer to the question, whether *J* or *Q* is the narrator, remains an uncertain and purely subjective one. The connection of the family, to whom the promise is given, with Paddan Aram is thus peacefully dissolved, and the progress of the sacred history, turned quite away from this its mother country, advances henceforth towards Egypt, where the family was to grow into a nation. Accompanied by the blessing of Laban, Jacob continues his journey, vv. 2, 3: *And Jacob went on his way and angels of Elohim met him, and Jacob said when he saw them: This is God's host, and he called the name of that place Mahanaim.* Angels of God, in whom he recognises a host of God given him as an escort, meet him (comp. 1 Chron. xii. 22), and he names the place after the angelic host added to his own, or perhaps after the protectors of his previous and future journeys, מַחֲנַיִם (two camps)—the name of a subsequent Levite city, in the territory of the tribe of Gad, north of the Jabbok. Here, according to a statement of Estori ha-Parchi, recently confirmed by Eli Smith, is still found between Jabbok and Jarmuch (ירמוך by Talmudic and Arabic corruption from 'Ιερόμαξ), upon a mountain terrace above the two-branched Wadi Jabes, a place called مَحْنَة *Maḥne.* Hitzig and Kneucker place Mahanaim farther northwards in the Jordan valley, where the Jarmuch flows into the Jordan, but where not a trace of the ancient name is to be found. The name מחנם is inscribed upon the Karnak tablet of the march of Shishak; the termination *ajim* might, as in יְרוּשָׁלַיִם and the like (comp. Köhler, *Gesch.* ii. 176), be a diphthongally formed *am* (Wellh.), but the name is in the Bible always written מַחֲנַיִם, and the Dual represents more aptly than the singular, the meaning and aim of what is related. Jacob's message to Esau, vv. 4–6: *And Jacob sent messengers before him to his brother Esau, to the land of Se'ir, the field of Edom. And he commanded them saying: Speak thus to my lord, to Esau: Thus saith thy servant Jacob:*

I have sojourned with Laban and stayed till now, and I have oxen and asses, flocks and men-servants and maid-servants, and I have sent to tell my lord, to find grace in thy sight. Esau then was already dwelling in שֵׂעִיר אֶרֶץ, though its final occupation and possession, related xxxvi. 6—8 from Q, and according to which it is here anticipatively called שְׂדֵה אֱדוֹם (comp. xxxvi. 6), did not take place till afterwards. A third name of the country in Targ. Jer. and Samar. is אֶרֶץ נבלה the Gebalene (*'Gebâl* = mountains). תֹּאמְרוּן is in the favourite *impf. energicum* of the Jahvistico-Deuteronomic style. The imperfect form אֱחַר (=אֶאֱחַר) is syncopated like אֱהַב Prov. viii. 17. The historical tense וָאֶשְׁלְחָה (as at Ezra viii. 16, Neh. vi. 3, 8) has the intensive *ah*, which enhances the vividness of the notion of the verb and occurs four times in the Pentateuch, Ges. § xlix. 2; Driver, § 72. שׁוֹר used here collectively, and whose plural occurs but once, Hos. xii. 12, is without example elsewhere. Report of the messengers and Jacob's precautionary measures, vv. 7—9: *The messengers returned to Jacob saying: We came to thy brother to Esau, and he also is coming to meet thee, and four hundred men with him. Then Jacob was greatly afraid and was distressed, and he divided the people that was with him and the flocks and the herds and the camels, into two companies, and said: If Esau comes to the one company and smites it, then the company that is left will escape.* The circumstance that Esau has such a host for offence and defence, is explained by his having to maintain himself in Mount Seïr, upon which he has set his mind, against the not yet subjugated and supplanted Horite aborigines. The reader is left as much in the dark as to Esau's purpose and disposition, as Jacob was. This advance, which caused Jacob so much fear, did not manifest any change of mind since xxvii. 41. The angelic manifestation at Mahanain still hovers before him, but the threatening reality is again encamped between him and this consolatory picture. Preparing for the worst, he divides his people and flocks into two companies, that if Esau should smite the one (מַחֲנֶה first *fem.* as at Ps. xxvii. 3, then *mas.* as at Zech. xiv. 15) the other לִפְלֵיטָה, *i.e.* to an escape, *i.e.* will be an escaped and preserved one. Nothing indicates a reference by this division to the Dual מחנים (Dillm.). Jacob does not however rest satisfied with this prudent arrangement, but by believing prayer grasps through the dark future the promise of God, vv. 10-13: *And Jacob said: God of my father Abraham and God of my father Isaac, Jahveh, who saidst unto me: Return to thy country and to thy home and I will do thee good—I am less than all the favours and all the truth which Thou hast showed to Thy servant, for with my staff passed I over this Jordan, and now I am become two companies. Deliver me from the hand of my brother, from the hand of Esau, for I fear him, lest he come and smite me, the mother with the children. And Thou didst say: I will surely do thee good and will make thy seed like the sand of the sea, which cannot be numbered for multitude.* The comparative מן of קָטֹנְתִּי מִכֹּל ver. 11, denoting distance, does not refer to incapacity of requital, but to unworthiness of reception. The חסד is in חסדים (only here in the Pent.) resolved into its manifestations; אמת (the faithfulness or truth which keeps its promises) did not admit of such a plural. "The mother with the children" is, as at Hos. x. 14, a proverbial expression in accordance with Deut. xxii. 6 (על, as at Ex. xxxv. 22, comp. on Ps. xvi. 2). The prayer is of one cast. Tuch thinks it unsuitable in the narrator, to make Jacob call upon God to keep His word. But to keep to His word the God who keeps His word, is the way of all true prayer. Upon what else can Jacob rely but upon the promise of God, and how else can he do so but by praying? With such prayer did Jacob chase away his fear, 14*a*: *And he lodged there that night.* There, viz. where he had received the message and undertaken the division into two companies. Since no וַיִּשְׁכֵּם follows, what is further related must be thought of as taking place during the night season, and this is also confirmed by ver. 23. What lies between 14a and 22b appears to be from E, but the analysis is not certain and is moreover unimportant. Preparations for appeasing Esau, 14b–22: *And he took of what he had in his possession a present for Esau his brother. Two hundred she-goats and twenty he-goats, two hundred ewes and twenty rams, thirty milch camels with their foals, thirty cows and ten bulls, twenty she-asses and ten foals, and delivered it into the hand of his servants in single separate droves, and said to his servants: Pass over before me and leave a space between drove and drove. And he commanded the first, saying: When Esau my brother meeteth thee and asketh thee, saying: Whose art thou and whither goest thou, and to whom do these before thee belong? Then say: To thy servant Jacob, it is a present sent to my lord Esau, and behold he also is himself behind us. And he commanded also the second, also the third, also all who followed the droves, saying: Just so shall ye speak to Esau, when ye meet him. And ye shall say: Also behold thy servant Jacob is behind us; for he thought: I will appease his face by the present, that goes before me, and afterwards see his face, perhaps he will accept my face. So the present went over before him, while he passed that night in the company.* "What had come to his hand" is to be explained according to יָדוֹ צֹאן the flock of his possession, Ps. xcv. 7. The proportion of ten to one in the selection of male and female animals is like 2 Chron. xvii. 11; comp. Varro, *de re rust*. ii. 3. The abbreviation וַעְיָרִים (for וַעֲיָרִים) is like יַעַר Job iv. 2. The verb פָּנָשׁ 18a (a syn. of פָּגַע) only occurs again in the Pent. at xxxiii. 8, Ex. iv. 24, 27; in יִפְנְשֵׁךְ 18b from יִפְנֹשׁ, a secondary form of יִפְגֹּשׁ 1 Sam. xxv. 20, the close of the first syllable is dissolved, comp. Cant. viii. 2, where Ben-Asher reads אֲנָהֶגְךָ and Ben-Naphtali אֶנְהָגֲךָ. In like manner is בְּמֹצַאֲכֶם modified from בְּמָצְאֲכֶם, the original combination of syllables being dissolved. The verb כִּפֶּר, ἐξιλάσκεσθαι, which, when the sinner is spoken of in relation to God, never has God or His wrath as its object (see the ground of the exposition in the Comm. on Heb. ii. 17), has here 21b the accus. of the person offended, and at Prov. xvi. 14 the accusative of the wrath. The Samar. Targum here translates אשפי and vi. 14 וחשפי, and hence assumes both here and there a like original meaning for כפר. To accept the face of any one 21b (comp. xix. 21) is equivalent to favouring his person and interests, receiving him favourably. The night of 22b is the same as that of 14a. That extracts from different sources are discharged into these statements is apparent from vv. 23, 24, where the two sources are seen flowing side by side: *And he arose up in that night and took his two wives and his two handmaids and his eleven children, and passed over the ford of Jabbok. And he took them and brought them over the stream, and brought over what belonged to him.* On בלילה הוא "in that night," comp. xix. 33, xxx. 16. Instead of אֶת־אֲשֶׁר־לֹו the Samar. has את כל אשר לו, which is involuntarily substituted for the pregnant briefer expression. Though יְלָדָיו, not בָּנָיו, is used, Dinah is left unnoticed. The Jabbok is not the Jarmuch (Ew.), nor mentioned by mistake in its stead (Hitz.), but (if we take 'Gebel-Aǵlûn as the place of the meeting with Laban) the eastern affluent of the Jordan (now called *ez-Zerḳâ* on account of its clear blue waters), into which it flows about 1½ leagues south-west of the place where it issues from the mountains. The Syrian caravan road leads to the ford of its upper course; traces of ancient buildings project half-hidden from the rushes and thickets of oleander; the district and the region about the banks of the ford testify that ancient civilisation was there active.

When Jacob was now again alone on the northern bank, he had to undergo a long and difficult conflict, ver. 25 : *And Jacob remained behind alone, and a man wrestled with him till the break of day.* What is here related, ver. 25 sqq., gave, in the opinion of the narrator, its name to the stream, for it is surely intentionally that he uses the *Niph.* נֵאָבֵק, not elsewhere occurring (from אָבַק radically related to חָבַק to hold fast to, to close with one another), hardly a denominative, from אָבָק dust: to make oneself dusty (LXX ἐπάλαιεν, comp. πάλη = pollen, pulvis, συγκονιοῦσθαι). Hence יֵאָבֵק is not in his mind equivalent to יָבַל, from בָּקַק evacuans aquas, but to יֵאָבֵל, according to the kind of syncope in מִלְּפָנוּ Job xxxv. 11, וַתְּזָרֵנִי 2 Sam. xxii. 40. The Samar. has in the Heb. text ויחבק, in the Targ. ואושש: he effected contact, *i.e.* a violent struggling embrace (Aphel of נשש *contrectare*, no denominative from גּוּשׁ clod, Job vii. 5, as Ges. in the *Thesaurus* assumes). Straining of the hip of him who was not to be prevailed against, ver. 26: *And when he saw that he prevailed not against him, he touched the socket of his hip; then was the socket of Jacob's hip strained, as he wrestled with him.* The unnamed sees that he לֹא יָכֹל לוֹ (comp. Ps. cxxix. 2), properly, that he is not equal, not superior to him, and he therefore gives him a blow on the socket of the hip, so as to strain it (וַתֵּקַע from יָקַע, وَقَعَ to fall, to fall out, to occur, LXX ἐνάρκησεν, torpuit, from ναρκάω, which does not exactly correspond, but rather *luxari*), the sinew of the hip undergoing during the wrestling so violent a strain, that Jacob was lamed in consequence. The wrestling having lasted long enough, without Jacob being conquered, the unnamed says, 27a: *Let me go, for the day breaketh.* But Jacob, divining and feeling that it is a Divine Being whose attack he has had to sustain, keeps hold of the man and cries out, according to Hos. xii. 5, with tears and supplications, 27b: *I will not let thee go unless thou bless me.* Then the marvellous Being says to him, ver. 28: *What is thy name? And he said: Jacob.* The question is only preparatory to the communication which follows, ver. 29: *Thy name shall no longer be called Jacob, but Israel; for thou hast fought with Elohim and with men, and hast prevailed.* Instead of the more usual יִקָּרֵא xvii. 5, xxxv. 10, we here read יֵאָמֵר. In אֲנָשִׁים Esau and Laban are thought of. In יָכֹל the *Hoph.* of כֹּל gives the imperfect form וַתּוּכָל, properly, *capax factus es*. The verb שׂרה to contend, is connected with the Arabic شَرَى, I., III., IX. (different from the √ שׁר to put in a row, *serere*, and שַׂר, Heb. and Babylonio-Assyr.: to rule). Ancient translators all render שָׂרִיתָ like the LXX ἐνίσχυσας, they did not understand the distinction between the verbs שׂרה to contend and שָׂרַר to rule (comp. וַיָּשַׂר Hos. xii. 5: he fought, from שָׂרָה = שָׂרַר, and on the other hand יָשֹׂרוּ Isa. xxxii. 1, they will rule); but Luth. correctly: *For thou hast fought with God and with men*. After this oracular saying, Jacob, on his part, also desires to know the name of the wondrous and, as he now the more certainly knows, Divine Being, with whom he has to do, vv. 29, 30: *Then Jacob asked and said: Tell me, I pray thee, thy name. And he said: Wherefore askest thou after my name?* He gives no answer, and yet answers: *And he blessed him there*. It is the same מלאך יהוה who replies to the same question from Manoah, Judg. xiii. 18: Wherefore askest thou after my name, which is Wonderful (יְהוּא פֶּלִי)? His name is not comprehensible for mortals, but the fact of blessing tells Jacob plainly enough Who is before him, viz. the Almighty Himself in His מלאך. His blessing has shed light upon the darkness of Jacob's soul. It was night there, but light appeared during the conflict, and now it is full bright day within and without, ver. 31: *Then Jacob called the name of the place Peniel; for " I have seen Elohim face to face, and my life was preserved."* The name פְּנִיאֵל (or פְּנוּאֵל with the connective sound *û*, like מְתוּ בֵתוּ) means, as the LXX translates it, εἶδος Θεοῦ. He has seen God and yet (contrary to the rule, Ex. xxxiii. 20) is preserved; the *impf. consec.* here denotes a result contrary to expectation, as at xix. 9, xlix. 24; Driver, § 74β. When Jacob now goes farther southwards with his family, ver. 32: *The sun rose upon him, as he went over Penûel, and he halted upon his hip*. A popular custom recalling this circumstance, ver. 33: *Therefore the children of Israel eat not of the sinew of the hip, which is in the socket of the hip, because he touched it.* Even here the subj. continues unnamed, as a mystery not to be unveiled. This sinew (*nervus ischiadicus*) has the name גִּיד הַנָּשֶׁה, العَرَقُ النَّسَا, as the torpifying or paralysing one, *i.e.* the one which causes such a condition, whether momentarily or permanently (see Ges. *Thes.* p. 921*b*); the Arab. نَسَا, which of itself already means the nerve of the hip, shows that הנשה is *gen. appositionis.* The straining, stretching, or crushing of this nerve would result in paralysis. The שחיטה (an allusion to ritual slaughter) understands by it the internal sinew of the so-called hindquarter, including the external, and the ramifications of both.

The meeting of the brothers now follows, xxx. 1–16. Esau approaches, and Jacob prepares for the worst, vv. 1–3: *And Jacob lifted up his eyes and looked, and behold Esau came, and with him four hundred men. And he divided the children unto Leah and Rachel and unto the two handmaids. And he placed the handmaids and their children foremost, and Leah and her children behind, and Rachel and Joseph last. And he himself went before them and bowed himself seven times to the earth, till he came near to his brother.* The verb חצה to divide, had at xxxii. 18 the meaning of separating, here 1*b* of sharing; he shared the children to their mothers, so that in the long train, the handmaids with their children went first, then followed Leah with hers, while Rachel with her only child Joseph closed the procession. Thus at the passage of the Jabbok he reunited the divided companies, and still so mistrusted Esau, as to place the members of his family at a distance from him, proportioned to the degree of responsibility in which he stands to them; nor has he really any reason for not mistrusting him, and at all events nothing can release him from the care for their safety, which his family have a right to expect. He puts himself at the head of the train, and on approaching his brother bows reverentially before him seven times. The הִשְׁתַּחֲוָיָה, προσκύνησις, fully performed, took place with

אפים ארצה, Gen. xix. 1, comp. 1 Sam. xxv. 23, 2 Sam. i. 2, hence, as is traditionally explained, with פִּשּׁוּט יָדַיִם וְרַגְלַיִם, extension of the hands and feet; or only suggestively by bending, as one about to prostrate himself (comp. 1 Sam. xx. 41). At all events Jacob meets his brother with such superabundant courtesy, as we nowhere else meet with in sacred history. It was politic but not hypocritical. He had truly sinned against him, and ought to feel ashamed. The external was the expression of the internal self-humiliation which he experienced, in remembering his fault. Esau makes less ceremony, for he has a comparatively better, and none too tender a conscience; he has let fall his resolve to slay Jacob. The freebooter life awarded him by his father, by which he too may be in his fashion powerful, pleases him. And now that the passion of revenge has spent itself, the brotherly affection, which was never extinct, is rekindled at the sight of Jacob, ver. 4: *Then Esau ran to meet him and embraced him, and fell on his neck and kissed him, and they wept.* The six points over וַיִּשָּׁקֵהוּ have the value of a critical ὀβελός, on which account this word is missing in many MSS. of the LXX. The Midrash however takes them as a mark of interrogation, which casts a doubt on the sincerity of this kissing, and would rather read וישכהו (he bit him); but this is against Esau's character. As all kinds of shadows pass across the piety of the son of promise, so on the other hand is the energetic son of nature capable of noble impulses and emotions. The Divine grace, which ruled in the paternal house, had not been without influence upon him also. He inquires after the women and children in Jacob's retinue, who all salute him with the utmost reverence, vv. 5–7: *And he lifted up his eyes and saw the women and the children, and he said: How are these related to thee? And he said: They are the children which Elohim has graciously given thy servant. And the handmaids drew near, they and their children, and they bowed themselves. And Leah also drew near and her children, and they bowed themselves.*

And last drew near Joseph and Rachel, and they bowed themselves. Here, as at ver. 11, Jacob calls the God who has so richly blessed him אלהים, and that in the midst of the Jahvistic text; it almost seems as if he purposely suppressed the name which God bears as the God of the history of redemption. Esau then inquires concerning the company which he had met—he had already heard from the shepherds that it was a present for himself, but this he ignores, vv. 8–11: *Then he said: What meanest thou by this company which I have met? And he said: That I may find grace in the sight of my lord. Then Esau said: I have abundance, my brother, keep what is thine! But Jacob said: Nay, I pray thee, if I have found favour in thy sight, receive my present from my hand, for for this cause have I seen thy face, as the seeing of the face of Elohim, and thou hast received me kindly. Take then, I pray thee, my blessing, which is brought to thee, for Elohim has dealt graciously with me and I have all. And he urged him. Then he took it.* In the question 8a, מִי stands by attraction (as at Judg. xiii. 17) for מה (xxxii. 28); it relates to the now united five droves (xxxii. 15 sq.). Esau declines the present; omitting the title of *my lord* used by Jacob, he says: יֶשׁ־לִי רָב, *i.e.* not only enough (יֵשׁ), but more than enough. Jacob however requests its acceptance: אִם־נָא expresses condition with the addition of request, as at xviii. 3, xxx. 27; the expression of the request follows in וְלָקַחְתָּ, according to Ges. § 126, note 1. On כִּי־עַל־כֵּן (where עַל־כֵּן כִּי might be expected) see on xviii. 5, here: because occasion and opportunity were offered me to bring thee a gift of homage, therefore have I seen thy face כִּרְאֹת פְּנֵי אֱלֹהִים. If Jacob here means to say, that as great a happiness has been bestowed upon him as if he had seen the face of God, this would certainly be "odious humility" (Kn.). But it must be explained in accordance with such passages as 1 Sam. xxix. 9, 2 Sam. xiv. 17. Jacob means to say that elohimish (we should say heavenly) kindness looks upon him from Esau's face, nor could he think otherwise; for he must have recognised in the disposition of his brother, thus changed against all expectation, the work of the God who hears prayer and disposes the hearts of men (comp. xxxi. 24 with Ps. xxxiii. 15), and so have seen in his, a reflection of the Divine kindness. אלהים and not יהוה was here too in J the Divine name appropriate to the meaning. Dillm. agrees with Wellh. that in 10b another meaning of the name פניאל is indicated, than that given in E, xxxii. 31. Jacob calls the present expressing his wish for a blessing בִּרְכָתִי, my blessing. הֻבָאת is equivalent to הוּבָאָה; āth = ath, is the original feminine termination; comp. the forms of verbs לא Deut. xxxi. 29, Isa. vii. 14, Jer. xliv. 33, Ps. cxviii. 23, and of verbs לה, where it is less frequent, Lev. xxv. 21, xxvi. 34; Ges. § 74, 75, note 1. חֻנַּי is contracted from חָנְנִי. A second reason is added with וְכִי, as at 1 Sam. xix. 4, Isa. lxv. 16. Esau had said: I have abundance; Jacob can, in the consciousness that Jahveh is his God, without hyperbole outvie him and say: I have all. By thus pressing Esau he induces him to accept the present. Then Esau remembers the onward journey and offers to escort him, but this Jacob declines, vv. 12–15: *Then he said: Let us journey and go onwards, and I will go in presence of thee. And he said to him: My lord knoweth that the children are tender, and the flocks and herds are upon me as giving suck, and if they are overdriven one day, all the sheep will die. Let my lord, I pray thee, go before his servant, and I will move forwards at my ease according to the pace of the cattle that is before me, and according to the pace of the children until I come to my lord to Seir. Then said Esau: Let me, I pray thee, place with thee a portion of the people that are with me; but he said: Wherefore! Let me find favour in the sight of my lord!* Esau will precede לִנְגֶד Jacob, so that the latter having him in sight may be sure of protection. But Jacob declines; he does not yet feel that this would be safe, is the remark of Kn. But could he who wrestled with God have so soon become again a designer and a coward? No; the vocation of which Jacob is conscious, by reason of the blessing of the first-born, obliges him, like Abraham in the presence of the five kings, just now to maintain his independence in the presence of Esau, and not to involve himself in any fresh obligation to him. Besides, the reasons for which he deprecates his escort are no empty pretence, for he does not desire that Esau should accommodate himself to the difficulties of his advance, and he is unable to accommodate himself to the warlike pace of Esau and his people, being obliged for the sake of the children and flocks to avoid overexertion: עָלַי עָלוֹת *lactantes* (as at Isa. xl.11, not *lactentes*, because properly *sustentantes*, see on Ps. viii. 3) *super me, i.e.* make special care incumbent on me, because in the condition of giving suck, and should any one overdrive them (*ûm* for *ûn*, as at xxvi. 15 and always), etc.,—the usual hypothetical construction with the Perf. in both prodosis and apodosis, xlii. 38, xliv. 29, comp. xxxi. 30, Ex. xvi. 21; Ges. § 155. 4*a*. The לְ of לְאִטִּי and לְרֶגֶל is that of measure; מְלָאכָה here means property = cattle, as perhaps also at 1 Sam. xv. 9, comp. *peculium, pecunia*, property consisting in cattle. Jacob's destination is Hebron, thence he seems to purpose visiting his brother in Seir: he deceives him by deceiving himself. Esau proposes to leave at least some of his people with him as an escort, but this too Jacob courteously deprecates as unnecessary. They consequently separate and depart in different directions, vv. 16, 17: *Therefore Esau returned on his way that day to Seir. And Jacob journeyed to Succoth and built himself a house and made booths for his cattle, therefore he called the name of the place Succoth.* The uninterrupted prosecution of his journey was not possible to Jacob, his household required forbearance and rest: only necessity makes this trans-Jordanic sojourn comprehensible. Jerome in his *Quaestiones* on this passage remarks: *Sochoth usque hodie civitas trans Jordanem in parte Scythopoleos.* There is actually still a place, ساكوت, south of

Beisân (= Bethseān = Scythopolis), "upon a low bluff at the end of the ridge above the *Wâdi el-Mâliḥ*" (Robinson in *DMZ.* vii. 1, p. 59). This *Succoth* lies *in parte Scythopoleos*, but not *trans Jordanem*. There must however have been also a Succoth on the other side of Jordan, which Jacob, coming from Mesopotamia by Mahanaim and Peniel and crossing over Jordan to Sichem, would pass. Sichem is emphatically called, xxxiii. 18, the first Canaanite town, *i.e.* the first place in the country west of Jordan which he reached. A Succoth situate *trans Jordanem* is also required: (1) Because a Gadite Succoth is named with Beth-Nimra and other east-Jordanic places, and this must have been, even on this account, on the left bank of Jordan, because the tribe of Gad had no possessions on its western side. (2) Because Gideon, Judg. viii. 4–8, having passed over Jordan, comes to Succoth and thence to Penuel. If then the Succoth, between which and Zarthan Solomon had the temple-vessels cast, lay in the neighbourhood of Scythopolis, 1 Kings iv. 12, upon the western side, so that we must distinguish between an eastern and a western Succoth, both בְּעֵמֶק Josh. xiii. 27, Ps. lx. 8, there must beyond all doubt have been one east of Jordan, and this is Jacob's Succoth. Kiepert's maps transpose it close to the left bank of Jordan above the Wadi Jabis; but then Jacob must have gone northwards and thus have twice passed the Jabbok, which may be admitted, although the narrative does not say so. It is more probable however that this Succoth on the left bank lay between the Jabbok and the high road, which leads from Salṭ in Gilead to Sichem (Köhler, *Gesch.* i. 147; Keil, Dillm.). Ver. 17 also bears in the עַל־כֵּן קָרָא (therefore he called) the mark of *J* (comp. xi. 9, xvi. 14, xix. 22, xxv. 30, l. 11).

Before proceeding farther, we would once more review the wonderful experiences of Jacob at Mahanaim and Peniel. At Mahanaim, on the threshold of the Land of Promise, is fulfilled to him what he had dreamed at Bethel, when on the point of leaving it. What he here experienced, is thus in the mind of the narrator no second dream-vision. The host of God has invisible reality outside himself (a reality made for the moment visible), as indeed already follows from its being appointed to protect him. Are we to judge otherwise concerning the occurrence at Peniel? It is for the most part transposed, as already by Eusebius (in the *Elogæ proph.*), to the sphere of the dream or ecstasy. "A mystic obscurity"—says Krummacher in his *Paragraphen zu der heil. Gesch.* 1818 —"rests upon this appearing, which is with peculiar simplicity represented not as a dream-vision, which it indisputably was, but as an historical event, and as such it may with full justice be esteemed, for does only the material, and that which is an object of sight and touch, belong to history, and is that which can neither be laid hold of nor comprehended excluded from it?" And Hengstenberg: "In an external conflict and struggle, victory is not obtained by prayer and tears as by Jacob, according to Hos. xii. 4 sq." Umbreit (*Studien u. Kritiken*, 1848) passes the final sentence: "If we try to explain the passage literally, darkness settles upon it, and we see no gleam of light, except the rising sun." Certainly the occurrence here related belongs not to outward and visible history, but to the spiritual life; but it is not on that account purely subjective. The Being with whom he contended was not present only to Jacob's imagination, it was not merely an attack caused by his own conscience, but an attack objectively real by God Himself. The מלאך (Hos. xii. 5) had not indeed flesh and bone, he opposed force to force in virtue of the power, which the spirit has over the material, just as our spirit also, though it has not flesh and bone, sets this in motion as it chooses. But that Jacob conquers God in the Divine man, is possible, because it is only with a certain measure of His omnipotence that God opposes him. And why does he wrestle with Jacob in this hostile manner? Because, as now comes clearly to light in view of the meeting with Esau, his possession of the blessing is not unspotted by sin. It is for this reason that he is attacked, and that not merely by his own conscience, which testifies against this sin, but by God Himself, who makes him feel it. But the faith in the depth of Jacob's heart breaks through sin and weakness and attack, grasps the mercy of his Adversary notwithstanding His hostile demeanour, and wrings anew from Him that blessing, threatened with annihilation, which he now obtains purified from dross, sanctified, transfigured as a Divine gift, a gift of grace. The straining of his hip was a reminder that his natural strength was nothing. What made Jacob invincible was, as the Divine touch proved, not his hip (Ps. cxlvii. 10), but his faith. It was by this that he anew obtained the blessing, which he had till now possessed as the acquisition of his carnal subtlety. For the blessing of the first-born, out of which he tricked Esau, could neither be the basis of a birthright valid before God, nor the root from which the holy nation was to grow. It becomes this in this conflict, in which Jacob re-obtains it as the prize of his victorious faith, and from which he comes forth with the new name of ישראל, which (of like meaning as it seems with שְׂרָיָה) does not directly signify the fighter of God, *i.e.* fighter with God (for, as Nestle, *Eigennamen*, pp. 30–63, has shown, אֵל is, in all personal names compounded with אל, intended as subject, not as object), but "God fights," yet so that this, by reason of the occasion, acquires the meaning of one with whom God fought and who thus had to fight with God; thus *e.g.* יִצְחָק means the laugher, but according to its meaning is the designation of him who was the object of laughter; also יבק (=יאבק) means the wrestler, but designates the stream where the wrestling took place. Thus Jacob is called ישראל as the man fought with by God, but connotatively as the man who sustained the fight with God. This name he henceforth bears, especially in *J*, but in none of the sources so exclusively as Abram and Sarai bear those of אברהם and שרה after they were given them by God, xvii. 5, 15. For these two names designate the transition into a new and ever-continuing position effected and appointed by the Divine will and promise, and therefore entirely abolish the former names. But the name יִשְׂרָאֵל denotes a spiritual demeanour determined by faith, beside which the natural, determined by flesh and blood, was henceforth to go on in Jacob's life. Jacob-Israel is herein the prototype of the nation descended from him.

THE SOJOURN IN SICHEM. SIMEON AND LEVI'S VENGEANCE FOR THE DISHONOURING OF DINAH, CH. XXXIII. 18–XXXIV.

The second portion of the third section of the Toledoth of Isaac, xxxiii. 18 to xxxiv., relates to the atrocity perpetrated by Simeon and Levi upon the Sichemites. Vv. 18–20 form the transition: *And Jacob came in peace to the city of 'Sechem which is in the land of Canaan, upon his journey from Paddan Aram, and he encamped before the city. And he bought the piece of ground, where he had pitched his tent, at the hand of the sons of Ḥamôr, the father of 'Sechem, for a hundred K'sîṭah. And he erected there an altar and called it " El God of Israel."* The LXX, Syr. Euseb. Jerome take שָׁלֵם as the name of a place, and Sâlim is actually the name of a village situated on a rocky eminence east of Nablus, certainly that near which John baptized, John iii. 23, and from which the valley of Salem, Judith iv. 4, had its name. But then עִיר שְׁכֶם would be in opposition to this שָׁלֵם, which is inadmissible (for that a daughter city should be called עִיר of the mother city is without authentication); hence of the two meanings: *in Salem* and *in pace* (see Rönsch, *Buch der Jubiläen*, pp. 141–143), which the Leptogenesis places together, שָׁלֵם has here the latter (whence Saadia translates: he came سَالِمًا to the city of Nabulus); שָׁלֵם is equivalent to שָׁלוֹם xliii. 27 (as the Hebræo-Sam. reads: *ujaba ja'akob šalom îr eškem*), or בִּשְׁלוֹם, in safety, he came to the city of Shechem as it was promised him, xxviii. 15, comp. 21. The territory of Sichem (situate, as אשר באר בנען states, in Canaan proper on the right of the Jordan) is already mentioned in Abraham's time, xii. 6; the then still new city was regarded as founded by Chamôr, a Hivite prince, and called after his son (Judg. ix. 28, comp. Josh. xxiv. 32). That father and son are called *Asinus* and *Humerus* recalls the blessing of Issachar, xlix. 14 sq., though the ancient position of Sichem upon the "shoulder" of Gerizim makes the allusion doubtful. In any case there is no need to refer the name חמור to an ass honoured as a deity (*DMZ.* xl. 156). Nor need we be astonished to find the חִוִּים, who dwelt in the period after Moses from the Antilebanon to Hamath, Josh. xi. 3, Judg. iii. 3, here in the midst of Canaan, where they formed a small kingdom, as in Gibeon, Josh. ix. 11, 19, they formed a small republic; Mount Ephraim may have been their original abode, whence they were subsequently driven northwards until they disappeared after the time of Solomon (1 Kings ix. 20). In the neighbourhood (אֶת־פְּנֵי as at xix. 13, Lev. iv. 6) of this Sichem Jacob encamped and bought the piece of ground on which he pitched his tent, from the ruling family of the בְּנֵי־חֲמוֹר אֲבִי שְׁכֶם (comp. Judg. ix. 28), for one hundred Kesitah (to which Josh. xxiv. 32 refers), as Abraham bought the cave of Machpelah from the Hethites for four hundred shekels, xxiii. 16 (both which purchases are entangled into one, Acts vii. 16). LXX, Onkelos, the Targ. Job xxiv. 11 and Jerome translate קשיטה by חוּרְפָּא lamb (comp. Samar. עורפא and with it the Syr. עורפן money)—a meaning which קשיטה must, according to *Gen. Rabba* c. 79, have really had in the common tongue. R. Akiba however relates (*Rosch ha-Shanah* 26a) that in Africa (certainly among the Carthaginians) he heard a coin called קשיטה, which is not improbable, قسط being applied to all sorts of designations of quantity. We are not obliged with Cavedoni to understand קשיטה of an uncoined piece of silver of the value of a lamb, or with Poole of a weight in the shape of a lamb (such weights occur indeed among the Egyptians, Assyrians, and also among the Persians, in the forms of lions, dogs, and geese), but קְשִׂיטָה means directly a weighed piece of metal, and one indeed, as shown by xxiii. 16, Job xlii. 11, of considerably higher value than the שֶׁקֶל, but not more particularly definable (comp. Madden, *History of Jewish Coinage*, 1864, p. 6 sq.). The piece of ground, acquired at this price by Jacob, was the plain extending at the east end of the narrow valley between Ebal and Gerizim, where Jacob's well and Joseph's grave, from one to two hundred paces north of the latter, are still shown (Josh. xxiv. 32). Upon this piece of purchased ground Jacob erects an altar, not a מַצֵּבָה, for the circumstance that הִצִּיב is used, xxxv. 14, 20, for the erection of a pillar, does not prove that here too מזבח was substituted for an original מצבה belonging to וַיַּצֶּב (Wellh. Dillm.). He calls the altar אֵל אֱלֹהֵי יִשְׂרָאֵל. Having returned in safety from a strange country, he again settles in Canaan, and according to his vow thankfully acknowledges the God whom he calls אֵל, and who appeared to him in Bethel, xxxi. 13, as *his* God, the God of Israel (see xxxii. 25 sqq.). The name אל אלהי ישראל as the name of the altar is meant, as it were, of its inscription. In the Mosaic period אל אלהי ישראל was changed into יהוה אלהי ישראל Ex. xxxiv. 23, the favourite name for God in the book of Joshua.

From בְּבֹאוֹ מִפַּדַּן אֲרָם xxxiii. 18a it is seen that R is here speaking in words from Q, to whom belongs also ver. 19, the counterpart to the purchase in Hebron, ch. xxiii., while on the other hand ver. 20, the counterpart to Ex. xvii. 15, may be derived from E. In the history of the vengeance taken on Shechem for the dishonouring of Dinah, which now follows in ch. xxxiv., and which the unconnectedly inserted notice xxx. 21 had in view, Q and J are the chief narrators. The accounts of both as met with by R essentially agreed. In both circumcision was made a condition to the Shechemites, after Dinah had in both been carried of and dishonoured by the young prince, but most anxiously demanded by him in marriage—in both she is taken, and is again taken back, 2*b*, 17*b*, 26*b*. In vv. 1-2, 4, 6, 8-10, 14-18, 20-24, *Q* is unmistakeable; the demand of circumcision is repeated, 15*b*, 22*b*, in the same words as in xvii. 10, and the transaction at Shechem is similar to that at Hebron, ch. xxiii. (comp. the twofold כל־יצאי שער עירו ver. 24, and the twofold כל באי שער עירו xxiii. 10, 18). Just as evident is *J*'s mode of statement at vv. 3, 5, 7, 11-12, 19, 25-26, 30-31. Certainly the term טָמֵא for dishonouring is authenticated elsewhere only in the Priest Codex and Ezekiel, but the formula נבלה עשה בישראל is Deuteronomic, Deut. xxii. 21, and נער=נערה (which in the Pent. occurs only once, Deut. xxii. 19) is each of the twenty-one times (in Gen. xxiv. 14, 16, xxviii. 55, 57, xxxiv. 3*a*, 3*b*, 12) Jahvistic or Deuteronomic. In *Q* Hamor, in *J* Shechem is the chief speaker, which is easily fitted together; it is clearly seen from vv. 8-10 (*Q*) and 11-12 (*J*), how the two accounts are placed side by side to complete each other. The case of the abruptly commencing portion, vv. 27-29 (with ver. 13), is peculiar; this like xlviii. 21 seems to come from *E*, who has related the conquest of Shechem only according to its external aspect, as a deed of arms by the sons of Jacob. This apportioning of sources seems to me more than probable, while Dillm. thinks otherwise, and Kuenen makes a different analysis. Evidence and agreement are here scarcely attainable.

Dinah visits the city from the new dwelling-place of her father, ver. 1: *Then Dinah, the daughter of Leah whom she bare to Jacob, went out to see the daughters of the land.* It is *Q* who thus begins: " Daughters of the land," like xxvii. 46, comp. " people of the land," xxiii. 12. The son of the prince of the land is captivated by her beauty, keeps her with him and dishonours her, ver. 2: *And 'Sechem the son of Hamor the Hivite, the prince of the land, saw her, took her, lay with her and humiliated her.* Cajetanus (Thomas de Vio) already remarks in his Comm. on Genesis: *Multis annis post reditum Jacobi ex Mesopotamia peractis hoc accidit et ad minus apparet quod anni fluxerunt decem, ut et Dina esset nubilis et Simeon et Levi ad bellum dispositi.* Such is also the view of Bonfrère, Petavius and Hengstenberg (*Auth.* 2. 352 sq.). Dinah was then, as also Demetrius in Euseb. *Præp.* ix. 21 computes, in her sixteenth year, *i.e.* assuming that she was born in the second seven years of the Aramæan sojourn. According however to the after calculation, given ch. xxx., she was in her fourteenth, Simeon in his twenty-first, and Levi in his twentieth year. It may be objected against both these statements of Dinah's age, that the time from Jacob's return to the selling of Joseph, which took place after Jacob's entrance into his father's house, amounts to only eleven years (from Joseph's sixth to his seventeenth year), and that one year is too short for the occurrence in ch. xxxv. But much can happen in a year; we must therefore adhere to the view, that Dinah's dishonour falls in the tenth year after the return to Canaan. Is אֹתָהּ with וַיִּשְׁכַּב the acc. of the object? According to xxvi. 10, xxxv. 22, Lev. xv. 18, 24 and other passages it seems so, and the *Keri* יִשְׁכָּבֶנָּה Deut. xxviii. 30, assumes that this pregnant construction of שׁכב (אֹתָהּ instead of the expected עִמָּהּ) is possible, nay usual. In Dinah's case matters were different from Thamar's, whom Amnon, after the satisfaction of his passion, hated as much as he had loved, vv. 3, 4: *And his soul clave unto Dinah, the daughter of Jacob, and he loved the damsel and spake to the heart of the damsel. And 'Sechem said to Hamôr: Get me this damsel to wife.* The young seducer only loved her whom he had seduced the more, soothed her with pleasant prospects of the future, and actually entreated his father to take him the damsel for a wife; for the marriage of children was, according to ancient domestic arrangement, the business of parents (xxiv., xxi. 21). Jacob hears what has happened, the sons of Jacob hear it, and meantime the wooer arrives, vv. 5–7: *And Jacob heard that he had dishonoured Dinah his daughter, and his sons were with the cattle in the field, and Jacob held his peace until they came. And Hamôr, the father of 'Sechem, came out unto Jacob, to commune with him. But the sons of Jacob came in from the field when they heard it, and the men felt grieved, and were very wroth, that he had wrought folly in Israel in lying with Jacob's daughter, which thing ought not to be done.* The dishonour of a sister was a matter which touched the brothers even more closely than the father. The expression 7*b*, there being as yet no people of Israel, sounds anachronistic, like Deut. xxii. 21, Judg. xx. 10, 2 Sam. xiii. 12 sqq., Jer. xxix. 23; but it is only so to a certain extent, since the family of Jacob with its dependants had already the semblance of a family developing into a nation (comp. xxxv. 6). עָשָׂה נְבָלָה is the standing expression for carnal transgressions, which are more accurately called זִמָּה, Judg. xx. 6, and תֶּבֶל; נבלה because the man who follows his carnal impulses in opposition to nature, honour and decency, is a paragon of folly. The potential יֵעָשֶׂה means here: so should it not be done, as at xx. 9, Lev. iv. 27 (comp. xxix. 26: so it is not wont to be done). Hamor now comes and woos for his son, vv. 8-10: *Then Hamôr spoke to them thus: The soul of my son 'Sechem is bound to your daughter; I pray you, give her to him to wife. And make ye alliances with us, give your daughters to us and take our daughters to you. And dwell with us—the land shall be open before you, dwell in and pass through it and settle therein.* "Your daughters" zeugmatically include the brothers, who are here especially concerned. אֹתָנוּ after "make ye alliances," cannot be meant as an acc. but stands for אִתָּנוּ (1 Kings iii. 1), for which also בָּנוּ or לְ would be allowable. סחר combined with the acc. like *vv. eundi*, is here meant of passing through the land as סֹחֵר (xxiii. 16), hence of liberty to trade (different from xlii. 34). נֵאָחֲזוּ to settle is, like אֲחֻזָּה, an expression of the Elohistic style, xlvii. 27, Num. xxxii. 30, Josh. xxii. 9, 19. The old prince is ready to fraternize with Jacob, but the young prince also, without waiting for Jacob's answer, places in the balance words, with which his love for Dinah inspires him, vv. 11, 12: *And 'Sechem said to her father and her brothers: Let me find grace in your eyes, and what you shall say to me I will give. Lay upon me a very high price and dowry, and I will give whatever you say—only give me the damsel to wife.* He will agree to everything to the highest מֹהַר bride-purchase money (Arab. *mahr*, Syr. *mahrâ*) and the largest מַתָּן bridal present (Gen. Rabba: פרא פרניך, παράφερνα, according to a common inaccurate use of this word of the gift of the husband to the wife, comp. Ex. xxii. 15 sq. LXX), if they will only give him the maiden to wife. It sounded extremely flattering to Jacob and his sons that their flesh and blood should be so highly esteemed. But if they had consented to the offer of Hamor, the family of Jacob would by blending with the heathen have forfeited their redemptive vocation; and if the brothers of Dinah had let the matter be settled with money, they would have defiled their more than princely nobility and sacrificed their moral feeling to Mammon. This they refuse to do, and appear thereby morally great; but their moral greatness is blackened, by passion making them inventive and inspiring them with a plan of revenge, which, unless God had presided over this entanglement of good and evil, might easily have proved the destruction of the sacred family, vv. 13-18: *Then the sons of Jacob answered 'Sechem with guile, and said, because he had dishonoured Dinah their sister. And they said to them: We cannot do this to give our sister to one that is uncircumcised, for that is to us disgraceful. Only on this condition will we consent unto you, if ye become as we are, that you let every male among you be circumcised. Then will we give our daughters to you, and will take your daughters to us, and we will dwell with you and become one people. And their words were acceptable in the eyes of Hamôr, and in the eyes of 'Sechem the son of Hamôr.* The sons of Jacob answered בְּמִרְמָה and said, because, etc. In any case אֲשֶׁר (as at ver. 27 = יַעַן) introduces the reason for their concealed plan of vengeance, and we must either read here, transposing the words, וידברו במרמה (Olsh. Schrad. Dillm.), or, which is less probable: וְיִבֶּר means here to act from behind, a Piel meaning of دبر to be or go backward (trans. to lead, to bring backward), proved for the Hebrew also by דביר (see on Ps. xxxviii. 2), and shown to be at least possible by 2 Chron. xxii. 10, where וַיְדַבֵּר, assuming the integrity of the text, has the meaning of murderous destruction. They cannot give their sister to one who is uncircumcised, because that (the state of uncircumcision) is a disgrace with them; but בְּזֹאת for this, *i.e.* this act on their part, they will consent unto them (נֵאוֹת) from אוֹת, not *imperf. Kal* like יָבוֹשׁ, but *imperf. Niph.* to agree about anything, allied to אָתָה, أتى, used in post-biblical diction as a participle: agreeing to, suitably) if they (the Hivites) become as they (the Jacobites) are, לְהִמּוֹל by all the males among them submitting to circumcision; then will they give to them their sister (וְנָתַנּוּ, *perf. consec.* according to Ges. § 126. 6, note 1), and unite themselves with them as one people. Shechem hastens to fulfil the condition, ver. 19: *And the young man deferred not to do the thing, for he had delight in Jacob's daughter, and he was the most honoured in all the house of his father.* The condition did not displease the two wooers. Shechem really loved Dinah, besides circumcision was the custom of most of the Canaanites and Egyptians, while heathen worship required far greater mutilations; the thousands of Roman proselytes who, according to Cicero, *pro Flacco,* c. 28, filled Italy, show how much more compliant antiquity was in this respect than modern times would be. The account as at present constructed here at once remarks that the young man, whose example would go far, because he was the most respected member of his family, made no delay (אֵחַר for אָחַר, like מֵאֵן). The different sources betray themselves by the circumstance, that in ver. 20 both first return home, and he would hardly undergo the operation previously. The princely pair now proclaim in the city, and indeed in the gate (the Oriental forum), the treaty entered into, vv. 20-24: *Then came Hamôr and his son ˈSechem to the gate of their city and spake thus to the men of their city: These men are friendly with us, and they will dwell in the land and go through it; and the land, behold it lies before them spacious towards the right hand and the left: we will take their daughters to us for wives, and we will give them our daughters. Only under this condition will the men consent unto us, to dwell with us, to become one people, that we circumcise every male among us, as they are circumcised. Their cattle and their property and all their beasts of burden, will not this be ours? Let us only consent to them, that they may dwell with us. Then to Hamôr and his son ˈSechem hearkened all that went out to the gate of his city, and all the males were circumcised, all that went out to the gate of his city.* שָׁלֵם xxxiii. 18 means to be in safety, here, to be in good relation, to stand on a peaceful friendly footing with (אֶת, comp. עִם 1 Kings viii. 61 and frequently). They give to Jacob and his family the praise of being thoroughly well-meaning people. Besides, the land is of such spacious extent (Ps. civ. 25) that they may go about in it, without becoming inconvenient; they next declare the certainly unwelcome condition which is to cost the Shechemites blood (נִמֹּלִים, partic. of the *Niph.* which like the praet. runs through the whole scale of vowels: נָמֵס, נָבֵר, נִמֹּל), but at the same time somewhat sweeten it by adding that their cattle, beasts of burden, and property in general (to be explained according to xxxvi. 6, Num. xxxii. 26) may be looked upon by them, the Hivites, as their own, or may in the end become theirs. This recommendation of the treaty, which Jacob and his family indeed must not hear of, although it was only a rhetorical artifice, inclined the Shechemites to consent, for self-interest is the door to all hearts, and all who went out to the gate of Shechem's city (xxiii. 10, 18) submitted to circumcision. The operation of circumcision is however no slight matter; it may, if unskilfully or incautiously performed, become dangerous through haemorrhage, caries, etc. Adults have therefore to lie in bed and keep quiet for three days, while frequently healing does not take place till from thirty-five to forty days. Hence, on the third, the critical day, the men of Shechem were all down (comp. Josh. v. 8), and thus fell victims to a sudden and malicious attack, vv. 25, 26: *And it came to pass on the third day, when they were sore, that the two sons of Jacob, Simeon and Levi, the brothers of Dinah, took each his sword and surprised the careless city, and killed every male. And Hamôr and his son ᵛSechem they killed with the edge of the sword, and took Dinah out of ᵛSechem's house and departed.* They came upon the city בֶּטַח, not as Luther, *thürstiglich*, i.e. rashly, *confidenter*, but to be referred to the city: in a condition free from care (comp. Ezek. xxx. 9), struck down every male, and especially the two princes, according to (κατά) the edge of the sword, *i.e.* letting this, which is conceived of as a mouth that devours, have its way. It was Simeon and Levi, the "two sons of Jacob," who carried out this sudden assassination, which their father disowned shortly before his death, xlix. 5–7. In vv. 27–29 however, the other sons of Jacob are also participators: *The sons of Jacob fell upon the slain and plundered the city, because he had dishonoured Dinah their sister. Their sheep and oxen and asses, and what was in the city and what was in the field, they took away. And all their property and all their children and wives they carried away captive, and plundered all that was in the house.* The beginning is abrupt (comp. on the other hand 7a) and ואת כל־אשר בבית drags behind, just as וידברו does in ver. 13; the refrain-like "because he had dishonoured (her)," common to vv. 13 and 27, proves that vv. 13, 27–29 are taken from a special source, which, turning away from the moral aspect of the matter, relates the conquest of Shechem, in the sense of xlviii. 22, as a deed of arms on the part of the whole family of Jacob. The two ואת 28b may be conceived correlatively like Num. ix. 14, the ו of וְאֵת 29b perhaps in the sense of *etiam*; but probably as in ver. 13 (read וַיְדַבְּרוּ בְמִרְמָה), so here too, a displacement of the text may have occurred, and the original text may have run: וְאֵת כֹּל אֲשֶׁר בַּבַּיִת שְׁבוּ וַיָּבֹזּוּ (comp. Obad. ver. 11, 2 Chron. xxi. 17). Now follows the continuation from *J*, which joins on to ver. 26, vv. 30, 31: *Then Jacob said to Simeon and Levi: Ye have troubled me, to make me to stink among the inhabitants of the land, the Canaanites and Pherizites, and yet I am a numerable people, and if they gather together against me, they will smite me, and I shall be destroyed, I and my house.* The verb עָכַר to shake together, *conturbare*, is found in the Jahvistic style also at Josh. vi. 18, vii. 25. הִבְאִישׁ to make evil, especially of evil odour, here with the accus. of the person, Ex. v. 21 with the accus. אֶת־רֵיחֵנוּ. "Canaanites and Pherizites" as the population of the country also at xiii. 7. מְתֵי מִסְפָּר numerable = few people, is Jahvistico-Deuteronomic (Deut. iv. 27); נִשְׁמַד (and וְהִשְׁמִיד) is a frequent word in Deut. (occurring elsewhere in the peroration of the law of holiness, Lev. xxvi. 30). Jacob laments the fatal deed, but they (Simeon and Levi) justify it, ver. 31: *But they said: Should one treat our sister as a harlot?* The verb עָשׂה *tractare*, as at Lev. xvi. 15 and frequently. הַכְזוֹנָה has כ *raph.* as at xxvii. 38, Job xv. 8, xxii. 13, and *Gaja* before the *Pathach* in distinction from the article, it is uncertain whether with ז *majusculum*, comp. Frensdorff, *Ochla-we-Ochla*, p. 88. Simeon and Levi have the last word, but Jacob speaks the last of all in his testamentary sayings. The most sinful part of it was, their degrading the sacred sign of the covenant to so base a means of malice. And yet it was a noble germ which exploded so sinfully. The Divine righteousness, which fashioned the subsequent history, turned this also to account. The energetic moral purity, which the two tribes display in these their beginnings, was sanctified by grace and profited all Israel. When this is considered, the view of the vengeance of Simeon and Levi, which underlies xxxiv. 27–29, xxxv. 5, xlviii. 22, and according to which this warlike occurrence was perhaps related in the 'ס מלחמות ה' Num. xxi. 14, will be found explicable. The unbending strictness, with which the history abstains from interposing any judgment or reflections, is admirable.

THE LAST EVENTS OF ISAAC'S LIFE, CH. XXXV.

The third and last section of the Toledoth of Isaac ends with the third portion, ch. xxxv. The contents of this chapter are as miscellaneous as Old Testament biographies in general, as also Arabic biographies, are wont to be towards their close. From Succoth Jacob went to the district of Shechem, every station bringing him nearer to his father's home. Between his arrival in Canaan however and his entrance into that home an interval of several years, during which he lived at a distance from his aged father, took place. 1. RETURN TO BETHEL AND DEATH OF DEBORAH, xxxv. 1–8, from *E*, without interpolations being (as by Dillm.) denied to him. The reason for his long sojourn in Shechem is unknown to us. An inner voice now directs the patriarch to leave the neighbourhood of Shechem, which had been so cruelly devastated, and to go to Bethel, where upon his flight he had had the encouraging dream-vision of the ladder reaching to heaven: *And Elohim said to Jacob: Arise, go up to Bethel and dwell there, and build there an altar to the God that appeared to thee, when thou fleddest from the face of thy brother Esau. Then Jacob said to his household and to all that were with him: Put away the strange gods which you have among you, and purify yourselves and change your garments. And we will arise and go up to Bethel, and I will erect an altar there to the God who heard me in the day of my distress, and was with me in the way that I went. Then they gave to Jacob all the strange gods which were in their hand, and the rings which were in their ears, and Jacob buried them under the terebinth which was in Shechem. And they journeyed, and a terror of Elohim was upon the cities that were round about them, and they did not pursue the sons of Jacob. So Jacob came to Luz, which is in the land of Canaan, the same is Bethel, he and all the people that were with him. And he built there an altar and called the place El Bethel, for there God manifested Himself to him, when he fled before his brother. There Deborah, Rebekah's nurse, died and was buried below Bethel under the oak, and they called its name the oak of weeping.* Before starting on the journey to Bethel, by which he obeyed the behest of God, and at the same time fulfilled a promise formerly made to Him, Jacob bids those belonging to both his narrower and wider family circle, to put away their "gods of the strange land" (נֵכָר, original form *nĭkăr*, like שֵׁעָר, עֵנָב), which had been long enough tolerated from his too indulgent affection for his wives, and to make fit preparation for visiting the holy place (Ex. xix. 14 sq.). There in Bethel is he to dwell, there is he, in conformity with his vow, to make this place a house of God, *i.e.* a place of worship, xxviii. 22, to build an altar to the God who heard him in the day of distress (comp. the saying Ps. xx. 2, which perhaps alludes to this passage of Genesis), and was with him on his way to the strange country. Then they gave to the patriarch all the strange gods (among which were Rachel's teraphim); they gave him also their earrings (which served as amulets or charms, Targums קָדְשַׁיָּא; comp. talisman = τέλεσμα), and he buried these things, which would profane the holy place, תַּחַת הָאֵלָה, in Shechem. The LXX adds καὶ ἀπώλεσεν αὐτὰ ἕως τῆς σήμερον ἡμέρας. The place overshadowed by this terebinth consecrated by Jacob, and perhaps already by Abram (xii. 6, comp. Deut. xi. 30), was in Joshua's time (Josh. xxiv. 26, where it is pointed הָאַלָּה, comp. on the other hand Judg. ix. 6) esteemed as a מִקְדַּשׁ ה׳, and Joshua there erected the memorial stone of the oath of covenant faithfulness to Jahveh here taken by the elders of the people. The ancient patriarchal injunction: הָסִירוּ אֶת־אֱלֹהֵי הַנֵּכָר, is purposely repeated in Joshua's address, xxiv. 23. Ver. 5, which joins on to xxiv. 27–29 and furnishes an indispensable explanation, explains how it was that Jacob could thus quietly prepare for and take his journey, and hence must not (with Dillm.) be denied to *E* as an insertion of *R* (the redactor). "A terror of Elohim," חִתַּת אֱלֹהִים (comp. 2 Chron. xx. 29, Zech. xiv. 14), *i.e.* one more than natural (according to heathen expression: πανικὸν δεῖμα), fell upon the cities round about, none ventured to pursue the sons of Jacob, who had smitten and plundered Shechem; and so Jacob arrived with all his household, which, especially now, when the women and children taken prisoners from Shechem were added to it, was so numerous that they could be called a עַם at Luz " in the land of Canaan " (comp. xlviii. 3). It is not strange (even though 6*a* were not *E*'s), but of deliberate purpose, that Bethel, the station which became so important on the outward journey, is here on the return journey, when it acquired new importance, so circumstantially designated, as at xxviii. 19, by both its new and its ancient name. He builds there an altar, and now calls the place of the altar, as formerly the whole spacious part in front of Luz, אֵל בֵּית־אֵל (comp. xxxiii. 20), in remembrance of the former Divine manifestation on his flight from Esau (comp. on the plural of the verb combined with הָאֱלֹהִים xx. 13). This is the fifth altar in the patriarchal history. Abraham erected one in the neighbourhood of Bethel, xii. 8, comp. xiii. 4, and one in Mamre near Hebron, xiii. 8; Isaac one in Beersheba, xxvi. 25; Jacob one in Shechem, xxxiii. 20, and one here in Bethel,—it is nowhere said that sacrifice was offered on these altars; they seem to be regarded by the narrator as places of devotion, not of sacrifice. Rebekah's nurse, who had followed her mistress to Canaan, xxiv. 59 (*J*), called, as we here first learn, Deborah, was then found among the followers of Jacob who journeyed with him; a circumstance for which we can imagine many reasons, but only by means of worthless conjectures. Being now of advanced age, she died at Bethel, and was buried

below Bethel, under the oak, which received the name of
אַלּוֹן בָּכוּת *oak of weeping*, or oak of mourning (וַיִּקְרָא, as at xxv.
26), probably the very tree which is called תֹּמֶר דְּבוֹרָה Judg.
iv. 5, perhaps also one and the same with אֵלוֹן תָּבוֹר 1 Sam.
x. 3. This Deborah must have been a faithful nurse and
family friend, since the house of Jacob so lamented her, and
both legend and history found her worthy of such perpetua-
tion. If, according to heathen legend, the nurse of Dionysos
(בָּכוּת, Βάκχος ?) is buried in Scythopolis (Plin. *h. n.* 5. 18),
and there is a grave of Silenos in the land of the Hebrews
(Pausan. *Eliaca*, c. 24), with which J. D. Michaelis already
combined xxxv. 4, these are, like the name and cultus of the
Bactylia, distorted echoes of what is here related. 2. THE
RENEWAL OF THE HONOURABLE NAME OF ISRAEL, vv. 9—15:
*And Elohim appeared to Jacob again on his return from Paddan
Aram and blessed him. And Elohim said to him: Thy name
is Jacob, thy name shall no longer be called Jacob, but Israel
shall thy name be. And Elohim said to him: I am El Shaddai,
be fruitful and multiply, a nation and a company of nations
shall arise from thee, and kings shall come out of thy loins.
And the land, which I have given to Abraham and Isaac, to thee
will I give it, and to thy seed after thee will I give the land.
And Elohim went up from him at the place where He had
spoken to him. And Jacob set up a pillar at the place where
He had spoken to him, a pillar of stone, and he poured thereon
a drink-offering and poured oil thereon. And Jacob called the
place, where Elohim had spoken to him, Bethel.* Elohim appears
again (עוֹד by *R* as a retrospect at xxviii. 11 sqq.) to Jacob
when returned from Aramæa (פַּדַּן אֲרָם), gives him the name of
Israel, and renews to him the promises given to Abraham,
ch. xvii., that גּוֹי וּקְהַל גּוֹיִם, a whole nation, nay a multitude of
nations, shall arise from him, and kings proceed from his loins
(מֵחֲלָצֶיךָ, as at 1 Kings viii. 19, 2 Chron. vi. 9, for which elsewhere יָצָא יֶרֶךְ xlvi. 26, Ex. i. 5, never מָתְנַי), and that He will
give to him and to his seed the land promised to the fathers

(אֶת־הָאָרֶץ) at the beginning and close of the verses, comp. the palindrome, ii. 2, vi. 9, xiii. 6, Lev. xxv. 41, Deut. xxxii. 43, and comp. on this figure, *Jesaia*, p. 408), calling Himself as He did, ch. xvii. (but never with respect to Isaac), אֵל שַׁדַּי. Elohim then goes up (וַיַּעַל just as at xvii. 22), and Jacob erects upon the spot, where this revelation was vouchsafed, a stone memorial pillar, pours out upon it a drink-offering, probably of wine (comp. Ex. xxx. 9), pours oil upon it, and calls the place בֵּיתְאֵל. This is the second time that the bestowal of this name is related, comp. xxviii. 19 (not the third time, since the name of the altar place אֵל בֵּיתְאֵל ver. 7 presupposes that the local name בֵּיתְאֵל already existed). Both these occurrences, the change of Jacob's name and the erection of a memorial pillar, have already been related by *E*, the former xxxii. 25 sqq., the latter xxviii. 18. Here the manner of *Q* is unmistakeable, though not unmixed.[1] The manifestation which Jacob experienced on his return journey from Aramæa is here comprised in one entire picture, and the erection of the pillar with the bestowal of the name Bethel is postponed in the same manner that the Synoptists retrospectively transpose the purification of the temple by Jesus, which took place at the first Passover, to the last. A libation is here added to the anointing of the memorial stone with oil, perhaps to make this consecration symbolically an expression of thankful joy. Jacob himself looks back, xlviii. 3 sq., to this appearing of God in Bethel. It is easily conceivable in the position which it occupies. Jacob has now again arrived at Bethel, whence he started; for what other purpose has God directed him to Bethel but to crown him, at this closing point of his history, as at its commencement, with promises of blessing? 3. BIRTH OF BENJAMIN AND DEATH OF RACHEL, vv. 16–20: *And they*

---

[1] According to Kuenen (*Einl.* § 13, note 4), the account of P² (= *Q*) is enlarged by *R* from *JE*, and Hosea is based upon *J*. It is certain that Hos. xii. 5, who there follows the course of events, intends none other than this very theophany in Bethel (not xxviii. 11 sqq.), and that his reference cannot be utilized for the date of *Q*.

GENESIS XXXV. 16—20.   231

journeyed from Bethel, and there was still a kibrah of land unto Ephrath, then Rachel travailed and had hard labour. And it came to pass, when she was in such hard labour, that the midwife said to her: Fear not, for this time too thou shalt have a son. When then her soul was departing—for she died—she called his name Ben-ôni, but his father called him Benjamin. And Rachel died and was buried in the way to Ephrath, the same is Bethlehem. And Jacob erected a pillar upon her grave, the same is the pillar of Rachel's grave to this day. With respect to the source of this portion, one thing is certain, viz. that 17b leads us to infer that it is from the same writer as xxx. 24, therefore from *J*, and also from the same as xlviii. 7 (which see). The noun בִּבְרַה (also Assyr.) is a measure of length from the stem כָּבַר (whence also כְּבָר long ago), and cannot be more closely defined; the Onkelos - Targ., which translates פְּרוּב אַרְעָא (properly a yoke or acre of land, from ܚܪܒ ܟܒܪ to plough), gives a precedent for a transposition of sound; the word means in general a considerable length, and probably, as may be inferred from this passage together with 2 Kings v. 19, an hour's journey, so that the Persian *Farsakh* or *Farsang*, παρασάγγης (Syr., Arab., Samar. *Tavus*), which according to Talmudic estimates amounts to four miles (*milliaria*), according to Arabic estimate to 12,004 ells, corresponds. Jacob was as near as this to Bethlehem when Rachel was seized with travail pains and had hard labour (*Piel* קִשָּׁה, here the intensive of the *Kal*: to be very hard, to have great difficulty, *Hiph.* as really transitive, to inflict or suffer hardship). The midwife (comp. xxxviii. 28) encourages her. When Joseph was born, Rachel had wished for another son, xxx. 24. She must now, in this hard birth-time, brace herself for the fulfilment of her wish. But she dies (מֵתָה *finitum*, as also xlviii. 7), and while dying names her new - born son בֶּן־אוֹנִי "son of my sorrow;" אָוֶן, from אָנַן to breathe, whence it means sometimes emptiness in a physical and ethic sense, sometimes exertion of strength, painful effort, and especially hard labour in childbirth (comp. Isa. xlii. 14). Jacob however called him בִּנְיָמִין (always according to the *Keri* and 1 Sam. ix. 1 one word, and with *i* in the first syllable as more homogeneous with the following י, comp. Arab. *ibn = binj*, here with י in the last syllable, but mostly written defectively בִּנְיָמִן) "son of prosperity," whether because this son was born in the time of his prosperous independence, or because he completed the fortunate number of twelve sons. The right side is, according to both Eastern and Western notions, the lucky side (*DMZ.* xxi. 601-604). It is true that there is no further authentication of the meaning fortune, power, prosperity (like يَمِين) for יָמִין, but much that is unauthenticated is elsewhere found in proper names. The ancient interpretation *filius dierum* is rejected by Jerome, while he himself explains *filius dexterœ hoc est virtutis*. "Son of the south" is more suitable (Ps. lxxxix. 13), in distinction from those born in Aramæa (Arab. *Schâm*, the left = northern) (Rashi); but Canaan nowhere bears this name. Jacob buried his beloved wife on the way to Ephrath-Bethlehem, and erected upon her grave a στήλη, of which the narrator says that it is to be seen "to this day." A chapel is now built over Rachel's grave, which the road from Jerusalem to Bethlehem, two leagues to the south, passes. It lies to the right, about 300 paces from the road, in a small hollow under a group of olive-trees. It is only half a league thence to Bethlehem; the burying-place and the birth-place would certainly not be exactly the same (with which xlviii. 7 is also compatible). 1 Sam. x. 2 however is in apparent contradiction with this specification of the place, which in the time of Jesus was thus and no otherwise understood, Matt. ii. 16—18. Then. v. Lengerke, Kn. Graf, Hitz. Dillm. and others (see the articles "Rachel" in Riehm's *HW.*, and Ryssel, *Untersuchungen* über *Micha*, 1887, p. 247) get rid of the contradiction by expunging הִיא בֵּית לֶחֶם here and at xlviii. 7 as incorrect glosses, and placing Ephrath in the territory of Benjamin, between the Ramah of Samuel and the Gibeah of Saul. But at 1 Sam. x. 2 we have צֶלְצַח, where, according to this hypothesis, we should have expected אֶפְרָת; the "less known"[1] Benjamite Ephrath having been invented purely in the interests of criticism (Köhler, *Gesch.* i. 150); and it is an incorrect inference from Micah iv. 8 (see Caspari, *Micha*, p. 151), that the station מִגְדַּל־עֵדֶר ver. 21, leads us only to the neighbourhood of Jerusalem, and not quite to that of Bethlehem. The tower of the flocks (for the protection of the flocks, comp. 2 Kings xviii. 8, 2 Chron. xxvi. 10) is in the neighbourhood of Bethlehem, where tradition also, since the time of Jerome, though uncertain as to the exact locality, places it, 20 minutes east of the city (Tobler, *Bethlehem*, p. 255 sqq.), and אֶפְרָת (with *He local* אֶפְרָתָה, the usual form out of Genesis, Ruth iv. 11, Micah v. 1) is Bethlehem (as is also evident from 1 Chron. iv. 4), the native city of David; it shares the name אֶפְרָתָה only perhaps with Kirjath-Jearim (see on Ps. cxxxii. 6), which however lay out of the route of both Jacob and Saul, assuming that Ramah of Samuel is one with Ramathajim Zophim = Ramah of Benjamin, the position of which, two leagues north of Jerusalem, is now occupied by the village *er-Râm*, situate upon a cone-shaped hill east of the road to Nablus. Keil combines 1 Sam. x. 2 with the elsewhere testified situation of Rachel's grave, by supposing that the city, 1 Sam. ix. 6, where Saul finds Samuel, is not Ramah (Ramathajim Zophim). But this is very improbable, אֶרֶץ צוּף ver. 5 pointing to the Ramah or double Ramah, distinguished from other Ramahs by the additional name צוֹפִים. The contradiction in question between 1 Sam. x. 2 and Gen. xxxv. 20, xlviii. 7, must be acknowledged, for in 1 Sam. x. 2 Rachel's grave is transposed into the territory of Benjamin,

---

[1] So Eugen Hermann, *Prolegomena zur Gesch. Sauls* (1886), p. 38.

and this never extended so far southwards as the neighbourhood of Bethlehem, where, according to Gen. *id.*, Rachel was buried. Jer. xxxi. 15 is also favourable to the local definition of 1 Sam. x. 2, according to which Samuel sends Saul back to Gibeah (now *Tuleil el-Fûl*, Bean hill). For he makes there Rachel, the ancestress of the tribes of Joseph and Benjamin, rise from her grave at Ramah and lift up her voice in lamentation over the depopulated land of her children. רָמָה is that Ramah of Benjamin, where the exiles of Judah and Benjamin assembled after the catastrophe of Jerusalem (Jer. xl. 1). Thus no other expedient is left, than to admit the existence of two traditions concerning the burial-place of Rachel, one of which placed it at the borders of Benjamin, the other in the neighbourhood of Bethlehem, which indeed bore the name of בֵּית לֶחֶם אֶפְרָתָה (Micah v. 1), or simply אֶפְרָת from the district in which it lies. Rachel died in about the 50th year of her age, at latest in the 106th year of Jacob's, so that Benjamin would be at the time of the migration into Egypt at least 24 years old.

4. JACOB'S FURTHER JOURNEY, AND REUBEN'S DISGRACEFUL ACT, vv. 21, 22a: *And Israel journeyed and pitched his tent beyond the tower of the flocks. And it came to pass, when Israel dwelt in that land, that Reuben went in and lay with Bilhah, his father's concubine, and Israel heard of it.* Jacob may have tarried some considerable time at the station beyond *Migdal 'Eder*, though not so long as at Shechem. בִּשְׁכֹּן has a dageshed כ contrary to rule (see on Ps. xl. 15). Reuben here carnally transgresses against Bilhah, the פִּילֶגֶשׁ (see on xxii. 24) of his father. On Reuben's incestuous act nothing further is said but, in preparation for xlix. 4, that Israel heard of it. In this portion, vv. 21, 22a, the threefold repetition of ישראל (after יעקב had preceded at 20a) is striking; so also is the abrupt וישמע ישראל for which the space in the middle of the verse (פסקא באמצע פסוק) makes as it were a break; after it a Pethûche (פ), just as at Deut. ii. 8 a Sethûme (ס), begins in

the middle of the verse (see Buxtorf, *Lex. Talm.* under
פרינמא).¹ The LXX fills up the space by καὶ πονηρὸν ἐφάνη
ἐνώπιον αὐτοῦ (comp. on iv. 8). These פסקאות, of which
three occur in the Pentateuch and twenty-eight from Joshua
to Ezekiel (most of them in the books of Samuel), are mentioned in neither the Talmud nor Midrash, and hence seem to
be an arrangement of the post-Talmudic Masoretes, which
was however only imperfectly carried out. 22a is doubly
accentuated: יִשְׂרָאֵל has Athnach and also Silluk, according
as from ויהי to ישראל is read as a half or as a whole and completed verse. Those who read ver. 22 by themselves conclude it with ישראל, but those who read it in public hasten
past its objectionable contents, and conclude with שְׁנֵים עָשָׂר
(see Heidenheim *in loco*, and Geiger, *Urschrift*, 372 sq.).
5. List of the sons of Jacob, according to their mothers,
vv. 22b–26 (parallel with 1 Chron. ii. 1, 2): *So then the sons
of Jacob were twelve.* The *impf. consec.* joins on to the
account concerning the second son of Jacob by Rachel.
Hereupon follow the twelve, according to their mothers, and
within this division, according to their ages (in accordance
with chs. xxix. and xxx.). The list closes, 26b: *These are the
sons of Jacob, which were born to him in Paddan Aram* (יֻלַּד
instead of יֻלְּדוּ xxxvi. 5, according to Ges. 143. 1b). This,
strictly speaking, applies only to the eleven, and not to
Benjamin; but it is referred to him also as completing the
number twelve, and as supplementing the eleven; besides, he
too was born, not in the house of his grandfather, but on the
home journey from Aramæa. The list is from *Q*. It would
be too improbable to suppose that he regarded Benjamin also
as born in Haran. 6. Jacob's arrival at his father's
house, and the death of the latter, vv. 27–29: *And*

¹ This halving of the verse before ויהי is ancient. R. Chaninah b. Gamliel
was listening in the synagogue of Cabul to the Methurgeman, who was about to
translate 22a, and called out to him: Stop, only translate אחרון, *i.e.* the second
half! *Megilla* 25d. The Orientals however placed Silluk with Soph pasuk
after וישמע ישראל (see Baer's edit. of the five Megilloth, p. v.).

Jacob came to Isaac his father, to Mamre of Kirjath-Arba, the same is Hebron, where Abraham and Isaac sojourned; and the time of Isaac's life amounted to one hundred and eighty years. And Isaac departed and died, and was gathered to his people old and full of days, and his sons Esau and Jacob buried him. Continuation from *Q*. Isaac at this time dwelt in Elone Mamre, near the city הָאַרְבַּע, *i.e.* of the Anakite chieftain of that name (comp. הָעֲנָק Num. xiii. 22 and frequently, הָרָפָה 2 Sam. xxi. 16 and frequently), the subsequent Hebron, which (already dedicated by Abraham, xiii. 18) remained a place of worship down to the time of the kings (2 Sam. xv. 7). The name Hebron was the usual one in the time of the narrator (comp. Josh. xiv. 15, Judg. i. 10). City of Arbaʿ was the more ancient name, Mamre that of the site of the terebinths upon its territory (comp. xxiii. 19 with xiii. 18). It is strange that Jacob should not till now have come to Mamre. Could he have been a decade in Canaan without seeing his aged father? Certainly not. But it was now that he first came to him to dwell entirely with him. Did Jacob and his mother ever meet again? Pressel thinks so, but the silence of the narrative favours Grossrau's view:[1] "Rebekah had indeed hoped that, when Esau's wrath was mitigated, she should be able to send for her favourite son; but no message of this sort reached Jacob, and when he returned through his own resolve, Rebekah was buried." The Toledoth of Isaac are now closed at ver. 28 sq. This was not as yet the chronological place for recounting Isaac's death; for if we admit the dates not derived from *Q* in the history of Joseph into the chronological web of *Q*, the following relations of time result. Jacob having been born in Isaac's 60th year, xxv. 26, and Isaac living, as we are here told, to be 180, Jacob would be 120 when his father died; and as Jacob was 130 years old when he was pre-

---

[1] In his *Commentary on Genesis* (1887), p. 262 sq., in which he tries to show that Genesis was written by one author, Moses.

sented to Pharaoh, xlvii. 19, Isaac died only 10 years before the migration into Egypt. And since from 9 to 10 years (the 7 fruitful and 2 of the barren years) elapsed between Joseph's elevation in his 30th year, xli. 46, and the migration, Isaac did not die till about the period of Joseph's elevation. Besides, since at Joseph's elevation in his 30th year 13 years had elapsed since he was sold in his 17th year, Isaac was, when Joseph disappeared, 167 years old. Hence he shared for 13 years the grief of his son Jacob for the loss of Joseph, and his life ended in the deep unilluminated darkness of this sorrow. The history buries him thus early in order to pass on over his grave to the new great turn in the history of Israel. Hitherto the history of Jacob has been always subordinated to the history of Isaac, from which Jacob starts and to which he returns. But now that he has become the father of twelve sons, from whom the twelve-tribed nation of Israel descends, his own independent Toledoth may begin. The history of the patriarchs outlives itself by losing itself in an old age of scarcely any historical importance. But for the patriarchs themselves it was of the greatest importance. They became thereby full of years. They longed to have done with this world, they longed therefore for the other world. The other world was night to them, for the sun of the New Testament Easter morn had not yet risen, but the star of the name of Jahveh shed a light for them also upon the other world. The וַיֵּאָסֶף אֶל־עַמָּיו (here said ver. 29 of Isaac, xxv. 8 of Abraham, xlix. 33 of Jacob) tells us more than that their corpses were gathered to the corpses of their people. Their souls were associated with the souls of their people in Hades, and because heaven would be no heaven without God (Ps. lxxiii. 25), so too was Hades no hell for those who had God in their hearts.

IX.

THE TOLEDOTH OF ESAU, XXXVI.

(Parallel with 1 Chron. i. 35 sqq.)

ESAU and Jacob joined hands once more over the corpse of their father. Thence their ways separated without ever again meeting. Hence Esau is finished off in this ninth and last but one chief division of Genesis. The Toledoth of Esau precede Jacob's as, xxv. 12 sqq., those of Ishmael preceded Isaac's. The historiographic course of Genesis is not however the only motive for this arrangement. It has besides this the historical motive, that the development of the branches broken off from the good olive tree, and growing up independently, far outstripped the development of this good olive tree itself. Just as secular greatness in general grows up far more rapidly than spiritual greatness, so did Ishmael and Edom become nations long before Israel. It is on this account also that the Toledoth of Esau precede those of Jacob. The important genealogico-ethnographic section is "a model of the manner and method in which Q was accustomed to produce the material he had in hand, these being elsewhere obscured by the rending asunder of his portions" (Dillm.). Nevertheless, although the systematic arrangement of the portion has come down to us undisturbed, the interposing hand of the redactor may be discerned — (1) in that the title, ואלה תלדות ver. 1, is repeated at ver. 9; it is very probable that, in the text of Q, xxxvi. 6–8a (as far as בהר שעיר) and xxxvii. 1 originally stood after xxxv. 29. The redactor so expanded the introduction which followed the title, ver. 1, that its repetition after the expanded introduction seemed to him necessary. (2) The names of Esau's three wives differing from xxvi. 34, xxviii. 9, are owing to his interposition. It is a matter of hesitation whether the names, as contained in the historical work of Q, have been preserved there or here in ch. xxxvi. The hand of R having elsewhere interposed within vv. 2-8, the names here may also be derived from another source. Then, having once given the preference above Q to this other source, the three names would have to be altered accordingly throughout vv. 10-18. On certain other passages, whose origination from Q is open to question, we shall speak in their respective places.

Title, ver. 1: *And these are the generations of Esau, the same is Edom.* For הוא אדום we have ver. 43 אבי אדום; in Q, as far as we know him, no cause is stated why Edom became a proper name of Esau. The title is now, in the first place, followed by an introductory passage. 1. xxxvi. 1-8 (parallel with 1 Chron. i. 35). THE FIRST BEGINNINGS OF THE RACE DESCENDED FROM ESAU: *Esau took to him wives of the daughters of Canaan: 'Adah, daughter of Êlon the Hittite, and Oholibamah, daughter of 'Anah, granddaughter of Ṣib'on the Ḥivite, and Bâsmath, Ishmael's daughter, the sister of Nebajoth. And 'Adah bare to Esau Eliphaz, and Bâsmath bare Ré'uël. And Oholibamah bare Jé'ûš and Ja'lam and Koraḥ—these are the sons of Esau, which were born to him in the land of Canaan. Then Esau took his wives and his sons and his daughters and all the souls of his house and his cattle and all his beasts, and all his possessions, which he had made his own in the land of Canaan, and went into a land . . . away from Jacob his brother. For their substance was too great for them to dwell together, and the land of their sojournings as strangers was not able to bear them, because of their cattle. So Esau dwelt in Mount Sê'ir; Esau the same is Edom.* This עשו הוא אדום takes 1b up again and gives us reason to expect that what lies between the two will show signs of the revising hand. The perf. לָקַח is related as a circumstantializing premiss to the main fact וַיֵּלֶךְ וגו׳, and is in itself (like יָדַע iv. 1) only Pluperf. with reference to this, but here it is at the same time such with reference to what has already been related. The name of the country after אֶל־אֶרֶץ ver. 6 is omitted: שֵׂעִיר (Syr.) not אדום, for שֵׂעִיר אֶרֶץ (ver. 30, xxxii. 4) is with respect to אֶרֶץ אֱדוֹם (ver. 16 sq., xxi. 31) the narrower notion: the former in its strictest sense is the hill country in the south of Judah westward of the Arabah (now inhabited by the Azazim), while the latter includes also the chain (جبال) and الشراة) stretching on the eastern side of the Arabah from the Dead Sea to the Ælanitic Gulf (Kn. Dillm.). The LXX, Sam. correct the defective ארץ into מארץ כנען, which tells nothing. There, according to *JE*, Esau already dwelt in Mount Seir, at Jacob's return from Aramæa, xxxii. 4, xxxiii. 14, 15. It is here in *Q*, ver. 6 sq. (comp. with the expression, xii. 5, xxxiv. 23, xiii. 6), that the separation after the return is first carried out. The names of the three wives differ in ver. 2 sq., and xxvi. 34, xxviii. 9: (1) עָדָה בַּת־אֵילוֹן הַחִתִּי, for which at xxvi. 34 we have בָּשְׂמַת; (2) אָהֳלִיבָמָה בַּת־עֲנָה בַּת־צִבְעוֹן הַחִוִּי. הַחִוִּי here is, as ver. 24, together with 20, shows, an error of transcription for הַחֹרִי. The name of this second wife is given, xxvi. 34, as יְהוּדִית בַּת־בְּאֵרִי הַחִתִּי. The Gentilic appellation החתי (instead of חחרי) may be taken as the most general designation of the heathen population dwelling around the family of Isaac; for not only at xxviii. 1, comp. xxvii. 46, but here also, the two wives are called בְּנוֹת כְּנָעַן. Only an ingenuity leaning upon any random support will combine בְּאֵרִי and עֲנָה (Hengst.), though Oholibamah is, notwithstanding 25*b*, really the daughter of ʻAnah, the well discoverer. For the appellation בַּת־צִבְעוֹן makes her the grand-daughter (Luther, *neffe = neptis*) of Zibeon, and so the daughter of the Anah mentioned, not at ver. 24, but at ver. 25. The combination of two בת, one meaning daughter, the other grand-daughter, is striking;

it is however repeated ver. 14, and is found yet a third time ver. 39, so that it has to be regarded as linguistically possible; but ancient translators (here in ver. 2, LXX, Samar. Pesh.) all incline to the exchange of בת for בן. And how about יהודית instead of אהליבמה? The difference is here so great, that Ewald regards Judith the Hethite and Oholibamah the Horite as two different persons; but it is too unanimously testified that Esau had three, not four wives. Hengstenberg appeals to the fact that in the East women often change their names at marriage; and Kurtz also explains the difference of the names by "the great fluctuation especially in female names in the East." Perhaps it is with reference to this double name יהודית=אהליבמה, that Ezekiel ch. xxiii. calls the kingdom of Judah Oholibah; for it may be supposed that the text of the Pentateuch in the time of Ezekiel already contained these irreconcilable statements concerning Oholibamah. (3) בָּשְׂמַת בַּת־יִשְׁמָעֵאל is called xxviii. 9 מָחֲלַת. The Samar. leaves the names עדה and אהליבמה unaltered, but changes בשמת here throughout ch. xxxvi. into מחלת. It may be said that Basmath bore besides the name מחלת, or that this (from חֲלִי, synon. עֲדִי jewels) was the surname of 'Adah. Still, however we may reconcile and combine, there still remains a discrepancy, which must be set to the account of the non-concurrence of historical tradition in this respect, and we owe it to the redactor that this has been preserved undiluted. After a repetition of the title, ver. 9, in which, in accordance with the tendency of these Toledoth towards national history, we have אבי אדום in place of the הוא אדום of ver. 1, and which is linked to ver. 8, and what precedes by בהר שעיר, the next passage, 2. xxxvi. 9 – 14 (parallel with 1 Chron. i. 36, 37) treats of THE THREE MAIN BRANCHES OF THE EDOMITES. The names of the sons and grandsons of Esau are here personal names, about to become the names of tribes, hence the repetitions from No. 1. The two wives, who bore but one son each, form as many tribes as they had grandsons; from Oholibamah, on the contrary, proceeded three tribes after her three sons. In ver. 12 עֲמָלֵק is designated as the son of Eliphaz by Timna', a Horite concubine. Is he then to be regarded as the ancestor of the Amalekites? But these already, xiv. 7, appear as lords of the northern portion of the *Tih* between the Negeb and Egypt, and at Num. xxiv. 20 they are called as the most primitive, or also (comp. Amos vi. 1) as the chief nation רֵאשִׁית גּוֹיִם, as at 1 Sam. xxvii. 8, with reference to the land of *Shur* (*i.e.* the desert *El-'Gifâr*) towards Egypt יֹשְׁבוֹת הָאָרֶץ אֲשֶׁר מֵעוֹלָם. The Arabic legend also, the historical value of which cannot however be estimated very highly, refers the eponymous ancestor of the '*Amâlika*, whom it calls '*Imlâk* ('*Amlâk*) or '*Imlîk*, to another Semitic origin, and transposes their rule from Jemen to Syria to times so ancient, that their name may be a general designation of the people of primitive antiquity. Hengstenberg, on the contrary, following Josephus, who, *Ant.* ii. 2. 1, calls Ἀμαληκῖτις a portion of Idumæa, adheres to the view that the entire Amalekite nation is here referred to an Edomite origin (*Authentie des Pent.* ii. 302 sqq.). The truth probably lies in the middle. An Edomite tribe proceeding from Timna', the concubine of Esau, which mingled with the Amalekites, and brought within the Edomite circle of peoples, the name of that ancient people is here called Amalek. For "the remnant of the Amalekites that escaped," whom the Simeonites destroyed at some undefined time before the Babylonian exile, 1 Chron. iv. 42 sq., dwelt in Mount Seir (see Nöldeke, *Ueber die Amalekiter*, 1864, comp. *DMZ.* xxiii. 297). The Chronicler, 1 Chron. i. 36, seems to reckon תִּמְנָע and עֲמָלֵק among the sons of Eliphaz, but ותמנע תמלק 36*b* only range there as figures of what is related Gen. xxxvi. 12. 3. xxxvi. 15–19. The אַלּוּפִים DESCENDED FROM EDOM. This is the special appellation of the Edomite (and Horite) phylarchs or chieftains, which is transferred to the Jewish only by Zechariah (ix. 7, xii. 5 sq.): it is a denomin. from אֶלֶף Micah v. 1, thousandhood (comp. عشير tribe, family), or more generally (from אָלַף to join oneself) society. The form (comp. רְחֹבוֹת, חָנָה) does not agree with taking the word as meaning tribe (Kn.) or canton (*DMZ*. xii. 315-317), as it has everywhere a personal meaning (*e.g.* Ex. xv. 15). Of Esau's five sons, those of Adah (Eliphaz) and Basmath (Reûel) are fathers of seven and four אלופים, the three sons of Oholibamah being directly such, thus making fourteen chiefs of tribes. אַלּוּף קֹרַח ver. 16 however has come in from ver. 18, and should, as by the Samar., be expunged: there then remain thirteen, not twelve. Their number becomes twelve if, with Dillm., we expunge אַלּוּף עֲמָלֵק, with which 12*a* also falls away as an insertion. Amalek is indeed descended from neither of the three legitimate wives; hence, when this is considered, the אלופים descending from these are actually twelve. תֵּימָן (Obad. ver. 9, Amos i. 12, Jer. xlix. 7, 20, Hab. iii. 3) became the name of a district and town (ver. 42) in north-eastern Idumæa; Jerome places a town Θαιμάν, *quinque millibus*, from Petra (Ritter, xiv. 128 sq.).

צְפוֹ (צְפִי in Chron.) recalls الصَّافِيَة the name of a village and of a rivulet flowing into the Dead Sea, southwards from which Gebalene (جِبَال), *i.e.* northern Idumæa, is entered (Ritter, xiv. 1031). This rivulet is also called *el-Kurâhi*, with which Kn. compares קֹרַח; but the important town قَرْح, in the Wadi el-Korâ, is more likely (Wetzstein, *Nordarabien und der syr. Wüste*, p. 123). More uncertain is the comparison of תִּמְנָע as a local name, ver. 40, with *Thamana* of the *Notitia dignitatum*. This is certainly the same as Theman or Thamara (see on xiv. 7). There is nothing to be said of אוֹמָר (vv. 11, 15), פִּעְתָּם (vv. 11, 16), נַחַת (vv. 13, 17), זֶרַח (*id.*), שַׁמָּה (*id.*) and מִזָּה (*id.*). קְנַז too (vv. 11, 15, 42) is unknown as an Edomite tribe. Othniel is called בֶּן־קְנַז, and Caleb, who gave to him, his younger brother, his daughter to wife, bears the surname הַקְּנִזִּי, and a race dwelling in the south of Canaan are called Kenizzites, xv. 19, their geographical proximity favouring a

historical connection with the Edomite קֵן. The middle term
הקנזי xv. 19 is however to us indefinable. The last words,
הוא אֱדוֹם 19b, have wandered from their right place after עֵשָׂו
(comp. 8b and the displacements xiv. 12, ii. 19). 4. xxxvi.
20–28 (parallel, 1 Chron. i. 38-42). SURVEY OF THE DESCEND-
ANTS OF SEIR THE HORITE, the ancestor of the חֹרִים, $T\rho\omega\gamma\lambda o\delta\acute{\upsilon}\tau a\iota$,
the aborigines of the mountainous country abounding in caves,
who were extirpated by the Edomites, see Deut. ii. 12, 22,
(comp. the descriptions Job chs. xxiv., xxx., which perhaps
relate to a gipsy-like decayed remnant of the Horites), and
on the other hand Gen. xiv. 6, where they appear as still an
independent people in possession of their Mount Seir. Seven
sons of Seir are named, and the sons of these, together with
two daughters, who are expressly mentioned : Timna', the
" sister of Lotan," and so the daughter of Seir, who, according
to 12a, was, as the concubine of Eliphaz the son of Esau, the
mother of Amalek ; and Oholibamah, " daughter of 'Anah,"
who, according to ver. 20, was the sister of Zibeon, and not,
as ver. 2 requires (where the second בת must mean grand-
daughter), his daughter, for Oholibamah is surely the there
named wife of Esau. We have here a rude discrepancy. At
25b, Oholibamah is brought before us as the daughter of 'Anah
the son of Seir, while according to ver. 2 she is the daughter
of 'Anah son of Zibeon, and thus of another and subsequent
'Anah. But to expunge 25b, as an erroneous gloss, on this
account (Kn.) is surely unnecessary; the statement should stand
at the end of ver. 24, and has thence erroneously come into
ver. 25. It is an easier accommodation which makes עֲנָה and דִּישׁוֹן
the names of both sons and grandsons of Seir (Dišon the son of
'Anah, 'Anah the son of Zibeon) ; the recurrence of the names
is not strange ; Tuch conjectures that the two grandsons of Seir
are also cited in ver. 20 sq. as his sons, because they formed
independent tribes with chiefs of their own. 24b says of
'Anah the grandson of Seir, that this is the 'Anah who, when
he was feeding the asses of Zibeon his father, found the יֵמִים

in the wilderness. Luther translates: *who found mules in the wilderness*, this being the ancient Jewish meaning, according to the consonance of ἡμίονοι and ἥμισυ, whence it would designate hybrids from a stallion and a female ass, or from a male ass and a mare—*mulorem nova contra naturam animalia*, which Jerome refers to as an old Jewish view: "the race of Esau," says a Midrash, "was not only itself given to illegal connections, but also seduced the animals to them." But it speaks against this interpretation—(1) that מָצָא used thus by itself can only be meant of a local finding; (2) that 'Anah was feeding asses and not horses also; (3) that mongrels of both are elsewhere called פְּרָדִים (Aram. כּוּדְנְיָא). Still less tenable is the identification of ימם with the race of the אימים, as Samar. and Onkelos translate and Ephrem explains it (Lagarde, *Orientalia*, ii. p. 58). יֵמִם are probably *hot springs* (akin perhaps to יוֹם, Assyr. *û-mu, im-mu*, day, named according to חֹם היום), whence the Syrian translates ܚܡܝܼܡܹܐ (Diodor. of Tarsus: πηγήν), perhaps the sulphur springs of Kalirrhoë (the ancient Lesa', x. 19) below the *Zerka Maein*, about two leagues on the eastern side of the Dead Sea. Here a warm spring flows in the ground, and receiving from several parts an increase of seething water, deposits abundance of sulphur. In favour of this meaning of ימם (LXX. ἰαμείν) is Jerome's information, that this is also in the Punic the word for *aquæ caldæ* (if he does not confuse ימם with חַמִּים, Arab. حَمَّامَات), as are also the wording and situation of what is related. The addition that 'Anah was just then keeping his father's asses, may point out that the animals themselves contributed to the discovery, as the whirlpool at Carlsbad is said to have been discovered by a hunting dog of Charles the Fourth, who, while chasing a stag, got into a hot spring, and attracted the huntsmen by his howling. In ver. 24a we must, with LXX, Sam. Syr. and 1 Chron. i. 40, read אַיָּה instead of וְאַיָּה (unless perhaps a preceding name has fallen out), and דִּישָׁן 26a must be corrected, as in Chron., to דִּישׁוֹן (LXX, Pesh. Jer.). The ancient Semitic worship of animals inferred by Robertson Smith, in his article, "Animal Worship and Animal Tribes" (*Journal of Philology*, ix. 75 sqq.), from certain names of animals in this register of the descendants of Seir, is rightly rejected by Dillm. and Nöldeke as not demonstrable. The name שׁוֹבָל has been transmitted in *Syria Sobal* (Judith iii. 1, according to the Vulgate and Luther), corresponding with the name of the third province kept by the crusaders below *Arabia secunda*, viz. *'Gebâl* below *Kerek*. The fortress *Mons regalis*, founded by Baldwin, and surrounded by a forest of olive trees, is also called Sobal, or more correctly (see on xxv. 2) Sobak (thicket, as a bishopric: *Saltus hieraticus*). The Arab tribes ديش (compared by Kn.) are similar in sound to (וַיִּשָׁן, עֵיפָּמוֹ, חֶמְדָּן, עֲלָוָן) (the dwelling-places of these tribes are not against this comparison), and *Menochia* of the *Not. dign.* and the district of *Μουνυχιάτις* westward of Petra in Ptol. with מְנָחַת. עֲקָן recalls the בְּנֵי יַעֲקָן, after whom a wilderness station is named, Num. xxxiii. 31, Deut. x. 6; אֶרָן the *Areni* in Plin. vi. 32. But that עוּץ, named with אֲרָן 28b as a son of Dishan, should have given his name to the אֶרֶץ עוּץ (הָעוּץ), has against it x. 23, xxii. 21; this עוּץ being certainly an individual of no further significance of the Horite race[1] conquered by the Edomites. The other names also defy national and provincial explanation. 5. xxxvi. 29 sqq. THE SEVEN HORITE PRINCELY RACES FORMED FROM THE SEVEN SONS OF SEIR. *These are*— runs this concluding sentence in the style of Q (while the anticipation 21b seems inserted from a more recent hand)— *the chiefs of the Horites* לְאַלֻּפֵיהֶם *as their* (the Horites') *chiefs in the land of Seir are each called* (the ל is that of the relation of the individual to the whole and of the whole to the individual, frequent in enumerations). Perhaps the vocalization לְאַלְפֵיהֶם

---

[1] *An is*, as in Horite proper names, a favourite ending in the inscriptions brought from Têmâ by Euting. See the Oxford *Studia Biblica* (1885), p. 214.

(Dillm.) would better correspond with the intention of the author. 6. xxxvi. 31–39 (parallel with 1 Chron. i. 43–50, comp. the apocryphal close of the book of Job in LXX). THE EIGHT KINGS OF EDOM DOWN TO THE TIME OF THE NARRATOR. The title, ver. 31: *And these are the kings that reigned in the land of Edom before there reigned a king over the children of Israel.* It does not necessarily follow from this, that the writer lived till the time of the Israelite kingdom,[1] though it looks like it; and it cannot be denied that the author of the historical work beginning with בראשית ברא represents, as compared with *J, E* and *D*, a more recent stage in the development of Mosaism, and thus has the commencement of Israelite kingship far behind him. It is however still a question, whether in this list of kings he transposes himself to the standpoint of the time of Moses, or whether he brings it down to the beginning of the Israelite kingdom (*i.e.* to Saul-David); for that he brings it down to his own actual present is excluded both by the brevity of the list, which contains only eight kings, and by the fact that the independence of Edom and the continuance of its native sovereignty ceased with Saul and David. The author of these Toledoth is the same, who delights to record the promises of kings arising from the patriarchal race (xxxv. 11, xvii. 6, 16); he expressly notices that Edom became a monarchy earlier than Israel, that the shoot which was cut off sooner attained such maturity, independence and consistency, than the seed of the promise. In these Toledoth he has hitherto been going backwards, to describe the Idumæan hill country according to its former inhabitants; he now goes forward and brings the history of Edom to a certain point. None of the eight kings is the son of his predecessor, their places of origin are also different. Hence Edom was an elective monarchy; the chiefs

---

[1] In this matter I agree with E. C. Bissell in his important work, *The Pentateuch, its Origin and Structure* (New York 1885), p. 141, especially as I, like himself, regard the law of the king in Deut. xvii. as ancient Mosaic.

of the tribes were, according to Isa. xxxiv. 12, the electors, and the dignity of the אלופים was hereditary in noble families. The name of the first king בֶּלַע בֶּן־בְּעוֹר sounds provokingly like the name of the seer בִּלְעָם בֶּן־בְּעוֹר; his native city was דִּנְהָבָה (LXX Δενναβά), a local name which cannot be pointed out as Edomite, but which is testified to as occurring in the neighbouring lands. Kuenen notes besides Δαναβά in Palmyrian Syria (in Ptol. and in Assem. *Bibl. Or.* iii. 2), Δαυάβη in Babylonia (in Zosimus, *Hist.* iii. 27), *Dannaia* and *Dannaba* in Moab (by Jerome on this passage testified in Lagarde's *Onom.* 114 sq.). The second king is יוֹבָב בֶּן־זֶרַח of בָּצְרָה; according to the LXX (at the close of the translation of the book of Job, comp. Jul. Africanus in Routh, *Reliquiæ*, ii. 154 sq.), Job is said to be one and the same with this Jobab ben Zerah (ben Re'ûel), — an untenable conjecture, although there may be some relationship between the names יוֹבָב, יוֹב xlvi. 13, *Juba*, Ἰόβας (the name of a Mauritanian king) and אִיּוֹב. The native place of King Jobab, בָּצְרָה, has been rediscovered as a village with ruins under the diminutive name *el-Buṣaire* in 'Gebâl (different from the similarly named ancient town in Auranitis, celebrated in ecclesiastical history, viz. Hauran, the birthplace of the Emperor Philip the Arabian). The third king is חֻשָׁם of the אֶרֶץ הַתֵּימָנִי, the province of Têman in the northern part of Edom. The fourth king is הֲדַד בֶּן־בְּדַד, who is more particularly designated as *he who smote Midian in the field of Moab*, whence Hengst. rightly infers that the time of his sovereignty is not to be placed far after the Mosaic period; for after Gideon, the Midianites almost disappear from history (comp. Kautzsch, art. "Midian" in Riehm's *HW.*), and it is improbable that the field of Moab should have been a place of battle between the Midianites and Moabites in later post-Mosaic history. Kn. combines the ridge of hills ضُوَيْنَة on the east side of Moab (Burckhardt, *Syr.* 638) with עֲוִית the birthplace of Hadad. The fifth king is שַׂמְלָה, of the otherwise unknown מַשְׂרֵקָה, which apparently signifies place of Sorek vines. The sixth king, שָׁאוּל, would be a foreigner if הנהר, in the name of his native town רְחֹבוֹת הַנָּהָר, had to be understood of the Euphrates; but a smaller river (2 Kings v. 12), a canal (Ezek. i. 3), and even non-perennial Wâdi (see on xv. 18) may also be called a נהר, and an Idumæan *Robotha* is mentioned by Eusebius, Jerome, and the *Notitia dign.* as still existing in their time. The seventh king is בַּעַל חָנָן (which is equivalent to the Punic חַנִּיבַעַל, *Hannibal*), his father was called עַכְבּוֹר (again a name of an animal); there is no statement of his birthplace. Of the eighth king, on the contrary, the city, wife, wife's mother, and grandmother are given, without וַיָּמָת being added, as though he were still living when this list was written. His name is הֲדַר. In the text of Chronicles it is like that of the fourth king, הֲדַד, just as the LXX 1 Kings xi. 14 writes Ἀδερ for הדד of the Hebrew text. הדר Ἀδαδ, not הדר Ἀδερ (Justin : *Adores*), is an Aramaic, and therefore not an Idumæan name of God (see *Zeitschrift für Keilschriftforschung*, ii. 165 sq., 365). A proper name הדר (ornament) perhaps existed beside it, or owes its existence simply to the misunderstood הדר. The native city of the last-named king was פָּעוּ, for which the LXX gives Φογώρ, therefore פעור, which accords in sound with the Edomite ruins *Fau'ara* (Ritter, xiv. 995). This eighth king has nothing to do with the Hadad of the time of Solomon; for though the latter was an Edomite of royal blood, he married a daughter of Pharaoh, and was never king of Edom (1 Kings xi. 14–22). It might rather be supposed that the last-named was that king of Edom, of whom Moses in vain requested permission to pass through his land, Num. xx. 14. And there is nothing against the view that Q is here communicating a document, whose original author was a contemporary of Moses and survived to the entry into the promised land. Now follows—7. xxxvi. 40 sqq.

(parallel with 1 Chron. i. 51 sqq.) A LIST OF THE EDOMITE אַלּוּפִים, *according to their families, according to their places, with their names.* To what purpose is this second list? We had above, vv. 15–19, the names of fourteen (thirteen) Edomite אלופים, here the names of eleven, among which only two (קְנַז and תֵּימָן) agree with the former. The Chronicler introduces the list with the words: *Then Hadad died and,* etc., which sounds as if after Hadad's (Hadar's) death the kingship became extinct, and the old tribal constitution, with its hereditary aristocracy, went on (Bertheau). In any case this list gives, without respect to the kingdom, a survey of the districts into which the land was divided in the time of its author; the former list was historico-genealogical, this is geographico-statistical (Dillm.). The title, in which the chief tone falls upon לְמְקֹמֹתָם, is in the style of Q, who however took this list of districts, as well as the list of kings, from an ancient source. The chiefs of קְנַז and תֵּימָן occurred also in the other list. The concubine of Eliphaz is called תִּמְנָע, and אָהֳלִיבָמָה the daughter of 'Anah is the Horite wife of Esau, vv. 2, 14, 18, 25; עֲלָה (for which in Chron. עֲיָה) is one and the same name as עַלְוָן, one of the grandsons of Seir, 23*a*. The remaining six names are new. Nothing worth saying can be told concerning יְתֵת, מַגְדִּיאֵל and עִירָם, for which the LXX has Ζαφωίν. In פִּינֹן (פּוּנֹן), on the contrary, we at once recognise that encampment of Israel where Moses set up the brazen serpent, Num. xxi. 9 sq., comp. xxxiii. 42 sq., celebrated, under various Greek and Latin forms of the name, for its mines, to which, during the Diocletian persecution, a multitude of Christians, to whom the dedication of the *Apology* of Origen is addressed by Pamphilus, were sent for penal servitude (*ad æris metalla quæ sunt apud Phænum Palæstinæ damnati*). After the fifth century it became the seat of a bishopric, not quite two leagues distant from Dedân. According to Jerome, אֵלָה is certainly no other than Elath, or, as it is called, xiv. 6, אֵיל פָּארָן.

מִבְצָר is not Petra (Kn.), which is called סֶלַע, 2 Kings xix. 7: the LXX has for it Μαζάρ, on which Eusebius (Lagarde, Onom. 277) makes the credible remark, ἔτι καὶ νῦν κώμη μεγίστη Μαβσαρὰ ἐπὶ τῆς Γεβαληνῆς, ὑπακούουσα τῇ Πέτρᾳ. The list of chiefs and districts closes with the subscription: *These are the chiefs of Edom, according to their dwellings in the land of their possession*, while the concluding endorsement, *this is Esau, the father of Edom*, looks back at the whole many-membered Toledoth—this great nation that dwelt in the land of the Horites, with its chiefs and kings, proceeded from him.

The register of the race of Esau-Edom is now followed by a verse, which joins No. 9 of the Toledoth with No. 10, xxxvii. 1: *And Jacob dwelt in the land of the pilgrimage of his father, in the land of Canaan.* Esau, as formerly Lot, vacated it, and thus was fulfilled the purpose and promise of God (xvii. 8). If this verse had originally stood after xxxvi. 8, it would have begun וַיֵּשֶׁב יַעֲקֹב. As it at present stands, it points back to it, for the purpose of forming the transition from the one Toledoth to the other.

X.

THE TOLEDOTH OF JACOB, XXXVII.-L.

THAT the title: *These are the generations of Jacob*, should be followed by: *Joseph was seventeen years old, and was feeding the flock with his brethren*, seemed so strange to ancient expositors, that they felt obliged to regard this superscription as the subscription of xxxv. 23-26, and as referring thereto past the parenthetical portion ch. xxxvi. A Lapide however closely approximates to the right state of the case, when he says: *Quasi dicat: deinceps enarrabo posteros Jacobi eorumque casus, eventa et gesta, maxime Josephi.* The תולדות יעקב are, according to their proper notion, the history of Jacob in his sons, not merely in Joseph, though chiefly in him. It is utterly contrary to the meaning of the title to regard chs. xxxvii.-l. as the history of Joseph, for then ch. xxxviii. would be a disturbing episode, which it by no means is. The matter is, on the contrary, divided as in the תולדת יצחק (xxv. 19). There Jacob, here Joseph, is the active principle of the history that follows. The twelve sons of Jacob are the seed-corn of Israel. Egypt is the foreign land, where a nation is to develop and come to maturity from the twelve. To precede his family thither, and there to prepare a shelter for Israel during its development, was Joseph's high vocation. Sold into Egypt, he makes a path to Egypt for the house of Jacob; and the same land, in which he grew to man's estate, was imprisoned and attained high rank, became for his family the land of their ripening into a nation, and of their deliverance. The history of Joseph is so far the opening of the history of Israel, and a type of the path of the Church and the Church's Head from humiliation to exaltation, from bondage to freedom, from suffering to glory. The treatment he received from his brethren, turned by the message of God to their safety and that of the nation descending from them, is a type of the treatment Christ received from His people, which the counsel of God turned to the world's salvation, and will at last turn to the salvation of Israel.

The Toledoth of Jacob, which include the history of Joseph, are divided into four sections. The first section reaches from the selling of Joseph into Egypt to his elevation, chs. xxxvii.–xli.; the second, from the first appearance of his brethren before him to his declaration of himself, chs. xlii.–xlv.; the third, from the migration of the house of Israel to Egypt to their prosperous settlement and increase in Goshen, chs. xlvi.–xlvii. 27; the fourth, from Jacob's entreaty to Joseph to bury him in Canaan to the burial of Jacob and death of Joseph, chs. xlvii. 28-l. The beginnings of these sections (xxxvii. 1, xlii. 1, xlvi. 1, xlvii. 28) show that Jacob still rules the history, though, with the exception of ch. xxxviii., there is none in which Joseph's name is not the more prominent.

"The sources from which R (the redactor) composed this last division of Genesis are, for the first two sections, almost exclusively B (El^1) and C (J). The plan and the greater part of the execution of this noble, almost dramatically arranged history of Joseph is from B. But R has also delighted in adopting and artistically working into it matter from C, whose narrative was on the whole similar though in particulars different, and in parts more excitingly told and with more didactic insight. Not till xlvi.-l. is A (Q or El^2) again made much use of, and there the three sources flow on together." We cannot deny our concurrence with the net results of the analysis thus formulated by Dillmann, although we must acknowledge our own inability to follow in detail his acute and almost clairvoyant disentanglement of the various threads.

There is more for us than for him which is beyond the limits of the knowable, as will be at once shown in the restraint we have felt obliged to impose upon ourselves in our analysis of ch. xxxvii. It is however undeniable that the redactor, without glossing over their differences, has here combined different accounts into one. In the one account Joseph is, according to the proposal of Reuben, cast into a pit, from which he intends to deliver him, but a passing caravan draws him out of it and takes him to Egypt. In the other account it is Judah who counsels against the slaying of a brother and causes him to be sold to a passing caravan. In the one account these merchants are called מְדָנִים or מִדְיָנִים 28*a*, 36, and in the other יִשְׁמְעֵאלִים 25, 27, 28*b*. But whether they are two different accounts, according to one of which Joseph was hated by his brethren for his tale-bearing, and according to the other for his dreams, is to us questionable. We shall not however conceal in this matter what speaks in favour of a working up together of different accounts, which do not by their matter exclude each other.

JOSEPH SOLD INTO EGYPT, CH. XXXVII.

The first verse wants nothing of internal unity, xxxvii. 2 : (*These are the generations of Jacob:*) *Joseph, being seventeen years old, was feeding the flock with his brethren; and he was a young servant with the sons of Bilhah and with the sons of Zilpah, and he brought evil report of them to their father.* The syntactic state of the three sentences is essentially the same as i. 2, 3 ; the perf. sentence with the noun sentence ruled by it precedes and circumstantializes the main fact וַיָּבֵא, at which the period aims. There is also a close connection in matter. It is first said generally that Joseph, being seventeen years old, was feeding the flock with his brothers (for בצאן is obj., רעה being, after the manner of verbs of ruling, construed as at 1 Sam. xvi. 11, xvii. 34); the brothers here are without distinction the sons of his father's two wives and two concubines. Then this statement is particularized by saying, that he was given to the sons of Bilhah (Dan and Naphtali) and to the sons of Zilpah (Gad and Asher) as a נַעַר (אֵת as a preposition being here repeated). Nothing can be done with the meaning youth; any one's נַעַר is, according to the custom of the language, his young servant, Judg. vii. 10, ix. 54, xix. 13.¹ דִּבָּה is not so indifferent a word as report, but means (from דבב to sneak, Assyr. and Aram. to lay in wait, to harass) slander, scandal. דִּבָּתָם הָרָעָה, which might mean the slanderous conduct of the brothers, is purposely not said; the more appositional co-ordination of the indefinite רָעָה (as at xliii. 14, Ezek. xxxiv. 12, Ps. cxliii. 10, Ges. § 111. 2*b*, comp. my commentary on the Psalms on 2 Sam. xxii. 33) suggests rather taking the brothers as object. That Jacob should let his comparatively more remote sons be thus secretly overlooked by Joseph, was the consequence of his affection for him, ver. 3: *And Israel loved Joseph above all his sons, for he was born to him in old age, and he made him a garment reaching far down.* The narrator, who after xxxv. 10 intelligently interchanges the names יִשְׂרָאֵל and יַעֲקֹב, is *J*. Benjamin as still very young is left out of consideration; but Joseph had been born seventeen years before, after the two Aramaean septennaries, when Jacob, who was of full age when he migrated to Aramaea, had already entered the age of the זְקֻנִים. On כְּתֹנֶת see on iii. 21. A כתנת פַּסִּים is one reaching to the end of the arms and down to the feet, the ends of the legs; for פַּס יָד Dan. v. 5, 24 is the more exact designation of the hand as distinguished from the arm, and אֲפָסַיִם Ezek. xlvii. 3 (from פַּס = אֶפֶס = אָפֵס) mean the extremities, viz. the lower (אפסי רַגְלַיִם), hence (with respect to the skeleton) the ankles, which agrees with כְּתֹנֶת פַּסִּים; it is called a χιτὼν καρπωτός

¹ Unless 'את־בני זלפה וגו followed, וְהוּא נַעַר might be taken, as by Rosin (*Jubelschrift* on Zunz's 90th birthday, 1884), as a preliminary adverbial sentence (comp. xviii. 8, xxiii. 10): when he was still young he brought . . . thus giving a retrospective motive for the sale in his seventeenth year.

(LXX, Aq. 2 Sam. xiii. 18), *i.e.* reaching down to the wrist (καρπὸς χειρός), and also ἀστραγάλειος (Aq. here), *i.e. talaris* (from *tali*), reaching to the ankles, hence a χιτὼν ποδήρης and at the same time χειριδωτός (provided with sleeves).[1] The כתנת פסים is, according to 2 Sam. xiii. 18, a kind of מְעִיל, and is there mentioned as the distinguishing costume of the unmarried daughters of a king. This preference for the favourite dislocated the brotherly relation, ver. 4: *Then his brothers saw that his father loved him more than his brothers, and they hated him, and could not say peace to him*, *i.e.* could not address him (דִּבֶּר, as at Num. xxvi. 3, with an accus. of the obj.) with the wish שָׁלוֹם לְךָ (prosperity be to thee!), hence they did not control themselves so as to give him a friendly greeting (comp. שָׁאַל לְשָׁלוֹם xliii. 27, Ex. xviii. 7, *i.e.* הֲשָׁלוֹם לְךָ, to put the question: Is it well with thee?).

We are now told how Joseph increased the hatred of his brothers by relating his dreams to them, ver. 5: *And Joseph dreamed a dream and told it to his brethren, then they hated him yet the more.* If vv. 5–11 are, as it appears, derived from another narrator, it is the redactor who links together the extracts from the two sources by the words, "then they hated him yet the more." This increase of hatred, on this fresh account, does not of itself exclude that which existed because of his father's preference. I cannot see that 5*b* is here unsuitable (Dillm.), the whole verse being related, as its theme, to what follows (like ii. 8 to ii. 9–15). The first dream, vv. 6, 7: *And he said to them: Hear, I pray you, the dream that I have dreamed: And lo, we were binding sheaves in the midst of the field, and, behold, my sheaf arose and also stood up, and, behold, your sheaves stood round about and bowed themselves before my sheaf.* Two וְהִנֵּה are found in one verse, xxix. 2,

---

[1] In the Mishnic and Syriac פַּס means not extremity but surface (see *Menachoth* i. 2: he has to stretch out his finger ידו עַל פַּס to the whole extent of the hand, *i.e.* without curving or doubling); Mühlau-Volk in Ges. *Lex.* 10th edit., seek to deduce the meanings cut off (terminate) and extend from the same root.

here there are three. The name for sheaf אֲלֻמָּה occurs only here and Ps. cxxvi. 6, and the denominate אָלַם only here. The dream of Joseph shows that his father, like his grandfather (xxvi. 12), combined agriculture and the rearing of cattle. Reception of the relation of the dream, ver. 8: *Then his brethren said to him: Shalt thou indeed be king over us, or shalt thou become our ruler, and they hated him still more for his dreams and his words*, i.e. on account of the arrogant tenor of such dreams and the insulting candour with which he related them. As Joseph had as yet told them but one dream, the plural חֲלֹמֹתָיו is striking; it must be understood as the categorical plur., but leaves room for the conjecture that 8*b* (and therefore 5*b* also, as results retrospectively) did not belong to the text of the excerpted sources. The second dream and its reception by his brethren and his father, vv. 9–11: *And he dreamed yet a dream and told it to his brethren. He said: Behold I have dreamed again, and lo, the sun and the moon and the eleven stars cast themselves down before me. And he told it to his father and his brethren; then his father rebuked him and said to him: What is this dream that thou hast dreamed—shall we, I and thy mother and thy brethren, indeed come to bow ourselves down to the earth before thee? And his brethren envied him, but his father kept the thing in mind.* The sentence וַיְסַפֵּר אֹתוֹ לְאֶחָיו is, in respect of the וַיְסַפֵּר אֶל־אָבִיו וְאֶל־אֶחָיו which follows in ver. 10, not only superfluous, but interrupting; accordingly the LXX takes καὶ διηγήσατο αὐτὸ τῷ πατρὶ καὶ τοῖς ἀδελφοῖς αὐτοῦ into ver. 9 and expunges it in ver. 10. In any case this second וַיְסַפֵּר (without אֹתוֹ) belongs to the original text, comp. וַיַּגֵּד 5*a*. By the eleven stars may certainly be meant eleven of the stars of the Zodiac (מַזָּלוֹת), for Joseph does not say אַחַד הֶעָשָׂר, because he thinks of himself as the twelfth. The sun is Jacob-Israel, the even stars the eleven brethren, and the moon the dead but forgotten and unlost Rachel. The dreams were images of future elevation of Joseph over the whole house of Jacob.

They came from Joseph's deeply gifted presentient mind (*Biblische Psychol.* p. 280 sq.) not without God, but the counsel of God was still concealed from human eyes. Hence this second dream brings upon the dreamer quite a harsh rebuke from his father. But while the brethren persevered in their suspicious jealousy, Jacob, without his affection for him being diminished, kept the thing in memory, שָׁמַר, LXX διετήρησε, like συνετήρει Luke ii. 19.

When then Joseph was on a certain occasion sent by his father to a distance to see after his brethren, they resolved, as soon as they saw him, to get rid of their hated brother by violence, vv. 12–18. It is at once perceived by the name יִשְׂרָאֵל that *J* is here the narrator, vv. 12 – 14: *Then his brethren went to feed their father's sheep in Sichem. And Israel said to Joseph: Do not thy brethren feed the flock in Sichem ? Up then, I will send thee to them ! He said to him: Here am I. And he said to him: Go now, see after the welfare of thy brethren and the welfare of the flock, and bring me back word. So he sent him forth from the vale of Hebron to Sichem.* When Jacob migrated to Aramaea, it was done from his father's house in Beersheba; and when after a long period he returned by indirect journeys to his father's house, it was in Hebron, one of the few cities of the Holy Land, which are situate in valleys. It seems strange that the sons of Jacob and their flocks should have gone so far north as the district of Shechem, the city which, since it was so murderously attacked by Simeon and Levi, was at strife with his family. The enmity of the Shechemites must have been in some manner appeased between the sojourn of Jacob in Shechem and in Hebron.[1] אֵת 12*b* is over-punctuated, and as to style might be dispensed with (comp. *e.g.* Isa. lxi. 5 with Ezek. xxxiv. 8). Joseph willingly consents to his father's proposal to send him

---

[1] Kuenen (*Einl.* § 13, note 7) conjectures that *R* with respect to *P²* substitut Hebron for some other city. But the burial of the three patriarchs in Ma· pelah near Hebron is not a mere view of *P²*, but a national tradition, w which l. 5 is only apparently in contradiction.

to Shechem (where we may imagine the brothers feeding their flocks in the plain of *Machnah* on the west of the city), to inquire after their welfare and that of the flocks (שָׁלוֹם welfare, then ambiguous, like *valetudo*). He accordingly goes to Shechem, in the neighbourhood of which however he seeks in vain for his brothers, vv. 15–17: *And a man met him, and behold he was wandering in the field, and the man asked him saying: What seekest thou? And he said: I am seeking my brethren; tell me, I pray thee, where they are feeding. And the man said: They have departed hence, for I heard them say: We will go to Dothajin. Then Joseph went after his brethren and met them in Dothan.* The classic style prefers to leave subjects and objects unexpressed, where they can be dispensed with. So here we have וְהִנֵּה תֹעֶה without הוּא, שְׁמַעְתִּי אֹמְרִים for שְׁמַעְתִּים (Samar.), comp. 4a וַיַּגֵּד he told (it), 10a וַיְסַפֵּר he related (it), 21a וַיִּשְׁמַע רְאוּבֵן and Reuben heard (it). A similar instance already, vi. 19, and here a little farther on, 21a, 25b, 27b, 32a. The question runs: What seekest thou? for the inquirer does not yet know that Joseph is seeking persons. The form of the name דֹּתָיִן interchanging with דֹּתָן is like עֶפְרַיִן, יְרוּשָׁלַיִם, שֹׁמְרַיִן, no Dual, but a diphthongal pronunciation of the termination *ān* (*âm*),[1] the Greek writing Δωθαείμ, or what is the same, Δωθαΐμ in the LXX, and Judith iv. 6, vii. 3. viii. 3 reproduces דֹּתָיִם; the name Δωταία, *id.* iii. 10, is the same hellenized. *Tell Dóthân*, a beautiful hill, at the southern foot of which bubbles forth a spring, about five leagues north of Sabastîja (Samaria), as Eusebius and Jerome already state, west of 'Gennin, and westward (see Bädeker, p. 237) of the road leading from Nabulus to 'Gennin, still marks the situation of the place. Seeing Joseph at a distance, the brothers agree to get rid of him, ver. 18: *They saw him afar off, and before he came near to them, they made him the object of a crafty plot to*

---

[1] See Wellhausen, *Composition des Hexateuchs*, on Gen. xxxii. 1–3 (מַחֲנָיִם); comp. Merx' *Archiv*, iii. 352.

kill him. Thus is הִתְנַכֵּל conceived with an accusative object instead of with בּוֹ Ps. cv. 25: "they treated him craftily" would not do full justice to the notion. If it is E who refers, vv. 5–11, the hatred of the brothers to Joseph's dreams, it is from him also that vv. 19, 20 are derived. *And they said one to another: Behold, this dreamer cometh! And now up, let us kill him and cast him into a pit and say: A wild beast has torn him to pieces; and we shall see what will become of his dreams.* The הַזֶּה enhanced to הַלָּזֶה [1] occurs in J, besides here only at xxiv. 65. The combination בַּעַל הַחֲלֹמוֹת is without an analogous example in the Pentateuch. בּוֹר (=בְּאֵר) is the pit as distinguished from בְּאֵר the well. The נִרְאֶה is just as scornful as לְמַעַן רְאֵה Isa. v. 19. When they have killed him and left his corpse to decay in a pit, they think it will then be seen how ridiculous were his high-flown dreams. But here too man's sin and God's plan are found to work together. The elevation dreamed of by Joseph becomes the means of his brethren's downfall, to become subsequently that of their uprising. God makes sin itself subservient to His plan, and thus a co-operating factor in the coming deliverance.

Postponement of the murder by Reuben, vv. 21, 22: *And Reuben heard it and delivered him out of their hand, and said: We will not take his life. For Reuben said to them: Do not shed blood, cast him into this pit, which is in the wilderness, and do not lay hand upon him —* (this he said) —*that he might deliver him out of their hand and restore him to his father.* Ver. 21 is, like ver. 5, an anticipative summary of what follows. Instead of הִכָּה נַפְשׁוֹ he smites the life of such an one (Lev. xxiv. 17 sq.), הִכָּהוּ נֶפֶשׁ with two accusatives (Ges. § 139, note), he smites his life, *i.e.* kills him (Deut. xix. 6 and frequently), is also used. It cannot be discerned from the style whether ver. 21 sq. is derived from J or E. But that their different accounts are farther on combined is seen from the merchants who took Joseph with them to Egypt being twice called

---

[1] The Samar. translates: the splendid (excellent) dreamer, comp. on xxiv. 65.

Ishmaelites (vv. 25, 28b) and twice Midianites (vv. 28a, 36); in ver. 28 the excerpts from the two sources strike sharply against each other. One source (E) related that Reuben dissuaded them from killing Joseph and advised them to cast him into a pit and to leave him to his fate, intending to take him out secretly and to help him to escape to Hebron. But that when after some time he came to look after him, he had disappeared; some passing Midianite merchants having drawn him out and carried him away, as Joseph himself says, xl. 15: I was secretly stolen out of the land of the Ibrim. The redactor gave the preference to the narrative of J, according to which Judah advised not to kill but to sell him to the Ishmaelites, subordinating to it and arranging in it what he derived from E. Next follows the casting into the pit, related in E and J, vv. 23, 24: *And it came to pass when Joseph was come to his brethren, that they took off from Joseph his garment, the garment reaching far down which he had on, and took him and cast him into the pit; and the pit was empty, there was no water in it.* They strip him of his long tunic (הִפְשִׁיט) with two accusatives, like הִלְבִּישׁ Ges. § 139. 1), because they mean to make it by and by the means of diverting suspicion from themselves. Like Joseph, Jeremiah also was cast into a pit wherein was no water, but Jeremiah sank in mire, Jer. xxxviii. 6. By the advice of Judah he is sold, vv. 25-27: *And they sat down to eat food; then they lifted up their eyes and saw, and behold a travelling company of Ishmaelites coming from Gilead with their camels laden with tragacanth and balsam and ladanum, upon the way to carry it down to Egypt. Then Judah said to his brethren: What profit have we that we slay our brother and conceal his blood? Up, let us sell him to the Ishmaelites, and let not our hand be upon him, for he is our brother, our flesh—and his brethren hearkened* (to it). The Midianites (who according to xxv. 2 are only a collateral tribe of the Ishmaelites proper) are called Ishmaelites, Judg. viii. 24, whence it appears that this had become a general designation of the desert tribes, who are elsewhere called עַרְבִים or (from badû, desert) Bedouins. אֹרְחָה (fem. from אֹרֵחַ a traveller, plur. אֹרְחוֹת Isa. xxi. 13, or, as if it were a fem. from אֹרַח, אֲרָחוֹת Job vi. 19) means that which is travelling, viz. a travelling company, called in Persian karwân. The caravan, which came within sight of Jacob's sons as they were resting and eating, was from Gilead, and its camels were carrying spices, which were then as now the chief articles of import of the Arabico-Egyptian caravan trade. נְכֹאת is tragacanth or tragant (see this article in Riehm's *HW.*), the resinous gum of the *Astragalus gummifer* and many other Palestinian kinds of astragali. צֳרִי (according to the formations רְאִי, דְּמִי) is not real balsam from the balsam tree, but (see *Mastix* in Riehm) the gum of the *Pistacia lentiscus, i.e.* the mastix tree. לֹט is *ladanum, i.e.* the aromatic gum (λήδανον, λάδανον) of the *Cistus creticus* (λῆδος, λῆδον). The caravan had crossed over Jordan at Beisan, as is still done, and was taking the high road which led from Beisan and Zer'in to Ramleh and Egypt, and entered west of 'Gennin the plain in which Dothan lies. Judah advised his brothers to sell Joseph to these travelling Ishmaelites, opposing, as Abravanel remarks, three reasons against depriving him of life. This murder would be criminal fratricide (אָחִינוּ בְשָׂרֵנוּ, an appositional connection according to Ges. § 113); and as it would bring them no profit —not even the satisfaction of revenge, since they would have to conceal the deed—there was no object to gain by it. His proposal found approval. *E* is now the narrator, 28*a*, and joins on to Reuben's counsel, who was purposing to deliver Joseph: *Then there passed by Midianite merchants, and they drew and lifted up Joseph out of the pit.* It is the meaning of *E* that the Midianites drew him up, but of the composition, as we have it, that the brothers did this, as the caravan was approaching, so that what now follows from *J* joins on to 28*a* without contradicting it. 28*b*: *And they sold Joseph to the Ishmaelites for twenty pieces of silver, and they brought Joseph to Egypt.* We must supply שֶׁקֶל or שְׁקָלִים (Lev. xxvii. 3,

2 Kings xv. 20). The average price of a slave was, according to Ex. xxi. 32, thirty shekels. A slave afterwards cost just as much (120 drachma = 30 tetradrachmic shekels) in the market of Alexandria (Joseph. *Ant.* xii. 2. 3),—the Midianites would of course make a profit by the transaction. Reuben's consternation, according to *E*, vv. 29, 30 : *Then Reuben came back to the pit, and behold Joseph was not in the pit; and he rent his garments and returned to his brethren, and said : The boy is not there, and I—whither shall I go ? !* He, the most responsible, because the eldest of the brothers, desired to rescue Joseph (22*b*, comp. xlii. 22), and now he sees to his horror that the expedient, by which he had thought to effect this, has turned out to Joseph's ruin. Henceforth the narratives of *J* and *E* concur. The text has chiefly the tone of *J;* the Midianites again mentioned at the close are a sure token of *E*. The sending of the blood-stained garment, vv. 31, 32 : *And they took Joseph's garment, and killed a he-goat, and dipped the garment in the blood. And they sent away the garment that reached far down, and brought it to their father and said : This have we found; see now carefully whether it be thy son's garment or not ?* A similar הַכֶּר־ of testing observation is found xxxviii. 25, xxxi. 32. The ה of הַכְּתֹנֶת is the interrogative, which before a consonant with Sheva cannot be other than הֲ, and this either with a Metheg like הֲכִמוֹנִי xxxiv. 31, or as here (comp. Ges. § 100. 4) with a following Dagesh. When the aged father sees the bloody garment of his favourite son, he immediately comes to the conclusion contemplated by the brethren, and mourns for him as one dead, vv. 33-35 : *And he looked carefully and said : My son's coat ! A wild beast has devoured him. Joseph is torn, yea torn to pieces. And Jacob rent his clothes, and put sackcloth about his loins, and mourned long for his son. And all his sons and daughters arose to comfort him, but he refused to be comforted, and said : Nay, I will go down to the world beneath mourning for my son. So his father wept for him.* That Joseph is torn to pieces is designated as

a fact by טֹרֹף, and as quite beyond doubt by the *inf. intens.* טָרֹף (*Kal* according to Ges. § 131. 3, note 2). In xliv. 28 אַךְ is added as a still further enhancement. Instead of קרע בְּגָדָיו, we have here קרע שִׂמְלֹתָיו, as at xliv. 13, a variation critically unimportant. Jacob grounds his rejection of the consolation of his sons and daughters (comp. above, p. 180) on כִּי־אֵרֵד. It is here and farther on in the history of Joseph, xlii. 38, xliv. 29, 31, that the *fem. noun* Sheôl (*masc.* only Job xxvi. 6, but then with a preceding predicate) is mentioned for the first time in the O. T. שְׁאוֹל, from שאל=שעל, שׁוּל, √ של, سل, to be slack, languid, to hang down, to sink down, means the hollow (see on Isa. v. 14, and xl. 12, בִּשְׁעֹלוֹ), and corresponds with *tian*, the deep, the Egyptian name for the subterranean world. The later usage of the language may have thought of the verb שׁאל to summon, and, as seems to follow from Prov. xxx. 15 sq., Isa. v. 14, Hab. ii. 5, have understood שׁאול of the place to which all terrestrial beings are summoned.[1] Thither is Joseph gone, thither, where human existence continues in a shadowy manner, will Jacob follow him; till then there is no more comfort or joy for him. אָבֵל is equivalent to בְּיָגֹן xlii. 38, xliv. 31; הִתְאַבֵּל 34b also means not merely mourning attire, but especially the grief of mourning (Num. xiv. 39). The sale of Joseph into Egypt, according to *E*, ver. 36: *And the Midianites sold him into Egypt, to Potiphar, a court official of Pharaoh, a captain of the guard.* מְדָנִים 28a are here called מְדָנִים, which, according to xxv. 2, is the name of a tribe nearly akin to Midian. So too פּוֹטִיפַר here and at xxxix. 1 is the shorter form of the name פּוֹטִי פֶרַע xli. 45, xlvi. 20;

---

[1] The name of this world below is in Assyrian *šuâlu* (written *šu-âlu*, as if it meant the powerful city); the verb *ša'âlu* means to question, to decide, to rule, and according to the Assyrian usage of language, the notion of a requisitionary summoning power for שׁאול is the result. The best word for it is the world beneath, for hell is equivalent to γέεννα. Luther himself felt this, when he exchanged " Hölle " (hell) in Gen. xxxvii. 35, xlii. 38, xliv. 29, 31 (as he sixty-seven times translates שׁאול), for " Grube " (pit). See Kamphausen's article on the subject in Zimmermann's *Theol. Literaturblatt*, 1872, Nos. 6, 7.

LXX Πετεφρῆς or Πεντεφρῆς (see Lagarde, *Genesis*, p. 20). The name (compounded from *p-et-e-ph-ra*) he who (*et = ent*) is the (*e = em*) sun-god's,[1] compare the names Πετεαμῆν, Πετεμπαμέντης, Πέτεσις and the shorter פֹּמָה (belonging to the goddess Muth). The sun-god is called *Pa* or *Pη*, with the aspirated article Memphitic *Φρη*. סָרִים, gelding (eunuch), which is also Babylonian and Himyaritic, means likewise by an obliteration of the fundamental meaning, a courtier in general, as the Arab. خَادِم means contrariwise first, a servant and then a eunuch. "Slayer" in the official title שַׂר הַטַּבָּחִים is not equal to butcher (Luth. in Comm. *praefecto laniorum*) or cook (LXX ἀρχιμάγειρος), but the executioners (comp. טבח Ezek. xxi. 15, Lam. ii. 21), the inflictors of capital punishment, were so called (Jer. *magistro militum*). Potiphar was captain of the bodyguard, who as such had to execute capital punishment on the condemned, like Nebuzaradan and Arioch, who bore the same title at the Chaldæan court. It was on this account that the State prison was under his supervision,[2] xl. 3 sq. In the time of Herodotus Pharaoh's bodyguard consisted of 1000 Hermotybians and 1000 Kalasirians, who were dismissed daily, so that the whole army might enjoy the advantages of the profitable service at the court. At the time however that Joseph came to Egypt, the military class was not yet organized.

The sale of Joseph took place in his seventeenth year, for this statement of his age xxxvii. 2 is certainly intended as the chronological setting of what is afterwards related. Joseph was born, xxx. 25, after the second 7 years of the Mesopotamian service had elapsed. This lasted 20 years, xxxi. 38; but granting that it is consistent with xxx. 25 to delay Joseph's birth to the sixth year after the 7+7, yet it

---

[1] The name *Ra* means, according to Brugsch, "the maker of existence" (*qui facit esse*), viz. to the perception of the senses; see the article on the Egyptian religion by Victor v. Strauss and Torney in the *Conserv. Monatsschr.* Aug. 1882.

[2] See the illustration of the white castle of Memphis (after the mosaic of Praeneste) in Cunningham Geikie's instructive *Hours with the Bible*, vol. i. (1881) p. 461.

could not possibly have been in the twentieth year, for Joseph at the return to Canaan was, according to xxxiii. 7, no longer a suckling. But supposing him to have been born after the 7 + 7 years, he would have been at the return a boy of 6. There would thus be 11 years between Jacob's return and Joseph's disappearance, during the far greater part of which Jacob would be not yet with his father, but at Succoth, Shechem, and in the district of Bethlehem. If then Jacob arrived at Haran in his seventieth year, we must raise these 11 years from the return of Jacob to the selling of Joseph to 17, for the 130 years of Jacob on his appearance before Pharaoh (xlvii. 9) can only be obtained by adding together the 70 years of Jacob when he migrated to Mesopotamia, the 20 years of his sojourn there, 17 years from his return to Joseph's disappearance, 13 years thence to his elevation, and 10 years thence to the migration into Egypt. But if Joseph were 6 years old at his father's return to Canaan and 17 at his own disappearance, it is impossible to admit 17 years between the return and this disappearance. Hence Jacob at his arrival in Haran cannot have been 70, but 76 (see Demetrius' statement in Euseb. *Præp.* ix. 21), and so 90 when Joseph was born, 107 when he disappeared, 120 at his elevation, and 130 at the migration to Egypt (130 = 76 + 14 + 17 + 13 + 10). Jacob's 107th year would be the 167th of Isaac, who lived to be 180. Hence the selling of Joseph happened only in appearance after Isaac's death. It was not in reality, but only to history, that he died long before that event.

It is historiographic art to break off in the history of Joseph at xxxvii. 36. We thus get to experience with him the comfortless darkness of the two decades, during which hopeless and sorrowful longing was gnawing at the heart of the aged father, and the secret curse of deadly sin deceitfully concealed was weighing on the souls of his children. Meantime another history is related, which seems, but is not an episode. For the superscription of this long tenth part of Genesis is not תולדות יוסף but תולדות יעקב, and the contents of ch. xxxviii. are of no less importance than the history of Joseph to the history of Jacob, nay, are even in causal connection with it. For the impulse to a new movement in conformity with the promise, which the history of the line of promise received in Joseph, found its occasion in the danger, manifest from ch. xxxviii., it was in, of settling itself in a manner contrary to the promise; and when it came to pass that the now separating paths of Jacob's family attained in his lost but re-found son to the unity of a new turning-point and goal, we need to learn how the family of Judah, which migrated with the rest into Egypt, and was to be the chief and ruling tribe, originated.

THE TWIN CHILDREN OF TAMAR AND JUDAH, CH. XXXVIII.

It is with a vague בָּעֵת הַהִוא that what follows, at least what next follows, is inserted during the period in which Joseph disappeared, and was regarded as lost, ver. 1: *And it came to pass at that time that Judah went down from his brethren and turned in to a man of Adullam, of the name of Hirah.* The hill country of Judah is thought of as the point of departure in וַיֵּרֶד; it was there that Jacob dwelt in Hebron, and that Judah and his brethren lived. 'Adullam, whose king is mentioned Josh. xii. 15, lay in the plain of Judah, Josh. xv. 35, north-west of Hebron, probably (see Bädeker, p. 212) one league south of Socho (*'Suwêke*). Here dwelt a Canaanite named חִירָה (which may mean "freedom," like חָרוּת, Syr. *ḥirûtha*), to whom (עַר, as at 1 Sam. ix. 9) Judah turned; וַיֵּט *devertit*, like ver. 16. It is unnecessary to understand וַיֵּט in this passage according to xii. 8, and to complete it by אָהֳלוֹ. Here in Adullam Judah married, ver. 2: *And Judah saw there the daughter of a Canaanite man, whose name was 'Sûa, and took her and went in unto her.* Having made a heathen his colleague, Judah went farther, and made a heathen woman his wife (as, according to xlvi. 10, did Simeon, as well as Ishmael and Esau). She was the daughter of a Canaanite named שׁוּעַ, and therefore not belonging to the little town of Adullam. We leave conjectural explanations of this name and of those which follow to the dictionaries. Judah's three sons by the daughter of Shua, vv. 3—5: *And she conceived and bare a son, and he called his name 'Er. And she conceived again and bare a son, and called his name Onan. And she yet again bare a son, and called his name Sêla, and he was at Chezîb when she bare him.* 1 Chron. ii. 3 sq. is a compendium of what is related here and to the end of the chapter. כְּזִיב is one with אַכְזִיב, Micah i. 14, in the plain of Judah, Josh. xv. 44, differing from the north-Palestinian אַכְזִיב (Ecdippa, now Zîb), Josh. xix. 29. That Chezîb is the birthplace of the מִשְׁפַּחַת הַשֵּׁלָנִי (Num. xxvi. 20) seems also pointed out by אַנְשֵׁי לֵכָב, 1 Chron. iv. 20, belonging to this branch of the tribe of Judah. Instead of the syntactically striking וְהָיָה, the LXX has αὕτη δὲ ἦν, hence וְהִיא. וַיִּקְרָא 3b, along with two וַתִּקְרָא, is also strange. The Samar. and Targ. Jer. read וּתִקְרָא all three times. The marriage of Er and his early death, vv. 6, 7: *And Judah took for his first-born 'Er, a wife, of the name of Tamar. And 'Er, Judah's first-born, was evil in the eyes of Jahveh, and Jahveh slew him.* Tamar (whose name means the palm, a common ancient figure for a woman of slender figure and for imposing female beauty) was undoubtedly a heathen, and indeed of unknown descent. Her husband, without leaving issue, died an early death as the penalty of his wickedness. The sin of Onan, vv. 8—10: *Then Judah said to Onan: Go in unto thy brother's wife, and enter into a brother-in-law's marriage with her, and raise up seed to thy brother. But Onan knew that the seed would not be his, and it came to pass whenever he went in unto his brother's wife, he destroyed it to the ground, lest he should give seed to his brother. And what he did was evil in the sight of*

Jahveh, and he slew him. What here appears as a custom became subsequently Mosaic law, viz. that when brothers dwell together, and one of them dies without leaving a son, her husband's brother (יָבָם *levir*) shall be מְיַבֵּם, *i.e.* enter into husband's brother (levirate) marriage with the widow, and her first-born shall bear the name of the deceased, that his name may not become extinct in Israel, Deut. xxv. 5 sq. Onan agreed to his father's demand, but through coveting the inheritance and out of malice [1] prevented its purpose. וְהָיָה is purposely said 9b, and not וַיְהִי, because not a single but a repeated occurrence is intended, as at Num. xxi. 9, Judg. vi. 3 (comp. xxx. 41); אִם, followed by a perf., has here as there a temporal signification, and the meaning of *quotiescunque* (comp. Ps. xli. 7). The expression to destroy to the ground is like Judg. xx. 21, 25. The *inf.* נְתֹן for תֵּת occurs again in the Pentateuch, Num. xx. 21. After the premature death of Onan also, Judah consoles his daughter-in-law with the prospect of Shelah, ver. 11: *Then Judah said to Tamar his daughter-in-law: Remain as a widow in thy father's house, until my son 'Selah is grown up. For he thought: lest he also die like his brothers. And Tamar went and remained in her father's house.* That a childless widow should return to her father's house (Lev. xxii. 13) has been at all times a natural custom. Thither does Judah direct his daughter-in-law, giving her hopes of marriage with his youngest son, who was not yet of marriageable age, but attracts her thither with this prospect, because he fears that marriage with her would be as fatal to Shelah as to Er and Onan. Meantime Judah also becomes a widower, and an opportunity arises for the carrying out of a crafty design by Tamar, ver. 12: *And after a long time had passed, Shua's daughter, the wife of Judah, died; and when Judah had ended his mourning, he went up to his sheep-shearers, he and Hirah the Adullamite, his companion,*

---

[1] לֹא in כִּי לֹא לוֹ has the emphatic Dagesh, as also at xix. 2.

to Timnah. In 13*b* it is Judah himself who is said, like Laban, xxxi. 19, to shear his sheep. It was an act performed in the presence and under the oversight of the owner of the flock, and was, like the vintage, a festival given by him to his servants (1 Sam. xxv. 11), to which guests also were invited (2 Sam. xiii. 23-27). Thus Judah here takes Hirah, his companion, with him. The LXX and Jerome read רֵעֵהוּ, which ver. 20 may seem to favour. There are three Timnahs (for which now *Tibneh*); that here meant is the one mentioned Josh. xv. 57, together with Gibeah, in the hill country of Judah (see Mühlau in Riehm), between Socho (*'Suwêke*) and Beth-shemesh (*'Ain 'Sems*), the Tibneh of the 12th route in Bädeker, p. 212. עַל, not of the place, but of the persons to whom they went up, is here combined, as at Josh. ii. 8, with עָלָה. Tamar hears of it, disguises herself, and places herself on the road to Timnah, vv. 13, 14: *And it was told Tamar, saying: Behold, thy father-in-law goeth up to Timnah to shear his sheep. Then she put off her widow's garments, and covered herself with a veil and disguised herself, and so sat at the entrance of 'Enajim, which is on the way to Timnah; for she saw that 'Sela was grown up, and yet she was not given to him to wife.* לִגְזֹז xxxi. 19 is here exchanged for the infinitive form לָגֹז. And instead of וַיִּתְּכָם xxiv. 65, we have here the active: she made a covering of her veil (as at Deut. xxii. 12, in opposition to which we find Jon. iii. 6: he spread sackcloth) in order not to be recognised as his daughter-in-law. וַתִּתְעַלָּף is not meant of ornaments (שִׂיחַ זוֹנָה Prov. vii. 10) (LXX, Onk. Syr.), but of disguising after the manner of a harlot (like עֲטִיָּה Cant. i. 7). She intended to appear, according to Canaanite custom, as a קְדֵשָׁה (Assyr. *kadištu*), i.e. one exposing herself in honour of Astarte, the goddess of love, and in this, according to ver. 21 sq., she succeeded. She seated herself at the entry of the village (hence פֶּתַח not שַׁעַר) 'Enajim, in order to escape by stratagem the disgrace of childlessness: *non temporalis usum libidinis requisivit.*

sed successionis gratiam concupivit (Ambrose). As דֹּתָם (דֹּתָן) and דֹּתָיִן (דֹּתַיִם) are interchanged, so is עֵינַיִם one with עֵינָם in the plain of Judah, Josh. xv. 34 (comp. here ver. 21 בְּעֵינַיִם). Ancient translators (Targums, Syr. Jer. Saad.), the LXX excepted (Αἰνάν), ignore that עינים (two fountains) is here the name of a town. R. Chanan in *Jalkut*, § 145, already correctly appeals to Josh. xv. 34. Judah sees her and is seized with carnal lust, vv. 15, 16: *Then Judah saw her and took her for a harlot, for she had covered her face. And he turned aside to her in the way and said: Come then, I will come in unto thee. For he knew not that she was his daughter-in-law. And she said: What wilt thou give me that thou mayest come in unto me?* His not recognising her as his daughter-in-law arose from her being veiled, and his taking her for a harlot from her disguise and her sitting on the watch. Then he turned aside to her (נטה as *e.g.* Num. xx. 17, and really like פָּרַד Hos. iv. 14) אֶל־הַדֶּרֶךְ where she was sitting by the way; LXX, ἐξέκλινε δὲ πρὸς αὐτὴν τὴν ὁδόν, הדרך as accus. of the more particular definition which Lagarde and Olsh. prefer. As the price of her compliance, she requires a kid; and as he cannot give her this at once, a pledge, vv. 17, 18: *And he said: I will send thee a kid from the flock; and she replied: If thou give me a pledge till thou send it. And he said: What pledge shall I give thee? And she said: Thy signet ring and thy cord and thy staff that is in thy hand. And he gave it to her and went in unto her, and she conceived by him.* She requires as a price a kid, the favourite sacrificial animal of Hetæri in the worship of the goddess of love (see Movers, *Phönizier*, i. 680); and as עֵרָבוֹן, a pledge (in Greek and Latin a word borrowed from the Semitic), three articles closely connected with his person, and therefore making him the more certainly recognisable. Judah's signet ring חוֹתָם is the only possible but still uncertain trace of the use of writing in the patriarchal history; the verb כתב does not occur in Genesis, and חתם in itself means only to close, to close up. The signet ring was worn on the breast (Cant. viii. 6) on a cord (פָּתִיל), a multiple one (whence ver. 25 הַפְּתִילִים, comp. עטרות of a multiple crown, Zech. vi. 11). The travelling or walking staff is here called מַטֶּה as distinguished from the natural stick מַקֵּל xxx. 37, xxxii. 11 (only accidentally sounding like *baculum*). "Every Babylonian—says Herodotus, i. 195—wears a signet ring and a staff cut by hand, and on every staff is something set upon the top, an apple, or a rose, or a lily, or an eagle, or something of the kind, for no one may carry a staff without a sign." The Jahvist testifies that this custom prevailed in Canaan also. Tamar now resumes her widow's garments, and the harlot, whom Judah causes to be sought for, is nowhere to be found, vv. 19-23: *And she arose and went away and put off her veil from her, and she put on the garments of her widowhood. And Judah sent the kid through his friend the Adullamite, to fetch the pledge from the woman's hand, and he found her not. Then he asked the men of her place, saying: Where is the hierodule that was at 'Enajim by the way? But they said: There is no hierodule here. And he returned to Judah and said: I have not found her; and also the people of the place said: There is no hierodule here. Then Judah said: Let her keep it, that we may not be a laughing-stock; I sent indeed the kid and thou hast not found her.* The connection הַקְּדֵשָׁה הִיא is like הוּא בַּלַּיְלָה xix. 33, comp. Judg. vi. 14, פֹּחַד זֶה and זֶה סִינַי Ps. lxviii. 9. Instead of the usual בָּזֶה (*e.g.* also xlviii. 9), בָּזֶה is only once written, 1 Sam. xxi. 10. Jerome aptly translates תִּקַּח־לָהּ by *habeat sibi*. It is apparent from Judah's unwillingness to let what he has done be known, that he was ashamed of it. When Tamar's condition was manifest, she was condemned to be burned, ver. 24: *And it came to pass after about three months, that it was told Judah saying: Thy daughter-in-law Tamar has played the harlot, and also she is with child in consequence of her harlotry. And Judah said: Bring her forth and let her be burned.* The מ of מִשְׁלֹשׁ is not preformative (according to the formation מִזְמוֹר, מִבְחוֹר) but prepositional: after three months, hence the same as מִשְּׁלֹשׁ; the constructive שְׁלֹשׁ stands here with a masc. as at Lev. xxv. 21 with a fem. It also sometimes occurs elsewhere that בְּ stands before a word provided with a preposition; see Lev. xxvi. 37, 1 Sam. xiv. 14, Isa. i. 26 and 1 Sam. x. 27, where we must read with the LXX בְּמָחֳדָשׁ "a month later," instead of בְּמַחֲרִישׁ. הִנֵּה does not here stand first in the announcement, but before the adjective הָרָה, the point of gravity of the announcement (comp. on the contrary xxii. 20). Judah as the head of the family pronounces the sentence of death, as Laban does xxxi. 32. Tamar being to a certain extent the betrothed of Shelah, who had not expressly resigned her, her yielding to another man was regarded as the unfaithfulness of a bride or a wife; but the punishment of death by burning pronounced upon her is not in accordance with the Mosaic penal law, which inflicts this penalty only upon carnal intercourse with a mother and daughter at the same time, and upon unchastity in the daughter of a priest, Lev. xx. 14, xxi. 9. The capital punishment to be inflicted upon the unfaithful wife is left undetermined, Deut. xxii. 22, but seems, like that of the newly-married woman found to be deflowered and of the betrothed who was proved unfaithful, Deut. xxii. 20 sq., 23 sq., to have consisted in stoning, and to have been, according to Ezek. xvi. 40, so also understood, comp. John viii. 5. Judah's profound confusion, vv. 25, 26: *She is brought forth, and at the same time she sent to her father-in-law saying: Of a man, to whom these things belong, am I with child; and she said: Look carefully, I pray thee, to whom the signet ring and the cord and the staff belong. Then Judah acknowledged and said: She is more righteous than I, for because* (that it thus happens) *I gave her not to my son Shelah. And he continued not to know her again.* The construction 25a serves to express what is contemporaneously done or experienced by the same subject, just as at 1 Sam. ix. 11; comp. the same scheme with a different subject in the account of the flood, vii. 6. On כִּי עַל־כֵּן, when we rather expect עַל־כֵּן כִּי, see on xviii. 5. It is noble of Tamar not to disgrace Judah publicly, and rather to go to death than at once to name him. Judah acknowledges the three pledges as his, and, struck by conscience, confesses that he is himself to blame for this result of the matter.[1] This public confession of his fault (comp. as to the expression that of King Saul, 1 Sam. xxiv. 18) is the first good trait that is related of Judah. There was no need for saying that now she was not burned, though there was for telling us that Judah left her in future unmolested. Tamar's twins by Judah, vv. 27–29: *And it came to pass at the time of her delivery, and behold, twins were in her womb; and it came to pass, when she travailed, a hand came to sight; then the midwife took and bound upon his hand a scarlet thread, saying: This came forth first. And it came to pass as he drew back his hand, and behold, his brother came out, and she said: How hast thou on thy part torn a rent! and they called his name Pereṣ. And afterwards came his brother forth, on whose hand was the scarlet thread, so they called his Zeraḥ.* The time of travail and the delivery itself, as the result, are distinguished. Whether וַיְהִי is conceived of with an indefinite personal subject: then he (it) stretched out a hand (Dillm.), which the retrospective עַל־יָדוֹ 28*b* seems to favour, or impersonally, then there was, *i.e.* appeared, a hand, is questionable; the possibility of this impersonal comprehension is apparent from Job xxxvii. 10, Prov. xiii. 10 (in opposition to which Prov. x. 24 may have to be read, as by Hitzig, יְחִי). It is unnecessary to read with Driver (*Heb. Tenses*, § 135. 6, note 2) כְּהָשִׁיב instead of כְּמֵשִׁיב; כְּמֵשִׁיב as a definition of time: as he was in the act of drawing his hand back, is defended by בְּפֹרַחַת as it (the vine) was in the act of sprouting, xl. 10: כְּהָיוֹתוֹ מֵשִׁיב=כְּמֵשִׁיב with בּ not of comparison but of time; in

---

[1] Because this is to his honour, this history is not only read in Hebrew, but also translated by the Methurgeman *Megilla* 25*b*.

post-biblical Hebrew this use of the participle instead of the *finitum* is of frequent occurrence, *e.g. Shabbath* ii. 5 כְּחָם=שֶׁחָם when he spares (comp. Rashi on the passage, and also Geiger, *Sprache der Mischnah*, § 24. 2), or: כ is *Caph veritatis* introducing the predicate: then he was (showed himself as) drawing back his hand. A piece of wool dyed, not purple but scarlet, with the dye of the cochineal gall-insect *coccus cacti*, is here called שָׁנִי. Without some such external identification as that employed by Tamar's midwife, there is really no certain token by which, after delivery has been completed, the first-born can be recognised. This time however it was of no avail, the turning of the one thus marked leaving space for the twin brother to come forth first. Jerome correctly takes עָלֶיךָ in the exclamation of the midwife in the sense of *propter te* (comp. xx. 3); פֶּרֶץ is not meant of *ruptura perinaei*, but only of a breaking through by means of push upon push; the accentuation seems to take עָלֶיךָ פֶּרֶץ as a sentence by itself, as at xvi. 5: upon thee lies the fault of the breach (Heidenh. Reggio)—but what follows upon מה must be taken together as an exclamation of puzzled astonishment. The name זֶרַח as well as פֶּרֶץ refers to something memorable from birth, the "brightness" alludes to the bright-coloured string; זֶרַח, a reference to the word crimson, Aram. זְהוֹרִי, זְהֻרִי (Rashbam, Heiden. and others), Assyr. *zarîr = zahrîr*. Instead of וַיִּקְרָא with the most general subject: they called, the Samar. Targ. Jer. I. and Syr. give both times וַתִּקְרָא.

It was thus, as this historic picture taken entirely from *J* relates, that the beginnings of the tribe of Judah were formed by a wondrous co-operation of human sin and Divine appointment. Perez, Zerah and Shelah are the three ancestors of the three chief families of the tribe of Judah at the departure from Egypt, Num. xxvi. 20. Through Perez, Tamar was the ancestress of the first and of the second David. How homely are the pictures of the ancestors of Israel! There is almost more shadow than light in them. National ambition played no part in, or with them. Not a trace of mythic idealization is to be seen. The ancestors of Israel do not appear as demi-gods. Their elevation consists in their conquering, in virtue of the measure of grace bestowed upon them, or, if they succumb, in their ever rising again. Their faults are the foil of their greatness with respect to the history of redemption. Even Tamar with all her errors was, through her wisdom, tenderness and noble-mindedness, a saint according to the Old Testament standard.

At the selling of Joseph in Dothan, Judah had apparently not yet separated from his brethren. Hence it must have been after this event that he made common cause with Hirah the Adullamite. Between Joseph's disappearance and the migration of the family of Jacob to Egypt, there are, as we saw on ver. 37, some twenty years. Within these two-and-twenty years or so, was the history of Judah and Tamar played out. When at xlvi. 12 two sons of Perez, one of the twin brothers, are named among those who came into Egypt, these are great-grandsons of Jacob, who, though born in Egypt, are regarded as coming into Egypt in their fathers (see on xlvi. 8 sqq.).

JOSEPH IN POTIPHAR'S HOUSE AND IN PRISON, CH. XXXIX.

The history of Jacob in his son Judah, related ch. xxxviii., is now followed by the continuation of his history in his son Joseph. Different hands were not to be discerned in ch. xxxviii., all was by *J* (*C*), even without the intervention of the redactor. Ch. xxxix., on the contrary, though throughout from *J*,—apart from xlix. 18 it is the only section of Joseph's history in which the Divine name יהוה appears, and that seven times,—has not remained in the same manner intact. It may be assumed, but cannot be sufficiently proved, that *E* (*B*) is here and there blended with *J* (*C*); the hand of *R* is however at once apparent in ver. 1, where the history of Joseph is again taken up from the point at which it had arrived at xxxvii. 36 : *And Joseph was brought down to Egypt ; and Potiphar, a court official of Pharaoh, captain of the guard, an Egyptian man, bought him of the hand of the Ishmaelites who had brought him down thither.* וַיּוֹרִדֻ is not used in continuation, for what is related is out of connection with ch. xxxviii. The more particular designation of the "Egyptian man," according to his name and dignity, is inserted by *R* from *E* in accordance with xxxvii. 36 ; for this writer gave the name and title of the master to whom the "Midianites" sold Joseph, while *J* merely says that he who bought Joseph from the "Ishmaelites" was an "Egyptian man," a distinguished person and a man of property, as appears from the account which follows. He made a profitable purchase; Joseph had good fortune, and brought it to his master, vv. 2–5 : *And Jahveh was with Joseph, and he was a prosperous man, and he was in the house of his Egyptian master. And his master saw that Jahveh was with him, and that all that he undertook Jahveh caused to prosper in his hand. And Joseph found favour in his eyes and served him, and he made him overseer over his house, and put all that belonged to him in his hand. And it came to pass from the time that he made him overseer over his house and all that belonged to him, that Jahveh blessed the house of the Egyptian for Joseph's sake, and the blessing of Jahveh was shown in all that belonged to him, in the house and in the field.* The second וַיְהִי 2*b* is striking, but it is, as ver. 20 shows, the style of *J*, as the expression of continuance in the given condition ; xl. 4*b* is by reason of the definition of time added to ויהי, not quite analogous. It was according to יהוה אִתּוֹ 3*a* that we explained אֶת־יהוה, iv. 1, of helpful support. The Egyptian master saw that Jahveh (equivalent in *J* to אלהים) was with him, made him his first servant, and placed everything under his eye and care. כָּל־יֶשׁ־לוֹ, all belonging to him, is possible, Ges. § 123. 3*a*, but the elliptical expression might rather be expected after the full one in vv. 5, 8. מֵאָז with a perf. following occurs in J at Ex. v. 23, ix. 24; בְּנֵלָל too is Jahvistic (xii. 13, xxx. 27), and elsewhere in the Pentateuch only Deuteronomic (Deut. i. 37, xv. 10, xviii. 12). הִפְקִיד, *praeficere*, is construed alternately with בְ (comp. Jer. xli. 18) and עַל (comp. xli. 34). It is regular that the predicate וַיְהִי in the *genus potius* should precede the subject בִּרְכַּת ה', Ges. § 147*a*, especially in the case of ויהי, which corresponds with the neuter "there was, there was shown." Joseph possessed his master's fullest confidence, and was a man of goodly appearance, ver. 6 : *And he left all that he had in Joseph's hand, and with him he troubled himself about nothing but the bread that he ate; and Joseph was beautiful in form and beautiful in appearance.* עזב אל (לְ?) to leave (to confide) to any one, is said, Job xxxix. 11, 14, comp. Isa. x. 3, here with בְּיַד of him to whom some property is entrusted. אִתּוֹ refers to Joseph. He let him take care for everything that another could take care for, so that nothing was left but his eating, which it was self-evident he must himself care for. The young superintendent of his house was factotum, he was handsome in form (growth) and appearance (countenance, complexion, hair); the narrator distinguishes in the same manner תֹּאַר and מַרְאֶה xxix. 17. In the Moslem legend he is esteemed from this time forward as the ideal of youthful male beauty; in Persian figurative language he is called *mâhi Kanâ'n*, the moon of Canaan. His master's wife falls passionately in love with him, ver. 7 : *And it came to pass after these things, that his master's wife raised her eyes to Joseph and said: Lie with me, I pray thee.* On נשׂא עֵינַיִם אֶל, Assyr. *naśâ înâ ana*, see the discussion in Luthardt's *Zeitschr.* 1882, p. 125, and Friedr. Delitzsch, *Prolegomena*, p. 48. She cast upon him love glances; אֵצֶל has the same root as وَصَلَ the association of love. There have been at all times and in all nations such women with adulterous lusts. De Rougé has given a similar history from the papyrus d'Orbiney, which is written in hieratic characters

(*Revue archéologique*, 9th year).[1] Joseph however had no ear for her unchaste proposal, vv. 8, 9 : *But he refused, and said unto his master's wife: Behold, my master cares with me for nothing in the house, and all that belongs to him has he given into my hand. He is not greater in this house than I, and he has withholden nothing from me but only thee, because thou art his wife, and how should I do such great wickedness and sin against God!* The relator does not say לֹא אָבָה, but, which better expresses the act of self-control, וַיְמָאֵן (Reggio). After the preceding מה לֹא, 8a means *quidquam*, as at Prov. ix. 13; the more emphatic expression for it is מְאוּמָה 9a (the French *point*). If we had אֵין instead of אֵינֶנּוּ 9a, this would state: there is none greater in this house than I; אֵינֶנּוּ has a personal subject: he is not greater in this house than I, *i.e.* he has placed me on a level with himself (comp. on Eccles. vi. 2, where the case is similar). The confirming בַּאֲשֶׁר (*quoniam*, since) occurs in the Pentateuch only here and ver. 23. That which is repugnant is also rejected with אֵיךְ at xliv. 8, 34, Ps. cxxxvii. 4. Joseph recognises the inviolability of marriage, and recoils from such faithless ingratitude towards his master. A last but unsuccessful attempt to seduce him, vv. 10–12 : *And it came to pass, as she persuaded Joseph day by day and he hearkened not to her, to lie by her, or to be with her, then it came to pass, about the same time, that he came in to do his work, and there were none of the men of the house within, that she caught him by the garment saying : Lie with me ; but he left his garment in her hand and fled and went out.* לִהְיוֹת עִמָּהּ used in the sexual meaning of συνελθεῖν, συνεῖναι, συνουσία, is perhaps from *E*, where what the woman desired might have been so expressed. Besides בַּיּוֹם הַזֶּה l. 20, כְּהַיּוֹם הַזֶּה occurs elsewhere also, *e.g.* Deut. vi. 24, comp. ii. 30: about this day, *i.e.* this time. His not snatching the garment out of her hands arose from respect,

---

[1] In the Moslem legend it has grown into the sentimental loves of Jusuf and Suleiha ; see the Hungarian work of E. Neumann, *A Mohammedan Jozef-monda* (Buda-Pesth 1881).

and his fleeing was a flight from temptation, lest he should succumb to it. הַבַּיְתָה 11a being meant of the inner part of the house, הַחוּצָה must certainly be understood not of the street outside the house, but of the more external part of the house itself; nevertheless, since בִּגְדוֹ is meant of the upper garment, we may also think of flight into the open air. The revenge of the rejected, vv. 13-15: *And it came to pass, when she saw that he had left his garment in her hand and fled out, that she called the men of the house and said to them thus: See, he has brought in unto us a Hebrew man to mock us; he came in unto me to lie with me, and I cried out with a loud voice. And it came to pass, when he heard that I lifted up my voice and cried out, that he left his garment with me and fled and went out.* That she does not give the man his proper name, but says "he," is a characteristic trait. A "Hebrew man" was, according to xliii. 32, xlvi. 34, no *epitheton ornans* in anti-Semitic Egypt. In בָּנוּ she comprises herself and the household, especially the females; "he" seems, by having brought this foreigner into the house, to have intended to risk their honour. It is with the design of not betraying the true state of affairs that she does not say: he left his garment בְּיָדִי, but אֶצְלִי. Having thus gained over the household, who would certainly not be inclined towards the favoured foreigner and strict overseer, she preserves the means of proof for the purpose of exciting her husband against Joseph, vv. 16-19: *And she let his garment lie by her until his master came in, and she spake to him just such words, saying: The Hebrew slave, whom thou broughtest to us, came in unto me to mock me. And it came to pass, when I lifted up my voice and cried, that he left his garment near me and fled out. And it came to pass, when the master heard the words of his own wife, which she spake to him, saying: Such and such things did thy slave unto me, that his wrath was kindled.* The narrator transfers himself to the standpoint of the wife, when he says: she waited till his (Joseph's) master came, not: till her husband and still less her lord came, for petticoat government was indigenous in Egypt, *Diodor.* i. 27. כַּדְּבָרִים הָאֵלֶּה 17*a*, pointing backwards, as at xxiv. 28, xliv. 7, means "such words;" here, according to the context, what was said having been already repeated, "just such words." In 19*a* the use is somewhat different, the formula there meaning "such things," as at 1 Sam. ii. 23; in Hebrew diction the notions word and thing are both included in דבר. Joseph's master was angry; the marriage laws of Egypt were, as *Diodor.* i. 78 says, severe; he did not however inflict their heaviest penalty on Joseph; his anger would certainly be more excited by the vexatious nature of the occurrence, since he would hardly regard his wife as truth itself, ver. 20 : *And Joseph's master took him and put him into the public prison, the place where the king's prisoners were imprisoned, and he remained there in the prison,* properly the house of the enclosure (=בית הסחר, as Hebraeo-Sam. reads), not: of confinement (as though סהר=סגר, سجن, whence *sign*, dungeon); the prison-house is thus called as being a fortress surrounded with a wall (Syr. *sáḥrethā*)—a designation which occurs (instead of בית הבּוֹר or בית הָאֲסוּרִים) only in the history of Joseph and in *J.* According to this narrator, Joseph's master is a wealthy private man, who is left unnamed, and he consigns Joseph to prison from his own house; while according to *E* he, viz. Potiphar, is captain of the bodyguard and has his official residence in the State prison. The addition אשר שם= (=אֲשֶׁר־אֲסוּרֵי (אֲסִירֵי) הַמֶּלֶךְ אֲסוּרִים) . . xl. 3, as at xxxv. 13, comp. on מָקוֹם Ges. § 116. 2) helps to accommodate the two accounts. Joseph's prosperity in the prison, vv. 21-23 : *And Jahveh was with Joseph and showed him favour, and worked him favour in the eyes of the keeper of the prison. And the captain of the prison delivered into Joseph's hand all the prisoners that were in the public prison, and everything that had to be done there was done by him. The captain of the prison looked after nothing in his hand, because Jahveh was with him, and whatever he undertook Jahveh made to prosper*

The expression וַיִּתֵּן חִנּוֹ בְּעֵינֵי is like Ex. iii. 21, xi. 3, xii. 36. To עֹשִׂים must be added in thought the most general subject, as at Isa. xxxii. 12 (Driver, *Hebrew Tenses*, § 135. 6): everything that they had to do there, he did, *i.e.* it was done by his orders and under his supervision. The enhancement כָּל־מְאוּמָה is found only here; ראה with the accusative means to see after anything, to make it one's business: the captain did not trouble himself about anything that was in his (Joseph's) hand, he left him a free hand, he trusted him blindly. The concluding words are, as it were, like the refrain to ver. 2 sq.

THE DREAMS OF THE TWO STATE PRISONERS, AND JOSEPH'S INTERPRETATION, CH. XL.

From ch. xx., the model portion for *E* (*B*), onwards, this narrator appears pre-eminently as the writer, from whom proceeds an account of the impulse given to the course of history by dreams. This already makes it probable that the narrative, which now follows, is chiefly derived from this source. To this leads also, in relation to xxxvii. 28*a* (down to מִן־הַבּוֹר), the statement of Joseph, "I was stolen out of the land of the Hebrews," and the statement found in xl. 3 in its variation from *J* (*C*), who makes Joseph's master deliver him up to the בֵּית הַסֹּהַר, outside his house. But apart from the harmonistic additions in vv. 3, 5, 15, according to which Joseph was put in the prison before the two officers of Pharaoh, *J* may be recognised by the style at xl. 1, comp. xxii. 1 and xl. 10 כְּפֹרַחַת, comp. xxxviii. 29. It seems to be *J* himself who is here relating after *E*.

Here for the first time we meet with the intervention of the king of Egypt in the history, and the question arises, whether this Pharaoh belongs to a national Egyptian dynasty, or to one of the three Hyksos dynasties—the first having the names of six kings—which, according to Manetho, preceded the eighteen native dynasties. The Hyksos—says an extract in Josephus, *c. Ap.* 1. 14, from Manetho's Egyptian history—invading Egypt from the East, subjected it, ruled it for 511 years, and receiving free egress, after being at length conquered by Misphragmuthosis and besieged by his son Tethmosis in Avaris (the border fortress erected in the east against the Assyrians), marched through the desert towards Syria, and, not daring to advance as far as Syria from fear of the Assyrians, who then ruled over Asia, founded Jerusalem in Judæa. The name $TK\Sigma\Omega\Sigma$, says Josephus, means, according to Manetho, βασιλεῖς ποιμένες, or, according to another copy of the historical work, αἰχμάλωτοι ποιμένες. Both explanations are linguistically legitimate, for *šasu* is the hieroglyphic name of a brave pastoral people involved in many ways with Egypt, and *šôs* means in Koptic (as in the common tongue) shepherd, while *hak* (often with the addition of the vowel *a*, and often also with the determinative of a sitting figure of a king) means in the monumental language prince (chief), and written with other hieroglyphics it means also prisoner (*DMZ.* xxxi. 453), like the Koptic *hôk*, to surround; *hêk*, surrounded. Julius Africanus has, instead of 511 years for the total duration of the three Hyksos dynasties (the first of which is stated by Josephus to have lasted 259 years 10 months), 284 + 518 + 151, hence nearly 1000 years. Another fragment in Josephus, *c. Ap.* i. 26 sq., relates that the lepers of Egypt being removed by Amenophis to the city of Avaris, where the Hyksos, driven away by Tethmosis, had dwelt 393 years before, rose up, under the Heliopolitan priest Osarsiph, afterwards called Moses, against the king, and after practising, with the help of the Solymitan Hyksos, whose aid they had invoked, all kinds of cruelties and abominable profanations of holy things, were at last, after the thirteen predicted years of their rule over Egypt had expired, expelled from Egypt to the borders of Syria by Amenophis, who had fled from them to Ethiopia and his son Sethon-Ramses. Manetho himself says (as Josephus twice brings forward) that this second narrative is derived not from original Egyptian sources, but ἐκ τῶν ἀδεσπότως μυθολογουμένων. Other authors give still more confused accounts: Chæremon (Joseph. *c. Ap.* 1. 32), that the unclean, who were expelled from the country by Amenophis, led by Tisithen-Moses and Peteseph-Joseph, joined themselves with those in Pelusium, and forced Amenophis to flee to Ethiopia, until his son Ramesses drove them, the Jews, to Syria. Lysimachus (*id.* 34), that under the Egyptian king Bokchoris, the lepers and those who had scabies among the Jewish people were drowned, and that the rest of this ungodly multitude, being cast out into the wilderness, went on to Ἱερόσυλα (city of the sacrilegious), afterwards called Ἱεροσόλυμα, burning and plundering on the way. Justin (*Hist.* xxxvi. 2, comp. *Pompeji Trogi Fragm.* ed. Bialowsky, p. 32), who takes Moses for the son of Joseph, says: *Aegyptii quum scabiem et vitiliginem paterentur, responso moniti eum cum ægris, ne pestis ad plures serperet, terminis Aegypti pellunt. Dux igitur exsulum factus sacra Aegyptiorum furto abstulit, quæ repetentes armis Aegyptii domum redire tempestatibus compulsi sunt;* Tacitus (*Hist.* v. 2): *Sunt qui tradunt, Assyrios convenas, indignum agrorum populum, parte Aegypti potitos mox proprias urbes Hebraeasque terras et propria Syriae coluisse.* Hence we are obviously to regard the Hyksos and Israelites as one people. Josephus boasts of their being his ancestors. H. Grotius, Herm. Witsius, Basnage, Perizonius and others are on his side. Hofmann in an article " Unter welcher Dynastie haben die Israeliten Ægypten verlassen " (in *Studien u. Kritiken,* 1839), and in his letter to Böckh on Egyptian and Israelite chronology (1847), has tried to show, that the Hyksos were the Israelites, transformed by Egyptian vanity into a conquering nation. But many ancient investigators, such as Cunæus, Scaliger, Pezronius, Bochart, Marsham, Jas. Usher, Frider. Spanhemius, already perceived that this view was untenable; and now the view of Ewald, that the Hyksos were

Hebrew tribes who penetrated into Egypt before the Israelite migration, may be regarded as generally prevailing. The papyrus Sallier I. (in Ebers, pp. 204-206) confirms this episode of foreign usurpation. The worship of *Sutech* (*Set*), which has since prevailed, and the horse which has since become native in Egypt, are characteristic. But while the combination of the Hyksos with Israel has failed, it is on the other hand almost universally acknowledged, that the lepers who, according to Manetho's second account, dwelt for a time with the Hyksos, were the Israelites. This view also has ancient advocates, and reaches back—as may be inferred from the narrative of Hecatæus of Abdera in Diodor. xL 3, comp. xxxiv. (ed. Bekk.)—to the early time of the Ptolemies. Schiller in his *Sendung Mosis* states it, but without considering that the dark colour of the tradition must be for the most part laid to the account of Egyptian national hatred. We have accordingly to distinguish between two expulsions of foreigners from Egypt: the casting off of the yoke of Phœnician or Arabic conquering invaders by a sovereign of the 17th or 18th Dynasty, according to Wiedemann, Amosis (Aḥmes), father of Amenophis I., and the Israelite exodus, represented as the removal from the country of a people who defiled it, under Menephthes (Merneptah, lower Egyptian Mernephtah), son of Ramses II. Miamun of the 19th Dynasty. The capital of the kingdom in the time of this pair of rulers was Thebes in Upper Egypt, the home of the dynasty; but they resided in Tanis, the ancient capital of the Hyksos in the eastern Delta, the chief place of the worship of Set, after whom the father of Ramses II. was called Seti. The period of the Hyksos was then long past. But was the king under whom Joseph came into Egypt one of the Hyksos or not? Greek chronographists and Barhebraeus call him Apophis (Apepi), a king of the 15th Manethonian, the 1st Hyksos Dynasty. Wiedemann in his Egyptian history, 1884, advocates the view that the Pharaoh of Joseph was a Hyksos, but a later one than this first Apepi. So too Dillm., who says that Joseph's elevation took place in the Hyksos period, not in the time of their first impetuous eruption, but when they had become Egyptianized.[1] But apart from the fact that the rule of the Hyksos is a still indefinable, confused and indistinct matter (*DMZ.* xxxix. 148), the view, that the Hyksos ruled in Egypt from Joseph to Moses, is opposed by the one grave objection, that the people of Egypt, to whom Israel was in bondage, appears throughout the Old Testament Scriptures as a foreign, and by no means kindred race, and that the aim of the migration of the house of Jacob to Egypt, viz. to grow up into a nation far from the danger of intermixture, excludes identity of origin.

It is striking that in the first account of Manetho in Josephus, the first king whom the Hyksos elected from among them is called *Salatis* (as also Σαίτης, ἀφ' οὖ καὶ ὁ Σαίτης νομός, regarded by Afric., Euseb. and the school of Plato as an objectionable various reading), and that at xlii. 6 it is said of Joseph (the all but sovereign of Egypt, see Artapanus in Euseb. *Praep.* ix. 23): ויוסף הוא הַשַּׁלִּיט עַל־הָאָרֶץ. These and other combinations, as 'Τκσῶς and אַנְשֵׁי מִקְנֶה xlvi. 34 (xlvii. 6), "Αβαρις or Αὔαρις (Hyksos fortress) and עִיר עָבְרִים (xl. 15), are however but *ignes fatui.* How very much we are groping in the dark with respect to the organization of the Hyksos sovereignty, and Israel's sojourn in and exodus from Egypt, is shown by Köhler's examination of the matter in his *History of the Old Testament*, i. 237–245. He finally considers it most probable that the migration of Israel must be placed before the invasion of the Hyksos, the Hyksos rule limited to a period of between two and three hundred years, and the exodus dated after the expulsion of the Hyksos, perhaps the middle of the 18th Dynasty.

[1] v. Strauss-Torney in his article, "Israel von Joseph bis Mose nach ägyp. Quellen," in the *Conserv. Monatsschrift* for 1880, places the immigration in the year 1944/3 under the Hyksos-Pharaoh Archles (Aseth).

Offences of Pharaoh's cup-bearer and baker bring them both into the prison with Joseph, vv. 1–3 : *And it came to pass after these things, the cup-bearer and baker of the king of Egypt offended their lord the king of Egypt, and Pharaoh was wroth with his two courtiers, with the chief of the cup-bearers and the chief of the bakers, and he gave them into the custody of the house of the chief of the body-guard in the prison, the place where Joseph was imprisoned.* The circumstantiality of the narrative shows that two accounts are here interwoven, with a careful preservation of their words, notwithstanding the tautology thence arising. The main fact which follows in וַיִּקְצֹף is introduced by וַיְהִי; the accessory fact precedes in the circumstantializing perf. חָטְאוּ, as at Ex. xvi. 22, Deut. ix. 11 sq., Jer. xxxvi. 16, Ezek. i. 1, though חָטְאוּ may also, according to the scheme xiv. 1 (see there), be regarded as the main fact at which וַיְהִי aims. קצף is the usual word for the anger of high-placed personages, *e.g.* Esth. i. 21, 1 Sam. xxix. 4. The Kametz of סָרִים (see on xxxvii. 36) is treated as immutable in סָרִיסָיו as in סָרִיסֵי, Esth. ii. 21, comp. פְּרִיצֵי Dan. xi. 14, and on the other hand as mutable in סָרִיסֵי 7*a* (as in סָרִים, xxxvii. 36, comp. פָּרִיץ Isa. xxxv. 9). The captain of the body-guard (executioners) dwelt, as we are here told, in the prison building, which was under his charge, and he gave the two aristocratic prisoners to his slave Joseph to wait upon, ver. 4 : *And the captain of the guard gave them into the charge of Joseph, who ministered to them, and they remained some time in custody.* As the accounts are before us for their mutual completion, the שַׂר בֵּית הַסֹּהַר xxxix. 21–23 is the subordinate officer of the chief commander of the executive, and the latter, the master of Joseph, disposes, in virtue of his right of possession, of those consigned to prison, and placed under the oversight of the keeper. Whether and in what connection the imprisonment of Joseph himself was related by *E*, must be left unsettled. יָמִים designates a lengthy period, as an indefinite number of days, iv. 3, Neh. i. 4, Dan. viii. 27, comp. 1 Sam. xxix. 3. We now see how Joseph preserved his undaunted character in a prison also, and how, as the reward of his fidelity, the wisdom of a prophetic spirit was implanted in his pure soul (Wisd. i. 4). He finds his two fellow-prisoners depressed on account of their dreams, which they are unable to interpret, and gets them to relate them, vv. 5–8 : *And both dreamed a dream, each his dream in one and the same night, each according to the interpretation of his dream, the cup-bearer and the baker of the king of Egypt, who were imprisoned in the prison. And Joseph went in unto them in the morning, and saw them, and behold they were sad. Then he asked the courtiers of Pharaoh, which were with him in the custody of his master, saying: Why are your countenances sad to-day? And they said to him: We have dreamed a dream, and there is no one to interpret it to us; and Joseph said to them: Are not interpretations God's? Tell it, I pray you, to me.* It is seeking for difficulties where there are none to take חֲלוֹם שְׁנֵיהֶם genitively, *somnium amborum* (Reggio); חֲלוֹם, formed according to יְאוֹר, יְסוֹד, חֲמוֹר, is not a connective form, but is here the acc. object governed by וַיַּחַלְמוּ (an accessory form to וַיַּחְלְמוּ, Ges. § 63. 2); פִּתְרוֹן (explanation interpretation from פתר, نثر) combines the notions of interpretation and meaning. Their saying: we have dreamed a dream (not: dreams), seems to proceed from their thinking that their dreams, which they had related to each other, were essentially identical. And with the complaint וּפֹתֵר אֵין אֹתוֹ is certainly combined the afterthought, that as prisoners they could not apply to the חַרְטֻמִּים. Joseph however directs them from men to God, "interpretations are God's," *i.e.* His affair and gift, and by requesting them to tell them to him, he puts it before them as possible that God will not withhold from him the ability which comes from Him alone. Here too the circumstantial character of the narrative manifests different hands. The dream of the cup-bearer, vv. 9–11: *And the chief of the cup-bearers told Joseph his dream, and said: In my dream, behold I had a vine before me. And in the vine were three branches, and while it was sprouting, its blossom also already shot forth, its clusters of blossom ripened to grapes. And Pharaoh's cup was in my hand, and I took the grapes and pressed them, and handed the cup into Pharaoh's hand.* On כְּפִרְחָהּ for כְּהִיוֹתָהּ פֹּרַחַת, see on xxxviii. 29. Sprouting, blooming and ripening coincided in a manner significant of the immediate fulfilment of what the dream imagery indicated. נִצָּהּ sounds like an inflection of נֵץ, which in the meaning blossom is warranted by Mishnic Hebrew (see Levy), but the construction with עֹלְתָה shows that it is intended as an abbreviated נֵצָתָה, as at פְּנֵי Prov. vii. 8 = פְּנֶיהָ; see on the abbreviation with an added suffix the comm. on Ps. xxvii. 5 (4th edit. p. '260). Viticulture, said to be derived from Osiris, was, as is evident from Ps. lxxviii. 47, cv. 33, comp. Num. xx. 5, already well known in Egypt from the times of the ancient kingdom, and the statement of Herodotus, ii. 77, must be limited accordingly. Strabo, Athenaeus and Pliny describe the various wines and wine lands of Egypt. Nor is it true that, in the time of Psammetichus only, new must was drunk and fermented wine forbidden. Plutarch, *de Iside*, c. vi., tells us the contrary. The people drank wine without restriction; the kings, as being also priests, only so much as the sacred writings allowed, but after Psammetichus this restriction ceased. The ancient monuments show us all kinds of utensils used in wine-making, busy grape-treaders, sleepy tipplers, even drunken women (*DMZ.* xxx. 407). Ebers sees in the pressed juice of the grape, which the cup-bearer hands to the king, a kind of cooling drink; this feature in the picture however has in itself no significance, but naturally resulted from the entire symbolism of the dream. Joseph's interpretation, vv. 12–15: *Then Joseph said unto him: This is its interpretation: The three branches are three days. In yet three days will Pharaoh lift up thine head and restore thee to thine office, and thou shalt give Pharaoh's cup into his hand according to the former manner, when thou wast his cup-bearer. Only mayest thou keep me in thy remembrance when it is well with thee, and do kindness, I pray thee, to me, and make mention of me to Pharaoh, and bring me out of this house.* For I was stolen away out of the land of the Hebrews, and here also have I done nothing that they should put me into the dungeon. "To lift up the head of any one" is also used at 2 Kings xxv. 27 of release from prison and rehabilitation; in Assyr. also *ullû rêšu* = to bring to honour (Friedr. Delitzsch, *Proleg.* 155). אֲשֶׁר, which xxxix. 20 meant "where" of place, here means "when" of time, as *e.g.* also at 2 Sam. xix. 25. The restriction with כִּי אִם־ (always with the אִם makkephed, except in the three passages, xv. 4, Num. xxxv. 33, Neh. ii. 2, where כִּי has Makkeph) is like μόνον ἵνα Gal. ii. 10. כִּי אִם is here also, as at Micah vi. 8, Job xlii. 8, the confirmation of an implied negative sentence: I ask of thee nothing but that thou mayest (only that thou mayest). Driver, § 119δ, stumbles at this modal sense of the perfect; but if something future has preceded, the perfect following כִּי אִם shares in the reference to the future, without כִּי אִם interrupting the otherwise regular *consecutio temporum*, 2 Sam. v. 6 (where we must translate *imo abigent te*), 2 Kings xxiii. 9. Hence the alteration of כִּי into אַךְ (Wellh. Driver) is syntactically unnecessary and not really preferable; for with this *verumtamen si memineris* "זְכֹר is placed under conditions, while Joseph evidently means to entreat it" (Dillm.). He calls the land of Canaan אֶרֶץ הָעִבְרִים, so as at the same time to state his nationality. He was able to call it this as the land where Abraham the Ibri (xiv. 13) and his descendants had dwelt.[1] And though he says he was stolen away (after xxxvii. 28*a*), not sold (xxxvii. 28*b*), he was still the victim of a crime which his brothers perpetrated on him;

---

[1] See Herm. Witsius' († 1708) remarks on the subject in S. J. Curtis' 'Sketches,' *Bibliotheca sacra*, 1885, p. 318 sq.

but concerning this he is purposely silent. In the account of his brothers' revenge, ch. xxxvii., the stone-lined rain-water pit, into which Joseph was cast, was called בוֹר by both narrators. Such pits were elsewhere also used as dungeons, on which account בוֹר became, as here, the general name for a dungeon or a vault serving as a prison.

The dream of the baker, vv, 16, 17: *And the chief baker saw that the interpretation was good, he said to Joseph: I too in my dream—and behold three baskets of white bread upon my head, and in the uppermost basket all kinds of food of Pharaoh's bakers' work, and the birds ate it out of the basket upon my head.* He means to say: I also saw a like thing in my dream, but immediately starts off to relate this like thing. To carry a basket on the head was the custom of Egyptian men (Herod. ii. 35), especially, as the monuments show, of bakers.[1] Onkelos mistakenly translates סַלֵּי חֹרִי as סַלִּין דְּחֵרוּ, baskets of the nobility, *i.e.* with fine bread; Rashi and others: broken baskets, baskets with holes in them; but חֹרִי is an *adj. rel.* (from חָוַר, akin to חרר חֻוּר *candere*, and then *candium esse*) and means like حَوَارَى white or fine flour and bread made of it (comp. חוֹרַי white cloth, Isa. xix. 9, and حَرِير silk as dazzlingly white). Targ. Jer. correctly has פִּתָּא נְקִיָּא, and so already has the Jerus. Gemara to *Beza* ii. 6. The מ of מִסַּל is partitive, like vi. 2. Joseph's interpretation, vv. 18, 19: *Then Joseph answered and said: This is its interpretation: The three baskets are three days. In yet three days will Pharaoh lift up thy head from thee and hang thee on a tree, and the birds shall eat thy flesh from off thee.* As in the quasi-blessing of Esau מִשְׁמַנֵּי is ambiguously repeated from the blessing of Jacob, xxvii. 39, comp. xxviii., so here יִשָּׂא אֶת־רֹאשְׁךָ has the sense of *auferet caput tuum*, while when said of the cup-bearer it meant *efferet*. Beheading was an

---

[1] See the chapter on bread-baking in Wœnig's *Pflanzen im alten Ægypte*, 1886, pp. 174–180.

ordinary capital punishment, and the hanging of the corpse upon a tree (stake) an enhancement of the punishment (in use also according to the Mosaic penal law, Deut. xxi. 22 sq.). That Joseph did not keep back so crushing an interpretation, is a proof on the one hand of his Divine certainty, and on the other of the courage which was combined with his truthfulness; in any case, he would feel that it was well for the unhappy man to be prepared for the worst.

The fulfilment of the interpretations, vv. 20–23: *And it came to pass on the third day, Pharaoh's birthday, that he made a feast for all his servants, and lifted up the head of the chief of the cup-bearers and of the chief of the bakers among his servants. He restored the chief of the cup-bearers to his office of cup-bearer, and he gave the cup into Pharaoh's hand. And the chief of the bakers he hanged, as Joseph had interpreted. And the chief of the cup-bearers did not remember Joseph—he forgot him.* The LXX rightly has ἡμέρα γενέσεως Φαραώ, and Targ. Jer. I. יוֹם גְּנוּסָא דפרעה; the *inf. Hoph.* הֻלֶּדֶת, which means the having been born (different from the *inf. Niph.* הִוָּלֵד, e.g. Hos. ii. 5, the being born), is as at Ezek. xvi. 5, comp. 4, combined with an accus. object. That the king's birthday was kept as a holiday in Egypt, is confirmed, at least for the Ptolemaic period, by the bilingual tables of Rosetta and Canopus. Rashi understands נשׂא ראשׁ 20*b* according to Ex. xxx. 12: he counted over his servants, and among them the two also. Then there would be an addition to the two meanings of *tollere caput* the third of *recensere*, which is improbable; the Targ. Jer. correctly renders it: he raised (רוֹמֵם) the heads of the two in different manners. מַשְׁקֶה 21*a* does not as a partic. mean the cup-bearer, but his office (כֵּן 13*a*). When the cup-bearer was reinstated in his office, his ingratitude made him have no effectual remembrance of Joseph, so that he really forgot him.

PHARAOH'S DREAMS AND JOSEPH'S ELEVATION, CH. XLI.

The chief source from which this narrative is obtained is the same as the preceding. E (D) may be recognised by such expressions as פֹּתֶר and פִתרון, which occur exclusively in these portions of the history of Joseph, and פַּ office, xl. 13, xli. 13, as also by the form קִרְבֶּנָה xli. 21 (E elsewhere also, xxx. 41, xxi. 29, xxxi. 6, xlii. 36, indulging in such emphatic prolongations), and the Divine name אֱלֹהִים xli. 15 sq. (where J would have suitably had יהוה), but especially by the particular, that Joseph is here called the servant appointed by the captain of the guard for the two State prisoners. As J would certainly also relate the elevation of Joseph through the verification of his interpretation of Pharaoh's dreams, the question arises whether many traces of a parallel text of J may not be more easily explained by the view, that we have before us the narrative according to E, as reproduced by J, than by supposing that R interpolated the text of E with additions from J.

Pharaoh's first dream, vv. 1–4: *And it came to pass after two full years, and Pharaoh dreamed, and behold he stood by the Nile. And behold, there came out of the Nile seven kine, beautiful of form and fat of flesh, and they fed in the reed grass. And behold, seven other kine came up after them out of the Nile, ill-favoured and lean of flesh, and stood beside the kine on the brink of the Nile. And the ill-favoured and lean-fleshed kine devoured the seven kine beautiful of form and fat of flesh.* The structure of the sentence is the same as at xlii. 35, comp. xv. 17, xxix. 25; the apodosis begins with וְהִנֵּה, and וּפַרְעֹה חֹלֵם is a preceding adverbial sentence (Driver, § 78). עֹמֵד is left after הִנֵּה without the subject being expressed, as at xxiv. 30, comp. הנה תעה xxxvii. 15 (Driver, § 135. 6). To שְׁנָתַיִם is added as the accus. of more exact definition יָמִים (Ges. 118. 3): two years of days are two full years, like חֹדֶשׁ יָמִים xxix. 14, a full month. יְאֹר, as the name of the Nile, may be an assimilated Egyptian word, in itself it is however Semitic, and used as much of the Tigris (Dan. xii. 5 sq.) as of the Nile, and even of mine-shafts (see Friedr. Delitzsch, *Hebrew Language*, p. 25). אָחוּ, on the contrary, is an indigenous Egyptian word: *achu* from *ach*, redupl. *achach* to become green, LXX ἄχι (with the more recent final *i*), which must have been so much transferred into Egyptian Greek that עָרוֹת Isa. xix. 17 is translated by τὸ ἄχι τὸ χλωρόν, on which Jerome remarks: *quid hic sermo significaret, audivi ab Ægyptiis, hoc nomine omne quod in palude viride nascitur appellari*. Instead of וַיִּקוּץ the Samar. has רקות, like the Masoretic text of ver. 19 sq., 27; וַיִּלּוֹת brought down, thinned, is a third synonym. The designation of the brink of the Nile by שָׂפָה is no poetic image; שָׂפָה means not only the edge of the mouth (the lips), but the rim of anything, that whereby it comes in friction or into contact with other things (see on the root on iii. 15). Pharaoh's second dream, vv. 5–7: *And he slept and dreamed a second time, and behold, seven ears of corn came up upon one stalk fat and well-favoured. And behold, seven ears, thin and blasted by the east wind, sprang up after them. And the thin ears swallowed up the seven fat and full ears—then Pharaoh awoke, and behold it was a dream.* The ־ in שִׁבֳּלִים from שִׁבֹּלֶת is like that in תִּקָבְנוּ from תָּקֹב Num. xxiii. 25. The adj. בָּרִיא healthy, strong, fat, is also applicable to ears, which can indeed be sickly and shrivel; such a sickness is the blight שְׁדֵפָה (שִׁדָּפוֹן), mostly caused in Egypt by the dreaded Chamsin, blowing from the south-eastern desert districts. The swallowing up of the first ears by the second is not really meant, for "the absolutely irrepresentable cannot be dreamed" (Heidenh.): the seven lean ears shot up above the others and so concealed them, that they had, as it were, vanished. Vain interrogation of native scholars, ver. 8: *And it came to pass in the morning that his spirit was troubled, and he sent and called all the scribes of Egypt and all the wise men therein. And Pharaoh told them his dream, and no one was able to interpret them* (the two dreams) *to Pharaoh.* In the similar history of Nebuchadnezzar's dream, the *Niphal* וַיִּפָּעֶם Dan. ii. 3 precedes the Hithpael וַתִּתְפָּעֶם with a similar recession of the tone. Pharaoh sends for all the חַרְטֻמִּים and all the wise men of Egypt. He did what Ptolemy, according to Tacitus, *Hist.* iv. 83, did in a similar case: *sacerdotibus Aegyptiorum, quibus mos talia intellegere, nocturnos visus aperit.* חַרְטֻמִּים (from the non-occurring sing. חַרְטֹם) is a Semitic word formed perhaps in consonance with an Egyptian one, a secondary formation from חֶרֶט pen, mode of writing, a writing, Isa. viii. 1. The LXX translates it ἐξηγηταί, *i.c.* according to Hesychius: οἱ περὶ ἱερῶν καὶ διοσημείων ἐξηγούμενοι. ἱερογραμματεῖς would be more suitable. Egypt was familiar with Manticism of every kind. The plur. אוֹתָם, referring back to אֶת־חֲלֹמוֹ, looks almost like a hint that the native scholars looked upon the essentially one dream as two different dreams, and were thereby led astray. Reference of the chief cup-bearer to Joseph, vv. 9-13: *Then the chief of the cup-bearers spoke to Pharaoh saying: I remember my sins this day. Pharaoh was angry with his servants and gave me into custody of the house of the captain of the guard, me and the chief of the bakers. Then we dreamed a dream in one and the same night, I and he, we dreamed each after the interpretation of his dream. And there was there with us a young Hebrew man, a slave of the captain of the guard; to him we told it, and he interpreted to us our dreams, according to the dream of each he interpreted. And it came to pass, as he had interpreted to us, so it happened; me he reinstated in my office, and him he hanged.* The combination אֶת דִּבֶּר is neither here nor at Ex. ii. 1, iii. 22 an accusatival one; אֶת is a preposition, as at xlii. 30, xxiii. 8. The LXX rightly renders τὴν ἁμαρτίαν μου ἀναμιμνῄσκω σήμερον, not: I bring it to mention, but (as at xl. 14) I bring it to remembrance; but he says חֲטָאַי (not חֲטָאִי), respectfully magnifying and not diminishing the offence, which had incurred the anger of Pharaoh. Instead of the first אִתִּי, the LXX, Samar. have the preferable אִתָּם. The genit. combination in the custody of the . . . is repeated from xl. 3. The intensive *ah* with the 1 *pl. impf.* וַתְּחַלְּמָה, which makes the historical statement only the more emphatic, finds its equal in וַנַּעְפָּה, Ps. xc. 10, and elsewhere occurs almost only in the 1 *sing.*, *e.g.* xxxii. 6, Ew. § 232g. אִישׁ כְּחֶלְמוֹ is, according to the scheme discussed in rem. on ix. 5, equivalent to אִישׁ בַּחֲלוֹם, as אִישׁ אֶל־שִׂקּוֹ xlii. 25 is the same as in the sack of each. Joseph's appearance before Pharaoh, vv. 14–16 : *And Pharaoh sent and called Joseph, and they dismissed him quickly from prison ; he shaved himself and changed his garments and came before Pharaoh, and Pharaoh said to Joseph : I have dreamed a dream, and no one can interpret it, but I have heard say of thee, that thou hearest a dream to* (at once) *interpret it. Then Joseph answered Pharaoh saying : It belongs not to me, God will answer what will profit Pharaoh.* The prison is here called בּוֹר, as at xl. 15. The LXX has ἀπὸ τοῦ ὀχυρώματος, *i.e.* according to xl. 14, xxxix. 20 מִן־הַבַּיִת. The unnamed subject of וַיְרִיצֻהוּ is as frequently (*e.g.* Zech. iii. 5, comp. Luke xii. 20) the attendants : they quickly dismiss (not fetch) Joseph, and, being free for his departure to the palace, he shaves himself (וַיְגַלַּח reflexive, like רָחַץ to wash oneself) and changes his garments ; for to shave off all hair from the body, was in Egypt a main article of cleanliness and purity ; and that no one should appear before a king in his work-day garments, is self-understood. With respect to shaving, Joseph had as yet had no reason for conforming to Egyptian custom. עָלֶיךָ *de te*, as at 1 Kings x. 6 : The king has heard say concerning Joseph, that he only needs to hear a dream, to be able at once to interpret it. He however refers the king, as he did (xl. 8) the two prisoners, from human intervention to God. בִּלְעָדָיו xli. 44 without the *excepto te* ; thus the בִּלְעָדַי forms a thought of itself : without me = I can do nothing at all (like I may (take) nothing at all, xiv. 24). God alone is able to do it, and He can give the power ; He will give as an answer (to me who inquire of Him) the welfare of Pharaoh, *i.e.* what shall be for his welfare. This sounds hopeful, though it does not prejudge. Pharaoh again repeats his double dream, vv. 17–24: *And Pharaoh said to Joseph: In my dream, behold I stood on the brink of the Nile. And behold seven kine rose up out of the Nile fat of flesh and beautiful of form and fed in the reed-grass. And behold seven other kine rose up after them, poor and very ill-favoured, and fallen away in flesh. I have not seen their like for badness in all the land of Egypt. And the fallen away and ill-favoured kine ate up the seven first fat kine. And they went into their inside, and it could not be seen that they had gone into their inside, and their appearance was ill-favoured as at the beginning—then I awoke. And I saw in my dream, and behold, seven ears shot up on one stalk, full and fair to see, and behold seven ears withered, thin and blasted by the east wind. And the thin ears swallowed up the seven good ears—I told it to the scribes, and none of them could give me an explanation.* In such repetitions Hebrew authors, and even poets in their refrains (see *Psalms*, 4th edit. p. 350), delight in small variations instead of literal identity. So *e.g.* xxiv. 42–47 with relation to xxiv. 11–24. It is a needless conjecture that the variations are worked in from the parallel text of *J* (Dillm.). In Pharaoh's repetition of his double dream the adjectives דַּלּוֹת, רַקּוֹת and צְנֻמוֹת as well as the greater detail, 19*b*, 21*a*, are new. On the sing. מַרְאֵיהֶן 21*a*, see Ges. § 93. 3, note 3. And on אַחֲרֵיהֶם 23*b*, instead of the more correct אַחֲרֵיהֶן, comp. xxxi. 9, xxxii. 16, and וַיֵּלְדוּ xx. 17. Joseph's interpretation, vv. 25–32: *Then Joseph said to Pharaoh: The dream of Pharaoh is one; what God intends to do he has announced to Pharaoh. The seven well-favoured kine are seven years, and the seven well-favoured ears are seven years. The dream is one. And the seven lean and ill-favoured kine, which came up after the former, are seven years, and the ears empty and blasted by the east wind will be seven years of famine. This is the word that I said unto Pharaoh: What God intends to do He has shown unto Pharaoh. Behold, seven years are approaching, a great plenty in the whole land of Egypt. And* *seven years of famine shall arise after them, and the plenty is forgotten in the land of Egypt, and the famine will consume the land. And the plenty will not be noticed in the land by reason of the famine following, because it is very grievous. And in respect of this that the dream was twice repeated to Pharaoh,* (this happened) *because the thing is settled with God, and God will speedily bring it to pass.* Osiris was to the Egyptians the God of the Nile, whose symbol was the bull (Diod. i. 51), and Isis-Hathor the goddess of the fertile and all-nourishing earth, whose symbol, the cow (Macrobius, *Saturn.* i. 19), was also that of the moon and the lunar year—hence the interpretation of the kine by fruitful or unfruitful years, according to the favour or disfavour of the Nile, was an obvious one; but it needed Joseph's divinely attested insight into the future, to answer not only for this apparently obvious and simple interpretation, but also for the results of fourteen years. On the determinated adj. with the undeterminated chief notion in שֶׁבַע פָּרֹת הַטֹּבֹת 26a, see on i. 31. Instead of דַקּוֹת the second seven ears are called 27b הָרֵקוֹת (the opposite of מְלֵאוֹת); רַקּוֹת is only said of the kine. In the remark that the seven empty ears are seven years of famine, *i.e.* will be proved to mean such, the centre of gravity in the meaning of the two dreams is anticipatively alluded to. The "word" (הַדָּבָר, comp. Acts xv. 6 in Luther's, and in our Hebrew translation) 28a is what he said 25b. קוּם "arise" (*oriri*), said of years, is a kind of personifying transference of the diction of Ex. i. 8. As the swallowing up is alluded to by וְנִשְׁכַּח, so by וְלֹא־יִוָּדַע is it signified that nothing of the seven fat morsels was perceived in the seven lean kine; the famine will be so great that the stores will visibly disappear. The elliptical brevity in ver. 32 is like xxxvii. 22 (*E*). עַל introduces that to which respect is had, as at Ruth iv. 7 (comp. לְ xvii. 20), and כִּי confirms the said state of matters (comp. on xviii. 20). Joseph's counsel, vv. 33–36: *And now let Pharaoh look for a prudent and wise man and set him over the land of Egypt. Let Pharaoh set to work and appoint overseers over the land, and take up a fifth part of the land of Egypt in the seven years of plenty. And let them gather all the food of these coming good years and heap up corn under the hand of Pharaoh in the cities, and let them keep it. And the food shall be for a store for the land for the seven years of famine which will come upon the land of Egypt, that the land be not ruined through the famine.* The jussive יְרָא has, according to the Masora, the tone upon the ultima (König, p. 561), and has on that account Tsere instead of Segol in the last syllable, as Abenezra expressly states in his two Grammars. In 34a we must not explain: *constituat Pharao et praeficiat praefectos* (Dillm.), which is tautological; Ges. rightly compares the Latin *fac scribas*, the object of יַעֲשֶׂה is what is afterwards specified, or also: עָשָׂה has in itself the completed sense of acting or setting to work; 1 Kings viii. 32, comp. Ps. xxii. 32, is similar. Pharaoh should take during the seven fruitful years the fifth part of the entire harvest, by means of commissioners, and store up this corn (בָּר) under Pharaoh's hand, *i.e.* in royal magazines, that the store of food thus laid up (אֹכֶל) may save the land from starvation during the years of famine. The verbal copiousness of ver. 35 may arise from the two accounts being here compressed into one, as in vv. 48, 49 (comp. xxvii. 44 sq., xxxi. 18). Elevation of Joseph to be the highest official in the land, vv. 37–40: *And the thing was good in the eyes of Pharaoh and in the eyes of all his servants. And Pharaoh said to his servants: Shall we find a man like this, in whom is the spirit of God? And Pharaoh said to Joseph: Since God has showed thee all this, there is none prudent and wise as thou. Thou shalt be over my house, and according to thy bidding shall all my people be ruled, only by the throne will I be greater than thou.* Arnheim translates 38a "will there be found;" but we have not הֲיִמָּצֵא, nor is נִמְצָא the *partc. Niph.*, for "will found be = exists" would be expressed in ancient Hebrew by יֵשׁ; Rashi already correctly gives: should we find, if we should go and seek for. To translate 40a "upon thy mouth shall all my people kiss" (Ges. Kn.), is impracticable; for though נשק to kiss = to do homage, is now also corroborated by the Assyrian, the kiss of homage is a kissing of the foot, not the mouth, for which כָּל־עַמִּי would certainly be an intolerable subj., and besides we find in Biblical Hebrew וַיִּשָּׁקֵהוּ or נָשַׁק לוֹ (he kissed him), but not נשק על פיו. נשק means to join, especially mouth to mouth, i.e. to kiss, but also to fit to (whence the armour a man puts on is called נֶשֶׁק), and here (but not at Ps. ii. 12) with an internal obj.: disponere (res suas), to submit to (comp. نظم نفسه); hence עַל־פִּיךָ like xlv. 21. הַפָּא is the accus. of more exact definition, according to Ges. § 118. 3. Honours are heaped on Joseph, and first the insignia of his office are bestowed, vv. 41, 42: *And Pharaoh said to Joseph: Behold, I have placed thee over the whole land of Egypt. Then Pharaoh took off his signet ring from his hand and put it on the hand of Joseph, and he clothed him in byssus garments and put the gold chain on his neck.* Ver. 41 was not absolutely needed after ver. 40, and may have been taken from the parallel source, but stands here as the solemn act of institution, following the declaration of Pharaoh's will (see on נָתַתִּי i. 29). טַבַּעַת like חוֹתָם, Arab. *chátim*, means the signet ring, which is confirmed as Egyptian by impressions from the signets of the Pharaohs, Cheops, Horus, Sabaco. בִּגְדֵי־שֵׁשׁ are garments of cotton (there were cotton plantations in ancient Egypt, see Ebers, *Durch Gosen zum Sinai*, 2nd edit. pp. 490–492), or also fine white cotton-like linen; for שֵׁשׁ, ancient Egypt. *schenti*, means both; while בּוּץ, ancient Egyptian *pek*, is the proper word for fine linen. Priestly garments, by which Joseph is here distinguished, might not be of woollen, but might be of either cotton or linen.[1] רְבִיד (רְבִד הַזָּהָב) from

---

[1] The white head-gear usual among the wandering tribes is now called شاش, properly the fine white cotton texture, of which it consists (*DMZ*. xxxii. 161).

רבד, רְבַל ,, √ רב to fix closely) is the gold chain usual as an official distinction, a mark, according to Elian and Diodorus, of the dignity of a judge, but here of like significance with the "golden collar" occurring on the monuments as a reward. Joseph is presented to the people as the highest representative of the king, who appoints him an almost absolute ruler with himself, vv. 43, 44: *And he made him ride in his second chariot, and they cried before him: Abrech; and he placed him over the whole land of Egypt. And Pharaoh said to Joseph: I am Pharaoh, and without thee shall no one lift up hand or foot in the whole land of Egypt.* As פֹּהֵן הַמִּשְׁנֶה is the second priest of highest rank after the כֹּהֵן הָרֹאשׁ, so is מֶרְכֶּבֶת הַמִּשְׁנֶה the next State chariot to the exclusively royal one. The call to show profound respect expressed in אַבְרֵךְ, is satisfactorily explained as an Egyptian cry assimilated to the Hebrew: "Cast thyself down!" The Coptic *abork*, imper. of *bor*, to cast down, with the suffix of the 2nd pers., means this (Benfey, *Verhalt. der äg. Sprache zum sem. Sprachstamm*, p. 302 sq.). In Hebrew אַבְרֵךְ is to be understood as the *inf. abs. Hiph.* of ברך (comp. אַשְׁכֵּים Jer. xxv. 3), whence Jose b. Dormaskith in *Sifri* (65a, ed. Friedmann) explains it by לברכים, and Jerome translates: *clamante praecone ut omnes coram eo genu flecterent*.[1] The Targum and Midrash, on the contrary, explain אברך as a compound from אב and רך *pater tener* (highly respected though young), which must be left out of consideration, or from אב and רךּ *pater regis* (see Rashi on this passage), which is in itself permissible,

[1] In Macropedius' *Josephus, sacra fabula*, the herald Thalthybius goes through the city with Joseph and proclaims: Σωτῆρα κόσμου regis edicto hunc jubeo vocarier Genuque flexo Ægyptiis ab omnibus adorarier; see v. Weilen, *Der ägyptische Joseph im Drama des XVI. Jahrh.* 1887. The view quoted by Köhler (*Gesch.* i. 156) from the *Speaker's Commentary*, that אברך means the same as the Hebrew שְׁמַח־נָא, has, notwithstanding its Egyptologic demonstrability, this first of all against it, that it does away with the kinship of meaning between the original word and its Hebraized form (comp. my *Jesurun*, p. 107 sq.). Still farther off is v. Strauss-Torney's explanation: "he who opens knowledge."

"father of the king" being actually the title which Joseph gives himself, xlv. 8b, and having other Oriental analogues as the title of the highest official at the side of the king. Apparently however it cannot be adopted, because רך = *rex* (*Baba bathra* 4a לא ריכא בר ולא ריכא, "not king and not king's son") is a borrowed Jewish word derived from the Latin. But Friedr. Delitzsch points out in his *Hebrew Language*, p. 26 sq., that *abarakku* is in Assyrian the appellation of the highest dignitary in the kingdom, and is ideogrammatically explained by "friend of the king;" even the goddess who is the supreme protectress of a sanctuary is called *abarakkatu*. Since neither a Hebrew nor an Egyptian medium is perceptible for the use of this Assyrian word,[1] itself inexplicable in Assyrian, some curious chance must certainly have had a hand in the matter.[2] The *inf. abs.* וְנָתוֹן continues the *finitum* in an adverbially subordinate manner as at Isa. xxxvii. 19, Ex. viii. 11, Lev. xxv. 14, Judg. vii. 19, Hagg. i. 6, Zech. iii. 4, xii. 10, Eccles. iv. 2. In ver. 44 is repeated what was already virtually stated at ver. 40, viz. that Pharaoh is king, but that Joseph is to be ruler. Joseph's change of name and marriage, ver. 45: *And Pharaoh called Joseph's name Ṣāphnath Pa'neaḥ, and gave him Asnat, daughter of Potiphera the priest of On, to wife, and Joseph went out over the land of Egypt.* The LXX paraphrases the name Ψονθομφανήχ, which, as Jerome testifies, and as is, with the exception of one letter, confirmed by the Coptic, means *salvator mundi*, *p-sot-om-ph-eneh* (from *sot*, *sôte* salvation, and *eneh* age, world), but the nasal *p-sont*, instead of *p-sot*, thus remains unexplained. It seems therefore more obvious to regard פענח as the Egyptian *anḫ* life, provided with the article (whence the temple quarter of Memphis was called *p-ta-anḫ*, the world of life), and with Rosellini, Lepsius, Ormsby and others, to

[1] The opposition of Halévy in *Recherches Bibliques*, No. vi. p. 24, must still let the fact stand that *abarakku* and *abarrakkatu* are, in Assyrian, the names of high dignity.
[2] See the *Assyrian Dictionary*, pp. 68–70.

explain the name as compounded of *sônt* to support, to preserve, and *anḫ*, "support (*sustentator*) of life" (צפנת=פֹּצְנַת). Josephus, *Ant.* ii. 6. 1, by explaining the name κρυπτῶν εὑρετής reproduces the impression made by the Hebraized word upon Jewish ears (see *Bereshith rabbah*, c. 90); the Jewish Pajtanim use פָּעְנֵחַ as a four-lettered verb, with the meaning to uncover, to reveal (*DMZ.* xxxvi. 402). The name of אָסְנַת (LXX 'Ασενέθ) apparently means one belonging to the goddess *Neith*, the Egyptian Athene; Brugsch, *Gesch.* p. 248, identifies it with *Snat* (*Sant*), a female name frequent in the ancient and middle kingdom. On the name of her father פּוֹטִי פֶרַע (one dedicated to the god Ra), we have already spoken at xxxvii. 36. He was a priest in אֹן (און), which the LXX rightly translate Ἡλιούπολις in the history of Joseph; they also thus render the synonymous אָוֶן Ezek. xxx. 17; while, on the contrary, the Cœlesyrian אָוֶן (Heliopolis) is paraphrased as Ὤν. In ancient Egyptian it was called *An* (*Anu*), or more precisely *Anumhit*, Anu of the north, in Coptic *Un* or *On*, which means light, according to Cyrill on Hos. v. 8 ἥλιος; the sacred name of the city was *ta-Ra* or *pa-Ra*, house of the sun (as at Jer. xliii. 13 בֵּית הַשֶּׁמֶשׁ, comp. on Isa. xix. 18). The worship of the sun was the most ancient form of the Egyptian religion; Amon-Ra was called, subsequently to Ahmes I., the king of the gods.[1] Joseph, the husband of the priest of the sun's daughter, has now become an Egyptian to the Egyptians, the favourite son of Jacob a ruler of the heathen; he is admitted into the priestly caste, to which the kings of Egypt also belonged, or into which they had to be admitted, if descended from the military caste. Thus raised to be ruler of the land, he

[1] See Krummel, *Die Religion der alten Ægypter*, 1883, p. 19 sq. One of the obelisks, which stood in front of the temple of the sun, the most ancient, erected by King Osirtases I., is still there; of the two others, which bear the names of Tutmes III., Ramses II., and Seti II., one now adorns the Thames Embankment in London, the other the public park in New York. See J. Leslie Porter's *Egypt, Physical and Historical*, 1885, p. 18 sq.

went out over the land of Egypt, יָצָא עַל as at Ps. lxxx. 6. This is now told once more in the words of another narrator, ver. 46: *And Joseph was thirty years old when he stood before Pharaoh king of Egypt; and Joseph went out from before Pharaoh and went through the whole land of Egypt.* The combination פַּרְעֹה מֶלֶךְ מִצְרַיִם occurs only here in Genesis, and is next met with Ex. vi. 11, and farther on in Q (*A*). To this narrator belongs the statement of age at xxxvii. 2, and consequently here also: hence from twelve to thirteen years elapsed between Joseph's sale and elevation. The tone of diction 46*a* is like that of xlvii. 7, and 46*b* like that of xlvii. 10. Joseph's arrangements during the seven fruitful years, vv. 47-49: *And the land bore in the seven years of plenty by handfuls. And he gathered all the food of the seven years, which were in the land of Egypt, and laid up the food in the cities, the food of the ground round about any city he laid up in that city. And Joseph heaped up corn as the sand of the sea, exceeding much, so that he left off numbering, for it was beyond numbering.* The noun קֹמֶץ, with its derivative קְמָץ, is native in the Minchah law, Lev. ii. 2 and onwards; the former means the hand forming a hollow for grasping, the latter to take away a handful (*manipulum* or *pugillum*). Consequently לִקְמָצִים (with an adverbial לְ in the sense of the Greek κατά or ἀνά, Ew. § 217*d*) here means, in such abundance that the whole hand was always needed for taking what offered itself, not: in bundles, *manipulatim* (Ges.), which does not give the notion of great abundance; but, if the expression may be allowed, in full-handed manner. In ver. 48 the undeterminated שֶׁבַע שָׁנִים is intolerable; it cannot mean *per septem annos*, for אֲבָל (without an article) points to a genitival relation, so that we have to write according to ver. 35 שֶׁבַע הַשָּׁנִים, or, since this does not elsewhere occur thus without an addition, שֶׁבַע שְׁנֵי הַשָּׂבָע (as at ver. 53). The LXX, Sam. take over שָׂבָע into the relative sentence: τὰ βρώματα τῶν ἑπτὰ ἐτῶν ἐν οἷς ἦν ἡ εὐθηνία (היה השבע) ἐν τῇ

GENESIS XLI. 50-52.

γῇ Αἰγύπτου. Heidenh., Reggio and others understand וַיִּקְבֹּץ and וַיִּתֵּן with the most general subject: they collected, they put; but that we have יֹסֵף in ver. 49 and not already ver. 48, just shows that the narrative is not of one cast. Joseph collected the whole produce of cereal food (אֹכֶל, viz. בַּר, comp. ver. 35) of the seven fruitful years, by placing granaries[1] in the cities for the harvest within their territories, and the corn to be stowed up was very much, like the sand of the sea (a usual hyperbole, xxii. 17, xxxii. 13), so that he left off keeping account of it, because of its enormous quantity. Joseph's sons by Asnath, vv. 50-52: *And there were two sons born to Joseph before the coming of the year of famine, which Asnath, daughter of Potiphera, priest of On, bare him. And Joseph called the name of the first-born Manasseh, for " Elohim has made me forget all my trouble, and all of my father's house." And the name of the second he called Ephraim, for " Elohim hath made me fruitful in the land of my affliction."* The passive יֻלַּד, with a plural subject following, is like x. 25 (*J*), comp. xxxv. 26 (*Q*), and the more particular statement with אֲשֶׁר (*quos, quem, quam*) without pronouns referring backwards, like xvi. 15, xxv. 12, xxxiv. 1 (*Q*). The year of famine is self-evidently the first of the seven. The Aramaico-Arabic form נַשַּׁנִי for נִשְׁנִי (comp. קַרְקַר Num. xxiv. 17 for קִרְקַר) is chosen because of its consonance with the name; נִשָּׁה is a causative *Piel*, like יָהַם Job xxxiii. 20. יָחֵל Ps. cxix. 49, מְנַשֶּׁה he who brings into forgetfulness, *i.e.* his former sorrows, and also the fate of his family, which had formerly caused him great anxiety.[2] אֶפְרַיִם means double fruitfulness, the Dual being used in Egyptian also in a superlative sense, *e.g.* double - Jbis = Jbis κατ' ἐξ., comp. שַׁחֲרִים

---

[1] מִסְכְּנוֹת Ex. i. 11, from סכן to take care of; see Friedr. Delitzsch, *Proleg.* p. 186.

[2] In a bilingual Cypriote inscription (in the possession of Colonel Warren), the erector of the dedicated image is called in the Phoenician text מנחם, in the Cyprio-Greek Μανασσης, which is certainly a confusion caused by the kindred meaning.

double dawn, 1 Chron. viii. 8, and the allusion to the meaning of the name Ephraim, Hos. xiii. 15.

It is strange, remarks Kn., that Joseph, who so affectionately loved and was equally beloved by his father, did not give him early notice of his safety and exaltation, but let a number of years pass by without doing so, and then only found occasion for this communication on the arrival of his brethren. This obvious objection is met by the consideration, that the news would have destroyed the peace of his father's family, so he went on trusting in God, who could bring all to a happy issue. In the first place his prophetic interpretation had to be confirmed by the result. This now took place, vv. 53–55: *And the seven years of plenty that was in the land of Egypt came to an end. And the seven years of famine began to come, as Joseph had said, and there was famine in all lands, but in the land of Egypt there was bread. And the whole land of Egypt was famished, and the people cried to Pharaoh for bread. And Pharaoh said to all the Egyptians: Go to Joseph; what he saith to you do.* In ver. 48a הָיוּ is used with respect to שָׁנִים ; here הָיָה in conjunction with הַשָּׂבָע. There was bread in Egypt, i.e. in the granaries; and when, after the consumption of private stores, the general scarcity was felt there also, Pharaoh referred those who supplicated his help to Joseph, who now opened the granaries and sold to natives and foreigners the corn there stored up, vv. 56, 57: *And the famine extended over all the face of the land: and Joseph opened all the storehouses and sold to the Egyptians, and the famine prevailed in the land of Egypt. And the whole population of the earth came to Egypt, to Joseph, to buy, for the famine prevailed in all the earth.* Ver. 56 ought to end with : לְמִצְרַיִם (Dillm.); it treats throughout of Egypt. The famine increased there, and at the same time in all the neighbouring countries. אֶת־כָּל־אֲשֶׁר בָּהֶם, all places wherein was found; the subj. is missing, just as when שלה xlix. 10 means: he whose is. Both phrases are as to style impossible. The Samar. adds בר (corn), but we also want האוצרות; perhaps אשר בהם is corrupted from אוצרות בר, whence the LXX has πάντας τοὺς σιτοβολῶνας. The verb שבר is a *denom.* from שֶׁבֶר food, perhaps as that which breaks hunger and thirst (Ps. civ. 11), according to Fleischer on Prov. xi. 26 what is crushed, ground, and means in *Kal* to buy food (comp. مَكَ to buy, from مَكَّـةِ, مِيرَة corn), *Hiph.* to sell food (comp. זבן to buy, *Pa.* to sell); in 56b however *Kal* is used with the meaning of *Hiph.* Notwithstanding this sale the famine increased; the *impf. cons.* וַתֶּחֱזַק has a contrastive meaning as at xix. 9 (comp. the *perf. cons.* Judg. xiii. 13). On the hyperbole כָּל־הָאָרֶץ " all the world," see on vii. 19. אֶל־יוֹסֵף is intended to be drawn to בָּאוּ. Such a common famine of Egypt and the neighbouring countries has often occurred, *e.g.* in the years 1064 and 1199 of our era. The monuments also testify to such years of famine (Brugsch, *Histoire d' Egypte,* i. p. 56). The danger was all the greater in presence of the condition of the canal and irrigation system of Lower Egypt. Strabo relates, that before the times of the Prefect Petronius, famine broke out in Egypt, through neglect of the waterworks, when the Nile rose only eight ells, and that eleven ells were needed for a specially good year, while he so managed, that ten ells only were needed for the best of harvests, and that eight caused no scarcity.

THE FIRST JOURNEY OF JOSEPH'S BRETHREN TO EGYPT WITHOUT BENJAMIN, CH. XLII.

With ch. xlii. begins the second section of the Toledoth of Jacob, extending from the first appearance of the brothers to Joseph's discovery of himself, ch. xlv. The chief narrator in ch. xlii. is *E;* see on ver. 38. Departure to Egypt to fetch provisions, vv. 1-4: *And Jacob saw that there was food in Egypt. Then Jacob said to his sons: Why look ye one upon another? And he said: Behold, I have heard that there is food in Egypt; go down thither and buy us thence food, that we may live and not die. Then Joseph's brethren, ten of them, went down to buy corn from Egypt. But Benjamin, Joseph's brother, Jacob sent not with them, for he said: Lest peradventure mischief befall him!* The Hithpahel התראה 1b is a reflexive of reciprocal meaning (comp. on ii. 25): to look at each other in a helpless, inactive manner. חיה to live, ver. 2b, is as frequently (xliii. 8, Num. iv. 19) equivalent to remain alive. The brethren of Joseph to the number of ten go down to the land of the Nile valley. So many go that they may get the more and to bring away the more. העשרה is not said; the translation above follows the accentuation. In יִקְרָאֻ֫ 4b קרא = קרה *contingere*, as at ver. 38, xlix. 1, Ex. i. 10, Lev. x. 19; comp., on the contrary, Gen. xliv. 29. Jacob from apprehension keeps back his youngest, and now also his only son by Rachel. The ten now appear before Joseph, and are recognised by him, but he is not recognised by them, vv. 5–8: *So the sons of Israel came to buy among those that came, for the famine was in the land of Canaan. And Joseph, he was the governor over the land, he it was who sold food to all the people of the land. Then came the brethren of Joseph and prostrated themselves before him, with the face to the earth. And Joseph saw his brethren and knew them, but he made himself strange towards them and spoke roughly to them, and said to them: Whence come ye? They said: From the land of Canaan, to buy food. Joseph knew his brethren, but they knew him not.* They appeared before Joseph among the many whom a like necessity drove to Egypt, and fell down before him with their faces to the earth; for he was the שַׁלִּיט (a word occurring elsewhere only in Ezek. and Eccles., and in Aramaic in Dan. and Ezra) over the land and director of the sale of corn. "The author," remarks Kn., "delights in testifying that Joseph was the lord or ruler of Egypt (vv. 30, 35, xlv. 8 sq. 26, xli. 40, 44), and it almost seems as if the legend of the Hyksos were transferred in the Hebrew tradition to the Hebrews. שַׁלִּיט is the same word as *Salatis* or *Salitis*, the name of the first ruler of the Hyksos in Egypt (Joseph. *c. Apion.* i. 14; Euseb. *Chr. Arm.* i. p. 224)." Joseph at once recognised his brethren, and remembered his dreams with respect to them: the sheaves and stars bowing down to him were vividly present to him; but they did not recognise their brother, whom they had not seen for about twenty years, and who had meantime grown up, become Egyptianized, and raised to an incredible elevation. He also studiously dissembled before them (נִכַּר) to fix one's eyes upon, to look keenly at, which might mean both recognition and non-recognition, whence the *Hithpahel* is both to make oneself known, Prov. xx. 11, and to make oneself unknown, like the *Niph.* Prov. xxvi. 24), spoke to them קָשׁוֹת harshly as to matter and tone, and let them, who said they came from Canaan and yet did not look like Canaanites, feel the Egyptian mistrust of foreigners. Joseph accuses them of being spies, and insists upon testing the truth of their exculpation by their sending for their youngest brother, vv. 9-17: *Then Joseph remembered his dreams which he dreamed concerning them, and said unto them: Ye are spies, to see the nakedness of the land are ye come. And they said: Nay, my lord, but to buy food are thy servants come. We are all sons of one man, we are honest men, thy servants have never been spies. And he said to them: Nay, surely to see the nakedness of the land are ye come. And they said: Twelve brethren, sons of one man in the land of Canaan are we thy servants, and behold the youngest is at the time with our father, and one is not. Then said Joseph to them: That is it which I spake to you saying: Ye are spies. Hereby shall ye be proved, that ye, as truly as Pharaoh lives, shall not go hence, unless your younger brother comes hither. Send one of you, that he may fetch your brother; but ye shall be imprisoned, that your words may be proved, whether there be truth with you or not, by the life of Pharaoh! surely ye are spies. And he put them in ward three days.* He calls them מְרַגְּלִים, those who go about for the purpose of espionage, a more ignoble word than תָּרִים (those who go about for the purpose of reconnoitring). They deny it; the ו of עֲבָדֶיךָ, as at xvii. 5b = כִּי elsewhere (כִּי אִם־). The form נָחְנוּ occurs again in the Pent. only Ex. xvi. 7, 8, Num. xxxii. 32, and out of it 2 Sam. xvii. 12, Lam. iii. 42. They bring to his consideration, that a father would not expose so many of his children at the same time to the danger of acting as spies. Joseph however insists that they have come to see the nakedness of the land (the order of the words is here such as it frequently is in interrogation, Judg. ix. 48, Zech. ii. 4, Neh. ii. 12). In ver. 13 it should be שנים עשר אחים אנחנו עבדיך (comp. ver. 32), the order of the words is inverted in a scarcely possible manner, or else a separative must be placed at עבדיך: Twelve of them are thy servants, brethren are we. הַקָּטֹן (of Benjamin) is a relative designation of age: *natu minor* (*minimus*). To say מֵת he is dead instead of אֵינֶנּוּ (like v. 24), goes against their heart and conscience. Joseph does not allow his accusation to be as yet silenced, 14b הוא אשר דברתי *hoc* (neutrally, as at xx. 16) *est quod dixi;* what they say of their two missing brothers strengthens the suspicion, to which he is giving feigned expression. By what he at once adds will he test them (בָּחַן) according to جَسَّ, properly to try by rubbing, especially on the touch-stone), he swears to them by the life of Pharaoh (Pharaoh lives = as truly as Pharaoh lives, חֵי an abbreviated חַי, as at Lev. xxv. 36) that they shall not be at liberty to depart unless they procure at once their pretended youngest brother; if they do not do this, they are, as he again asserts by the life of Pharaoh, really (כִּי Ew. § 330b) spies. Hereupon, in order to make them compliant, he puts them in prison for three days (אסף, like Isa. xxiv. 22 and elsewhere). The purpose of his behaviour to them is not, to make them atone for a time for the injustice they did him, but to find out, before he becomes to them an actual proof of Divine mercy, whether they regard themselves as deserving of Divine punishment for the crime they committed against him, and to convince himself, before he grants them his own forgiveness, that the other son of Rachel has not experienced like injustice at their hands. How faithfully is the constraint delineated, which Joseph imposes on himself by speaking so roughly, and by concealing his fellowship with them in the worship of one God under the oath by the life of Pharaoh! One feels how much his words contradict the feelings of his heart. On the third day he gives a milder form to the test to be applied, vv. 18-20: *And Joseph said to them on the third day: This do and live, I fear God: If ye are honest men, let one of your brothers remain in the house of your prison, but go ye, carry food for the famine of your houses, and bring your youngest brother to me, so shall your words be verified, and ye shall not die—and they did thus.* On the two imperatives: This do and live! see Ges. § 130. 2, and on אֲחִיכֶם אֶחָד (comp. xliii. 14) instead of הָאֶחָד (as at ver. 33), Ges. § 111. 2b. The other nine are to take home the corn of the famine of their houses, *i.e.* for the famine (Gen. of purpose as in מְטַר זַרְעֶךָ Isa. xxx. 23) of their families, and to return with their youngest brother, that so their words may be verified and they may escape death (death by starvation, not the penal infliction of death, to which the pretended harshness of Joseph nowhere rises); for he fears God and will not punish on mere suspicion. The brethren see the chastening hand of God in what they are experiencing, vv. 21, 22: *And they said one to another: Truly we are expiating on account of our brother, the distress of whose soul we saw, when he entreated us and we did not hear, therefore has this distress befallen us. And Reuben answered them saying: Did I not speak to you saying: Do not sin against the boy, but you did not hear me, behold therefore is his blood avenged.* From ver. 21 onwards follows the more particular narration of what was summarily anticipated in וַיַּעֲשׂוּ־כֵן ver. 20. While still standing before the unknown Joseph, they say to each other, that they are expiating the crime which they so unmercifully committed against their brother; אֲבָל truly, as at xvii. 19, אָשֵׁם making expiation, paying (Ezra x. 19), elsewhere worthy of penance. Reuben who, as was related in ch. xxxvii. from *E*, had saved Joseph's life, who was not present when he was sold, and must therefore have thought him dead rather than still alive, answers that he had said to them in vain: Do not sin (תֶּחֱטָאוּ with a helping Segol for תֶּחְטָאוּ) against the boy, and that now evidently his blood is required, *i.e.* from those who laid violent hands upon him (ix. 5). Joseph hears it and weeps, vv. 23, 24: *And they knew not that Joseph understood it, for the interpreter was between them. And he turned himself from them and wept; then he returned to them and talked with them, and took from them Simeon and bound him before their eyes.* They did not know, while they were thus talking together, that Joseph understood them, for הַמֵּלִיץ with the art., the interpreter usual in such cases, was between them (בֵּינוֹת, like xxvi. 28); but he well understood all, and withdrew a little from them and wept. Painful remembrance of the past, thankfulness for God's gracious dealings, unextinguished brotherly affection and joy at the penitent confession he had just heard—these were the emotions which found vent in tears. Then returning to them, he agreed with them that Simeon (purposely not Reuben, but the next oldest) should remain behind, and had him bound before their eyes. His provident dismissal of them combined with a fresh test, vv. 25-28: *Then Joseph commanded, and their vessels were filled with corn, and he had every man's money put again into his sack, and provender given them for the journey, and so it was done to them. And they laded their food upon their asses and departed. And one opened his sack to give his ass provender at the resting-place, and saw his money, and behold it lay uppermost in his sack. And he said to his brethren: My money is restored, and behold there it is in my sack—then their heart failed them, and they said trembling one to another: What hath Elohim done to us?* לְמַלֵּא might follow upon וַיְצֵא 25a, but the two possible constructions are intermixed. שַׂקִּים, כֵּלִים and אֲמְתָּחוֹת (which latter is the prevailing one in ch. xliii. sq.) are interchanged as the appellation of their baggage. The mistakeable וַיַּעַשׂ 25b, for which after וַיְמַלְּאוּ we should rather expect וַיַּעֲשׂוּ, is strange. Thus they laded their asses with their corn and departed. There were then already caravansaries or khans (the former from the Pers. سراى, the latter from the Pers. خان or خانه, which both mean *domus* and especially *diversorium*), i.e. sheds or cart-houses erected on the desert road. Into such a מָלוֹן (as at Ex. iv. 24 = מְלוֹן אֹרְחִים Jer. ix. 1) they entered. But when one of them opened his sack to give his ass provender, he found therein his money. This he told and showed it to his brethren (וְגַם הִנֵּה, as at xxxviii. 24)—then their courage failed them, and turning trembling to each other (חָרַד אֶל, a similar *constr. pregnans* to xliii. 33, Jer. xxxvi. 16) they acknowledge, that the chastening hand of God is at work in the matter. It is obvious that the others also opened their sacks—perhaps the source which is here accommodated to ver. 35 said so (Wellh. Dillm.). They return and relate their experiences, vv. 29–34: *And they came to Jacob their father to the land of Canaan, and told him all that had happened to them, saying: The man, the lord of the land, spake roughly to us and took us for spies of the country. And we said to him: We are honest men, we were never spies. We are twelve brethren, sons of our father, one is not, and the youngest is now with our father in the land of Canaan. And the man, the lord of the land, said to us: Hereby shall I know that ye are honest men, leave one of your brethren with me and take (corn) for the need of your houses and depart. And bring your youngest brother to me, so shall I know that ye are no spies, but honest men; I will give you your brother and ye may go through the land.* On their return to their father, they related to him all that had happened to them, and stated that everything now depended upon their bringing Benjamin with them. בְּ וַיְהִי ver. 30 means placing on a level; Ben-Naphtali here read כְּמַרְגְּלִים, but the *text. rec.*, which follows Ben-Asher, has כִּמְרַגְּלִים; the former reading is favoured by 1 Kings x. 27. In 33*b* we must read with the LXX ואת שֶׁבֶר רעבון ביתכם (as at 19*b*), for that רעבן may mean the needs of hunger cannot be inferred from passages like Neh. ix. 15, Ps. lxix. 22, lxxviii. 29. In 34*a* the second כִּי has regularly the meaning of *imo*. סחר 34*b* with an accus. as at xxxiv. 10, 21: to go through. A startling surprise, ver. 35: *And it came to pass: they emptied their sacks, and behold every man's bundle of money was in his sack; and they saw their bundles of money, they and their father, and they were afraid.* The discovery of one at the nightly resting-place was now repeated in the case of all. On אִישׁ צְרוֹר־כַּסְפּוֹ = צְרוֹר־כֶּסֶף אִישׁ, see on ix. 5. וַיִּירָאוּ and וַיִּרְאוּ is an obvious and frequent play upon the sound. The complaint of Jacob, ver. 36: *Then Jacob their father said unto them: Me have ye bereaved of children; Joseph is not, and Simeon is not, and ye would take Benjamin away; all comes upon me.* The perf. שִׁכַּלְתֶּם refers to Joseph, Simeon, and in anticipation of the worst to Benjamin. כְּלָּנָה for כֻּלָּן, as at Prov. xxxi. 29, comp. the forms xxi. 29, Ex. xxxv. 26. Reuben's voluntary pledge, ver. 37: *Then Reuben spake to his father saying: My two sons shalt thou kill, if I do not bring him home to thee; trust him to me, and I will bring him back.* He offers his two sons as a pledge (at the migration to Egypt he had four). "Give him to my hand," *i.e.* entrust him to me (as at 1 Sam. xvii. 22). Jacob however has no ear for this, ver. 38: *He said: My son shall not go down with you, for his brother is dead, and he alone is left; and if mischief befall him by the way that you go, you would bring down my grey hairs with sorrow to the grave.* The complaint is repeated, evidently from the same source, at xliv. 29-31, and certainly from the same source as the similar complaint at xxxvii. 35, viz. from *J*. It is evident how the first journey to Egypt terminated in *J*, from the repetition xliii. 3-7, xliv. 20-26, whence Wellh. and Dillm. conclude that the retention of Simeon as a hostage was not mentioned in the Jahvistic account. The account in ch. xlii. is as to its main features from *E*, but with insertions from *J*, to whom ver. 38 certainly belongs. If this verse is taken as an answer to Reuben's offer, as it stands here, the circumstance of Jacob's omission of all mention of Simeon furnishes of itself no critical conclusion,—it is explained by his preference for the son of Rachel; the one threatened loss banishes every other from his consciousness.

SECOND JOURNEY OF JOSEPH'S BRETHREN WITH BENJAMIN TO EGYPT, CH. XLIII.

This portion of the narrative gives from first to last the impression of being from *J*. Supposing that this narrator did not mention the retention of Simeon as a hostage, vv. 14, 23*b* appear as insertions from *E* (Dillm.). For the rest, all is of one cast and a genuine model of the Jahvistic style. Not very long time elapses before a fresh purchase of corn becomes a pressing necessity, vv. 1, 2 : *And the famine was sore in the land. And it came to pass, when they had consumed the corn which they had brought from Egypt, their father said unto them : Go again, buy us a little food.* Everything corresponds as to style with *J*: בָּבָר like *e.g.* xii. 10 ; לְ כִּלָּה like xviii. 33, xxiv. 15 and elsewhere ; מְעַט (a little), like xviii. 4, xxiv. 17, 43—a little food, for however much they might get, it will be but little in proportion to the need. Judah declares that they are willing to go, but not without Benjamin, vv. 3-5 : *And Judah spake to him, saying : The man protested, yea protested to us saying : Ye shall not see my face, unless your brother be with you. If thou wilt consent to send our brother with us, we will go down and buy thee food ; but if thou wilt not consent, we will not go down, for the man said unto us : Ye shall not see my face, unless your brother be with you.* The man (this הָאִישׁ used of Joseph is repeated in a striking manner farther on, and he is generally called הָאִישׁ and הָאֲנָשִׁים), says Judah, expressly declared (עוֹד to repeat, *Hiph.* to say again and again) that he would not suffer them to appear before him unless (בִּלְתִּי mostly *præter,* here *nisi,* as at Ex. xxii. 19) Benjamin were with them. Judah, from forbearance for his aged father, gives the mildest statement of what Joseph had said. Jacob's reproach, the justification of the brethren, and Judah's pledge, vv. 6–10: *Then Israel said: Wherefore have you done me this evil, to inform the man whether you had yet a brother? But they said: The man inquired, yea inquired after us and our family saying: Is your father yet alive? Have ye another brother? And we told him according to these words—could we then know that he would say: Bring your brother down? And Judah said to Israel his father: Send the boy with me, and we will arise and depart, that we may live and not die, both we and thou and our children. I will be surety for him, of my hand shalt thou require him; if I bring him not to thee again and set him before thee, I will be guilty before thee for ever. For if we had not delayed, we should have already returned twice.* The reproachful לָמָה has the tone upon the ultima, by reason of the following aspirate. The interrogative ה stands 6*b* ("whether yet") in an indirect question, as at viii. 8. They answered him as they were obliged to do, according to his questions (עַל־פִּי, as at Ex. xxxiv. 27, Lev. xxvii. 8, 18, Num. xxvi. 56, Deut. xvii. 10). With 7*b* comp. Jer. xiii. 12; נדע has here a past meaning by reason of the historical connection. In ver. 8 sqq. Judah again entreats his father, in consideration of the starvation with which they are threatened, to send Benjamin with them; he will be surety for him, and will, if he does not bring him back, bear the guilt of it all his life (וְחָטָאתִי, as at 1 Kings i. 21). כִּי־עַתָּה (surely then) stands in the apodosis of the conditional sentence as at xxxi. 42, Num. xxii. 29, 33, 1 Sam. xiv. 30, Job iii. 13. With this last saying Judah cuts the knot asunder. Israel submits to the inevitable, but at once knows also how to gain composure in God and to act wisely under the circumstances, vv. 11–14: *Then their father Israel said unto them: If there is nothing else, then do this. Take of the cutting of the land in your vessels, and take it down for a present to the man, a little balsam and a little honey, tragacanth and ladanum, pistachio nuts and almonds. And take double money in your hand, also the money returned in the top of your sacks take back in your hand, perhaps it was an oversight. And take your brother and arise, go back to the man. And God Almighty give you mercy before the man, that he may release to you your other brother and Benjamin; but as for me, let me be childless if I am to be so!* אֵפוֹא, though standing with the conditional sentence, logically belongs to the imperative, comp. xxvii. 37, Job ix. 24, xxiv. 25. It is remarkable that שֵׁי is never used in ch. xliii., and that אַמְתַּחָה always (six times) stands instead. מִזְמְרַת הָאָרֶץ is generally translated: Of the prize, *i.e.* the choicest productions of the country; so highly poetic an expression is however the more strange, since the ancient custom of the language always uses זמר and its derivatives exclusively with reference to Divine worship, and only שִׁיר in a wider sense (see Malbim on Ps. ci. 1)—hence זִמְרָה from זָמַר to pluck off the portion = produce, will here mean that which is cut off before the harvest = cutting. Dillm. compares the Arab. ثَمَر (fruits, LXX ἀπὸ τῶν καρπῶν τῆς γῆς), Dav. H. Müller (in Ges. *Lex.* 10th edit., p. 983) the Aramaic גֵּמַר *mirari*, hence *mirabilia* (syn. Arab. *'aǵdîb*). On צְרִי, נְכֹאת, לֹט see xxxvii. 25, where these three spices are mentioned as caravan wares. They are also to take with them וּדְבַשׁ = دِبْس, √דב to be compressed, thickened, grape syrup, *i.e.* must, boiled down to a third of its quantity, of which three hundred camel loads are still annually sent to Egypt from the neighbourhood of Hebron. בָּטְנִים pistaccio nuts, as Samar. Rashi, Tavus translate, the almond-like fruit of the *Pistacia vera*, Talm. בָּטְנָה, בּוּטְמָא, LXX τερέβινθον, certainly with the same meaning, since *botn*, Arab. *botm*, in the later usage of language designated both *Pistacia terebinthus* and *Pistacia vera*, and שְׁקֵדִים almonds, the fruit of the *Amygdalus communis*, which was more rare in Egypt. They were moreover to take double money with them, that which was required for new purchases, and that first purchase money, which certainly had come back to them only through an oversight (הַמּוּשָׁב according to the Masora with Pathach instead of Kametz). The combination כֶּסֶף מִשְׁנֶה is appositional, as at Ex. xvi. 22; comp. מִשְׁנֶה־כֶּסֶף ver. 15, the double in money (acc. of the more exact definition, Ges. § 118. 3), as at Deut. xv. 18, Jer. xvii. 18. Jacob's speech continues to ver. 14, as might be expected; but perhaps here the expression of resignation, as it was found in *E* (comp. xlii. 36), is preferred. The other brother, אֲחִיכֶם אַחֵר for הָאַחֵר, as at xlii. 19, comp. 33, is Simeon, who was left as a hostage. The concluding words are the expression of submission to the unalterable, comp. Esth. iv. 16 with 2 Kings viii. 4. Ges. § 126. 5, elsewhere an expression of the aimless, 2 Sam. xv. 20, 1 Sam. xxiii. 13, or of the boundless, Zech. x. 8. שָׁכֹלְתִּי has a pausal *ā* from *o* as in יֶחְפָּץ, יַחְבֹּשׁ and עָז for עֹז xlix. 3, יִמְרָה for יִמְרֹה xlix. 27, Ew. § 93. 3, comp. Hitzig on Isa. lix. 17. Journey and arrival, ver. 15: *And the men took this present, and double money took they in their hand, and Benjamin, and they arose and went down to Egypt and stood before Joseph.* With וְאֶת־בִּנְיָמִן comp. xxi. 14 וְאֶת־הַיֶּלֶד; Benjamin was then somewhat over twenty years of age. When Joseph saw him and was thus convinced that the brothers had done him no violence, he prepared a solemn reception for them, vv. 16, 17: *When Joseph saw Benjamin with them, he said to the steward of his house: Bring the men into the house and slay cattle and make ready, for the men shall dine with me at noon. And the man did as Joseph had said, and brought the men into Joseph's house.* Instead of טְבַח טָבָה we have טְבֹחַ טֶבַח dissimilarly vocalized. Meat formed in Egypt also a main element of food at both priestly and royal tables (Herod. ii. 37, 77). Their fear when brought in, and how it was allayed, vv.

18-25: *Then the men were afraid, when they were brought into Joseph's house, and said: Because of the money that was returned in our sacks the former time are we brought in, that they may roll upon us and attack us and take us for slaves, together with our asses. And they came near to the man that was placed over Joseph's house and spoke to him, at the entry of the house, and said: Oh, my lord, we came down once before to buy corn. And it came to pass, when we came to the resting-place and opened our sacks, behold the money of each was at the top of his sack, our money according to its weight; now we bring it back in our hand. And other money have we brought with us in our hand, to buy corn; we do not know who put our money in our sacks. And he said: Be of good courage, fear not, your and your father's God has given you treasure in your sacks, your money came to me. And he brought out Simeon to them. And the man brought the men into Joseph's house and gave them water, and they washed their feet, and he gave their asses provender. And they made ready the present, before Joseph came at noon, for they had heard that they should eat with him.* By תְּחִלָּה they mean their first (previous) Egyptian journey. Instead of הַמּוּשָׁב 12*b* we here have הָשָׁב, which better expresses that the How is to them unknown and incomprehensible. Because they fear to be treated as embezzlers of others' property (the accusation of being spies is out of question), they seek to prevent what they fear, by explaining the state of affairs to the steward at the door of the house, which they so dread to enter. At the place of halting for the night, they discovered to their terror the purchase money returned in their corn-sacks (for these must, xlii. 27 sq., be completed according to the meaning of *J*; comp., on the other hand, xlii. 35). The steward discreetly gives a wise and kind answer: Peace be to you, *i.e.* lay aside your care and anxiety, I had your money quite right, hence what you found is a treasure given you by your God (שָׁלוֹם לָכֶם in the O. T. always expresses encouragement and congratulation, in later Hebrew, as in Aram. and Arab., greeting). He then brought Simeon out to them, led them into Joseph's house, and showed himself ready to serve them in various ways. They were now expecting Joseph, with whom, as they heard and also believed, they were to dine at noon, and they laid out their present to the best advantage (outside in the hall). The meeting before the repast, vv. 26-31: *When Joseph came home, they brought him the present, which they had brought with them, into the house, and cast themselves down to the ground. And Joseph asked them of their welfare, and said: Is your aged father, of whom you spake, well, is he still alive? They said: Thy servant, our father, is well, he is still alive; and they bowed and made obeisance. And he lifted up his eyes and saw Benjamin his brother, his mother's son, and said: Is this your youngest brother of whom ye spake? And he said: Elohim be gracious to thee, my son!—Then Joseph made haste, for his affection was kindled for his brother, and he was forced to weep, and he went into the inner room and wept there. Then he washed his face, came out, restrained himself and said: Set on the meal!* The present which was בְּיָדָם was, according to xxiv. 10, xxxv. 4, what they had brought with them, and this they made ready for presentation. וַיָּבִיאוּ has *Mappik* in the א that it may be plainly pronounced as a consonant; this occurs also Lev. xxiii. 17, Job xxxiii. 21, Ezra viii. 18, Olsh. § 32*d*. The reverential salutation is designated as at xviii. 2, xix. 1 and frequently, and is at 28*b* combined with וַיִּקְּדוּ as at xxiv. 26, 48. When he sees Benjamin, his brother by the same mother, he makes inquiry, but without waiting for an answer greets him with a hearty: "Elohim be gracious to thee, my son" (יָחְנְךָ like Isa. xxx. 19 for יְחֻנְּךָ, Ew. § 251*d*). He was obliged, while thus speaking, to hasten, for—such is the literal meaning of 30*a*—his bowels רַחֲמָיו, LXX ἔγκατα (ἔντερα), here equivalent to organs of feeling = feelings (as at 1 Kings iii. 26, Prov. xii. 10, comp. Isa. lxiii. 15, Syr. *raḥmê* = σπλάγχνα 2 Macc. ix.

5 sq.), were glowing (for which Syr. ܐܬܓܘܙܠܘ *i.e.* נתגלגלו or אתגוללו they rolled themselves, *DMZ.* xxvi. 800, but see on Job iii. 5), *i.e.* he was overpowered by sympathetic affection and "he sought to weep," *i.e.* felt an irresistible impulse to do so (comp. a similar active expression for strong emotion, Isa. xiii. 8*a*), and went הַחַ֖דְרָה into a chamber (חֶדֶר), جَدَرَ from חָדַר to retire, to hide) and there gave vent to his tears. Then he washed his face, came back again, and, controlling his feelings, commanded the repast to be served. The feast, and the preference shown thereat to Benjamin, vv. 32–34: *And they set on for him apart and for them apart, and for the Egyptians who ate with him apart, for the Egyptians cannot eat with the Hebrews, for that is esteemed an abomination by the Egyptians. And they sat before him, the first-born according to his birthright and the younger according to his youth, so that they looked one at another astonished. And they took messes to them from him, and Benjamin's mess was five times greater than that of any of them, and they drank and were full in his company.* Joseph, as the illustrious head of the priestly order, was served apart, and the sons of Jacob and the Egyptians who ate with them apart, because Egyptians could not, *i.e.* might not, eat with Hebrews; this לֹא יוּכְלוּן (the form of the *impf. energicum* having slipped in) is Jahvistico-Deuteronomic, לֹא תוּכַל, used of moral impossibility, running through the whole of Deut.: xii. 17, xvi. 5, xvii. 15, xxi. 16, xxii. 3, 19, 29, xxiv. 4, comp. Ex. xix. 23. הוּא refers to eating with foreigners in general, which ancient Egypt repudiated both from superstition and national pride, *Diodor. Sic.* i. 67, even their knives, forks, and crockery were avoided as defiled through their participation of sacred animals, Herod. ii. 41, comp. Ex. viii. 22, much more eating in common with the shepherd people of the Hebrews. Thus then they sat before him arranged from the first-born down to the youngest, exactly according to their respective ages, at which they

looked at each other with the greatest astonishment (תָּמְהוּ אֶל) like חרד אל xlii. 28). מַשְׂאֹת is meant of messes for guests of honour, whom the entertainer pointed out. וַיִּשָּׂא "they bore," has an unnamed subject, as is usual where the servants in waiting are intended (*e.g.* xxiv. 33 in *J*, in opposition to which וַיְשִׂימוּ they did, xlii. 25, which may be from *E*). Benjamin's mess was five times greater (comp. the occurrence of this number with respect to Egyptian matters, xli. 34, xlv. 22, xlvii. 2, 24, Isa. xix. 18) than the mess of any of the others, just as the kings in Sparta were served with double portions, but οὐχ ἵνα διπλάσια καταφάγοιεν (Xen. *de rep. Laced.* xv. 4). The brothers drank and were drunk (to be understood in the sense of Hagg. i. 6), עִמּוֹ feeling themselves at ease in his presence. The anxiety of conscience, which they experienced at the sight of the strange Egyptian lord, was now lost in a heartfelt delight, which was to them as inexplicable. But Joseph, the unknown and yet so well known, who has the key to the mystery, delights himself in the intoxicating rapture of these dearest of all guests, whom the LORD has brought him, and praises that wonderful leading of God, the glory of which beams upon him from their happy faces.

THE LAST TEST, CH. XLIV.

Yet one last trial is inflicted by Joseph upon his brethren. He has convinced himself that they have not done external violence to Benjamin as they did to himself, but he desires to be finally assured that the hardness of heart and want of feeling, which had formerly plunged their father into the deepest grief for his child have now passed away, and that a similar deed is impossible to them. The pastor-like spiritual wisdom with which he masters his natural feelings, to tread with them the way of God, is admirable. The mode of delineation is like that of ch. xliii.; *J* is unmistakeable, and his text is here without admixture.

The brethren are dismissed with full sacks and with Joseph's cup, vv. 1–3: *And he commanded the steward of his house saying: Fill the sacks of the men with food, as much as they can carry, and put every man's money at the top in his sack. And my cup, my silver cup, place at the top in the sack of the youngest, and his corn money! And he did according to the saying of Joseph, which he spake. The morning became light and the men were sent away, they and their asses.* In this portion of the narrative also אַמְתַּחַת is used throughout for שַׂק, and אֹכֶל (here and ver. 25, as at xliii. 2, 20, 22) for בַּר; the energetic imperfect form יֻכְלוּן, as at xliii. 32, is also characteristic of *J*. What is aimed at is to accuse them of theft. The superabundance of what they get for their money will stamp the theft of the silver cup as all the more glaring a crime. An eventual abandonment of Benjamin was deprived of all shadow of justification, by the fact that property not belonging to them was found in the sacks of all. The juxtaposition: the morning became light (אוֹר Ges. § 72, note 1) and the men are sent away is similar to xix. 23 in *J*; it is the syntactic scheme of the contemporaneous which we already met with in *Q*, vii. 6. The pursuit and accusation, vv. 4–6: *They were just gone out of the city and were not yet far off, when Joseph said to the steward of his house: Up, follow after the men, and when thou hast overtaken them, say to them: Wherefore have ye returned good for evil? Is not this it, out of which my lord drinketh, and by which he is accustomed to predict? An evil deed have ye done therein. He overtook them and said these words to them.* 4*a* is likewise the scheme of the contemporaneous. The city is left unnamed; it would have been Zo'an (Tanis) if the Hyksos had then been ruling in Egypt, which, as we have seen on ch. xl., is improbable. Hence we shall have to regard it as Memphis, as Kn. also thinks, though as the supposed capital of the Hyksos. זֶה 5*a* refers to the cup; he purposely does not add הַגָּבִיעַ, he is certain of the fact of the theft, and takes it for granted that they will know what is in question. On שתה בְּ to drink in = to drink out of anything, see Ges. 154. 3a. By the second בּוֹ is meant, that by looking into this cup he was accustomed to investigate mysteries (נַחֵשׁ divinare οἰωνί-ζεσθαι, as the LXX translates here and xxx. 27). In Egypt, the land of soothsaying and magic (Isa. xix. 3, Kiddushin 49b), hydromancy, i.e. predicting from the appearances presented by the liquid contents of a goblet (κυλικομαντεία), a dish (λευκανομαντεία), or some other vessel, either alone or with something thrown into it, was customary. The cup, which is described to the men as Joseph's favourite cup and as a sacred vessel, is called גָּבִיעַ from its calyx-shaped form; it was a κιβώριον like the Egyptian goblets which narrowed downwards (*Athen.* xi. p. 477, comp. *Didymus Chalcenter.* ed. Schmidt, p. 75). Their offer, and the terrible and surprising discovery, vv. 7–13: *And they said to him: Wherefore speaketh my lord such things? Far be it from thy servants to do such a thing! We brought back to thee from the land of Canaan money which we found at the top of our sacks, how should we then steal silver or gold out of thy lord's house? With whomsoever of thy servants it is found, let him die, and let us also be henceforth bondmen to my lord. Then he said: Now then, as ye have said, so let it be: he with whom it is found shall be my bondman, and ye shall be free of punishment. Then they hastened and let down each his sack upon the ground, and opened each his sack. And he searched; he began at the eldest and ended at the youngest, and the cup was found in Benjamin's sack. Then they rent their garments, and each laded his ass, and they returned to the city.* Earlier Jahvistic portions furnish parallel expressions to all and everything here, e.g. to the repudiating אֵיךְ xxxix. 9. We should expect הַכֶּסֶף (Samar.) instead of בְּכַסְפֵּ at 8a, but it is not necessary (comp. the translation above). In 10a גַּם is placed first, though it logically belongs to a following member of the sentence as at 1 Sam. xii. 16, Hos. vi. 11, Zech. ix. 11, Job ii. 10. Joseph's steward does not wish to be so harsh, but to deal more gently. With ready alacrity they assisted him in the search, which he effected according to their ages, and they may have been already triumphing, that their innocence was manifested, when the cup was at last found in Benjamin's sack. Then they rent their garments, reloaded their asses, and instead of leaving Benjamin behind as a bondman, return to the city. On their arrival they all desired to share the fate of Benjamin, vv. 14–17: *Then Judah and his brethren went into Joseph's house, and he was still there, and they fell before him on the ground. And Joseph said unto them: What deed is this that ye have done? Did ye not know that such a man as I can divine? And Judah said: What shall we say to my lord, what shall we speak, or how shall we clear ourselves? God hath laid hold of the iniquity of thy servants, and we are now bondmen to my lord, both we and he in whose hand the cup was found. But he said: Far be it from me to do thus. The man in whose hand the cup was found, let him be my bondman, and as for you, go up hence in peace to your father!* Judah is placed foremost, because he had become surety for Benjamin. They find Joseph, who was expecting them, in a state of anxious suspense, still in the house. He addresses them harshly: they might surely have known that a man like himself would know how to find out what is concealed and would soon discover their deed. Judah does not contradict the accusation, the proof is overwhelming. He sees therein the hand of God, who is thus laying hold of and visiting upon them the still unavenged crime they committed against their brother. Joseph however does not admit that they ought all to become his bondmen, he will only retain Benjamin, the really guilty one, and the rest shall return to Canaan לְשָׁלוֹם (with לְ of condition, which forms an adverbial notion) peacefully, *i.e.* unmolested (1 Sam. i. 17, xx. 42). Judah's remonstrance, vv. 18–34: *Then Judah drew near and said: Oh, my lord, let thy servant, I pray thee, speak a word in my lord's ears, and let not thine anger burn against thy servant, for thou art equal with Pharaoh. My lord asked his servants saying: Have ye yet a father or a brother? And we said to my lord: We have an aged father and a young child born to him in his old age, whose brother is dead, and he only is left of his mother, and his father loveth him. And thou saidst to thy servants: Bring him down to me, that I may set mine eyes upon him. And we answered my lord: The boy cannot leave his father, for if he should leave him—his father would die. But thou saidst to thy servants: Unless your youngest brother come down with you, ye shall see my face no more. And it came to pass, when we had gone up to thy servant, our father, we told him the words of my lord. When then our father said: Go again, buy us a little food, we said: We cannot go down; if our youngest brother is with us, then will we go down, for we may not see the man's face except our youngest brother be with us. Then thy servant, my father, said unto us: Ye know that my wife bare me two. The one went away from me, and I said: Certainly he is torn to pieces, and I have not seen him since. Now ye will take this one also from before my face, and if an accident befall him, ye will have brought down my grey hairs with unhappiness to the grave. When then I come to thy servant, my father, and the boy is not with us, seeing his soul is linked to the boy's soul, it will come to pass, when he sees that the boy is not there, he will die, and thy servants will have brought down the grey hairs of thy servant, our father, with sorrow to the grave. For thy servant brought away the boy from his father and became surety, saying: If I bring him not back to thee, I will bear the blame to my father for life. Therefore let thy servant remain instead of the boy as bondman to my lord, but let the boy go up with his brethren. For how could I go to my father, except the boy be with me? Oh no, I cannot see the sorrow that will come upon my father.* We have already had, xliii. 20, the courteous בִּי with which Judah begins. He desires to speak בְּאָזְנֵי of the great lord, *i.e.* directly (without an interpreter) and audibly (comp. 1. 4, but also xx. 8 and xxiii. 16). Thou and Pharaoh —he says—are equal one to another (כְּ—כְּ, as at xviii. 25). יֶלֶד זְקֻנִים 20*a* is equivalent to בֶן־זְקֻנִים xxxvii. 3 (comp. on iv. 23), and the added קָטָן does not describe Benjamin as a little child, but as still in the bloom of youth (and born in his father's old age, comp. 1 Kings iii. 7, 2 Chron. xiii. 7). By וְאָשִׂימָה עֵינִי עָלָיו 21*b* Judah explains the desire to see Benjamin as one of gracious intention (comp. Jer. xxxix. 12, xl. 4). אַךְ 28*a* is affirmative, as at xxix. 14. בְּרָעָה 29*b* or בְּיָגוֹן 31*b*, xlii. 38, to go down to Sheol, is the opposite of בְּשָׁלוֹם xv. 15. The emotionally repudiative פֶּן 34*b* with the chief sentence understood is similar to xxxviii. 11, xlii. 4.—Judah's words are those of a heart which makes its owner eloquent, words subdued by wise moderation and overmastering grief, but manly and bold from a deeply-stirred feeling of duty, enhanced by the consciousness of his former guilt. Before him stands the lord of Egypt, whose heart he is trying to pierce; behind him are his prostrate brethren, all of whom he is representing. Judah was the most eloquent among his brethren. It was his eloquence that at last induced his father to entrust Benjamin to him, xliii. 8–10 ; he, by whose advice Joseph had been sold as a slave, condemns himself to slavery, for the sake of saving Benjamin. The change of disposition in his brethren has now been sufficiently tested, and a continuance of the restraint, which Joseph has put upon himself, is no longer possible. The force of both the pain and the rapture of love can no longer endure restriction. The moment for the most touching and sacred scene of recognition—a turning-point full of important results in the history of Israel—has arrived.

THE RECOGNITION, CH. XLV.

The chief narrator seems here also to be *J*, his account being however completed from *E*. The passage vv. 17–23 is that which is the most certainly derived from the latter. The Divine name אלהים (האלהים) decides nothing, for only at xlvi. 2 does *E*, and at xxxix. 2, 3, 5, 21, 23 does *J* announce himself by the former, calling the God who presides over the history of Joseph אלהים, and the latter calling Him יהוה. Joseph himself never calls Him יהוה (not even in ch. xxxix.), but six times האלהים and nine times אלהים. Pharaoh also, the brethren and Jacob call God אלהים (ה) with or without the article; and what is striking, Jacob, in a text derived from *J*, xlviii. 20, even calls the God in whose name he is blessing אלהים. Nor is ישראל for יעקב any safe criterion. Certainly this name makes us think in the first place of *J* (p. 225); but *E* also calls the sons of Jacob בני ישראל at xlii. 5, xlvi. 5, and here ver. 21. In ch. xlviii. the names are interchanged both in the parts taken from *E* and those taken from *J*, and is it then *J*, who at xxxv. 21 sq. says ישראל three times in one breath?

Joseph has hitherto suppressed his feelings, for the sake of carrying out the plan of simulation which he had devised. His object is now attained. He has convinced himself that Benjamin is still alive, and has not become like himself a victim of his brothers' envy. He has taken a deep look into his brothers' hearts and has found them changed for the better. He has heard them, and above all Reuben (the comparatively least guilty, yet still as an accessory not innocent), repent and bewail the crime committed against himself, which is now visited upon them. Their tender affection for their aged father, and their loyalty towards the only remaining son of Rachel, have been made manifest by Judah's speech. They cannot but regard Benjamin as the guilty one, who has by theft plunged them all into misery; but they do not load him with reproaches, they do not regard themselves as released from the promise given concerning him to their father, they take the blame upon themselves as for their common act. Their conduct under this last test is the clear reflection of their wakeful conscience, of their converted heart. At the same time he looks into the whole depth of his miserably deceived father's mourning of now twenty-two years' duration for himself, his lost son. By sympathy he is sharing the anxiety which that father is now certainly undergoing about Benjamin. Any longer continuance of the seeming callousness, which he has not even been able to maintain without intermingling in it various marks of kindness, would be the greatest self-torture, and is indeed in the overwhelming rush of emotion utterly impossible, ver. 1a: *Then Joseph could no longer restrain himself before all them that stood before him, and he cried: Make every one go out from me!* At the first sight of Benjamin it already became difficult to him to restrain himself (xliii. 31), but he did it because of the bystanders (נִצָּב עַל), as at xxiii. 2 and also xxviii. 13); he now commands them to retire, their presence being, as is shown by מֵעָלַי, an intolerable burden. He is thus left alone, and as the narrator, with profound consciousness of the significance of this scene in the redemptive history, adds, ver. 1b: *And there stood no one with him, while Joseph made himself known to his brethren.* The *Hithpa.* הִתְוַדַּע only again at Num. xii. 6, properly to make oneself known, comp. הִתְגַּדֵּל to make oneself great. It was a transaction so tender and sacred, that the presence of an observer could not but be regarded as a profanation, a mutual outpouring of hearts, which, beside God, Who knows all things, no one ought to hear, and indeed no one was capable of understanding, ver. 2: *Then he burst out into loud weeping, and the Egyptians heard it, and the house of Pharaoh heard it.* The Egyptians (הַמִּצְרִים=מִצְרַיִם) outside heard it, and the news that some extraordinary occurrence must have happened soon reached Pharaoh's palace. His first word is, ver. 3a: *I am Joseph*, and his next: *Is my father yet alive?* He has already often heard that he was alive and has himself already asked it, but it is the first and greatest need of his heart again to assure himself of it. *But his brethren*—continues the narrator, ver. 3b—*could not answer him, for they were dismayed before him.*

Then Joseph said to them, ver. 4a: *Come nearer to me, I pray you, and they came nearer.* And he said further, vv. 4b–13: *I am Joseph your brother, whom ye sold into Egypt; and now trouble not yourselves, think not that you must be angry with yourselves that you sold me hither, for Elohim sent me hither before you to preserve life. For there have now been two years of famine in the land, and there come yet five years, in which shall be neither ploughing nor harvest. So then Elohim sent me before you to preserve you a remnant in the earth and to spare your life for a great escape. Now then—it is not you that sent me hither, but God, and He has made me a father to Pharaoh*[1] *and lord of all his house, and ruler over the whole land of Egypt. Go up quickly to my father and say unto him: Thus saith thy son Joseph: Elohim hath made me lord of all Egypt, come down to me, tarry not. And thou shalt dwell in the land of Goshen and shalt be near me, thou and thy children and thy children's children and thy cattle and all that is thine. And I will nourish thee there, for there are yet to be five years of famine, that thou mayest not come to poverty, and thy household and all that is thine. And behold your eyes see, and the eyes of my brother Benjamin, that it is my mouth that speaketh unto you. And tell my father all my honour in Egypt, and all that you have seen, and hasten, bring my father hither to me.* On אֲשֶׁר ‥ אֹתִי (relative of the 1st pers.) see Ges. § 123, note 1. מְכַרְתֶּם corresponds with J's description of the procedure, according to which Joseph was sold by Judah's advice, xxxvii. 26, 27, 28b, comp. (according to E) xl. 15a. The peculiar חרה בְּעֵינֵי 5a also belongs to the style of J at xxxi. 35, besides which a similar example to זֶה שְׁנָתַיִם is also found at xxxi. 38, 41. The phrase שׂוּם שְׁאֵרִית 7a is like 2 Sam. xiv. 7. The לְהַחֲיוֹת which follows is combined with

---

[1] The Codex of R. Meir and that which was, as the Midrash on Genesis of Mose-ha-Darshan (in MSS. at Prague) says, preserved in the Severus synagogue at Rome, read here וישני, *i.e.* as it is explained וַיַּשְׁנֵי (and he lent me to Pharaoh that I should be a father to him), an incredible various reading (see A. Epstein in Gratz's *Monatsschrift*, xxxiv.).

לָכֶם in the sense of לָתֵת מִחְיָה Ezra ix. 8 sq.: to you for a great escape (comp. xxxii. 9 in *J* and the Assyr. *balâṭu* to live, properly to escape, to be preserved). They are the notions שְׁאֵרִית and פְּלֵיטָה, which subsequently attained so great importance in prophecy, which here appear by way of prelude in the mouth of Joseph, the type of Christ, the preserver of his family, and in it of the future nation (see Hoelemann in the *Sächs. Kirchen- u. Schulblatt*, 1873, No. 14). "Father to Pharaoh" is the title of the highest dignitary, who as first councillor is always near the king, comp. on אַבְרֵךְ xli. 43. מֹשֵׁל here corresponds with שַׁלִּיט in *E*, xlii. 6. Dwelling in Goshen (see concerning this district of Lower Egypt, situate at at all events on the east of the Nile, on xlvii. 27; the LXX translates in this passage ἐν γῇ Γεσὲμ 'Αραβίας), and therefore on the soil of Pharaoh's kingdom, Jacob is near his son, and incomparably easier to be reached, than at that time in Canaan. There he will nourish his family (כִּלְכֵּל, as at xlvii. 12, l. 21) and protect them from poverty in the years of famine which are still to come (תִּוָּרֵשׁ transformed from רוּשׁ=יָרֵשׁ hardly: taken possession of = to be without possession). "Your eyes see" sounds Deuteronomic, Deut. iii. 21, iv. 3, xi. 7, xxviii. 32, which is not strange in the Jahvistic style. Three times does Joseph (vv. 7, 8, 9) bring it forward to comfort them, that what they did, had been of God's disposing for their own good. What a thoroughly noble heart it was, that he opened to his brethren! When he had thus poured forth his heart, vv. 14, 15: *He fell upon his brother Benjamin's neck and wept, and Benjamin wept on his neck. And he kissed all his brethren and wept on them, and after this his brethren talked with him.* That עֲלֵיהֶם has not a causal (as *e.g.* at Lam. i. 16) but a local meaning is shown by the preceding "on his neck." It is not to be seen why ver. 15 should be from *E* (Dillm.), and not, like ver. 14, from *J* (comp. xlvi. 29, xxxiii. 4). It was now that the brothers first ventured to approach him, the string of their tongues is now loosened, and they are able to talk with him. The sacred history maintains in the history of Joseph all its greatness; here especially, in the scene of the recognition, all is nature, all spirit and all art; every word is as it were bathed in tears of sympathy, in the heart's blood of love, in the wine of rapture. Never, says Klopstock, have few words expressed more noble passion. The foil however of this history, so beautiful in itself, is the Antitype, Who sheds over it His glorifying light. For after the Jewish nation delivers Jesus into the hands of the Gentiles, the antitypical history of this fraternal treachery also discharges itself into adorable depths of the wisdom and knowledge of God. *Ad hoc enim* — remark Augustine, Rabanus Maurus and others on this subject—*Christus a Judæis traditus est gentibus, tanquam Joseph Ægyptiis a fratribus, ut et reliquiæ Israel salvæ fierent.*

The intelligence of the arrival of Joseph's brethren, which soon reached the palace, made a favourable impression upon Pharaoh, and therefore of course upon the court officials, ver. 16: *And the report was heard in Pharaoh's house, saying: Joseph's brethren are come! And it was pleasing in the eyes of Pharaoh and in the eyes of his servants.* The interposition of this information was needed by what follows in ver. 17; hence the narrator is not necessarily another than in ver. 2, but still *J* (comp. ייטב בעיני, xli. 37). The command of Pharaoh, vv. 17-20: *And Pharaoh said unto Joseph: Say to thy brethren: This do: lade your beasts and go hence to Canaan. And take your father and your families and come to me, and I will give you the best of the land of Egypt, and eat the fat of the land. Now thou art commanded* (to say to them): *This do ye: take you out of the land of Egypt waggons for your little ones and your wives, and set your father upon one and come! And let not your eyes rest regretfully upon your stuff, for the best of the land of Egypt is yours.* It was an act of gratitude for the king to invite the family of Joseph to Egypt; this free and honourable invitation implied the right of Israel to leave it also without obstruction. There is not a word of this invitation in xlvi. 28 sqq.; but this involves no contradiction, the matter there in question being the securing their possession of the land of Goshen, by reference to their occupation of shepherds; nevertheless since xlv. 28 sqq. is from *J*, xlv. 17—20 may be from *E*. טען to load, is ἅπαξ γεγρ. (comp. עמס על in *J* xliv. 13). בְּעִיר occurs also in the book of the covenant, Ex. xxii. 1, and elsewhere only Num. xx. 4, 8, 11, Ps. lxxviii. 48, Arab. بعير camels, as the chief element of property in cattle (*DMZ*. xxx. 674). On לברבאו comp. Isa. xxii. 15, Ezek. iii. 4; on the טוב interchanged with חֵלֶב of the land, 2 Kings viii. 9 (differing, as Dillm. remarks, from מֵיטַב הָאָרֶץ the best part of the land); and on עֵינְכֶם אַל־תָּחֹס Deut. vii. 16 and frequently, it is an expression native to Deut. within the Pentateuch. After צִוֵּיתָה we must with the Syr. supply אֱמֹר אֶל־אַחֶיךָ; but according to the LXX Jer. צִוֵּיתָה was incorrectly written for צַוֵּה אֹתָם (Dillm.). Execution of the royal command, and supplies for the journey, vv. 21-23: *And the sons of Jacob did so, and Joseph gave them waggons according to the command of Pharaoh, and gave them provision for the journey. To all of them he gave each man new raiment, and to Benjamin three hundred pieces of silver and five new suits of raiment. And to his father he sent on this manner, ten asses laden with the good things of Egypt, and ten she-asses laden with corn and bread and victuals for his father upon the journey.* Ancient Egypt was rich in vehicles and horses for both warlike and peaceful purposes, comp. l. 9 with Isa. xxxvi. 9. חֲלִפוֹת שְׂמָלֹת changes of raiment, then like بَدَل new garments in general, as at Judg. xiv. 12 sq., comp. ver. 19 and frequently. Instead of פְאֹת we have everywhere else פֵּאָת with a foretone Kametz; the meaning is the same, not like the LXX, Vulg.: as many changes of raiment, but so many presents, viz. the following. The dismissal, ver. 24: *So he sent his brethren away and they departed, and he said to them: Fall not out on the way,* viz. as to the share of one above another in the injustice committed which had now to be confessed to their father, or from envy at the preference of one above another. The LXX and all ancient translations correctly give μὴ ὀργίζεσθε, while on the other hand the explanation : Tremble not, *i.e.* be of good cheer on the way, gives here a superfluous and moreover an inaptly expressed thought. The arrival, the announcement and the impression made, vv. 25–28 : *And they went up out of Egypt and came to the land of Canaan, to Jacob their father. And they told him saying : Joseph is yet alive, and he is governor over the whole land of Egypt ; and his heart was numbed, for he believed them not. And they told him all the words of Joseph, which he had said unto them, and he saw the waggons which Joseph had sent, then the spirit of Jacob their father revived. And Israel said : Enough, Joseph my son is still alive. I will go and see him before I die.* With וַיְ the announcement turns into an *oratio obliqua*. וַיָּפָג לִבּוֹ does not mean : his heart remained cold (Kn. Arnh. Keil), but it became cold, it stared at the fabulous narrative without being able to grasp it as true. But when he recognised, in the words and conduct of Joseph as they were related to him, the image of his son, and when the waggons, which were before him, brought to his eyes his rank and wealth, he exclaimed, esteeming rank, wealth and presents as nothing : Enough (briefly, as at 2 Sam. xxiv. 16, 1 Kings xix. 4 for רַב־לִי), my son Joseph is alive, and faith and love renewing his youth : I will go and see him before I die. Jacob believed not—then the spirit of Jacob their father revived and Israel said—what a judicious change of name ! The feeble old man says : I will go and see him, as if he needed the aid of no one in going to Egypt. Joseph is the one thought in which he is absorbed. This one thought he follows like a magnet, turning neither to the right hand nor the left. But this Jacob to whom the spirit of his youth thus returns is Israel. It is the nation of that name whose migration to Egypt and its birth there is decided by this אֵלְכָה.

THE REMOVAL OF ISRAEL TO GOSHEN IN EGYPT, CH. XLVI.

Here begins that third section of the Toledoth of Jacob which extends from the migration to Egypt to the prosperous sojourn and increase in Goshen, ch. xlvi.–xlvii. 27. 1. REMOVAL OF THE FAMILY OF JACOB, xlvi. 1-7. This is the first of the three portions of which ch. xlvi. is composed. The account down to ver. 5 is by E, and its amplification, ver. 6 sq., by Q. That J has a share in ver. 1 sq. is inferred from Beersheba being, according to E, the dwelling-place of Jacob, and not merely the intermediate station. But this assumption cannot be proved (comp. on xxxvii. 14). 1b is also similar to xxxi. 54, and 2a to xx. 3. In vv. 3-5 indeed the tokens of E are incomparably more abundant; in the first place, ver. 5, comp. xlv. 19 (where at the same time 21a showed that ישראל for יעקב is no decisive sign against him), and 3b, comp. xxi. 13. Parallels are also furnished in E to conspicuous particulars of style, while, on the other hand, ver. 6 sq. is a transition to the following catalogue of names similar in style to the second Elohist. The departure, ver. 1: *And Israel departed with all that he had and came to Beersheba, and offered sacrifices to the God of his father Isaac.* Travelling from Hebron, xxxvii. 14, in the direction of Egypt, Jacob arrives at Beersheba (בְּאֵרָה שֶׁבַע, comp. xxviii. 2), where were the tamarisk planted by Abraham, xxi. 33, and the altar of Isaac, xxvi. 25. There he offered sacrifices to the God of his father Isaac (according to xxxi. 54, sacrifices with a sacrificial repast, the only passage, apart from ch. xxxi., where the patriarchs appear as sacrificing), just when he was, certainly not without a deep feeling of melancholy mingled with his joy, about to leave the Land of Promise. Manifestation of God in Beersheba, vv. 2-4: *And Elohim spake to Israel in a vision of the night, and said: Jacob! Jacob! And he said: Here am I. Then He said: I am El, the God of thy father, fear not to go down into Egypt, for I will there make thee a great nation. As for me, I will go down with thee to Egypt, and I will also bring thee up again, and Joseph shall close thine eyes.* The plur. מֻרְאֹת is the intensive plur. expressive of grandeur and importance. The *inf.* רְדָה stands midway between רָדָת and רְדָה, according to לֵדָה, דֵּעָה, the ancient original form *ridat*, and גֶּם־עֲלֹה is like גַּם־אָכֹל, xxxi. 15, both in *E*, comp. אַף, Isa. xxxv. 2, and on the *inf. abs.* of *Kal* with *Hiph.*, Ges. § 131, note 2. However high Joseph might stand in Pharaoh's favour, Egypt was still a foreign land, and it would not be without apprehension that Jacob would contemplate his own and his descendants' future. His heart would cleave to Canaan, which was his native land by nature and his true home by promise. Hence it is that the Divine encouragement vouchsafed him takes the form of an assurance, that he does not go to Egypt alone, nor without hope of return. Thus reassured he continues his journey, ver. 5 : *And Jacob rose up from Beersheba, and the sons of Israel took their father and their little ones and their wives in the waggons which Pharaoh had sent to carry him.* In an Egyptian painting there is a representation of an Ethiopian princess returning to Thebes, the capital, in a waggon, under a sunshade attached to it, with her servant guiding the two cows harnessed to it. The body of the vehicle, resting on two wheels, is only just large enough for two persons, as are also the frequently depicted state chariots and war chariots (מֶרְכָּבָה and רֶכֶב, Egypt. *markabuta*). The waggons which Joseph sent were, on the contrary, certainly four-wheeled conveyances, like that of the chamberlain, Acts viii., who, though surely not without servants, yet asked Philip the deacon to sit beside him. In such waggons drawn by oxen did the women and children of the patriarchal family travel with their aged father. The cattle were driven, and the rest of their goods packed upon asses and camels. Thus they came to Egypt, vv. 6, 7 : *And they took their cattle and their goods, which they had gotten in the land of Canaan, and came to Egypt, Jacob and all his seed with him. His sons and his sons' sons with him, and his daughters and his sons' daughters and all his seed brought he with him to Egypt.* It is the same kind of statement as at xii. 5, xxxi. 18, xxxvi. 6, comp. also on אִתּוֹ vii. 7, 13, and other passages.

Here follows the second of the three portions of which ch. xlvi. consists: 2. A CATALOGUE OF THE NAMES OF THOSE WHO MIGRATED TO EGYPT, vv. 8–27. Kuenen (*Einl.* § 6, note 1) regards this as a piece of patchwork put together from Num. xxvi. In our opinion its author is *Q*, who is characterized both by פַּדַּן אֲרָם and יֹצְאֵי יְרֵכוֹ (ver. 26 as at Ex. i. 5, comp. Gen. xxxv. 11, elsewhere only at Judg. viii. 30); nor is וַיֵּלֶד אֶת־ ver. 20 against him, for he thus writes at Num. xxvi. 60; also (as the Jahvist does, iv. 18) *R* may have interposed here and there, but nothing can with certainty be shown to be of his insertion, except the relative sentence in ver. 20, and that not from its contents, but from the syntactic harshness of the annexation. The words יַעֲקֹב וּבָנָיו are the title and theme of the table, which is arranged, as it were, in four columns. Jacob stands at the head, and his sons are classified according to his four wives, Leah, Zilpah, Rachel, Bilhah; all is clear, it is only strange, but not doubtful, that in ver. 15 Jacob is reckoned in with the בְּנֵי לֵאָה (with these, because his seed began with them), instead of being added to them. Under Leah stand Reuben with four sons = 5; Simeon with six = 7; Levi with three = 4; Judah with five sons, of whom 'Er and Onan are, as is remarked, omitted, as having died in Canaan, and two grandsons, as a compensation for the two sons who died childless = 6; Issachar with four sons = 5; Zebulun with three = 4; and Dinah (who, having fallen, remained single, and moreover did not become a mother). She is hence mentioned alone, and is included in the computation as being also the eldest of the daughters, ver. 7. Thus we have $5 + 7 + 4 + 6 + 5 + 4 + 1 = 32$, but with Jacob, **33**.

Under Zilpah stand Gad with seven sons = 8; Asher with four sons, a daughter (Serah, who, like Dinah, is enumerated for a special reason) and two grandsons = 8. Hence **16**. Under Rachel, Jacob's wife κατ' ἐξ.: Joseph with two sons = 3; Benjamin with ten = 11, consequently **14**. Under Bilhah: Dan with one son = 2; Naphtali with four = 5, consequently **7**. These together (33 + 16 + 14 + 7) make 70 souls. The catalogue however reckons at first, ver. 26, only 66 descendants of Jacob (who "came forth out of his loins," comp. xxiv. 2), leaving out of the computation Jacob and Joseph with the two sons of the latter, whom the family that migrated to Egypt found there. If however Jacob and Joseph, with Ephraim and Manasseh, are added, there are **70**.[1] And Joseph's sale into Egypt being, as he himself regarded it, xlv. 2, only a sending thither beforehand, the account is quite right when it says finally, ver. 27b: *All the souls of the house of Jacob which came into Egypt* (אֲשֶׁר בָּאָה=הַבָּאָה, see Ges. § 109) *were seventy*. The same number is given Ex. i. 5, Deut. x. 22. The LXX however, comp. Acts vii. 14, reckons ἑβδομηκονταπέντε, counting, in accordance with its enlargement of ver. 20 (which omits בֶּכֶר the son of Ephraim, Num. xxvi. 35), three grandsons and two great-grandsons of Joseph, and at last, ver. 27, by the addition of 9 Josephites to the 66 descendants of Jacob makes the number 75.

So far all is clear. But taking the statement literally, that the sixty-seven—for this is their number including Jacob and excluding Joseph with Manasseh and Ephraim—came to Egypt, difficult questions arise. Since there are only about two-and-twenty years between the sale of Joseph and the migration of Jacob,[2] and the birth of Judah's twin children

---

[1] According to ancient Jewish explanation the meaning is, that when they came into Egypt, by including among them Joseph and his two sons and Jochebed who were born בֵּין שׁוּרַיָּא (*i.e.* at the wall of Sesostris at the eastern boundary of Egypt), there were 70 of them; see Targ. Jer. and Rashi on xlvi. 26, and Brüll's *Jahrbücher für jüd. Lit. u. Gesch.* 1883, p. 100 sq.

[2] Kanzleirat Paret, in his work on *The Era of the World*, 1880, p. 24, in

takes place after the former event, Perez, who, according to ver. 12, came to Egypt with Hezron and Hamul, must have been born and already have begotten two sons within these twenty-two years. This is not impossible, but with regard to patriarchal custom improbable. A greater difficulty arises from the fact of ten sons being awarded to Benjamin (according to the LXX: three sons with five grandsons and a great-grandson). Benjamin appears indeed in the preceding history not as a boy in the ordinary sense of the word, but at all events as still a young man. His birth took place, as we saw, p. 234, in the 106th year of Jacob (the last before Joseph's disappearance), and perhaps some years earlier. Hence, at the time of the migration he was perhaps twenty-four years old (according to Demetrius in Eus. *Praep.* ix., twenty-one ἐτῶν κή), and as such might as well be called נַעַר as Joseph when nearly thirty, xli. 12, comp. xlvi.; Absalom is also called נַעַר 2 Sam. xvii. 32, and Solomon, 1 Kings iii. 7, calls himself נַעַר קָטֹן, while at xiv. 24 נְעָרִים are men fit for war. But this was an age at which, even if he is made, as by Grossrau, a polygamist, he could hardly have already had, and certainly according to the impression made by the preceding narrative had not had, ten sons. Nor is this indeed the meaning of the list. The rude contrast said to exist between A (Q) and C (J), by the former making Benjamin a man above thirty, and the latter representing him as a young boy, is improbable in itself, and is done away with by the obvious view (Hengstb., Reinke and others), that those grandsons of Jacob, who were not born till after the migration, are regarded as members of his family, who came into Egypt in their fathers. The expres-

which he relies for chs. v. and xi. on the numbers of the LXX, thinks that the sojourn in Egypt amounted to 400 years, to 430 if we date it from Joseph's arrival there; for that from Joseph's sale to the settlement of the family of Jacob in Egypt there elapsed 30 years. But the statements, xxxvii. 2, xli. 46, xlv. 11, give 13+7+2 years, which cannot be extended to 30. Paret is however right in saying that 215 years are insufficient for the number of the people assumed, Ex. xii. 37, comp. Köhler, *Gesch.* i. 164 sq.

sion of the catalogue is consequently cautious, it does not say עִם־יַעֲקֹב but לְיַעֲקֹב (לְבֵית־יַעֲקֹב) 26a, 27b. "This view," objects Kn., "is inadmissible; the narrator reminds us only in the case of Manasseh and Ephraim that they were born in Egypt; he makes this remark repeatedly, and hence with special purpose (vv. 20, 27, Ex. i.)." But the remark with respect to Manasseh and Ephraim distinguishes these two, as found in Egypt, from those who migrated thither. That many of those named were not born to their fathers till after the latter had come to Egypt, is not contrary to either the object or meaning of the list. From xlii. 37 (E) we know that Reuben had two sons at the time of the second journey to Egypt, but the list reckons four as coming to Egypt with their father. We see by the counterpart, Num. xxvi., what the author was concerned about: he desired to show that the roots of the subsequent nation were transplanted to Egypt in the family of Jacob; he names the ancestors of the families, who were at the time of the exodus the most notable and numerous (as many as five were then already extinct). In such enumerations the power of the idea over the materials is shown. The sacred historians enclose their materials in the frame of significant numbers. Ten is the number of the finished whole, upon which is impressed the characteristic of sacredness by multiplication with seven, the number of disclosed unity, and especially of the Divine glory. The number 70 (= 7 × 10) stamps the little band of emigrants (Deut. xxvi. 5) as the holy seed of the people of God.

The list of names, Num. xxvi., differs in many respects from that of Gen. xlvi. The LXX modifies the latter by the former. Two of the sons of Benjamin appear, Num. xxvi., as his grandsons. And ten names of the same persons there differ more or less. The deviating pairs of names are either two different names of the same meaning, as צֹחַר and זֶרַח, יוֹב (from אוֹב=آب) and יָשׁוּב, or slightly differing forms of the same name, as יְמוּאֵל and נְמוּאֵל, צְפִיוֹן and צְפוֹן, אֲרוֹדִי and אֲרוֹד,

חֻפִּים and חוּפָּם, or the abbreviated and the full name, as אֲחִי and אֲחִירָם, or apparently various readings of the tradition, as אֶצְבּוֹן and אָזְנִי, מֻפִּים and שְׁפוּפָם, חֻשִׁים and שׁוּחָם.[1] Other differences are found in the lists of the Chronicler, and especially in the portion 1 Chron. vii. 14–29 comp. Num. xxvi. 28–37, which carries on the genealogical table of the descendants of Joseph beyond Gen. xlvi. (comp. xlviii. 6).

After the list, xlvi. 8–27, whose contents and object extend beyond the immediate present, the narrative is again taken up, and the third of the three portions of ch. xlvi. now follows.
3. THE MEETING AND RECEPTION IN GOSHEN. The narrator is J, as is at once perceived by the prominence given to Judah. Judah sent before, ver. 28: *And Judah he sent before him to Joseph, to give information before him to Goshen, and they came to the land of Goshen.* Instead of לְהוֹרֹת the LXX, Sam. Syr. read לְהֵרָאוֹת, which Wellh. Dillm. pronounce to be *Niph.*: that he (Joseph) might appear before him (Jacob). It is indeed fitly said, 29b, of Joseph, the ruler of Egypt, that he appeared before (showed himself to) his father; but the lower cannot without discourtesy and irreverence send word to the higher to appear before him. The translation too of Arnheim and others: that he might show the way to Goshen before him, is impossible; for that would only have meaning and purpose if Jacob and his family had gone directly after him, which is excluded by שָׁלַח. The purpose of sending the energetic and fluent Judah was, that he might take information to Goshen of the approaching arrival of the family. Both לְפָנָיו refer to Jacob; the second includes the obj. of הוֹרֹת: information before him, is that of his speedy following (comp. Ex. xxxv. 34: to instruct, to give information). Luther too

---

[1] If Alfred Jeremias, *Die Babylonisch-assyr. Vorstellungen vom Leben nach dem Tode* (1887), p. 123, is in the right, when he says that Zion is called אֲרִיאֵל Isa. xxix. 1 sq., with reference to the Babylonio-Assyrian *Aralû*, which on the one side is the seat of God (comp. Ps. xlviii. 3), and on the other conceals within it the world beneath, the proper name אֲרְאֵלִי (here and Num. xxvi. 17) might be compared with the Greek proper name Ὀλύμπιος.

gives this explanation of the ambiguous words: *ut doceat Juda et significet fratri Joseph adventare patrem et hortetur eum ut veniat in Gosen;* the LXX, taking the commission of Judah as an announcement to Joseph, translates with more exact designation of the place of meeting: τὸν δὲ 'Ιούδα ἀπέστειλεν ἔμπροσθεν αὐτοῦ πρὸς 'Ιωσὴφ συναντῆσαι αὐτῷ καθ' 'Ηρώων πόλιν εἰς γῆν 'Ραμεσσῆ. The Memphitic translation has: "at Petom the city in the land of Ramses." The excavations of E. Naville (1883) in Tell el-Maskhuta make it overwhelmingly probable, that it was not the store-city Ramses, but Pithom (*i.e.* the place of the god Tuen) that was situate there. The inscription EPO CASTRA upon a stone, which was found in a wall of the Roman settlement hard by the ruins of Pithom, speaks in favour of Hero (Herôônpolis) being a more recent city near Pithom.[1] It may well be supposed that the meeting between Jacob and Joseph took place here, the latter coming from Memphis for the purpose. On the arrival of Jacob and his family, Joseph hastens to welcome his father, ver. 29 : *And Joseph made ready his chariot, and went up to meet his father to Goshen, and he appeared before him and fell upon his neck, and wept on his neck a long time.* The עלה, generally used of the journey from the valley of the Nile to Canaan, stands here for that from the interior of Egypt towards the wilderness; and the וַיֵּרָא, elsewhere only used of Divine appearances, corresponds with the התודע with respect to the brethren. The high-pitched expression serves to designate the solemnity of the meeting. He who falls upon his neck seems to be Joseph, but perhaps it is Jacob (Reggio), after Joseph had made himself known to his uncertain and anxious father (comp. the change of subject, Ps. lxxii. 15). עוֹד (from עוּד, عاد *redire*) means, as at Ruth i. 14, Eccles. vii. 28, again and again, repeatedly and continually. The aged father's overwhelming joy, ver. 30 : *Then*

[1] See Dillmann's article on "Pithom, Hero, Klysma," in the *Report of the Royal Academy of Sciences*, xxxix., 1885.

Israel said to Joseph: Now let me die, since I have seen thy face, that thou art yet alive. A similar הַפַּעַם as at ii. 23, xxix. 34, xxx. 20, at the attainment of a wish. Advice to the newly-arrived, vv. 31–34: *And Joseph said to his brethren and to his father's house: I will go up and tell Pharaoh, and will say to him: My brethren and my father's house, which were in the land of Canaan, are come to me. And the men are shepherds, for they have always been keepers of cattle, and they have brought with them their flocks and their herds and all that they have. When then Pharaoh shall call you and ask you, What is your occupation?* say: *Thy servants have been keepers of cattle from our youth up till now, we as our fathers—that ye may dwell in the land of Goshen, for every shepherd is an abomination to the Egyptians.* The last words also form part of Joseph's address. Kn. lays stress upon צֹאן, in distinction from בָּקָר, for sheep and goats were not among the Egyptians customary sacrificial animals, because their flesh did not form part of the priestly and royal diet, and because woollen fabrics were esteemed unclean by the priests and not used for the apparel of the dead. But the conclusion, that shepherds and goatherds were therefore תּוֹעֵבָה in a high degree to the Egyptians, is not confirmed. Only swineherds were such (Herod. ii. 47), and they were nevertheless reckoned together with cowherds among the seven castes (Herod. ii. 164), both together forming the herd caste (Diod. i. 74). The name βουκόλοι is only an appellation *a potiori*, for pictures of goat-keeping and sheep-tending appear on the monuments, together with representations of cattle-rearing, while among the herds appear together with asses and horned cattle, also sheep and rams, goats and he-goats by thousands; goats, wethers and he-goats are being driven over the newly-sown fields, to tread the seed-corn into the soil; and the flesh of sheep and goats is customary and favourite food. In xlvii. 17 not only horned cattle, but also flocks of small cattle, are mentioned, together with horses and asses, as property of the Egyptians.

Hence the statement of Joseph can only be a strong expression for the depreciation of the shepherd caste as the lowest, and not for the depreciation of non-Egyptian nomads (Dillm.), for the reason 34*b* sounds unlimited (comp. on the contrary xliii. 32). Graul in his *Travels*, ii. 171, remarks, that the shepherds and goatherds on the monuments are depicted accordingly — they are all long, lean, haggard, sickly and almost ghost-like forms, recalling the famished appearance of those Indian castes who are similarly contrasted with the well-fed appearance of the agricultural Brahmanic state. Joseph hopes that Pharaoh, when he learns their occupation, will the more readily allow them to dwell in Goshen, far away from the centre of the country, that fertile district which his brotherly affection intended for them (xlv. 10), while Pharaoh had only offered in general terms to give up to them "the best of the land" (xlv. 18, 20). At the same time Joseph's wisdom sought to prevent his brethren from coming to the court and having too much inclination for, and contact with the Egyptians; he took care for this beforehand, by affixing to them a *vitium originis* (v. Moser).

THE SETTLEMENT OF ISRAEL IN EGYPT, AND THEIR PROSPEROUS AND CONTINUED EXISTENCE THERE DURING THE EXTREMITY OF THE FAMINE, CH. XLVII. 1—27.

The narrator from ver. 1 onwards is *J*, but *R* seems from vv. 5–11 to have kept to *Q*; מֵיטַב 6*a*, 11*a*, occurs again indeed only in the Book of the Covenant, Ex. xxii. 4, and אֶרֶץ רַעְמְסֵס is without further confirmation in the Hebrew text. The LXX has it once more, xlvi. 28, in a Jahvistic connection. If however *Q* has a share in the composition, vv. 5–11 almost entirely, and ver. 27, belong to him. Only *J* and *E* have claims to the rest, without its being possible to effect any certain division.

Joseph now announces to Pharaoh the arrival of his family,

ver. 1: *And Joseph came and told Pharaoh, and said: My father and my brethren and their sheep and their oxen and all that they have are come from the land of Canaan, and behold they are in the land of Goshen.* He thus did as he had told his brethren, xlvi. 31 sqq., he would, when he also instructed them how to behave towards Pharaoh. The audience and the king's decision, vv. 2-6: *And out of the body of his brethren he took five men and presented them unto Pharaoh. And Pharaoh said unto his brethren: What is your occupation? And they said to Pharaoh: Thy servants are shepherds, both we and our fathers. And they said to Pharaoh: To sojourn as strangers in the land are we come, for there is no pasture for thy servants' flocks, for the famine is sore in the land of Canaan, so thy servants wish to dwell in the land of Goshen. And Pharaoh spake unto Joseph saying: Thy father and thy brethren are come to thee. The land of Egypt is before thee, in the best of the land make thy father and thy brethren to dwell; let them dwell in the land of Goshen, and if thou knowest that there are able men among them, place them as chief herdsmen over my property.* In 2a מִקְצֵה (with ף *raphatum*) as at Ezek. xxxiii. 2 and מִקְצוֹת 1 Kings xii. 31, has still its undiluted original meaning: out of the collective whole (this is conceived of as the circumference, comp. xix. 4); מִקְצָת for the meaning: a part (some), is in use both in the Talmud and already at Neh. vii. 70, Dan. i. 2. On the number five, see on xliii. 34. It is characteristic of the Egyptian custom and way of looking at things, that the first question which, as Joseph had expected (xlvi. 33), is put to them by Pharaoh, relates to their occupation. They answer, ver. 3 sq., truthfully and discreetly according to Joseph's directions. רֹעֵה is a generic singular, Ges. § 147c, but certainly a mere error of transcription for רֹעֵי. Pharaoh grants their request to be allowed to dwell in Goshen, by authorizing Joseph to settle his relatives wherever he chooses, in the best part of the land, therefore in Goshen as they desire it, and directs him, if he knows of competent men among them, to make them chief keepers of the royal cattle (which were consequently in Goshen as the best pasture land). The audience of the five not taking place in Joseph's presence, the information given by Pharaoh to Joseph contains nothing inappropriate, hortatory being easily transposed into recapitulatory speech. It is however evident from the text of the LXX, a text apparently as they found and not as they arbitrarily corrected it (Wellh. Dillm. Kuen.), that in the Hebrew text two accounts are interwoven, that of J and that of Q, who has been continuing from xlvi. 27 (Dillm.). That Q also related the presentation of Jacob to Pharaoh, results even of itself from the analysis of vv. 5–11, and is confirmed by the LXX, in which ver. 5 of the Hebrew text is preceded by: ἦλθον δὲ εἰς Αἴγυπτον πρὸς Ἰωσήφ Ἰακὼβ καὶ οἱ υἱοὶ αὐτοῦ καὶ ἤκουσε Φαραὼ βασιλεὺς Αἰγύπτου καὶ εἶπε Φαραὼ πρὸς Ἰωσήφ κτλ. Jacob presented to Pharaoh by Joseph, vv. 7–10 : *Then Joseph brought his father and set him before Pharaoh, and Jacob blessed Pharaoh. And Pharaoh said to Jacob: How many are the days of the years of thy life? And Jacob said to Pharaoh: The days of the years of my pilgrimage are a hundred and thirty years; few and evil have been the days of the years of my life, and have not attained to the days of the years of my fathers in the days of their pilgrimage. And Jacob blessed Pharaoh, and went out from before Pharaoh.* Not till after the brethren had given account to the king of the external concerns of the family, because Jacob was himself too old and infirm to act independently in this new turn of domestic affairs, did Joseph bring in his father also. The aged Jacob greets the king with a blessing. When the latter asks him how old he is, he calls the hundred and thirty years of his life מְגוּרַי, for Abraham lived to be one hundred and seventy and Isaac one hundred and eighty years old (xxv. 7, xxxv. 28), and he feels himself, as the perf. לֹא הִשִּׂיגוּ shows, near the end. He had moreover a right to mention the

רָעִים he had experienced; for hard work, long and profound grief and also much self-inflicted misery lay behind him. He regards his own and his father's unsettled homeless earthly life as a pilgrimage, compared with the rest beyond, which, because hidden with God, is his true home, Heb. xi. 13–16, comp. Ps. cxix. 19, 54, xxxix. 13, 1 Chron. xxix. 15. The narrator is silent as to what further questions on the part of Pharaoh followed this answer; he only tells us that Jacob departed blessing Pharaoh, as he had also thus greeted him. The settlement, ver. 11: *And Joseph settled his father and his brethren and gave them a possession in the land of Egypt, in the best of the land, in the land of Ramses, as Pharaoh had commanded.* The land of Goshen is here called אֶרֶץ רַעְמְסֵס, for which, Ex. i. 11, the רַעַמְסֵס is vocalized in pause as a tri-syllable; the appellation of the eastern pasture land alternates in the Hebrew text, and hence furnishes to analysis no characteristic of a source.

The settlement takes place during the seven years of famine, which furnish the outer frame of the narrative. The narrator (it is uncertain which) finishes this off, to return to the closing period of the scarcity, ver. 12: *And Joseph provided his father and his brethren and all his father's house with bread, in proportion to the children.* The verb כִּלְכֵּל is, according to Ew. § 283b, combined with a double acc., and לְפִי הַטָּף means properly in proportion to the little ones (who would eat most, and whom one would be most unwilling to see wanting), hence according to the size of each family. What is now related, vv. 13–26, is no interpolated episode, but shows us the influential activity of Joseph in Egypt at its culminating point. The famine increased, and all the ready money came into the royal treasury, vv. 13, 14: *And there was no bread in all the land, for the famine was exceeding sore, and the land of Egypt was exhausted and the land of Canaan by reason of the famine. And Joseph collected all the money that was found in the land of Egypt and in the land of Canaan for the food which they bought, and Joseph brought the money into Pharaoh's house.* All the store of money in both countries came into the State treasury, which stood at the king's disposal. Egypt and Canaan were both quite exhausted by reason of the continuance of the famine: וַתֵּלַהּ from לָאַהּ=לָהָהּ, whence differing in form לָהַהּ Prov. xxxi. 18, syn. לָאָב Zech. xiv. 18, where v. Hofmann acutely conjectures that וְלָאֲבָה or וְלָאָבָה was the original: thus it (Egypt) was utterly dried up. As those who were famished could pay no more money, Joseph takes the cattle, which they possess, as payment, vv. 15–17: *So the money failed out of the land of Egypt and the land of Canaan; then came all the Egyptians to Joseph saying: Give us bread, for why should we die in thy presence? our money is at an end. And Joseph said: Give your cattle, and I will give you for the value of your cattle, if the money is at an end. And they brought their cattle to Joseph, and Joseph gave them bread in exchange for the horses and for the cattle of the flocks and the cattle of the herds and for the asses, and satisfied them with bread for the value of all their cattle that year.* אָפֵס used here and at Ps. lxxvii. 9, Isa. xvi. 4, xxix. 20, is without further confirmation in the Pentateuch. נִהֵל used here 17*b* in the sense to appease, to quiet, proceeds from the meaning to rest, to lie down, which Friedr. Delitzsch (in the *Athenaeum*, 1883, p. 569 sq., and often since) has shown to be the root-meaning of נהל, Assyr. *nahâlu*, synon. of *nâḫu* and *rabâṣu*, according to which 2 Chron. xxxii. 22 is also explained, without our needing to read וַיְנַהֵל לָהֶם, hence: he satisfied them with bread. The further offer to which they are compelled by want next year, vv. 18–20: *And that year ended, and they came to him in the second year and said to him: We cannot conceal from my lord, but* (must tell) *that our money and possession in cattle is gone to my lord, there is nothing left in the sight of my lord but our bodies and our land. Why should we die before thine eyes, both we and our land? Buy us and our land for bread, and we and our land will be* *slaves to Pharaoh, and give us seed, that we may live and not die, and that the land may not lie waste.* And Joseph bought all the cultivated land of Egypt for Pharaoh, for the Egyptians sold each man his field, because the famine compelled them; so the land became Pharaoh's. The peculiar expression וַתְּהִם הַשָּׁנָה has its equal only at Ps. cii. 28. אֲדֹנָי is used as *Monsieur* is, though several are speaking. כִּי אִם־ is not to be separated: "that as . . ." it is the usual "but," to be explained by means of an ellipsis (*e.g.* after solemn affirmations, 2 Sam. xv. 21, 1 Kings xx. 6, 2 Kings v. 20). They offer themselves and their lands as payment; the latter to become crown property, themselves bondmen; גְּוִיָּה (everywhere else corpse) here as at Dan. x. 6, Ezek. i. 11, 23, Neh. ix. 37. To die and to become slaves is by a zeugma referred also to the land, as the latter expression is at xliii. 18 to the asses. The intrans. Kal form תֵּשַׁם from שָׁמֵם is found also Ezek. xii. 19, xix. 7. We translate ver. 21 according to the LXX: *And he made the people bondmen from one end of the realm of Egypt to the other.* Such is the thought which we expect according to ver. 20, viz. that Joseph made the people themselves vassals to Pharaoh. The LXX answers to this expectation, and like the Sam. and Hebr. Sam. translates: καὶ τὸν λαὸν κατεδουλώσατο αὐτῷ εἰς παῖδας. Hence it must have read (comp. also Jerome): ואת־העם העביר אתו לעבדים, *i.e.* according to a like causative meaning of the Hiphil, as at Jer. xvii. 4: and he made him (viz. Pharaoh) enslave the people to slaves; Houbigant, Kn. Dillm. Reuss, Kamph. (*Jenaer LZ.* 1876, p. 170) find this reading correct, and in fact it entirely obviates the difficulties of the Masoretic text. The latter can mean nothing else, than that Joseph translocated the agricultural population from one end of the kingdom to the other. הֶעֱבִיר to cause to depart from one place to another. The translocation took place for the sake of removing from the soil those whose property it had hitherto been, and of thus avoiding future disturbances. But what is the meaning of לֶעָרִים? According to Onk. Rosenm.

Ges. Tuch, Reggio : from one city to another (מֵעִיר לָעִיר 2 Chron. xxx. 10); but אֶל־הֶעָרִים, which we expect instead of לֶעָרִים, if it is to be a statement of the place whither, could not have this meaning. Perhaps לֶעָרִים of the Masoretic text is to be understood distributively: according to each city (like לַחֹמֶשׁ every fifth, 26a, comp. Josh. vii. 14), and what is meant is, that he divided the whole people among those towns in which the granaries at that time were, and which were also subsequently to form the centres of appointed districts, νομοί (comp. xli. 48). But however it may be explained, the expression is too scanty and inexplicit—the authentic text is that reproduced by the LXX. Exemption of the landed property of the priests, ver. 22: *Only the land of the priests bought he not, for the priests had an appointed portion from Pharaoh, and ate their appointed portion, which Pharaoh gave them, therefore they sold not their land.* The lands of the priests were inalienable; nor did they need to alienate them, since they were besides protected from famine; חֹק a legal appointment, something legally appointed, here both times in the latter concrete sense, as at Ps. lxxxi. 4 and Prov. xxxi. 15. Taxation of the people, vv. 23–26: *And Joseph said to the people: Behold, I have bought you this day and your land for Pharaoh; here is seed for you, and sow ye the land. And it shall come to pass at the ingatherings that ye shall render a fifth to Pharaoh, and four parts shall belong to you for the sowing of the field, and for your food, and that of your households and children. And they said: Thou hast saved our lives, let us find grace in the eyes of my lord, and we will be bondmen to Pharaoh. And Joseph made it a law to this day in the land of Egypt, that to the amount of a fifth should belong to Pharaoh, only the land of the priests, that alone became not Pharaoh's.* The demonstrative הֵא 23b occurs again only Dan. ii. 43, Ezek. xvi. 43, comp. הָא Dan. iii. 25. The ב of בַּתְּבוּאֹת is the temporal, at the ingatherings, *i.e.* as often as the harvest is gathered and brought home. We already had יָדֹת in the meaning "parts" at xliii. 34 (five parts

= five times). אֹתָהּ 26a refers neutrally to what has been just related, and to this Joseph gave the character of a fixed ordinance. The soil of Egypt was, from this time onwards, partly royal domain and partly the property of the priestly caste. According to Diodor. i. 73, it was divided into three parts, the third belonging to the warrior caste. According also to Herodotus (ii. 168), it was among the privileges (γέρεα) of the warriors to have their own share of landed property, every warrior receiving for his own twelve excellent ἄρουραι exempt from taxation. The Scripture narrative however tells us nothing of the exemption from taxation and landed property of the soldiers, because this appointment was of later origin; it was cancelled by Sethos the priest of Hephaestos, when he came to the throne (Herod. ii. 141). We cannot expect a remembrance that it was through Joseph that all the land in Egypt became the property of the crown, from those who report according to the statements of Egyptians. According to Herod. ii. 109, Diodor. i. 73, it was Σέσωστρις (Σεσόωσις) who divided the country into thirty-six νομοί, and made it over by square measurements to the Egyptians for a yearly tribute (comp. Artapanus in Euseb. *Praep.* 9. 23). That a certain allowance of provisions was, as the scriptural report declares, given by the king to the priests, and that this obviated the alienation of their lands in the years of famine, was an ordinance which may have been afterwards annulled, because their landed property more than sufficiently supplied their wants. Diodorus at least (i. 73) reports, that the Egyptian priests defray the expenses of the national offerings and support themselves and their servants out of the revenues of their lands. Herodotus also says (ii. 37) that the priests have no need to use their private property (τῶν οἰκηίων) for their support, but that their sacred bread is baked for them, and that each (ἑκάστῳ) has daily a quantity of goose and beef for his consumption, that grape wine is also given them, viz. the produce of the farming of the order—that each lives very well, and at the expense of the community. The proceedings of Joseph preserved, in the first place, the interest of the king and respected the privileges of the priests, but abolished the free peasant class. It is left to the readers to pass their moral and politico-economical verdict upon them. Joseph undoubtedly had in view no less the good of the country than that of the king, when changing the disproportionately divided landed property into uniform parcels of copyhold liable to rent. Besides, the tribute of a fifth was, with the astonishing fertility of Egypt, a very tolerable burden. Nevertheless G. B. Niebuhr is in the right when he says, that the history of Joseph is a dangerous model for crafty ministers. Nor can Ebrard and others be contradicted when they assert, that in Joseph's financial speculation, as well as in Jacob's bargaining for the birthright, one of the unamiable sides of Semitic (Jewish) hereditary peculiarity comes to light.

Ver. 27 now returns to the family of Jacob in Goshen, of whom we certainly have to think as not exempted from the fee levied upon the whole country: *And Israel dwelt in the land of Egypt, in the land of Goshen; and they settled therein, and they were fruitful and multiplied.* The close, especially 27b, is in the style of Q (xxxiv. 10, xxxv. 11).

We have now arrived at the place for discussing more particularly, than has hitherto been done at xlvi. 28, the province of Goshen (LXX Γεσέμ, Artapanus in Euseb. Καισάν, Κεσσάν). It is to be sought for in Lower Egypt on the east side of the Nile. Its eastern boundary was the desert of Arabia-Petraea leading towards Philistia (Ex. xiii. 17, comp. 1 Chron. vii. 21), on which account the LXX translate, xlv. 10, xlvi. 34, Γεσὲμ 'Αραβίας. On the west it extended as far as the Nile, for the Israelites had abundance of fish, Num. xi. 5. Which part of the Nile was its western boundary will be determined, according as the question, Which was then the royal city? is answered. For Goshen was not very far from this, since Joseph there had his family near him, xlv. 10, and there was easy and rapid intercourse between Goshen and Joseph's dwelling-place, xlvi. 28, xlviii. 1 sq. Num. xiii. 22, comp. Ps. lxxviii. 12, 43, is appealed to, to show that Tanis צֹעַן was then the capital (Bochart, Hgst. Baumg. Kurtz); but this testimony holds good only for the time of Moses, not for the time of Joseph. In his time Memphis (on the left bank of the Nile south of the subsequent Cairo),[1] Hebr. מֹף or נֹף (see on Isa. xix. 13), founded, according to Herodotus, ii. 99, before Menes, was the royal city with its famed Ptah-temple, which stood where are now found the monuments, and among them the Colossus Ramses (the Sesostris Colossus of the ancients) at Mitrahîne. Philo also thinks of Memphis. In or near to Goshen lay, at the time of the exodus, the cities פִּתֹם and רַעְמְסֵס, magazine-cities,[2] provisioned fortresses, in the building of which the Israelites were compulsorily employed, Ex. i. 11. Goshen is at xlvii. 11 anticipatively called אֶרֶץ רַעְמְסֵס (Targ. Jer. אַרְעָא דְפִילוּסִין), from Ramses, the place of assembly and departure at the time of the exodus, Ex. xii. 37, Num. xxxiii. 5. Pithom is Πάτουμος, past which flowed, according to Herod. ii. 158, the canal from the Pelusian branch of the Nile to the Red Sea (παρὰ Πάτουμον τὴν 'Αραβίαν πόλιν); it was a city dedicated to the god Tum, the ruins of which, as E. Naville has shown (see on xlvi. 29), are concealed in the Tell el-Maskhuta; while, on the other hand, Lepsius[3] and others take this for the situation of Ramses (*Pa-Ramses-Miamun*), and transfer *Pa-Tum* to the neighbourhood of the Tell Abu Sulêman. In any case Goshen lay to the west of the Wadi Tumilât, which originally belonged to the desert, and the cities of Pithom and Ramses about denote the line of the southern boundary of Goshen.

[1] See A. Wiedemann's essay, "The Age of Memphis," in the Biblico-Archæological *Proceedings*, 1887, pp. 184-190.

[2] Magazine is the Arabic مَخْزَن, עָרֵי מִסְכְּנוֹת are cities with stone houses, whence the people are provided for (from סכן to provide for, Friedr. Delitzsch, *Proleg.* 186).

[3] *Zeitschr. für äg. Sprache u. Alterthumskunde*, 1883.

Its eastern boundary was, according to Ebers, the Isthmus of Suez and the line of fortifications that protected the country against its eastern neighbours. Of the western boundary the extreme southern point was the city of Heliopolis, the northern that of Tanis. On the north it was terminated by the Menzale lake and the marsh of Pelusium. Hence it would reach westward as far as the Tanitic branch of the Nile. But perhaps it did not extend so far either westward or northward; it may have been bounded on the west and north by the Pelusian branch of the Nile; and Fakus (according to Ebers,[1] *Pa [Pha] Kos* = גֹּשֶׁן) have been its northern point. The district thus bounded comprised both desert and cultivated land. At present the Pelusian branch of the Nile is quite choked up with sand, and the country is less frequently covered by the Nile, but the region of Bubastos, as far as the entrance of the Wadi Tumilât, and for the greater part the latter itself, the Wadi Sebabiâr and other districts, are still capable of cultivation, while there are some which are like luxuriant gardens. The region, whose name partly coincides with Goshen, اللورة الشرقية (the eastern district), is still one of the most fertile and lucrative provinces. Its capital is *Belbês*, according to which Makrizi determines the western boundary of Goshen. North-east of it lies *Sadîr* (between Abbasîe and Chasbi), by which Saad., the Arabic translators and Samar. render גֹּשֶׁן; in the neighbourhood of this Sadir, Arab tribes were settled, as Makrizi (*Ueber die in Aeg. eingewanderten Stämme*, ed. by Wüstenfeld, p. 39 sqq.) states, like Israel in ancient times.[2] Of the whole period between the 130th and 147th years of Jacob's life

---

[1] See his *Durch Gosen zum Sinai*, 2nd edit. p. 519, and "Historical Truths of Israel's Sojourn in Egypt," in the *Sunday School Times*, 1887, No. 18 (in which he always identifies Rameses, for the building of which the '*Aperu* are dragging bricks, with Tanis, and the '*Aperu* with עברים).

[2] We leave out of consideration the view, which Cope Whitehouse, in the *Proceedings* of the Biblico-Archæological Association, 1885–86, seeks, after the precedent of Jablonski (in the *Pantheon Aegyptiorum*), with great confidence whimsically to confirm, that Goshen was Fajûm, with the adjacent districts of the Nile valley, in a northern direction towards Gizeh and Heliopolis.

nothing further is told us, than that Israel settled and increased in this district.

TESTAMENTARY DISPOSITIONS OF JACOB,
CH. XLVII. 28—XLVIII.

From this sketchy remark, in which the threads of the history of Israel are again taken up, the narrator proceeds to the testamentary dispositions of Jacob. The fourth section of the Toledoth of Jacob commences here. Jacob has become much older since his entry into Egypt, and feels that his death is near, vv. 28–31: *And Jacob lived in the land of Egypt seventeen years, so that the days of Jacob, the years of his life, amounted to one hundred and forty-seven years. And the days of Israel drew nigh to death, and he called his son Joseph and said to him: If I have found grace in thine eyes, put, I pray thee, thy hand under my thigh and deal kindly and truly with me: Bury me not in Egypt, but let me lie with my fathers, and take me out of Egypt and bury me in their burying-place —and he said: I will do according to thy word. And he said: Swear unto me; and he swore to him, and Israel stretched himself upon the head of the bed.* Apart from ver. 28, we have the text of *J*, according to whom Jacob's wish and intention with respect to his burying is related; the direction is here given to Joseph and repeated to the twelve, xlix. 29–32, according to the text of *Q*. How Jahvistic the style is, is shown by parallels such as "the days draw nigh to death," Deut. xxxi. 14; אָם־נָא xviii. 3 and frequently, the kind and manner of the corporeal oath, as at xxiv. 2; חֶסֶד וֶאֱמֶת xxiv. 49, xxxii. 11; "to lie with (עִם) the fathers," as at Deut. xxxi. 16, and in the kindred Deuteronomistic remarks in the book of Kings, 1 Kings ii. 10. Jacob desires Joseph to put his hand under his thigh, and thus to assure him on the ground of the covenant of circumcision made with Abraham, the actual proof of faithful love, that he will not bury him in Egypt, but with his fathers in Canaan (1. 4)—in the promised land, which is appointed to be the place of the promised redemption. Joseph swears. His aged father had sat up in his bed for the purpose. And after Joseph has sworn, Israel (for so is he called at this solemn moment) stretches himself upon the ראשׁ הַמִּטָּה. To rise from the bed, sitting up in which he had talked with Joseph, and cast himself upon the ground, to thank God for the proof of His mercy involved in Joseph's sworn promise, was not possible to him, because of the infirmity of age. Hence he imitates the הִשְׁתַּחֲוָיָה by turning himself (like David, 1 Kings i. 47) in the bed, and stretches himself towards its top, worshipping with his face downwards, Vulg. *adoravit Deum conversus ad lectuli caput.* Böhmer, on the contrary: he bowed himself at the head of the bed in the direction towards its foot. According to a different vocalization, LXX (Syr. It., comp. Heb. xi. 21): προσεκύνησεν 'Ισραὴλ ἐπὶ τὸ ἄκρον τοῦ ῥάβδου (הַמַּטֶּה) αὐτοῦ = αὑτοῦ, as Rabanus Maurus remarks. According to this reading he made use of the staff, with which he had walked all his life (xxxii. 11), to raise himself in the bed, and now worshipped upon it, while calling to mind God's help during his pilgrimage and its end in another world. This passage, xlvii. 28-31, is the first portion from the last days of Jacob.

The second, ch. xlviii., relates his adoption and blessing of his two grandsons. The narrative as we have it accredits itself as a mosaic from all three sources: vv. 3-6 (7) is from *Q*, all the rest from *JE*, but so that notwithstanding editorial intervention, the portions respectively derived from *J* and *E* can still be distinguished. Following Dillm. and Budde (art. on Gen. xlviii. 7 and the adjoining sections in Stade's *Zeitschr.* iii. 56 sqq.), we separate them as follows: *J*, 1 sq. 8 sq. 13 sq. 17-19; *E*, 10-12, 15 sq. 20, 21 sq.; Kuenen claims for *E*, vv. 1 sq. 8-12, 15 sq. 20-22. In the introduction to ch. xlv. we already stated, that here in ch. xlviii. neither ישראל (for יעקב) nor אלהים (for which we expect

יהוה ver. 20) is a certain token of a source. What is decisive both here and elsewhere is, that the two threads of the narrative, which R (perhaps already the redactor of JE) intertwined, can be separated. The case of ver. 7 is peculiar. Budde brings forward the conjecture, that in xlix. 31 ואת־רחל originally stood also after את־לאה, that a redactor expunged this, and for it inserted the wording of xlviii. 7 from xxxv. 16a, 19. The conjecture is supported by the expedient, that according to Q Rachel also was buried in the cave of Machpelah. But we are certainly told that Rachel died on the journey from Aramaea to Canaan, was buried in the neighbourhood of Ephrath, and by no means at Hebron; and her death being the consequence of the birth of Benjamin, xxxv. 26, must be accommodated to this. If xlviii. 7 is really a "lost post," it must have become such some other way.

The aged and bed-ridden patriarch carried out this confirmation by oath of his desire, xlvii. 29, in anticipation of his approaching death. He is now actually ill, the end seems imminent, and Joseph is summoned, vv. 1, 2: *And it came to pass after these things, when Joseph was told, Behold, thy father is sick, and he took his two sons with him, Manasseh and Ephraim. And when they told Jacob, and said: Behold, thy son Joseph has come to thee, and Israel strengthened himself and sat up in bed.* Both וַיֹּאמֶר and וַיַּגֵּד have the most general subject, as at xliii. 34, and, according to the extant text, xlii. 25 also.[1] The interchange of the names יעקב and ישראל is not everywhere so significant as here. Jacob lies down sick, Israel draws himself up. On the arrival of Joseph, Jacob begins to speak of the blessing and the promises of God, by reason of which he raises Joseph's two sons, as though they were his own, to the station of ancestors of two independent tribes in the nation descending from him, vv. 3-6: *And Jacob said to Joseph:*

[1] Jewish expositors in such cases explain וַיֹּאמֶר הָאֹמֵר=וַיֹּאמֶר, and this corresponds with the spirit of Semitic speech (see Driver in the *Expositor*, 1887, p. 260).

El 'Saddaj appeared to me and blessed me in Luz in the land of Canaan, and said to me: Behold, I make thee fruitful and numerous, and make thee a company of peoples, and give this land to thy seed after thee for an everlasting possession. Now then, thy two sons, which were born to thee in the land of Egypt, before I came to thee to Egypt, are mine, Ephraim and Manasseh shall be mine like Reuben and Simeon. And thy seed, which thou hast begotten after them, shall be thine, after the name of their brethren shall they be called in their inheritance. The manifestation of God, to which Jacob looks back, is that which was vouchsafed to him in Luz-Bethel after his return from Aramaea, xxxv. 6 sq., 9–15; the wording of the promise, however, is more closely in unison with that given to him when going to Aramaea, xxviii. 3 sq. The placing of Ephraim first, in opposition to their succession in age, ver. 1, comp. xli. 50–52, is done in accordance with the express declaration of purpose which follows farther on. Jacob places Ephraim and Manasseh on a level with his own first and second born sons as independent heads of tribes, while, on the contrary, Joseph's other sons form no separate tribes, but are to be reckoned as belonging to the tribes of their brethren. Jacob's speech is interrupted by a reference to Rachel, Joseph's mother, ver. 7: *And as for me—when I came from Paddan, Rachel died from me in the land of Canaan, in the way, a kibra of land before Ephrath, and I buried her there on the way to Ephrath, which is Bethlehem.* In the presence of Joseph, the remembrance of his never-forgotten wife thrills powerfully through him. It is as though he wanted to lead Joseph to his mother's grave, and there to give him or receive from him a promise. His regarding Ephraim and Manasseh, who were by birth natives of Egypt, as his immediate sons by Rachel, also redounds to the honour of this prematurely lost wife. It is essentially thus that Kn. also explains the apparently uncaused, and in any case abrupt close of Jacob's speech. Budde sees in ver. 7 as thus explained "a sentimentally dramatic picture" which was not to be expected in a historical book, and least of all in *Q*. But even if it is less coloured up, the fact still remains that it is in Joseph's presence that the remembrance of Rachel forces itself upon the patriarch, and that the reason for his self-interruption is to be sought for in וַיַּרְא 8a, while, on the contrary, in *Q*'s own text the request to bury him with his fathers in the cave of Machpelah, xlix. 29–32, is joined on to xlviii. 7 (Nöld. Dillm.). Omitting in thought the introduction commencing וַיְצַו וגו' xlix. 29a, which was induced by the interstratification of xlviii. 8–xlix. 28, the וַאֲנִי here fitly continues the אֲנִי there: he buried Rachel in Ephrath, but yet desires to rest with his fathers in Hebron. מֵתָה עָלַי implies that he possessed her, and that by dying she was torn from him; פַּדָּן alone for פַדַּן אֲרָם occurs nowhere else, but why should not this abbreviation be possible? הוּא בֵּית לֶחֶם, on the contrary, is a gloss, but in itself not a false one, taken over from xxxv. 19 (see on this passage). The patriarch, who was almost blind, interrupts himself, now first perceiving that he is not with Joseph only, vv. 8, 9: *And Israel beheld Joseph's sons and said: Who are these? And Joseph said to his father: They are my sons whom Elohim hath given me here. And he said: Bring them hither to me that I may bless them.* The narrator is *J*: בָּזֶה *hoc loco*, as at xxxviii. 21 sq., Ex. xxiv. 14. וַאֲבָרֲכֵם has in Baer pausal Segol according to the Masora (as at יְרַחֵף Deut. xxxii. 11), against which Tsere is witnessed for by Num. vi. 27. His grandsons brought to Jacob, embraced by him, and led away, vv. 10–12: *And the eyes of Israel were dim from age, he could not see, and he brought them nearer to him, and he kissed them and embraced them. And Israel said to Joseph: I did not think to see thy face again, and behold Elohim hath given me to see thy seed also. Then Joseph led them away from his knees and bowed himself in his presence to the earth.* The patriarch had sat up in the bed as one about to rise, so that he could take the two between his knees, kiss them, and press them to his heart (יָשֵׂם and חָפֵץ with a Dat. as at xxix. 13), from which it by no means follows, that the narrator thought of them as little children; they were youths, but still under age and under the guidance of their father. The *inf. constr.* רְאוֹת is like עֲשׂה equally used for עֲשׂוֹת xxxi. 28, l. 20, Ges. § 75, note 2. פָּלַל elsewhere to decide, to judge, has here the more general signification of thinking, and the 1 *sing. perf.* is in the pausal form פִּלָּלְתִּי, occurring in only four verbs, see Koenig, *Lehrgeb.* i. 189. It is questionable whether לְאַפַּי refers to Joseph, so as to be equivalent, as at Num. xxii. 31, to אַפַּיִם elsewhere (*e.g.* xlii. 6), or to Jacob, and is so equivalent to לְפָנַי, which is, according to 1 Sam. xxv. 23, comp. 2 Sam. xviii. 28, not less permissible, and seems to me preferable. The LXX has καὶ προσεκύνησαν αὐτῷ (not αὐτόν as in Lagarde, 1883). The prostration is here the reverent expression of Joseph's thankfulness to Jacob for the affection shown towards his two sons. In the present combination of the extracts from different sources, the thankfulness is at the same time a request. For he leads them back to his father, who blesses them, giving to the younger the preference above the elder, vv. 13, 14: *Then Joseph took the two, Ephraim in his right hand to Israel's left, and Manasseh in his left hand to Israel's right, and brought them near to him. Then Israel stretched out his right hand and laid it upon the head of Ephraim, although he was the younger, and his left upon the head of Manasseh: he crossed his hands; for Manasseh was the first-born.* The perf. שִׂכֵּל stands syntactically (as at שָׂם xxi. 14), where the part. would also be allowable. Luther translates like Onk. Saad. Græc.-Ven.: and did thus wittingly with his hands; on the other hand, the tradition of both the Greek and Latin Churches takes this laying on of hands of Jacob as being in its correct translation: he entwined, *i.e.* crossed them, one of the most ancient types of the cross, LXX ἐναλλάξ, and similarly Syr. Targ. II. Ar.-Samar. Tavus Vulg., from שׂכל, *complicare* = שׂכל (شكل) in אֶשְׁכֹּל (סִגֹּל) a plait, a cluster of grapes. This is the first blessing by laying on of hands recorded in Holy Scripture. By means of laying on his hands, he who performs this places himself in a relation of mutual action with him who is the subject of it. This act is, according to its most obvious purpose, the vehicle by which something is conveyed and received. With hands laid on crosswise, Jacob, whose wish coincides with the counsel of God, now proceeds in the power of faith to bless Joseph in his children, vv. 15, 16: *And he blessed Joseph, and said: The God in whose presence my fathers Abraham and Isaac walked, the God who hath tended me as a shepherd since my existence to this day, the angel who redeemed me from all evil, bless the lads, and let my name and the name of my fathers Abraham and Isaac be named through them, and let them increase in multitude in the midst of the land.* The picture of God as a shepherd is suggested to Jacob by his own pastoral vocation; we meet with it again in the psalms of David, and especially of Asaph. The expression מֵעוֹדִי עַד־הַיּוֹם הַזֶּה recurs in the section on Balaam, Num. xxii. 30. בָּהֶם 16a would not be meant differently from xxi. 12, hence in the sense of a secondary cause (comp. ix. 6a). Ephraim and Manasseh, by becoming independent tribes, propagate the names of their three ancestors, with the promises attached to these names. Targ. II. takes the two הָאֱלֹהִים vocatively and: "the angel . . . bless . . ." as the supplication, but certainly יְבָרֵךְ is the common predicate of the complex notion which forms the subject. The subject, whose blessing is desired, is a threefold one; but as results from the omission of the conjunctive ו, which was to be expected at least in the third place with הַמַּלְאָךְ, and from the singular predicate (to which Novatian, *de trinit.* ch. xv., already draws attention), a single one; the מַלְאָךְ also is thought of as *Deus de Deo:* it is God revealing Himself in the appearance of an angel, God the Redeemer who at last, as God in Christ, fulfils mediatorially the counsel of redemption. When however Jacob in the act of blessing lays his right hand on Ephraim's head, this appears to Joseph an unconscious mistake, vv. 17-19: *And when Joseph saw that his father laid his right hand on the head of Ephraim, it was displeasing in his eyes, and he laid hold of his father's hand to remove it from the head of Ephraim to the head of Manasseh. And Joseph said to his father: Not so, my father, for this is the first-born, lay thy right hand upon his head. But his father refused, and said: I know, my son, I know; he also shall become a people, and he also shall become great; but his younger brother will be greater than he, and his seed will become a fulness of nations.* On יַד יְמִינוֹ hand of his right side, comp. Ps. cxxi. 5, and on תָּמַךְ of grasping and holding the hands, Ex. xvii. 12. Jacob refuses to change his hands; he knows well, viz. that Manasseh, not Ephraim, is the first-born, but the latter will be more powerful than he. This was not fulfilled in the immediate future, for at the numbering, Num. xxvi. 34, Manasseh was 20,000 above Ephraim. Subsequently however, together with the retention of the name יִשְׂרָאֵל, Ephraim gave his name to the whole kingdom, and was from the time of the Judges the greatest of the tribes in power and extent. In מְלֹא הַגּוֹיִם the determinate adheres to the second member of the *st. constr.* (as at xvi. 7, see on this matter remarks on ix. 20), and גוֹיִם refers, as at xxxv. 11 (comp. עַמִּים xxviii. 3, xlviii. 4), to the tribes of Israel; הֲמוֹן גּוֹיִם xvii. 5 has a wider meaning, and indeed that of τὸ πλήρωμα τῶν ἐθνῶν, Rom. xi. 25. The blessing continued, ver. 20: *And he blessed them that day, saying: With thee shall Israel bless, saying: Elohim make thee as Ephraim and as Manasseh—he set Ephraim before Manasseh.* The speech is addressed to Joseph, who is thus abundantly blessed in Ephraim and Manasseh. The blessedness of both became proverbial (comp. on xii. 3, and the cursing formula, Jer. xxix. 21 sq.). The last word of blessing to Joseph, vv. 21, 22: *And Israel said to Joseph, Behold, I die, but Elohim will be with you and bring you back to the land of your fathers. And I have given to thee one tract of land above thy brethren, which I took from the Emorite with my sword and my bow.* By שֶׁכֶם ridge of land, is at all events meant a part of the Canaanite mountainous district; אַחַד is the more quickly uttered form of word, which in closely connected speech occurs also elsewhere, and very frequently in this numeral, *e.g.* 2 Sam. xvii. 22, without a relation of annexation (see Philippi on the *Status constructus*, p. 59). On the use of עַל in עַל־אַחֶיךָ "beyond thy brethren," see on Ps. xvi. 2. הָאֱמֹרִי here as at xv. 16 is the favourite general name in *J* for the population of Canaan (comp. Ezek. xvi. 3). But—and this is the main question requiring an answer—what is meant by לְקַחְתִּי? Jacob —says Tuch—looking prophetically forward over four centuries and beholding as present the state of things after the conquest of the Promised Land, rightly says, as the representative of his descendants, אֲשֶׁר לָקַחְתִּי וגו׳ in the *perf. proph.* "Nevertheless," he continues, "the unusual expression שֶׁכֶם is chosen for the very probable purpose of playing upon the name of the well-known place of the same name [so Jerome: *pulcre allusit ad nomen*]. For *Sichem* was really situate in the portion of Joseph, Josh. xxi. 21, and was specially consecrated to his memory by the fact that his bones were buried there, Josh. xxiv. 32, in the field purchased by Jacob, xxxiii. 19." We could not in our retrospective view of ch. xxxiv., and especially xxxiv. 25 sq., comp. xxxv. 5, help remarking, that the vengeance of the sons of Jacob upon Sichem had a bright side, on which it was represented by *E*, and to this xlviii. 21 sq. also refers. Sichem seems indeed to have prematurely become a town with a predominantly Israelite population, an "ancient tribal possession."[1] But in the intention of this composition of extracts from sources, as it has come down to us, and in which xlviii. 22 and xlix. 5 – 7 are in all but direct contact, לְקַחְתִּי cannot be so understood as to make Jacob appropriate to himself on its brighter side the deed of arms of his sons. לְקַחְתִּי must be conceived of—as by Tuch—as spoken in the power of a prophetic self-consciousness raised

[1] See A. Eckstein, *Gesch. u. Bed. der Stadt Sichem* (1886), p. 18 sq.

above itself. Kuenen's former conjecture לא בחרבי (not with my sword, but by means of honourable purchase) is very tempting, as it removes all difficulty.

JACOB'S PROPHETIC SAYINGS CONCERNING HIS TWELVE SONS
CH. XLIX.

The third portion, ch. xlix., carries on the history of Jacob's last days and records his last words. These have been called, and not incorrectly, the blessing of Jacob, for xlix. 28 refers back to them. They are however introduced at ver. 1 as a prophecy, and are indeed both: words of prophecy as disclosures made by God concerning the future history of redemption; words of blessing as wishes strong through faith, and bringing within themselves the energy for their accomplishment. In lofty words, which already indicate his solemn frame of mind, the patriarch summons all his sons (Joseph included), vv. 1, 2: *And Jacob called his sons and said: Assemble yourselves, that I may announce to you what will befall you at the end of the days. Come together and hear, ye sons of Jacob, and hearken to Israel your father.* קרה (to befall), xxiv. 12, xxvii. 20, xlii. 29, xliv. 29, is also exchanged for קרא at xlii. 4, 38. From the standpoint of the present, the future may be regarded either as that which lies before us, which is coming (הָאֹתִיּוֹת Isa. xli. 23, xliv. 7, הַבָּאִים Isa. xxvii. 6), or also as that which lies after us (Greek τὰ ὀπίσω), whose development is still kept back, and will come after the present course of time, will succeed it (Orelli, *Hebr. Synonyma der Zeit u. Ewigkeit*, p. 14), hence as אַחֲרִית (Assyr. adverbially *aḥrátaš* the future), which as the opposite of the beginning of time means the end of time (the last time), or as the opposite of the present, the time following (the time to come). It has this latter meaning, *e.g.*, at Jer. xxiii. 20 and also Deut. xxxi. 29, though it there already designates not the time to come in general, but in an eschatological sense, like ἐν ὑστέροις καιροῖς, 1 Tim. iv. 1. Mostly however אַחֲרִית הַיָּמִים denotes the final future, the extreme end, but this not merely as the last epoch at the end of the course of time, but as that final period, lying entirely beyond the present course of development, which will bring the work of God to its full and final realization. In such wise also, that the notion varies in proportion to the stage of development, to which the work of God has advanced in the present, and to the horizon of the present thereby given, and the range of vision thereby determined. For in the prophetic prospect, the final redemption is ever combined with the promised event of the immediate future; both advance in close union even when they do not perceptibly coincide, and the progress of the expected redemption is such, that it is by this immediate future, when it is realized and shows itself to be only a portion of that work of God which is in a process of development, that the fulfilment of the glorious and most glorious, which is yet in arrear, is pledged, and a deeper understanding of it brought about. Thus the view of Jacob, who is borne by the spirit of prophecy beyond the sojourn in Egypt, is fixed upon the promised possession of Canaan by the nation of the twelve tribes. To him this stands in the foreground of the אחרית הימים; it is the watchword of his hopes; all that follows stands on a line with this one fundamental hope, as in a picture painted without perspective. It is just in this circumstance that we have a strong proof that no mere recent fiction is before us. At a period which evidently and palpably was not as yet the promised end of the days, no one would have put into Jacob's mouth a prophecy concerning it as the end of the days; while, on the other hand, he could not, according to the tenor of the promises made to the patriarchs, but concentrate all his expectation of redemption in the promised possession of the land. By the criticism, indeed, which either denies miracles, whether in the spiritual life or in history, or as much as possible attributes them to natural causes, these prophetic sayings will be *à priori* regarded as a *vaticinia post eventum*, or as Hupfeld expresses it, as a prophetic myth. Ewald insists upon the "truth which since 1828 he has publicly taught, and which will always force itself upon every better mind, that these sayings belong to the time of Samson" (*Jahrb.* 5. 238). Anger and Dillm. also make the time of the Judges their horizon. But we may with good reason regard the parallels in the Song of Deborah (Judg. ch. v.) as well considered and effective references, while borrowings of this kind would make the author of Gen. xlix. 3-27 show a poverty of thought which he by no means manifests. Hupfeld and others still now deeply depreciate ch. xlix. And Kuenen (*Einl.* § 13, note 16) agrees with Renan and Land in regarding these as sayings of different periods here worked up into a whole. If everything is regarded as prediction invented from after events, it must be indeed looked upon as such patchwork. We too might deal with such criteria, but are kept from so doing by our inmost convictions. Neither in the Old Testament nor the New, is the non-reality of historical or spiritual miracles the necessary consequence of critical analysis. But if prophecy is no delusion, testamentary words of a prophetic character might be expected from the departing ancestor of the chosen people; and if his discourse to his sons consisted of single sayings applying to individuals, it is quite comprehensible that these sayings, and consequently the blessing which was composed of them, should have remained in the memory and on the lips of the twelve tribes. And when and for what purpose should this blessing have been invented? The saying concerning Reuben affixes on him a blot, for the preservation of which subsequent history furnished no reason. The saying concerning Simeon and Levi is depreciative and reproving in a manner only conceivable from the pre-Mosaic standpoint. The saying concerning Zebulun contemplates an extent of the territory of his tribe, which was not realized either in the time of Joshua or under the Kings. And the saying concerning Issachar gives a picture of this tribe differing from the Song of Deborah, Judg. v. 15a. So too can ver. 23 also be understood without being a reflection of Syrian warfare.

The patriarch knew his children, knew the circumstances of their birth, knew the dispositions they had manifested, and was therefore naturally capable, so to speak, of casting their nativity.[1] And his blessing bears throughout the mark of the date claimed for it, and of that spontaneity, both human and Divine, which distinguishes the prophecy of the redemptive history from heathen Manticism. For all such prophecy is of an ethic nature, and for that reason no deluding spell; the history is the product of the interaction of God and man, and hence something different sometimes comes forth from what prophecy had predicted by promise and threat.

It cannot be determined from which of the three main sources of the Pentateuch the redactor has taken this prophetic portion. In itself, and especially by reason of יהוה ver. 18, it suggests our regarding J as the source; but the framework, vv. 1 and 28, leads to Q, who is not absolutely excluded either by יהוה ver. 18 nor by ver. 28b (see there).

The first saying, xlix. 3 sq., passes sentence upon Reuben and determines his future. In every genealogical table of the twelve, from xxxv. 23 to 1 Chron. v. 1, Reuben stands first, as the first-born among the sons of Jacob; hence, looking back with joy and sorrow to his Aramaean servitude, he greets him: רְאוּבֵן בְּכֹרִי אַתָּה כֹּחִי וְרֵאשִׁית אוֹנִי, *Reuben, my first-born, thou, my might and the first-fruits of my strength.* He is the product of Jacob's full manly strength, and the first offspring

---

[1] Such is the assumption, correct in itself, upon which Heinr. Mosler, in his work, *Die jüdische Stammverschiedenheit*, 1884, defends the authenticity of Jacob's blessing, with much profound insight, which is however overgrown with oddities. So too does Diestel, *Der Segen Jakobs*, 1853, who thinks that the sayings are connected with the position and conduct of the twelve during the sojourn in Egypt.

of his generative power after a long and unspotted celibacy (רֵאשִׁית אוֹן, as in legislative prose, Deut. xxi. 17, comp. Ps. lxxviii. 51, cv. 36). And how Reuben towers as the first-born above his brethren! He is יֶתֶר שְׂאֵת וְיֶתֶר עָז, *pre-eminence* (properly superabundance) *in dignity and pre-eminence in power* (עָז, not an adjective, but, as the order and parallelism show, the pausal form of עֹז, comp. xliii. 14), *i.e.* precedence, both in respect and power, is due to him above his brethren, a position excelling theirs in both respects. But Reuben has deprived himself of his privilege: פַּחַז כַּמַּיִם אַל־תּוֹתַר, *Boiling over like water, thou must have no pre-eminence, i.e.* not as boiling over, or because thou art such. The words פחז כמים are a descriptive and, at the same time, a confirmative apposi-tion of the subj., which is more probable than taking it vocatively (Oh, boiling over like water!) or making it form a noun sentence by itself (viz. a boiling over of water is come to pass). The Hebraeo - Sam. obliterates the plasticism of poetic diction by changing פחז into פחזת, whence most ancient translators, except Symm., render it according to the reading ὑπερζέσας, and Graec. Ven. κοῦφος ὡς ὕδωρ. The moral nature of Reuben is notified in a rapid picture, his characteristic is passion, like bubbling up, boiling water (פחז, not *subsilire*, of which also Targ. Jer. Deut. xxxii. 15 is no confirmation, but *bullire, fervere*, not related to פּוּ, נוּ to spring up, but, on the contrary, a shade of the √ פח to breathe, to blow, comp. فاخَر to swell, of the inflation of pride). The Samar. translates, in accordance with the original meaning, אֻרְתְּעַתְּ (from רְתַע=רָתַח), also Symm., whose ὑπερζέσας is a participle giving the reason (which Field exchanges for the less apt ὑπερέζεσας), the LXX more freely: ἐξύβρισας, in the sense of Ezek. xlvii. 5 ἐξύβριζεν τὸ ὕδωρ = גאו המים. Because he indulges his sensuality, he incurs the loss of precedence, and the reason is now .more particularly stated: *For thou didst go up to the bed of thy father, then didst thou defile*, i.e.

didst perpetrate a deed, defiling that which should have been sacred to thee—the verb חִלַּלְתָּ is left without an object, this (יְצוּעִי, for which, according to 1 Chron. v. 1, the Chronicler read יְצוּעַי, plur. like מִשְׁכְּבֵי Ges. § 108. 2, note 2) being made the object of an independent sentence (comp. a like case with the subj. Ps. lxxii. 17b). Deeply annoyed, Jacob turns from this criminal encroachment of Reuben upon the rights of his father and chief, xxxv. 22, as from an intolerable sight, and speaking to himself says only, with hollow voice, יְצוּעִי עָלָה: he went up to my bed! The first blessing is thus limited to Reuben's not being expelled from the number of the twelve, but in other respects it is changed into the curse of degradation. According to Deut. xxi. 17 (the passage in which ראשׁית אונו occurs), a double portion of the inheritance was the due to the first-born, and he was naturally the representative of the family and had precedence among his brethren. The deep and important results obtained by the birthright, are shown in the history of Esau and Jacob. Reuben thus loses not merely the property, but the rank of the first-born—he loses that position in the national and redemptive history which properly belonged to him. We are told 1 Chron. v. 1 sq., to whom Reuben's privileges were transferred: Joseph received the בְּכֹרָה, *i.e.* the double portion of the inheritance, but the princely position went to Judah. Jerome, together with the Targums and Midrash, reckons not only *regnum* and *hæreditas*, but also *sacerdotium*, among the privileges of the first-born, and hence translates (being herein Luther's predecessor): *prior in donis major in imperio*. But 1 Chron. v. 1 sq. shows that only *regnum* and *haereditas* are here under consideration. It was by the providential leading of God, whose plan hovers over all free human action, that the double inheritance was transferred from the first-born of Leah to the first-born of Rachel. But that what was here brought to pass by God's righteous government, may not be imitated by human caprice, the Thorah, Deut. xxi. 15–17, forbids the preference of the first-born son of the beloved wife before that of the hated one. The blessing of Moses, Deut. xxxiii. 6, takes up the words of Jacob concerning Reuben so far as to promise him indeed continuance, but (since there is no necessity for making וְיְהִי=וְאַל־יְהִי with Ges. Baumg. Graf and others) fewness of numbers and general insignificance. This history fulfilled. That Reuben had at the second numbering, Num. xxvi. 7, when compared with the first, Num. i. 21, suffered the loss of 3000 men, cannot, in view of the still more considerable losses of other tribes, come into consideration; but the fact, that in the time of the Kings from David onward only a Moabito-Ammonite and no longer a Reubenite region east of Jordan is spoken of, certainly does. The tribe of Reuben had not wholly died out, 1 Chron. v. 6, but had become quite powerless, and had already so entirely vanished from the sight of Isaiah, that his elegiac lamentation, ch. xv. sq., has only Moab as such for its subject, without any regard to his Reubenite fellow-countrymen. History knows nothing of the deeds of this tribe beyond the victories of the Reubenites and Gadites over Sihon king of the Amorites, and a victorious campaign against the Hagarens in the time of King Saul, 1 Chron. v. 8-10, 18-22. In post-Mosaic times its national importance soon sank to nothing, no judge, king, or prophet being designated as a Reubenite.

Now follow the second and third sons of Leah, ver. 5: שִׁמְעוֹן וְלֵוִי אַחִים *Simeon and Levi are brothers*. Brothers in the fullest sense of the word, not merely of the same parents, but of the same nature, as was shown by the treacherous and cruel vengeance which in common they inflicted on the Shechemites: כְּלֵי חָמָס מְכֵרֹתֵיהֶם *instruments of violence are their slaughter weapons*. The Hebraeo-Sam. and perhaps Onkelos also read כִּלּוּ for כלי : their slaughter weapons have executed violence. It was חמס, *i.e.* a deed of violence by the stronger against the weaker and unarmed; for, that they might be able to take vengeance upon them, they first rendered the

Shechemites incapable of defending themselves. The meaning murderous weapons is in any case the most obvious for מכרתיהם; the Midrash (*Bereshith rabba*, c. 99 and elsewhere) remarks, that in Greek חרבות swords, are called מכירין, *i.e.* μάχαιραι (Goth. *mêkja*, from the √ μακ to pierce, Lat. *mac-tare*), with which Donaldson also (*Jashar*, pp. 128, 196) regards it as one and the same word "changed by Greek mercenaries of David (1 Chron. xi. 36, Καῦρος ὁ μαχαιροφόρος)" into Hebrew. But מְכֵרָה is no more μάχαιρα than the Assyr. *pilakkua* is the Greek πέλεκυς; it comes from בָּרָר (after the formations מְאֵרָה, מְנָרָה, מְקֵרָה), which means to dig (for which usually בָּרָה) and to round (comp. פַּרְפַּר=בִּרְבֵּר, Arab. كَرّ, properly of the ricochetting ball كُرَة), both meanings being combined in that of a round digging or boring out, so that it might also be used of the weapon which bores a round gaping wound, like נָקַר and בָּאַר Ps. xxii. 17, comp. thereon, p. 233 of the Comm., according to the LXX, Pesh.; the verbs ὀρύσσειν and *fodere (hastâ)—stimulo fodere bovem* is even said—also admit the sense of piercing. Tuch, Baumg. explain otherwise: twistings, from בָּרָר, which however means to round and not to twist; de Dieu, Schultens, Maurer: intrigues, from מָכַר=مكر, without any support in Hebrew diction; Kn. Luzzatto, Merx and others: marriage contracts, after the Syr. ܡܟܪ *desponsare* (with reference to xxxiv. 15 sq.); but then כְּלִי is not suitable. Schröter gives another meaning (*DMZ.* xxiv. 525): their signs of recognition, from נכר (so that the punctuation would have to be מַכְּרוֹתֵיהֶם). It would be better to explain with Targ. II. III. Syr.: their nature *indoles*, but Ezek. xvi. 3 (comp. also Isa. li. 1) is not sufficient to prove this meaning for the word, and כלי חמס shows itself to be the predicate, not the subj. The meaning instrument of piercing is the most certain. Dillm. denies to the verb כרר the meaning to pierce, and would rather understand a curved instrument, from כרר to be round, hence something of a sabre. Perhaps the Assyrian, in which בור in the meaning to cut, to hew, to fell, is a syn. (Friedr. Delitzsch, *Proleg.* 121), gives the decisive casting vote. Jacob, who had already, xxxiv. 30, made bitter complaints of the deed of Simeon and Levi, here on his death-bed repudiates all share in it, ver. 6*a*: *Into their council, my soul, come thou not ; with their assembly, my honour, be thou not united.* On סוֹד, see on Ps. xxv. 14: it means compression, *constipatio*, in the sense of concentrated closeness, impervious to light, and consequently both the secret meeting and the secret matter. תֵּחַד is *impf. Kal* of יָחַד, and כְּבֹדִי here as at Ps. vii. 6, xvi. 9, xxx. 13, lvii. 9, cviii. 2, used of the soul as the glory of man, the Divine image, is as the name of the soul *feminine*, as is also *e.g.* עָפָה as the name of the wind, and בַּרְזֶל as that of a fetter. On the misconception or intentional setting aside of כבוד, the name of the soul, by ancient translators, see Geiger, *Urschrift*, p. 319. Reason for this repudiation, ver. 6*b*: *For in their wrath they slew men, and in their self-will they maimed oxen.* Unrestrained self-will, which disregards truth and justice, is here, as at Dan. viii. 4 and frequently, called רָצוֹן. On the exegetical and historical connection of the translation *suffoderunt murum* (שׁוּר) in Jerome, see Fürst in *DMZ.* xxxv. p. 132 sq. The LXX, as it already lay before the Itala, has ἀπέκτειναν ἀνθρώπους and ἐνευροκόπησαν ταῦρον, hence שׁוֹר, not שׁוּר (as Onk. Aq. Symm.: τεῖχος). According to Herder and others, שׁוֹר is said here to mean figuratively (as at Deut. xxxiii. 17) the same as אִישׁ: they slew the princes of Shechem together with the people like defenceless animals, whose sinews had been cut, and Reuss thinks it possible that שׁוֹר is an image of the male population maimed by circumcision. Since however, according to xxxiv. 27—29, they took possession of the flocks and herds, and cared more for vengeance than for booty, עִקְּרוּ שׁוֹר is meant in its literal sense: they cut the knee tendons (LXX ἐνευροκόπησαν) of the oxen, whom they either could not or would not bring away, for the purpose of laming them and making them useless, which is also called in Arab. غَدَر. This treacherous and cruel act of vengeance though inflicted on Canaanites, is pronounced by Jacob to be a sin worthy of condemnation, ver. 7: *Cursed is their anger, which was so fierce, and their wrath, which was so cruel. I will divide them in Jacob, and scatter them in Israel.* The predicates עַז and קָשָׁה (unbending and inexorable) are also interchanged, Cant. viii. 6. The Hebraeo-Sam. (which the other Samaritan texts follow) has here changed ארור into אדור (=הדור praiseworthy) and עברתם into חברתם (their association) to get rid of the curse (*DMZ.* xx. 160–162); the prayer of Judith also in ch. ix. (see thereon Fritzsche) begins by praising the righteous retribution executed by her ancestor Simeon (with Levi). The patriarch solemnly repudiates all share in this massacre. The punishment of Simeon and Levi is division and dispersion. Their fierce resentment is deprived of the support of an independent territory, and their despotic violence of a prerequisite of political power. The cities of Simeon lay as a powerless and almost nameless enclosure within the territory of the tribe of Judah (Josh. xix. 1–9, ch. xv.), and when the descendants of Simeon found their dwelling-places no longer sufficient, they emigrated in two companies and conquered dwelling-places and pasture lands outside the Holy Land (1 Chron. iv. 38 sqq.). Simeon is left quite unmentioned in the blessing of Moses, Deut. xxxiii., and disappears almost entirely after the disruption of the kingdom.[1] Levi received no territory of his own, the Levites being scattered among all the tribes, within which the law, Num. xxxv. 1–8, allotted to them forty-eight cities. Subsequently this scattering became a means of the clerical vocation of the tribe of Levi, here it appears as the punishment of a brutal fanaticism. This penal sentence on the two brothers is a proof of the great antiquity of the blessing. The blessing

---

[1] The Midrash תדשא says: שמעון לא העמיד לא מלך ולא שופט בשביל עון הַזְּנוּת, with reference to Num. xxv. 14; see Epstein, *Beiträge zur jüd. Alterthumskunde* (1887), p. 24.

of Moses, Deut. xxxiii., is silent concerning Simeon, and speaks quite otherwise of Levi. The difference between the two periods at once strikes the eye.

No blessing without a shadow has attached to the first three sons; an unobscured blessing now comes with so much the greater intensity upon Judah, the fourth son of Leah. The Samar. Targum tries as much as possible to turn the blessing of Judah into an insult (*DMZ.* xxx. 348). It is indeed true that Judah's previous life had not been unspotted; he sinned against Joseph, he sinned with Tamar, but these sins are now expiated, and they bore within them reasons in mitigation of their guilt. For it was Judah who wanted to sell Joseph rather than to shed his blood; it was he whose nobleness of mind towards his father and brethren made him so irresistibly eloquent before Joseph; and though not inaccessible to sensual temptation, he was, as the transaction with Tamar shows, of an heroic character ennobled by the fear of God. To him is transferred the princely dignity of the first-born, which Reuben had forfeited (1 Chron. v. 2). His name, according to xxiv. 35, signifies the being praised; this *nomen* Jacob takes hold of as an *omen* and explains it as a prognostic of Judah's future, ver. 8: *Judah—thee shall thy brethren praise: thy hand upon the neck of thine enemies! thy father's sons bow down before thee.* The *pers. pro.* stands first as *nom. abs.*, as *e.g.* at Deut. xviii. 14*b*, comp. אָנֹכִי xxiv. 27 (Ges. § 145. 2). Judah will be the ever victorious; his enemies flee, but they do not escape him, he grasps them by the throat (Job xvi. 12). His heroism procures him the homage and respect of his brethren, and that not only of his five brethren by the same mother (see on xxvii. 29), but of all the sons of their common father. Judah obtains this exaltation above his brethren by the lion-like nature which God bestows upon him: גּוּר אַרְיֵה יְהוּדָה *a lion's whelp is Judah.* Jacob has now before him the person of Judah, the ancestor of the lion tribe, hence he compares him to a young lion.

But his view is immediately transferred to the tribe in the full strength of its maturity: *from the prey, my son, hast thou gone up—he stoops down, he couches like a lion and like a lioness, who would rouse him up?* Jacob in spirit beholds his son as having become that to which he is destined. On רבץ see on iv. 7. Scripture is rich in names and images of lions, for it was then easy to become by personal observation acquainted with the lion, which has now almost disappeared from the lands of the sacred history. As a lion, which after he has obtained his prey goes up (עָלָה in its first meaning, not as at Isa. liii. 2, Ezek. xix. 3, in the sense of growing up) from the forest dwelling to the forest mountain to his den (Eccles. iv. 8, comp. ὀρεσίτροφος, the epithet given to the lion in Homer), so does Judah return from all his conflicts to his dwelling-place; there he couches in proud repose like a lion and like a lioness (who is still fiercer in defence of her young), who would venture to stir him up and to occasion fresh conflicts? The historical greatness of Judah is now further described, the image of the lion being laid aside, ver. 10: *The sceptre shall not depart from Judah and the leader's staff from between his feet, until he comes to Shiloh, and to him devolves the obedience of the peoples.* The LXX, Targum Samar. Saad. Gr. Ven. and the ancients in general understand מְחֹקֵק personally of a leader in peace or war, as at Judg. v. 15 and elsewhere, and as שִׁבְטֵי 2 Sam. vii. 7 (=σκηπτοῦχοι) is perhaps meant; and מִבֵּין רַגְלָיו is accordingly used as at Deut. xxviii. 57 of the coming forth from the maternal womb (comp. the euphemisms, Isa. vii. 20, xxxvi. 12, and Homer's πίπτειν μετὰ ποσσὶ γυναικός, *Il*. 19. 110 = to be born), hence a ruler from the maternal womb of Judah, a not impossible expression, Judah being conceived of not as an individual but as a tribe, which at once bears and begets. Luther otherwise: *noch ein meister von seinen Füssen*, in which מְחֹקֵק is (as in *lawgiver* of the English A.V.) understood, according to סָפְרָא of the Targums, with reference to the circumstance that *scribæ inter pedes regum aut magistratuum sub illis sedere solent.*

The Mecklenburg *Kirchenblatt*, 1885, p. 5: the territory upon which he walks—an impossible rendering, for the ground is not between, but under the feet. Considering that מחקק has no less frequently the meaning ruler's staff, suggested by the parallel שֵׁבֶט (Num. xxi. 18, Ps. lx. 9), than the personal meaning ruler; secondly, that a long staff held by the upper end is the insignium of the Assyrian kings, and that the Persian king represented in a sitting posture upon the monuments of Persepolis holds it between his feet; and thirdly, that the choice of more dignified expressions than the objectionable מִבֵּין רַגְלָיו (especially so as a declaration concerning an ancestor) were furnished by the language (see xlvi. 26, xxxv. 11, Jer. xxxiii. 26, Ps. cxxxii. 11), on which account the Hebraeo-Samar. writes מבין דגליו (from his banners), it must be explained: Judah will ever bear the sceptre, and the ruler's staff ever rest between his feet. Ever—for that ver. 10 awards the princely position to Judah, not merely for a period but for ever, is already required by the character of the saying as purely one of blessing. It is not meant that Judah shall bear the sceptre till the new turn of things and then lose it, or as the passage is already explained by Justin, *Apol.* i. 32, and in the Clementine *Hom.* iii. 49, and is still explained, *e.g.* by F. T. Bassett, Grossrau and others, that the Messiah will come at a time when the sceptre has departed from Judah, *i.e.* when the Jewish people have fallen into subjection to the heathen, which, according to Verbrugge (1730), was definitively fulfilled by the issue of the revolution under Hadrian. In an Advent festival play by Hans Sachs (written Dec. 8, 1730) it is by this saying interpreted in this sense, that the Jewish Rabbi is finally overcome by the Christian doctor. But עד in this blessing cannot possibly be such an exclusive "till." Nor, on the other hand, is there any reason for translating with Hitzig (*Bibl. Theologie*, p. 153), G. Baur and others: "as long as he shall come to Shiloh," for though עד שׁ (Cant. i. 12) and עד *seq. infin.* (Ex. xxxiii. 22, Judg. iii. 26, Jon. iv. 2, comp. 2 Kings ix. 22) may mean "as long as," yet עד כי nowhere expresses limited duration, but the *terminus ad quem*. Still less do we need, with an ancient MS. in Pinsker (*Zur Gesch. des Karaismus*, p. סף), to draw עד to what precedes with *Athnach* instead of *Jethîb* (not . . . for ever, for he will come . . .), but עד־כי with the *impf.* following has the same temporal sense as עד אֲשֶׁר " until that " (elsewhere followed by a *perf.* of gradative meaning, xxvi. 13, xli. 49, 2 Sam. xxiii. 10, 2 Chron. xxvi. 15), and here denotes the turning-point to which Judah's greatness lasts, not then to cease, but to be enlarged to sovereignty over the peoples, comp. on this use of עַד xxvi. 13, xxviii. 15, Ps. cx. 1, cxii. 8. ἕως Matt. v. 18. יִקְּהָה is neither equivalent to תִּקְוָה (LXX, Syr. Vulg.) nor to the Talmudic קְהִיָּה assembly (both Arabic translations), but as at Prov. xxx. 17, obedience, from יְקָה وَقَى (for which also יְקָה وَقَى, whence the *nom. pers.* יָקֶה, the obedient, the pious); here, as at Prov. xxx. 17 with *Dagesh dirimens*, a connective form, not of יְקָהָה, but יִקְהָה (وَقَهَ), like קִרְבָה the approach and נִצְרָה (parallel שְׁמְרָה) the watch, Ps. cxli. 3. עַמִּים might mean the Israelitish tribes, as at Deut. xxxiii. 3, Hos. x. 14 and frequently. But the leadership of the tribes was already awarded to Judah in לא יסור וגו', and the question as to whether he would maintain this with respect to the peoples around was pressing; hence עמים will not have the meaning of Deut. xxxiii. 3, but of Deut. xxx. 17. But if the nations of the world are intended, this suggests taking שִׁילֹה (such is the Masoretic writing, see Frensdorff, *Masora magna*, p. 322 sq., besides which however שִׁלֹה and שִׁלוֹ occur in MSS.) as a name of the Messiah. Jacob has before him in his sons the twelve-tribed nation. A nation however needs a single leader. This suggests taking שׁילה personally. The king of the latter days exalted above the heathen might be meant as at Num. xxiv. 15 sqq.; moreover, the Messianic interpretation of שילה has the recommendation of being ancient (*Sanhedrin* 98b).

But it rests in its traditional form upon an explanation of the word which cannot be accepted. When the Samar. texts write שלה, and Onkelos, Targ. Jer. II. Syr., whom Aphraates, Ephrem, Bar - Hebræus (see his Scholia published by R. Schröter in *DMZ*. xxiv.) and Saadia follow, translate: *donec veniat Messias cujus est regnum*, Aquila and Symmachus (comp. *Constitut. apost.* 6. 11): ᾧ ἀπόκειται (whom it is reserved for and belongs to, viz. ἡ βασιλεία), Peshitto: *is cujus illud (sc. regnum) est*, all these proceed upon the assumption that שילה (the Masor. reading) or שלה (an ancient variation) is equivalent to אֲשֶׁר לוֹ=שֶּׁלּוֹ. The translation also of the LXX (Theod.), ἕως ἂν ἔλθῃ τὰ ἀποκείμενα αὐτῷ (continuing: καὶ αὐτὸς προσδοκία ἐθνῶν), proceeds from the reading שִׁלֹּה, only it does not directly make the person of the Messiah the subject, on which account Justin, *Dial.* c. 120, would willingly stamp the ᾧ ἀπόκειται of Aq. and Symm. as the original reading of the Alexandrine translation. Eusebius (*Eclog. proph.*) rightly explains ἕως ἂν κομίσηται (according to the context, not the Messiah, but Judah through Him) τὴν κατὰ τῶν ὅλων βασιλείαν. With שילה = אֲשֶׁר לוֹ agrees the saying of Ezek. xxi. 32, where the utter destruction of the royal crown, which had been so shamefully desecrated in Zedekiah, is predicted עַד־בֹּא אֲשֶׁר־לוֹ הַמִּשְׁפָּט וּנְתַתִּיו, *i.e.* till He comes to whom the government belongs, and on whom Jahveh bestows it. But this אֲשֶׁר לוֹ of Ezekiel (LXX ᾧ καθήκει, strangely without any rendering of המשפט) is certainly only such a modification or bending of שילה as Jeremiah also frequently allows himself when borrowing older passages of Scripture. For it is impossible that שילה should be equal to שֶׁלּוֹ, and the same must be said of שלה also, for, not to mention that לו=לה cannot be authenticated, אֲשֶׁר=שׁ as the first letter of a proper or quasi-proper name is also unexampled, and שִׁלֹּה (for which we should at least expect with reference to שבט or מחקק, שֶׁלּוֹ הוּא) cannot of itself mean the same as מי שהמלכות שלו "he to whom the kingdom is due." Wellhausen indeed (*Gesch*. p. 375) manages to help the שִׁלֹה to become a subject by expunging לוֹ and then translating: till He comes to whom the obedience of the nations is due—this is however no untying, but a cutting in twain of the knot. Stade (*Gesch.* p. 160) further enhances still more the violence practised, by the conjecture that ver. 10 is a post-exilic addition. Another ancient view (Targ. Jer. I. Jepheth, Abulw. Kimchi[1]), which derives שִׁילֹה from שָׁיל, like עִירֹה from עָיִר, and this שָׁיִל from שָׁלָל=שִׁילֹה (whence the Talmudic שָׁלִיל, Arab. سَلِيل foetus, young) and שִׁלְיָה (whence שִׁלְיָה afterbirth), must, if for nothing else, be rejected because this designation of the Messiah (according to Jos. Kimchi and Dav. Costelli in his *Il Messia*, 1874: of King David) as the son of Judah, would be among all possible designations the most ignoble. Comparatively more attractive is the solution שַׁי לוֹ (to whom the consecrated offerings of the nations belong, according to Ps. lxviii. 29, in the Midrash *Lekach tob* on the passage) and Lagarde's שְׁאִילָה=שִׁילֹה "his prayed for or longed for one;" while, on the contrary, Jerome's *donec veniat qui mittendus est* is a bold *quidproquo*. There is no need of such byways and ventures for understanding שִׁילֹה of the Messiah. If שִׁילֹה is a proper name, it designates the Messiah as the bearer or bringer of rest, and is synonymous with שְׁלֹמֹה, which according to 1 Chron. xxii. 9 is equal to אִישׁ מְנוּחָה, and the Samar. translator of the Pent. into Arabic (Abu-Sa'id) actually translates שִׁלֹה, سُلَيْمَان, referring the prediction to Solomon. So too Donaldson: *Habemus vatem Salomoneum, sui temporis laudatorem*. Luther explains somewhat differently, and referring to שָׁלָה prosperity and welfare, translates: *der Held*, as "one who prospers, who freely carries out his plan;" but the meaning: the peaceful, peaceful kingdom, peacemaker,

---

[1] So too Samuel ben Chofni in the Arab. Comm. of Israelsohn (Petersburg 1886) on Gen. chs. xli.-l.: שילה = ولده ونسله (his son and descendant). This Gaon does not mention the explanation שֶׁלֹּו at all. Paulus Cassel (*Messianische Stellen*, 1885) even explains: scion, from שלח=שלה.

certainly a more appropriate name for the Messiah, is a far more obvious one. For at Micah v. 4 He is called שָׁלוֹם, as at Eph. ii. 14 εἰρήνη, Isa. ix. 5 שַׂר־שָׁלוֹם, and at Zech. ix. 9 sq. he comes to Zion as the King of Peace. The ending would then be the same as in the proper names שְׁלֹמֹה דֹּדוֹ יִדּוֹ and others, whose *oh* or *ô* is weakened from *ôn*, and though שָׁלָה cannot be regarded as the verb lying at the root (from which the noun must have been שָׁלִיןֹ, or if we compare שִׁילוֹחַ קִימוֹשׁ פִּידוֹר קִיטוֹר, יְשִׁילוֹ=שִׁלוֹ), yet שׁגל, synonymous with שָׁלָה, can, and this means to hang down loosely, to be unstrung, to rest, whence שִׁילֹה as a proper name means a quiet, homelike place, inviting to rest (comp. גִּלֹה Josh. xv. 51, from גִּיל), or a peaceable happy person bringing peace and happiness, without our needing to have recourse to Rödiger's expedient, that שִׁילֹה (LXX Judg. xxi. 12 and frequently Σηλώμ with Σηλώ) is weakened from שִׁילוֹם. At all events it is a proper name, for a *nomen appell.* שׁילה, with the meaning of rest or place of rest, would be unique as to formation; even אֲבַדֹּה Prov. xxvii. 20 (*Chethib*), as a name of Hades, being rather a *n. pr.* than a *n. appell.* The language has the nouns שֶׁלִי (not שָׁלָה) שָׁלְוָה שָׁלוֹם מְנוּחָה, with the meaning of rest. To take it as an appellative: till rest comes (Neum. Hofm. Reuss), or: till he comes to the resting-place, seems with such a store of synonyms inadmissible.

But the שִׁילֹה of our passage is no ἅπ. γεγρ., and the first question of all must be, what שִׁילֹה or, as it is everywhere else written, שִׁלֹה (שִׁלוֹ) means elsewhere. It is there the name of an Ephraimite town in the country on this side Jordan (hence שִׁלֹה אֲשֶׁר בְּאֶרֶץ כְּנַעַן Josh. xxii. 9, xxi. 2, Judg. xxi. 12), the ruins of which are still to be seen, in conformity with the statement Judg. xxi. 19, "on the north of Bethel, on the east side of the road that goes up from Bethel to Shechem, on the south of Lebonah (Lubbân)." They still bear the name of Sêlûn (Σιλοῦν in Josh.[1]), and lie upon a bare height above the village Turmus Aja, which is situate on a plateau enclosed

---

[1] See G. Böttger, *Topographisch-hist. Lex. zu Josephus* (1879), p. 231.

on all sides by hills. When the name of this town is used as an accus. of direction, it is said just as here בֹּא שִׁלֹה Josh. xviii. 9, 1 Sam. iv. 12, הביא שלה Judg. xxi. 12, 1 Sam. i. 24, שלח שלה 1 Sam. iv. 4, הלך שלה 1 Kings xiv. 2, 4. The next thing then surely is to see whether "till he (Judah) comes to Shiloh" gives a meaning agreeable to the context and to history. It has been objected against this geographical comprehension of שִׁילֹה, which has been preferred by Herder and since him by many others, that the name Shiloh did not originate till Joshua's time, and that the place was formerly called תְּאֵנָה (Hgst.), or that תְּאֲנַת שִׁלֹה, in the meaning of "meeting at the resting-place," was the full name then given it (Hofm.); but the Taanath Shiloh of Josh. vi. 6, in Euseb. and Jer. *Thanath* (*Thenath*), now *Ain Tânah*, is a northeastern border town of the territory of Ephraim, differing from Shiloh. It was the name of a place already existing, which Jacob made, as he did the names of his sons, an omen of the future. Why should he, who had resided for a period near Shechem, not have known of this mid-Palestinian Shiloh? At ver. 13 he names צִידֹן, and at ch. xlviii. uses the word שְׁכֶם district, with an allusion to Shechem, just as he here uses the word שִׁילֹה not without consciousness of its meaning of place of rest. But the question is—(1) Did Judah maintain this stated supremacy among the tribes till the twelve-tribed nation assembled at Shiloh? and (2) Was Shiloh the turning-point from Judah's tribal to his national sovereignty? With respect to the *first* question, it is not against an affirmative answer, that, first Moses, a Levite, and then Joshua, an Ephraimite, were the leaders of the people on their march to Canaan—for Moses and Joshua were what they were not by reason of their descent from this or that tribe, but in virtue of the Divine choice personally resting on them; and the question here is as to the relation of the tribes to each other. Nor is it any contradiction, that Reuben, Gad and half of Manasseh marched before (לפני) Israel (Num. xxxii. 17, Deut.

iii. 18 and frequently)—for they marched before the other tribes, but not at their head. The primacy of the tribe of Judah among the tribes was really that which Jacob predicted. At the first numbering of the people in the wilderness of Sinai, Judah appears as the most numerous of all the tribes, Num. i., and at the second in the plains of Moab he had, notwithstanding the judgments meantime inflicted, increased, Num. xxvi. In the order of encampment he is the first tribe of the three, who form the front of the square encamped about the sanctuary, and hence the bearer of the first of the four chief standards, Num. ii.; and when the signal for starting was given, the three tribes (Judah, Issachar and Zebulun), which together were called the camp of Judah, were the first to move, Num. x., comp. ii. 9. Judah also maintained this position during the wars of conquest under Joshua; for when the conquered country was divided, it was Judah who in Gilgal received first of all the tribes his hereditary territory, Josh. xv. The camp was then transferred to Shiloh in the heart of the country. Here the tribes assembled, Judah at their head; here the sanctuary was set up and the division of the land completed. This coming to Shiloh undoubtedly forms the boundary between two periods of Israel's history. We only need to read how the assembling of the people at Shiloh is related, Josh. xviii. 1: " And the whole congregation of the sons of Israel assembled themselves together at Shiloh, and set up the tent of meeting there, *and the land was subdued before them.*" Is not the coming to Shiloh here held up as a deeply cut mark in the history of Israel? Then was fulfilled what Moses had in his blessing entreated for the tribe of Judah, Deut. xxxiii. 7: "May Jahveh hear the cry of Judah and bring him home to his people—his hands contended for himself, and thou art his help against his oppressors " (see the Targums and Volck on this passage). The coming to Shiloh, till which Judah had not ceased to stand at the head of the tribes, was the commencement of the settlement and possession; שִׁילֹה became what its name denoted, the resting-place of Israel, comp. Josh. xxi. 42, xx. 4 with xviii. 1.[1] The *second* question is, whether after Judah, the נָגִיד (1 Chron. v. 2) of the tribes, had come as a victor to Shiloh the וְלוֹ יִקְהַת עַמִּים was fulfilled. This too is confirmed, if only we do not forget that Jacob's prediction, like all prophecy, has regard to the climax of the time following and overlooks the interval which elapses. It is not necessary, in order to regard the prophecy as fulfilled, that the tribe of Judah should, after Shiloh became the head and centre of the tribes, have always maintained and exercised its princely rights; it is sufficient that the time of the Judges shows single fulfilments of the prophecy. For when Joshua was dead, the tribe of Judah was called to take the precedence in the war against the Canaanites, Judg. i. 1 sq., and afterwards in the war against Benjamin, Judg. xx. 18; and when the people submitted to that rule of individual judges imposed upon them by circumstances, it was Othniel, of the tribe of Judah, who was the first of the series, Judg. iii. 9. Besides, did not Judah, after being, during the disorganized period of the Judges, kept back from its dignity as the chief tribe, become the royal tribe of Israel? Elohim chose not the tribe of Ephraim, as it is said Ps. lxxviii., but chose the tribe of Judah, the hill of Zion which He loved. David and Solomon, through whom the victorious conflicts and peaceable sway promised to him were gloriously fulfilled, were of the tribe of Judah. What Israel experienced under David and Solomon was not indeed as yet the period of final and unfading glory.

[1] Driver, in the *Expositor*, 1885, vol. vii., and in his exegetical studies on Gen. xlix. 10 in the *Cambridge Journal of Philology*, vol. xiv., thinks himself obliged to understand שֵׁבֶט in its strict meaning of "a royal sceptre" (but comp. Num. xxi. 18), and therefore finally acquiesces in the explanation according to the LXX: till His (Him appointed to Him by promise) shall come (which Briggs also follows in his *Messianic Prophecy*, 1886). We are thankful for the information, that the explanation *quousque veniat Silo* of Seb. Munster's translation (1534) and that of Herder, after the precedent of W. G. Teller (1766), are in circulation.

But did not the kingship of Judah, given Him according to promise, become the tree from which Jesus Christ, the predicted Zémach, grew? Πρόδηλον γὰρ ὅτι ἐξ 'Ιούδα ἀνατέταλκεν ὁ κύριος ἡμῶν, Heb. vii. 14. In Him Judah is for ever the Adored, the Victor, the King, the universal Ruler. For though it is true that the super-terrestrial existence of the exalted Redeemer, as such, is one which is also super-national, yet the earthly history, from which He proceeded and rose on high, was not thereby undone. Even in heaven the seer, who was transported thither, was comforted by one of the elders before the throne with the words: Weep not; behold, the Lion of the tribe of Judah hath overcome, Rev. v. 5.

Thus the prophecy has Christ as the goal of its fulfilment; it is Messianic without our needing to understand שִׁילֹה personally. Judah is the subj. of יבא, and remains such in ver. 11 sq., which describes the full blessing of Judah's peaceable possession, when he shall have come to Shiloh: *Binding his foal unto the vine, and his ass's colt unto the choice vine, he washes his raiment in wine and his mantle in the blood of the grape. His eyes dark with wine, and his teeth white with milk.* Judah binds without concern (in Judah they bind) the wild foal to a tree bearing good fruit instead of a stake—the fruitfulness of the land is so great that there is no anxiety to prevent damage. אֹסְרִי with the ancient and almost always accented connective sound, stands before a word with a prepos., as at Ex. xv. 6, Ps. cxi. 5, Obad. 3, Isa. xxii. 6, Micah vii. 14, Lam. i. 1, Ps. cxxiii. 1 and frequently, and בְּנִי has the same connective sound as the first member of the stat. constr. as at xxxi. 39. Besides לְפֶּמוֹ, شَقَة, לְשֹׂרֵקָה designates a special kind of good wine from the light red colour of its grapes, or rather of their juice. For light red is in Syria and Palestine the colour of the so-called white wine, while the red wine is black *vino nero*. On the perf. 11*b* as expressing the abstract present, see Ges. § 126. 3. סוּתֹה is contracted from סוּיְתֹה, from סָוָה to wrap round, not maimed, from בְּסֹאתֹה as the Samaritans read. The connective form לְבִי follows the analogy of אֲבָל Ps. xxxv. 14, Olsh. § 167b. Then—for this is the meaning of these images—begins a time of happy and prosperous peace. The disquietude of battle will then be at an end. Judah rides upon the animal of peace, and the land is full of vines, the seed of peace (Zech. viii. 12), and abounds in wine. The eyes of Judah then no longer flash with eagerness for the battle, but are dimly dark (חַכְלִילִי) adj. after the formation שְׁעַרוּרִי, from חָבַל, ﺣﻜﻞ, ﺣﻠﻚ to be firm and close, then to be dark (Assyr. akâlu[1])) with wine, and his teeth white with milk, his mouth being full of this childlike and rural nourishment. To understand the two מִן comparatively: his eyes have a darker fire than wine, and his teeth are whiter than milk, gives a trait more adapted to Canticles than to this context. Judah has finished his conflicts, and now enjoys in confident peace the abundance of his land. The territory of Judah was favourable for the culture of the vine (Josh. i. 7 sqq., iv. 18, 2 Chron. xxvi. 10), especially the hilly district of Hebron and Engedi (Num. xiii. 23 sq., Cant. i. 14), and not less so for cattle-breeding, especially the excellent pasture land at Carmel and near Tekoa (1 Sam. xxv. 2, Amos i. 2, 2 Chron. xxvi. 10). And such a simple, idyllic, peaceful life was indeed, during the period of the Judges, the happy lot of Judah above all the other tribes. In the times of David and Solomon all Israel shared in the prosperity of Judah, 1 Kings v. 5. But with Solomon it came to an end. The Ephraimite Shiloh was not yet the turning-point to true and lasting prosperity. Hence vv. 10, 11 are also eschatologic. The promise of peace bestowed upon Judah, was first fulfilled in Him who entered rejoicing Zion riding upon an ass and spake peace to the nations, and not perfectly and enduringly in Him, till not only

[1] See Friedr. Delitzsch in Zimmern, *Babyl. Busspsal.* p. 115.

He Himself, in whom the history of Judah is recapitulated, shall have entered into the κατάπαυσις of the other world, but shall also have fetched His Church into that κατάπαυσις of the other world, which is the heavenly counterpart of the שִׁילֹה of this world and of the full enjoyment of earthly peace. The prophecy sounds as if it were national, temporal, earthly; but viewed in the history of its fulfilment, it discloses relations and facts of a spiritual, eternal and heavenly nature.

If the succession of birth were observed, Dan and Naphtali, the two sons of Bilhah, and then Gad and Asher, the two sons of Zilpah, should follow Judah. Instead of this, the four already named sons of Leah (Reuben, Simeon, Levi and Judah) are followed by her two other sons, and in suchwise that, as in the blessing of Moses, the sixth, Zebulun, precedes the fifth, Issachar. The blessing pronounced upon Zebulun, ver. 13: *Zebulun—near to the coast of the sea shall he dwell, yea he, near to the coast of the ships, and his side leans on Sidon.* The והוא occurring three times in ch. xlix. is justified at ver. 19, and to a certain extent at ver. 20, by the contrast; here it is only a corroborative *idemque;* this rather pleonastic than emphatic use of the personal pronoun recalls the style of Hosea. The territory of Zebulun at its western extension never directly reached the Mediterranean (see Josh. xix. 10–16), nor did that of Asher to whom the לְחוֹף יַמִּים Judg. v. 17 is, in accordance with Josh. xix. 20, transferred. It was shut in on the north in the direction towards Sidon and on the west towards the Mediterranean by Asher. Thus the fulfilment did not come up to either the wish or the prophecy, as *e.g.* Acco and Sidon also, which were allotted to the tribe of Asher, remained in the possession of the Canaanites, Judg. i. 13, Josh. xix. 28. Besides עַל the reading עַד (Targ. Jer. Samar. and Codices) is also found. The plur. יַמִּים does not refer to the western sea and to the sea of Kinnereth, but means (comp. Gen. i. 10) the main sea, as is evident from

Judg. v. 15. In what sense his position with respect to the main sea is a blessing to Zebulun is indicated in חוֹף אֳנִיּוֹת. It is through his nearness to the sea that he becomes a prosperous tribe, rejoicing in the blessings of marine commerce; a tribe which, as Deut. xxxiii. 19 says of him and of his neighbouring brother Issachar, sucks the accumulated abundance of the seas and the hidden treasures, which are carried from the sandy coast into the interior.

Zebulun is followed by his elder brother. The saying concerning Issachar, ver. 14: *Issachar is a bony ass, stretching himself between the sheepfolds.* Geiger's conjecture חמור גֵרִם (an ass of burden of foreigners), approved by Schröter and Olsh., does not give the meaning put upon it, for which we should on the contrary have expected instead of גרים, זרים or נכרים; nor is it true that חמור גֶרֶם means an emaciated ass, the expression points to a strong-boned ass. הַמִּשְׁפְּתָיִם, the square sheepfold, is an image of the country within which Issachar, contented with material advantages and enjoyments, and indifferent to the honours of victory and independence, quietly employs and takes care of himself, ver. 15 : *He saw rest that it was good and the land that it was pleasant, and bowed his shoulder to the burden and became a serving task-worker.* Instead of the neutral טוב (good, or: a good) the Samar. needlessly corrects טובה. The phrase "to become מַס־עֹבֵד," *i.e.* a serving (task-working) tributary, is found also in historic prose, Josh. xvi. 10, 1 Kings ix. 21. The bright side of the saying is, that Issachar will become a robust and hardy race, and receive a pleasant country, inviting to comfortable repose (according to Josh. *Bell.* iii. 3. 2 also, τὸν ἥκιστα γῆς φιλόπονον, the attractive Lower Galilee with the lovely and fertile plain of Jezre'el) (the Midrash understands by נעים, Nain in the west of the so-called Lesser Hermon). The dark side, that he is no freedom-loving פֶּרֶא, but a willingly labouring חֲמוֹר, who, through his tendency to gain and comfort, will rather submit to the yoke of foreign sway, than risk his profits and possessions by warlike efforts.[1] Ritter finds here described the occupation of the nomadic tribes in the neighbourhood of Phœnicia, who furnished the Phœnicians with their caravan horses, and were their carriers; for the territory of Issachar, to which belonged the great plain of Jezre'el towards Beisân, lay on the high caravan road between Phœnicia and the Jordan, leading to Arabia and Damascus (*Erdkunde*, xvi. 19). At all events the yoke upon the neck (Isa. x. 27) is no blessing, and הָיָה לְמַס עֹבֵד to be bound to villeinage, to be, as it were, taxable in labour, does not become Israel, the nation called to free dominion, 1 Kings ix. 22, comp. Prov. xii. 24, but the Canaanites, upon whom was inflicted the curse of bondage, Josh. xvi. 10, 1 Kings ix. 20 sq., and the enemies of Israel in general, so far as they are not utterly extirpated, Deut. xx. 11.

After the six sons of Leah comes the turn of the sons of the handmaid, whose sons were born before Rachel's own sons, and first of Dan whose *nomen* Jacob makes an *omen* of his future, ver. 16: *Dan shall judge his people as one of the tribes of Israel.* By עַמּוֹ is meant Israel, as at Deut. xxxiii. 7, he will defend this as an independent tribe, without being lost among the other tribes; on the contrary, he will stand up with them for the rights and honour of the nation notwithstanding his smallness, for what he lacks in power he will compensate for by stratagem, ver. 17: *Dan is a serpent in the way and a horned snake in the path, which bites the necks of the horse, and he that rideth it falleth backwards.* The ו of וַיִּפֹּל is, as frequently, consecutive without being conversive. לִרְכֹּב can scarcely mean the carriage driver (L. Geiger), but in its direct

---

[1] The war-ass indeed stands in Arabic (حمار الحرب) *DMZ*. xxxvi. 272) on a level with the war-horse, so that not only the notion of endurance but also that of eagerness for battle is combined, *e.g.* in the surname حمار الجزيرة "the ass of Mesopotamia," borne by the Chalif Merwan II. (*DMZ*. xxxiv. 735). On the other hand, the stupidity of the ass is proverbial in the East also (*DMZ*. xl. 266 sq.).

reference to סוּס, as also at Ex. xv. 1, the rider *equo vehentem*. שְׁפִיפֹן (from שָׁפַף to rub the ground, to creep) is according to Jerome *cerastes* (κεράστης), *i.e.* the horned viper. This viper has the brownish yellow colour of the sand, from which it protrudes its knot-like antennæ, and inflicts its deadly bite on any one treading on it unawares (Diod. 2. 49, 20. 42, Plin. 8. 23, Solinus, p. 136, ed. Mommsen); it is called in Arabic مُقَرَّن (the horned) or (according to Curt Vogel in *Vom Fels zum Meer*, 1881, November) لَفَّاح *Leffâḥ* (the striker, *i.e.* biter). The territory of Dan lay between Judah and Ephraim, and only attained in some degree its requisite size by the relinquishment of some of their cities by these two tribes. Dan was nevertheless an independent tribe like any other, and held his own against Canaanites and Philistines, with whom he was by his bold craftiness involved in constant strife. This trait of character in Dan shows itself in the expedition described ch. xviii., and reaches its climax in the romantic chivalry of Samson. The patriarch, beholding the nation that descends from him imperilled by obstinate conflict with the nations of the world, and the future salvation threatened together with it, looks up in prayer to Jahveh, ver. 18: *I hope for Thy salvation, Jahveh!* The name of Jahveh does not exclude the possibility of Jacob's blessing being derived from Q or E. Jacob's end is indeed the threshold of the Mosaic period, the sign manual of which is this name. In no case is ver. 18 a heterogeneous insertion (J. D. Mich. Vatke). It is just the prophetic glance of the seer at the history of the tribe of Dan, which he beholds involved in obstinate and enduring conflict with the Philistines, so far his superiors in numbers and military power, which is changed into an upward glance to the God of salvation. The meaning of לִישׁוּעָתְךָ קִוִּיתִי יהוה cannot well be better developed than in the Jer. Targum: "Yet not to the redemption wrought by Gideon, the son of Joash, does my soul look, for it is temporal; not to the redemption wrought by Samson, the son of Manoah, is my longing directed, for it is transitory; but to the redemption which Thou hast promised to bring to Thy people, the seed of Israel, through Thy word. To Thy redemption, O Jahveh, to the redemption of the Messiah, the Son of David, who will one day redeem Israel and bring him back from exile, to *that* redemption is my sight and my desire directed, for Thy redemption is an everlasting redemption." The patriarch expects the full and final redemption of Israel from all hostile powers, not from man, but from an act of Jahveh Himself.

Then having, as it were, obtained from Jahveh's fulness new power and matter for blessing, he turns to Gad, his first son by Zilpah, ver. 19: *Gad—a warlike throng shall press upon him, and he shall press upon their heel*. The verb גדד (גוד), with which the name גָּד is here brought into combination, means to cut into, to press upon, to attack in a hostile manner (with an acc. following as at Hab. iii. 16, or עַל as at Ps. xliv. 21). Gad had to dwell beyond Jordan and there to endure much from the Ammonites, half of whose territory was taken possession of by him (Josh. xiii. 24–28), and from the marauding desert tribes in general, but faithful to his name he will victoriously resist their raids (غَزَوَات), putting the hostile troop to flight, following on their heels and slaying the fugitives. Saying concerning Asher, Jacob's second son by Zilpah, ver. 20: *From Asher comes fat, his bread, and he yields royal dainties.* To understand "from Asher (*i.e.* as to what comes from Asher)—his bread is fat" is forced; לַחְמוֹ is in apposition to שְׁמֵנָה: fat, fat food as his daily nourishment. But all these sayings begin with the mere name of the person to be blessed; and we must, with Scheid, Bleek, Kn. Olsh. take over the מ of מֵאָשֵׁר to עקב (עֲקֵבָם their, the oppressors' heels), so that the saying may begin more smoothly: Asher—fat is his bread. On וְהוּא see on ver. 13. The produce of his soil is so abundant, that besides feeding on the fat himself, he furnishes kings with the dainties of their tables. שְׁמֵנָה is meant to recall שָׁמֵן, according to Deut. xxxiii. 24, Asher dips his foot in oil. His territory in the low lands of Carmel along the coast of the Mediterranean (Judg. v. 17) up to the more mountainous districts of Sidon, was one of the most fertile of lands, and yielded excellent corn, wine and oil. Saying concerning Naphtali, Jacob's second son by Bilhah, ver. 21: *Naphtali is a hind let loose, one who is the bringer forth of goodly words.* Two things are here allotted to Naphtali: unrestrained agility of movement and the gift of refined and agreeable speech. The former alludes to the independent possession of a mountainous district, in which he ranges unfettered, and the latter marks him as the poetic and eloquent tribe of Israel; of this however no evidence can be produced except that the song of Deborah, Judg. v., is introduced as the song of Deborah and of Barak the Naphtalite—by the commendation "Naphtali upon the high places of the field," ver. 18, it enters into relation with the blessing of Jacob. אַיָּלָה שְׁלֻחָה means a hind let loose, left to itself (comp. עָזוּב Deut. xxxii. 36), roaming about at will; the point of comparison is not, as in the image of the gazelle 2 Sam. ii. 18, 1 Chron. xii. 8, swiftness, but as at Hab. iii. 19, the happy state of freedom. Hence ancient translators (Targ. III. Syr. Saad. Pers.) have incorrectly allowed themselves to be led by שְׁלוּחָה to the notion of a messenger, and to make the image represent Naphtali's successful qualification for the vocation of a messenger. The LXX reads differently and translates: ὡς στέλεχος ἀνειμένον, ἐπιδιδοὺς ἐν τῷ γεννήματι κάλλος, i.e. like a tall stem supplying beauty in the fruit. It cannot be certainly determined upon what wording of the text this is founded: στέλεχος seems to be a generalizing rendering of אֵילָה (although this is translated τερέβινθος xxxv. 4 and στέλεχος is more closely defined Job xxix. 18: ὥσπερ στέλεχος φοίνικος), and ἐν τῷ γεννήματι points rather to בַּפְּרִי than to אִמְרֵי (Wipfel). In no case can στέλεχος fat himself, he furnishes kings with the dainties of their tables. שְׁמֻנָה is meant to recall שֶׁמֶן, according to Deut. xxxiii. 24, Asher dips his foot in oil. His territory in the low lands of Carmel along the coast of the Mediterranean (Judg. v. 17) up to the more mountainous districts of Sidon, was one of the most fertile of lands, and yielded excellent corn, wine and oil. Saying concerning Naphtali, Jacob's second son by Bilhah, ver. 21: *Naphtali is a hind let loose, one who is the bringer forth of goodly words*. Two things are here allotted to Naphtali: unrestrained agility of movement and the gift of refined and agreeable speech. The former alludes to the independent possession of a mountainous district, in which he ranges unfettered, and the latter marks him as the poetic and eloquent tribe of Israel; of this however no evidence can be produced except that the song of Deborah, Judg. v., is introduced as the song of Deborah and of Barak the Naphtalite—by the commendation "Naphtali upon the high places of the field," ver. 18, it enters into relation with the blessing of Jacob. אַיָּלָה שְׁלֻחָה means a hind let loose, left to itself (comp. עזוב Deut. xxxii. 36), roaming about at will; the point of comparison is not, as in the image of the gazelle 2 Sam. ii. 18, 1 Chron. xii. 8, swiftness, but as at Hab. iii. 19, the happy state of freedom. Hence ancient translators (Targ. III. Syr. Saad. Pers.) have incorrectly allowed themselves to be led by שלוחה to the notion of a messenger, and to make the image represent Naphtali's successful qualification for the vocation of a messenger. The LXX reads differently and translates: ὡς στέλεχος ἀνειμένον, ἐπιδιδοὺς ἐν τῷ γεννήματι κάλλος, i.e. like a tall stem supplying beauty in the fruit. It cannot be certainly determined upon what wording of the text this is founded: στέλεχος seems to be a generalizing rendering of אילה (although this is translated τερέβινθος xxxv. 4 and στέλεχος is more closely defined Job xxix. 18: ὥσπερ στέλεχος φοίνικος), and ἐν τῷ γεννήματι points rather to בפרי than to אמרי (Wipfel). In no case can στέλεχος ἀνειμένον mean *virgultum resolutum* (Jer.) or *truncus ex quo virgulta* (βλαστήματα) *prodeunt* (Schleusner), but on the contrary *stirps procera* (from ἀνιέναι, to cause to grow). Hence Bochart, Lowth, Herder, Ew. Olsh. Dillm. read and translate: Naphtali is a slender terebinth, one who bears a pleasant crown; for Naphtali's territory—as Hofmann explains the image—rises from the Lake of Gennesareth to Mount Lebanon; the roots of the terebinth rest by the lake, pleasant cities are the branches which it casts forth, and Mount Lebanon, to which it extends like an arch, is its crown. The Masoretic text however has the testimony of Targums and the Samar. in its favour; besides, with this figure we should expect הַתְּכָנָה, and moreover שָׁלִיחַ in the meaning of stretched, slender, is uncorroborated and linguistically improbable.

The sayings concerning the sons of the handmaids close with Naphtali. They began with Bilhah's son Dan and terminate with her son Naphtali, Zilpah's two sons, Gad and Asher, standing between them. Rachel's own sons, Joseph, born in Aramaea, and Benjamin, born on the way to Ephrath, form the conclusion (xlviii. 7). Joseph is the deliverer, the stay, the pride of his family; it has really come to pass that the sun, moon and stars, *i.e.* his father, mother and brethren, bow down before him; the blessing pronounced upon him flows from the fulness of grateful love, and is therefore the most comprehensive of all, vv. 22-26. The image, with which it begins, is perhaps occasioned by the name אֶפְרַיִם, ver. 22: *The son of a fruit-tree is Joseph, the son of a fruit-tree by a fountain, whose branches run upon the wall*, or if we esteem the chief point of the comparison to be not support and shelter by means of a prop, but productive power and elevation: *over the wall*. Both "up" and "over" are implied in עֲלֵי. The absence of Makkeph cannot be the reason that בֵּן and בֵּן are pointed with Tsere, for the word with *Mahpach*, *e.g.* at xvii. 17, is equally pointed בֵּן without Makkeph; the pointing takes בֵּן as a plur., בָּנוֹת branch, as fem., and פֹּרָת=פָּרָה (with āth for ath as in עֲשָׂת Lev. xxv. 21, זִמְרָת and the like) as an adj. to it (Targ. Rashbam: a growing son, Rashi: a noble son), which is linguistically impossible. The connection is genitival (hence בֵּן־פֹּרָת), son of a fruit-tree (= פֹּרִיָּה, Isa. xvii. 6, of the olive tree, usually of the vine). In India also daughters and branches are interchangeable words (Roberts, *Oriental Illustrations*, p. 55). Aeschylus, *Oed. Col.* 701, calls the olive treè παιδοτρόφος with respect to its fruits. The sing. צְעָדָה comprises in a whole the branches, which are compared to daughters (comp. Zech. vi. 14, John i. 20). We can hardly entertain the notion that שׁוּר is in some way connected with שׁוֹר a bullock, the emblem, according to Deut. xxxiii. 17, of Joseph (*DMZ.* xxiv. 539, see Volck, *Segen Mose's*, on this passage). On the other hand, Ps. lxxx. 16 is not out of relation; for Ps. lxxx. is, as it were, a commentary on the comparison of Joseph to a young vine. Who is to be understood by the פֹּרָת the fruit-tree, whether Rachel or Jacob or all Israel, is not the question; בן פרת is a perceptibly indivisible image. Luth. translates: *Die Töchter treten ein her im Regiment* (of the daughter cities of the two tribes of Joseph), which, even if it were שׁוֹר instead of שׁוּר, would be linguistically impossible. What now follows is no retrospect to the past experiences of Joseph, the warlike imagery being inappropriate to express Joseph's victory over the persecutions he endured both at home and in Egypt. The historical tenses express something future, which is present to the mind of the patriarch as an accomplished fact, vv. 23, 24: *The archers sorely pursue him and shoot at him and make war upon him. But his bow remains in firmness and the arms of his hands move nimbly by the hands of the Mighty One of Jacob, from thence, the shepherd, the stone of Israel.* The LXX, Sam. translate וַיָּרֻבּוּ from רִיב to make war, but וָרֹבּוּ from רָבַב, a עֵי mid. O. like וְרִי Isa. i. 6, and רֹמוּ Job xxiv. 24, Ges. § 67, note 1, is more significant. בְּאֵיתָן is equivalent to בְּמָקוֹם אֵיתָן at a place of firmness, from which he neither swerves nor falls. פָּזַז is the same as the Arab. فزّ to be nimble, active. His arms are called the "arms of his hands," as ruling his hands and imparting to them elasticity and energy (comp. Ps. xliv. 3). Luther already remarks on בַּעֲלֵי חִצִּים: *hos viros sagittarum intelligo non tribum Juda, ut alii volunt* (the Midrash understands it, according to Ps. cxx. 3, of his slanderous brethren) *sed Syros, qui vehementer afflixerunt hoc regnum et fuerunt insignes sagittarii;* we have indeed to think chiefly, but not exclusively, of the Syrians. In מִידֵי אֲבִיר יַעֲקֹב וגו׳, מִידֵי is inconvenient. Olsh. approves of Lagarde's conjecture מִשְּׁדֵי. As the words stand, the מִן of מִידֵי designates the cause or source of this invincible defence: from the hands of the אֲבִיר יַעֲקֹב (a Divine name occurring also in Isa. and Ps. cxxxii.), these hands strengthening and supporting his (Joseph's) hands. The terms that follow are permutative: from thence (מִשָּׁם, *i.e.* from God, like שָׁם֫ Eccles. iii. 17, with God, hence, according to the meaning, ἄνωθεν): the shepherd (xlviii. 15, comp. the echo of this Ps. lxxx. 1), the stone (אֶבֶן, as elsewhere צוּר: the immoveable foundation and protection) of Israel. The Syr. reads מִשֵּׁם, according to which Oettli[1] proposes: מִשֵּׁם רֹעֶה אֲבִיר יִשְׂרָאֵל, but this מִשֵּׁם (from the name = the disclosed fulness of strength) is without analogy, and אֶבֶן יִשְׂרָאֵל as a bold variation leaning on צוּר יִשְׂרָאֵל (2 Sam. xxiii. 3, comp. Isa. viii. 14) must be esteemed possible. Luther translates: *aus jenen* (the Josephite tribes) *sind komen Hirten und Steine in Israel, i.e.* great rulers and prophets. But the rulers of a people are called shields, pillars and the like, not stones. The moderns see in אֲבִיר יַעֲקֹב, which they translate the "ox of Jacob," an after influence of the ancient Semitic worship of the ox, as in אֶבֶן יִשְׂרָאֵל of the ancient Semitic worship of stone fetishes or baetylia, but the appellations are in no need of such intervention by the history of religions. Ancient Jewish explanations already attempt to make אֶבֶן יִשְׂרָאֵל

---

[1] *Theol. Zeitschr. aus d. Schweiz von* Friedr. Weiß, 1885, p. 147 sqq.

dependent as an obj. on רֹעֶה; so does Dillmann, who, reading רֹעֶה, explains with Herd. Ew.: Shepherd of the stone of Israel, which would be equivalent to the God of Bethel—very improbable, since אֱלֹהֵי ought in this sense to stand instead of the misleading רֹעֶה. The blessing now turns from the descriptive to the supplicatory tone, the מִן, referring to the cause in the former sentence, still at first continuing, ver. 25: *By the God of thy father—may He help thee—and with Shaddai —may He bless thee, with blessings of heaven above, blessings of the deep couching beneath, blessings of the breast and of the womb.* It is unnecessary, either with Ew. § 351a, Dillm. and others, to alter, according to the LXX, Syr. Sam. Vulg., the וְאֵת, used as at iv. 1, v. 24, into וְאֵל, or, with Kn., into מֵאֵת, or to take it under the after influence of the מִן (comp. Isa. xlviii. 9, 14, xlix. 7, and perhaps liii. 8) in the sense of וּמֵאֵת; for "by the God of thy father" and "with Shaddai" (used instead of אֵל שַׁדַּי only again in the Pent. in the sayings of Balaam) continues the thought of whence and in whose fellowship the bow and arms of Joseph would be so invincibly strong; וִיבָרְכֶךָ is developed in the acc. which follows (comp. ver. 28). The combination שָׁמַיִם מֵעָל is like xxvii. 39, Ps. l. 4. Rain and dew from above, springs and moisture from beneath, shall shed their fertilizing powers on Joseph's territory, and his cattle shall never fail in productiveness and abundance of milk. It is superabundance which Jacob desires for Joseph, ver. 26: *The blessings of thy father tower above the blessings of my parents even to the boundary of the everlasting hills, may they come upon the head of Joseph and upon the crown of the illustrious among his brethren.* The LXX already combines הוֹרַי עַד, and the Sam. translates שׁוּרֵי עַד (טוּרֵי סְעַד=הֲרֵי עַד); a varying translation of Targ. III. combines parents and hills in הוֹרַי ("above the blessings with which Abraham and Isaac, who were like the hills לְטוּרַיָּא, were blessed "); and Rashbam, like S. J. Rapoport (on Freund's *Hülfsbuch*, 1866), takes הוֹרַי as a collective plural like חוֹרַי, חֲשׁוּפַי in the meaning hills. Since however *hōr* appears elsewhere only in proper names as a dialectic form, we must adopt the view that הוֹרַי is either softened or miswritten from הָרַי (as perhaps שׁוּרָי Ps. xcii. 12 is from שָׁרָי). That עד הורי is meant for "everlasting hills" (Ges. Win. Tuch, Kn. Dillm. and others) is certainly, as supported by Deut. xxxiii. 15, comp. Hab. iii. 6, very probable. In the text as we have it הוֹרִים means *parentes*, in which sense it is common in post-biblical and also in biblical Hebrew, as הוֹרָה mother (Cant. iii. 4, Hos. ii. 7) shows (comp. Arab. *ummáni*, probably both mothers = parents); and תַּאֲוָה, which elsewhere means *concupiscentia* (from אוה), may be taken in the sense of *terminus* (from אָוָה Num. xxxiv. 10 = תָּאָה Num. xxxiv. 7 sq., תָּוָה 1 Sam. xxi. 14, Ezek. ix. 4). According to this traditional text, the patriarch intends to say, that he so far surpasses the blessings bestowed on him by his parents, in his blessings of Joseph, that the latter tower above the former like the highest summits of the everlasting hills—but wherein did this superabundance consist? Here the answer is wanting. But if we read הררי עד, תאות deprived of the prep. עד will now mean not the boundary mark, but as the parallel word to בְּרְכֹת, will (without our needing, with Olsh., to correct it to the equally plural תְּבָאוֹת) mean the charm, *i.e.* the charming endowment "of the everlasting hills" with all that is beautiful, enjoyable and useful, a meaning confirmed by Deut. xxxiii. 15 (וּמִמֶּגֶד גִּבְעוֹת עוֹלָם), and the sense will be, that the blessings which Jacob inherited far exceeded the bestowal of an elevated and excellent hill-country, which is also confirmed by xxvii. 27–29. Reuss rightly says: *La bénédiction morale du patriarche vaut encore mieux que la bénédiction materielle de la nature.* In this view גָּבְרוּ is understood historically, while in the Masoretic reading he who blesses would mean that he is now grasping at a blessing beyond what he himself received. Thus, however we explain it, the blessings implored upon the head of Joseph, on the crown of the נְזִיר among his brethren, are superabundant. לְרֹאשׁ and not בְּרֹאשׁ is purposely said, because בְרֹאשׁ (or עַל־רֹאשׁ) is the usual expression for the coming down of a curse upon the head of some one, and לְרֹאשׁ for the coming down of a blessing (Deut. xxxiii. 16, Prov. x. 6, xi. 26). נָזִיר means separated (from נֵזֶר, نذر), and the question is, whether Joseph is here and at Deut. xxxiii. 16 said to separate from his brethren (Onk. Pers. Gr.-Ven.) on account of his chastity and self-denial, and thus a Nazir in the moral sense (Jer. Saad. Ar.-Sam. Luth.), or on account of his acquired power and elevation in Egypt, and thus as a dedicated one = prince (Targ. II. and III. LXX), unless the word in this sense is perhaps combined with נֵזֶר diadem (Sam. Syr. Arnheim). As the transference of this word to the moral region in general is not to be proved, נזיר designates Joseph as elevated to princely rank, and as by means of Ephraim and Manasseh the inheritor of this precedence in power and dignity.

After this long saying concerning the blessing of Joseph, in which grateful affection struggles for utterance, follows all the more briefly the saying concerning Benjamin, Joseph's own brother and the second son of Rachel, ver. 27: *Benjamin—a wolf that tears, in the morning he devours the prey and in the evening he divides the spoil.* The comparison with the ravening wolf has apparently a touch of moral criticism, as that of Issachar with the bony ass has a touch of irony. The LXX translates λύκος ἅρπαξ; but טָרַף does not properly mean *rapere*, but *carpere*, and according to the context *decerpere* (viii. 11) or *discerpere* (xxxvii. 33). אָכַל טָרֹף Num. xxxiii. 24 may be also said instead of אָכַל עַד, for what has been torn or is being torn (bitten) is called טֶרֶף. The Fathers (since Tertullian) have dreamt in a contrast between 27*a* and 27*b*, but morning and evening together give the notion of incessant victorious spoiling. What a warlike tribe Benjamin became is shown in the time of the Judges by his participation in the contest for freedom under Deborah, Judg. v. 14, and by his war with all the other tribes, waged indeed in an unrighteous cause, Judg. ch. xx. sq. Ehud the judge may also be regarded as an example of the warlike character of this small tribe, but above all King Saul, who everywhere appears surrounded by his brave and armed tribe (1 Chron. viii. 40, xii. 2, comp. 2 Chron. xiv. 7, xvii. 17) and accompanied by his heroic son Jonathan, and whose victorious deeds had in the history of Israel the significance of a pioneer's.

All these are the tribes of Israel, says ver. 28 retrospectively, *twelve, and this is what their father spoke unto them and blessed them, each with what was conformable with his blessing he blessed them*. The interpunctuation of 28a is correct, שְׁנֵים עָשָׂר is brought in afterwards, "together twelve." In 28b the circumstantial expression " with what was conformable with his blessing" appears strange, perhaps אֲשֶׁר is corrupted from אִישׁ (Olsh.) : man by man according to his blessing (that appertaining to him), compare the erroneous אֲשֶׁר corrected in the *Keri*, 2 Sam. xxiii. 21, Num. xxi. 30. This closing verse is in the style of Q (comp. i. 27, Num. i. 44). That it excludes Q as the narrator of the twelve sayings (Kn. Dillm.) is without foundation—the retrospect assumes that the sayings concerning Reuben, Simeon and Levi conceal blessings behind the form of curses. There are twelve tribes, not thirteen, for the double tribe of Joseph is reckoned as one, as at Deut. xxvii. 12, comp. xxxiii. 13. More frequently however, *e.g.* Num. ch. i. sq., xiii., Ezek. xlvii. 13, xlviii. 4 sq., Ephraim and Manasseh are counted as two tribes, and the number twelve maintained, by the tribe of Levi, which as the priestly tribe was scattered among all the rest without separate territory, solid unity, or political importance, being left unmentioned and unrepresented. There are however other computations which seem strange. In the blessing of Moses, Deut. xxxiii., Simeon is passed over, and the number twelve made up by the double tribe of Joseph counting as two and Levi being expressly reckoned. And in the prophecy of Ahijah, 1 Kings ch. xi., where the one tribe which is left to the house of David is the tribe of Judah, the ten tribes are thus made up, Levi is left out of consideration, and Benjamin, which partly by territory and entirely by inclination belonged to the northern kingdom, is added (Köhler, *Gesch.* ii. 457) to Ephraim, Manasseh, Issachar, Zebulun, Naphtali, Asher, Gad, Reuben and Dan; the tribe of Simeon, which never had a settled territory and remained without political independence, being left out of the computation. The number twelve in like manner results in the Apocalypse ch. vii., but here Simeon is specified, and on the other hand Dan is enigmatically passed over. Everywhere twelve remains undiminished and unexceeded as the sign manual of the covenant people.

Jacob's last request and his departure, vv. 29–33: *And he charged them, and said to them: I shall soon be gathered to my people, bury me with my fathers in the cave which is in the field of Ephron the Hittite, in the cave which is in the field of Machpelah, which is in front of Mamre in the land of Canaan, which Abraham bought together with the field from Ephron the Hittite for a possession of a burying-place. There they buried Abraham and Sarah his wife, there they buried Isaac and Rebekah his wife, and there I buried Leah.—The field bought and the cave therein from the sons of Heth. And when Jacob made an end of charging his sons, he drew his feet into the bed and departed, and was gathered to his people.* The sentence אֲשֶׁר קָנָה וגו׳, in which אֶת־הַשָּׂדֶה is antecedently intended, is defended from the suspicion of being a gloss by l. 12 where it is repeated; but ver. 32, which joins with nothing, is a marginal note in explanation of "the cave with the field" 30*b* which has been admitted into the text; it shows at the same time that all the three אֲשֶׁר in ver. 30 are meant to refer to the cave. It is here expressly said that Isaac, Rebekah and Leah had been buried in the cave of Macphelah. He must renounce lying near Rachel, because the neighbourhood of her grave was still in the hands of the Canaanites. His drawing his feet into the bed refers back to xlviii. 2, although his sitting up, as there mentioned, need not necessarily be conceived as continuing beyond xlix. 1. On וַיֶּאֱסֹף אֶל־עַמָּיו see on xxv. 8. He died in full consciousness, without a struggle, comforted by the hope of the salvation of Jahveh, willingly passing into another world to join his fellow-ancestors of that people for whom he knows this salvation of Jahveh was intended, and hiding in him his personality, as that of which he could not be deprived. It is intentionally that the brief וַיָּמָת is omitted, the last moments of the ancestor of Israel are kept back as long as possible, the reader is to see and feel that he departs from this world in a manner consistent with his piety and dignity. We already know from xlvii. 28 the length of his life in this world.

THE BURIAL OF JACOB AND DEATH OF JOSEPH, CH. L.

It is evident from the junction of 12 sq. with xlix. 29 sqq. (*Q*) and of ver. 4 (וַיְדַבֵּר וגו')–11 with xlvii. 29 sqq. (*J*), as well as from the similar kind of statement in vv. 19, 23 and xxx. 2 sq. (*E*), that *R* has here brought together the three main sources, but no certain separation into *J* and *E* can be carried out, especially since judgment is divided as to xxxiii. 18–20, and the use of the Divine name here (comp. the introd. to ch. xlv.) affords no support. In the closing portion too, ver. 15 sqq., which is by general acknowledgment traced to *E*, much is also found which is Jahvistico-Deuteronomic, and which we could not set to the account of *R*.

Joseph with the corpse of his father, ver. 1: *And Joseph fell upon his father's face, and wept upon him and kissed him.* Thus was fulfilled the promise, xlvi. 4. The embalming, vv. 2, 3: *And Joseph commanded his servants, the physicians, to embalm his father, and the physicians embalmed Israel. And forty days were passed thereat, for so long is the time of embalming accustomed to last, and the Egyptians mourned for him seventy days.* The physicians (LXX ἐνταφιασταί = ταριχωταί) are called Joseph's עֲבָדִים, not because they belonged to a caste subordinate to him, the priest (for a caste of physicians was probably first found under Psammetichus), but because physicians in his private service are intended; moreover it was the subordinate priestly class of the pastophori (Egypt. the Kolchyti) who, being according to Clem. Alex. in possession of the last six (medical) of the forty-two so-called Hermetic books, performed the embalming and burial of corpses and the worship of the dead in the grave chapels. These executed the embalming (חֲנֻטִים) in the customary forty days, and the Egyptians mourned for the dead seventy days (these forty included). Diodor. i. 91 reckons more than forty days for embalming (another reading is thirty); Herodot. ii. 86, 88 exactly seventy; the shortest delay, if the greatest possible haste was made, would have been forty. The corpse was opened by an incision in the side, the intestines and the brain were taken out and separately preserved in vessels (canopi). The drying (mummyizing[1]) of the body was promoted by the insertion of bituminous material, it was wrapped in numerous bandages and layers of byssus or linen, and, after remaining seventy days in the house of those to whom it belonged, was enclosed in a coffin and buried.

Pharaoh's permission to bury the dead out of the country obtained, vv. 4–6: *When the days of mourning for him were passed, Joseph spoke to the house of Pharaoh saying: If I have found grace in your eyes, speak, I pray you, in the ears of Pharaoh saying: My father made me swear, saying: Behold, I die—in my grave which I have digged for myself in the land of Canaan, there shalt thou bury me. And now I would go up and bury my father and return again. And Pharaoh said:*

---

[1] The word "mummy," in use since the thirteenth century, is derived from the Persian *mûm*, wax, and travelled back to the Persian in the foreign form *mûmia* = μουμία as the name of a medical remedy.

Go up and bury thy father as he made thee swear. The form בְּכִית (with בְּכוֹת xxxv. 8) is like שְׁבִית Num. xxi. 29. Joseph does not himself go at once to Pharaoh, but, desiring to go out of the country with all his family and a great retinue, he first seeks, for the sake of avoiding malicious insinuations, to dispose Pharaoh's surroundings to favour his request. Besides, etiquette forbade him, a mourner (and therefore unshorn and unadorned), to appear in his own person before the king. That Joseph makes his father describe the grave in which he desired to be buried as prepared by himself, is an abbreviation suited to the brevity of the communication. The verb כרה means to dig, and according to Deut. ii. 6, also to bury, whence the Syr. ܟܒܪ| translates (*emi*), but a grave being spoken of " I digged " (LXX, Targ. Jer. Jerome, Gr. Ven.) is according to the custom of the language the more obvious, and is confirmed by 2 Chron. xvi. 14. The king and the court did not need to be acquainted with details, and Onk. correctly renders the word by אֲתִקְנֵת (I have prepared), which is what is meant. The escort and mourning solemnity, vv. 7–11: *Then Joseph went up to bury his father, and with him went up all the servants of Pharaoh, the elders of his house and all the elders of the land of Egypt. And the whole house of Joseph and his brethren and the house of his father, only their little ones and their flocks and herds they left in the land of Goshen. And there went up with him both chariots and horsemen, and the host was a very imposing one. When they were come to the threshing-floor of Atad, which is beyond Jordan, they made there a great and very imposing mourning solemnity, and he ordered a mourning of seven days for his father. And when the inhabitants of the land, the Canaanites, saw the mourning in the threshing-floor of Atad, they said: This is a great mourning of the Egyptians, therefore they called the name of it Abel-Mizraim, which is beyond Jordan.* The principal courtiers and state officials journeyed with him, to show the last respect to the father of the chief ruler of Egypt (זָקֵן is here a name of dignity, as at xxiv. 2). Chariots and horsemen (comp. Ex. xiv. 9, xv. 19, and above on xii. 16) enhanced the pomp and served as escort. It was a very great, i.e. imposing מַחֲנֶה. They took the indirect route through the wilderness round the Dead Sea, because they desired, without touching upon Philistia and Idumea, to shorten as much as possible the passage through foreign and mistrustful states. They halted in Goren-Atad (אָטָד a thorn ῥάμνος, as Dioscorides explains it, and גֹּרֶן gathering-place, viz. of the corn for threshing) beyond Jordan, and Joseph there ordered a seven days' mourning for his father. The place was afterwards called, in allusion, as the narrator thinks, to this mourning (אֵבֶל) of the Egyptians, אָבֵל מִצְרַיִם, the plain of the Egyptians. V. Raumer, Ritter, Kn. and others are indeed of opinion that this Goren-Atad is said to have lain בְּעֵבֶר הַיַּרְדֵּן from the point of view of the funeral procession, and so on the west side of Jordan, as required by the statement of Jerome: *Area Atad locus trans Jordanem, in quo planxerunt quondam Jacob, tertio ab Hierico lapide, duobus milibus ab Jordane, qui nunc vocatur Betagla, quod interpretatur locus gyri, eo quod ibi more plangentium circumierint in funere Jacob.* The *trans Jordanem* here can only be a quotation from this passage, for the distance stated points to the western side, where was the ancient בֵּית־חָגְלָה, situate on the southern boundary of Benjamin toward Judah, whose position has been ascertained by the discovery of the well and castle of Hagla ¾ of a league south-east of Jericho and 1½ leagues from the Dead Sea. Not equally certain however is the identity asserted by Jerome of *Area Atad* and *Betagla* (בֵּית־חָגְלָה) in his possible indeed, but in this instance far-fetched interpretation of חגלה (which means partridge), by *gyrus* (circular motion). This might be reconcilable with ver. 10, where בעבר הירדן may proceed from the view-point of the funeral procession, but not with ver. 11, according to which אבל מצרים אשר בעבר הירדן, *the plain of Egypt on the other side of Jordan*, became the usual name of the locality (עַל־פְּנֵי קָרָא), as at xxxiii. 17). Hence we must regard Goren Atad or Abel Mizraim as some place unknown on the east of Jordan, to which the attention of the Canaanites, the inhabitants of the country (on this side), which was the goal of the journey, was attracted by the unusual mourning solemnity performed by so many distinguished foreigners. Conclusion of the funeral journey from Q, vv. 12, 13: *And his sons did to him as he had commanded them, and his sons brought him to the land of Canaan and buried him in the cave of the field of Machpelah, which Abraham bought together with the field for a possession of a burying-place of Ephron the Hittite before Mamre*. From the floor of Atad the procession passed over Jordan by the most southerly of its three fords, situate below the sea of Tiberias (the upper of which was at Beisan, the middle one from Nablus to Salt, the lower at Gilgal), to bring the patriarch, in accordance with his last will, to Canaan, and they buried him there in the hereditary grave, which undisputedly belonged to him. The abrupt בָּנָיו 12a shows that the brief narrative in Q was thus continued in adjunction to xlix. 33. The blending with *JE*, as it is before us, states, what is besides obvious, that the transference of Jacob to Hebron was performed by his sons alone, the Egyptian retinue being left behind.

Return from the burial, ver. 14: *And Joseph returned to Egypt, he and his brethren and all that went up with him to bury his father, after he had buried his father.* It is the text of *J*, in which Joseph, as was according to xlvii. 30 sq. to be expected, is the chief figure in the burying. The anxiety of the brethren, ver. 15: *When then Joseph's brethren saw that their father was dead, they said: If now Joseph should treat us as enemies and should requite us all the evil which we did to him!* The narrative here proceeds according to *E* with assistance from *J*. It is a hypothetical sentence in the tone of an exclamation (here beginning with לוּ as Ps. xxvii. with

לִגְלָא), in which is latent the apodosis: what would then become of us? Deputation of intermediaries to Joseph, vv. 16, 17: *And they sent a message to Joseph saying: Thy father commanded before his death saying: Thus speak ye to Joseph: Forgive, I pray thee, the crime of thy brethren and their sin, for they did evil to thee, and now, we pray thee, forgive the crime of the servants of the God of thy father. And Joseph wept when they spake to him.* Certainly their father would not once only, but often, have impressed upon them this duty in the case of his death, and at the same time have allayed their anxiety by such counsel. There is no need for supposing that this was expressly related in either *E* or *JE*.

אָנָּא has Pazer on the tone syllable and Munach on the penultima instead of the countertone Metheg; in Ex. xxxii. 31 also (the only passage of the Pent. where it occurs in *J* besides here) it has emphatic double accentuation (König, *Lehrgeb.* i. 678 sq.). On נשׂא with a dative obj. comp. xviii. 24, 26. In the וְיָעְתָּה which follows is inserted the foundation for their request, viz. the oneness of his and their God. It was with tears that Joseph received their message, and they now come themselves, vv. 18-21: *Then went also his brethren and fell down before him and said: Behold, we will be thy slaves. But Joseph said to them: Fear not, for am I in the place of Elohim? You meant indeed evil against me, but Elohim meant it for good, to do as it is this day, to preserve a great nation alive. Now then fear ye not: I—I will nourish you and your family. Thus he comforted them and spoke to their heart.* The question הֲתַחַת אֱלֹהִים אָנִי meant at xxx. 2: have I the power, here: have I the right, to interpose in God's dispensation, and both times: am I not bound to submit to God? The form of the *inf. constr.* עֲשֹׂה is like רְאֹה xlviii. 11, comp. רְדָה xlvi. 3. The promise אֲכַלְכֵּל וגו' sounds, if we compare xlv. 11, xlvii. 12, as if the famine were still continuing, but what had occurred once might occur again, even if not for so great a length of time; hence it is unnecessary to ascribe to *E* a different chronology (Kn. Dillm.); besides, the narrator here may just as well be *J* as *E*, for it is not certain that xlv. 7 is from *E*, comp. לְהַחֲיוֹת xix. 19, עַם־רָב Num. xxi. 6, דִּבֶּר עַל־לֵב xxxiv. 3, and בַּיּוֹם הַזֶּה Deut. ii. 30, iv. 20 and frequently, for the style of *J*, especially here, is the nascent style of *D*. Remainder of Joseph's life, his last will and his burying, vv. 22–26: *And Joseph remained in Egypt, he and the house of his father, and Joseph lived an hundred and ten years, and Joseph saw the sons of Ephraim of the third generation; the sons also of Machir, the son of Manasseh, were born upon Joseph's knees. And Joseph said to his brethren: I die, and Elohim will certainly visit you and bring you up out of this land into the land which He sware to Abraham, Isaac and Jacob. And Joseph took oath of the sons of Israel saying: Elohim will visit, yea visit you, and ye shall bring up my bones hence. And Joseph died an hundred and ten years old, and they embalmed him, and they put him in a coffin in Egypt.* The sons of Machir, the son of Manasseh (Num. xxvi. 28 sq.), are the great-grandsons of Joseph, hence בְּנֵי שִׁלֵּשִׁים do not mean children of the third generation to the exclusion of the ancestor, *i.e.* great-great-grandsons (=רִבֵּעִים), but great-grandsons, so that שִׁלֵּשִׁים is not a proper but an appositional genitive (Tuch, Kn. Dillm.). The question, why it is not also stated through which of the sons of Ephraim (Num. xxvi. 35) it was that Joseph became a great-grandfather,[1] is settled by the circumstance, that none of the sons of Ephraim were equal in historical importance to Machir, the son of Manasseh (see Num. xxxii. 39 sq., Deut. iii. 15). To be born on any one's knees is equivalent to being received into his or her bosom with paternal or maternal joy (xxx. 3). On the fulfilment of what Joseph caused to be promised to him with an oath, see Ex. xiii. 9, Josh. xxiv. 32. After וַיַּחַנְטוּ with the unnamed

---

[1] Started and answered in a needlessly circuitous manner in Lion Gomperz' *Nachgelassenen Schriften* (Wien, Lippe 1887).

subject of the persons employed (see on xli. 14), the sing. וַיִּ֫שֶׂם with a similarly general subject is harsh (comp. however xliii. 34, xlviii. 1 sq.), and a *Keri* וַיָּ֫שֶׂם would have been still better applied here than at xxiv. 33 (König, *Lehrgeb.* i. 435 sq.). He was embalmed and laid בָּאָר֖וֹן בְּמִצְרָֽיִם. A stone coffin is still called اران (اُرَان), in Bedouin ران, which also occurs, written ארנא, in Hauranian inscriptions (*DMZ.* xxii. 264). It is here, as the article shows, the sarcophagus in common use in Egypt, which might consist, like that of Mycerinus discovered in the third pyramid, of the wood of the *ficus sycomorus*, but was mostly of stone, frequently of porphyry, from the porphyry quarries still to be seen of the oasis of *Bethin* in the Sinaitic peninsula. The Haggada (in the Talmud, Midrash and Targum) turns it into a metal coffin, which was sunk in the Nile for its greater security.[1]

במצרים — with this statement, in itself self-comprehensible, in its connection with the whole subject significant, the first book of the Thorah closes. Israel is still in Egypt, and is there in full process of growth into a nation, waiting to be brought thence according to promise. When it became free from bondage and entered Canaan there entered with it, as the Talmud frequently reiterates, two ארונות, the ark of the ever-living One and the coffin of the dead Joseph. The latter was now standing ready for conveyance, and Jacob, the father of twelve tribes, was already buried in the Promised Land. The impulse of faith was in those days towards Canaan. Canaan was then the present form of the blessing of salvation. Itself of an earthly nature, it acquired as the promised gift of grace, a spiritual and to a certain extent a heavenly character. Buried there, the patriarchs believed that they rested in the love of God. Marching thither, Israel hoped to enter into the peace and glory of God.

---

[1] See J. H. Bondi, *Dem hebräisch-phönizischen Sprachzweige angehörige Lehnwörter in hieroglyphischen und hieratischen Texten* (1886), pp. 120–128.

The primitive history began with the formation of the heavens and the earth from the original chaos, the patriarchal history with the bringing forth of Abraham from the chaos of the heathen world. The primitive history ended in the Semites as well as the Japhethites and Hamites being sunk in heathenism; the patriarchal history ends in the deliverer and preserver of the house of Jacob being placed in his coffin. This "coffin in Egypt" is the coffin of all the spiritual joy of Israel in Egypt. The deep silence of history settles like a dark night upon the succeeding centuries. During these Israel has no redemptive, but only a secular history, until at last the hour of deliverance strikes, and the dumb tongue of history again begins to speak.

END OF VOLUME II.

www.ingramcontent.com/pod-product-compliance
Lightning Source LLC
Chambersburg PA
CBHW022113290426
44112CB00008B/656